## THOMAS KENEALLY

# AMERICAN SCOUNDREL

Thomas Keneally has won international acclaim for his novels *Schindler's List* (the basis for the movie and winner of the Booker Prize), *The Chant of Jimmie Blacksmith, Confederates, Gossip from the Forest, The Playmaker, Woman of the Inner Sea,* and *A River Town,* and for his work of nonfiction *The Great Shame.* He lives in Sydney, Australia.

## ALSO BY THOMAS KENEALLY

### FICTION

*The Place at Whitton*
*The Fear*
*Bring Larks and Heroes*
*Three Cheers for the Paraclete*
*The Survivor*
*A Dutiful Daughter*
*The Chant of Jimmie Blacksmith*
*Blood Red, Sister Rose*
*Gossip from the Forest*
*Season in Purgatory*
*A Victim of the Aurora*
*Passenger*
*Confederates*
*The Cut-Rate Kingdom*
*Schindler's List*
*A Family Madness*
*The Playmaker*
*To Asmara*
*Flying Hero Class*
*Woman of the Inner Sea*
*A River Town*

### NONFICTION

*The Great Shame and the Triumph of the Irish*
*in the English-Speaking World*

*Outback*
*Now and in Time to Come*
*The Place Where Souls Are Born:*
*A Journey to the Southwest*

### FOR CHILDREN

*Ned Kelly and the City of Bees*

*International acclaim for Thomas Keneally's*

# AMERICAN SCOUNDREL

"Entertaining. . . . Fast-paced."          *—The Wall Street Journal*

"An especially lively and compelling account of an extraordinary life."          *—The Seattle Times*

"Provocative. . . . [Keneally] shows himself . . . adept at biography. . . . [He] breathes full and controversial life into a famous military engagement."          *—The Economist*

"Engaging. . . . Keneally deftly conveys the atmosphere of fervent in pre–Civil War Washington. . . . [He] has the advantage of a novelist's sense of pace, a mellifluous prose style and a profound sympathy for both his main characters."
*—Sunday Times* (London)

"A fascinating look at a time when powerful men could get away with virtually anything."          *—Houston Chronicle*

"A memorable account of Sickles' life, and the political, social and military world in which he lived. Keneally has given us an engaging biography."          *—The Oregonian*

# AMERICAN
# SCOUNDREL

# AMERICAN SCOUNDREL

## THE LIFE OF THE NOTORIOUS

## CIVIL WAR GENERAL

## DAN SICKLES

# THOMAS KENEALLY

ANCHOR BOOKS

A DIVISION OF RANDOM HOUSE, INC.

NEW YORK

FIRST ANCHOR BOOKS EDITION, MAY 2003

*Copyright © 2002 by The Serpentine Publishing Co., Pty. Ltd.*

All rights reserved under International and Pan-American Copyright Conventions. Published in the United States by Anchor Books, a division of Random House, Inc., New York, and simultaneously in Canada by Random House of Canada Limited, Toronto. Originally published in hardcover in the United States by Nan A. Talese, an imprint of Doubleday, a division of Random House, Inc., New York, in 2002.

Anchor Books and colophon are registered trademarks of Random House, Inc.

Title page illustration used by permission of The Granger Collection, New York.

The Library of Congress has cataloged the
Nan A. Talese/Doubleday edition as follows:
Keneally, Thomas.
American scoundrel : the life of the notorious Civil War General Dan Sickles /
Thomas Keneally.
p. cm.
1. Sickles, Daniel Edgar, 1819–1914. 2. Legislators—United States—Biography.
3. United States. Congress. House—Biography. 4. Murder—Washington (D.C.)
5. Generals—United States—Biography. 6. United States. Army—Biography.
7. Gettysburg (Pa.), Battle of, 1863. I. Title.
E415.9.S53 K46 2002
328.73'092—dc21
[B] 2001043078
CIP

Anchor ISBN: 0-385-72225-7

*Author photograph © Kerry Klayman*
*Book design by Dana Leigh Treglia*

www.anchorbooks.com

Printed in the United States of America
10  9  8  7  6  5  4  3  2  1

To all my American Keneally cousins—

New Yorkers, New Englanders, Minnesotans,

Texans, and Californians

# Acknowledgments

IN ASSEMBLING THE MATERIALS FOR THIS TALE, I RE-
ceived the best of help from the New York Public Library, especially
from Elizabeth Deifendorf, Director of the General Research Division,
and Mary Bowling, Curator of the Manuscripts Division, and their respective staffs. I must make special mention of Ruth Carr and her genial
personnel in the History and Genealogy Room at the library.

Sickles documents held by the New-York Historical Society were
made available through the kind offices of the society's Library Director,
Margaret Heilbrun. Bruce Kirby, Manuscript Reference Librarian at the
Library of Congress, helped me find ready access to the library's relatively large holdings of Sickles-related materials.

As ever, my wife, Judy, and my daughter, Jane, working with an ef-
ficiency the author could rarely aspire to himself, helped assemble both
original and secondary Sickles material. And I cannot put down my pen
without thanking my agent, Amanda Urban, for her support of the project, and my editor and publisher, Nan Talese, who made the editorial
process a delight.

# AUTHOR'S NOTE

MY FASCINATION WITH THE TALE RECOUNTED IN THESE pages began with Australia and Ireland, and specifically with an Irish political prisoner named Thomas Francis Meagher, transported on a life sentence to Australia in 1849. Meagher was young, famous, eloquent, wealthy, and charming. He had brought back to Ireland from the French republic of Lamartine the tricolor, now the flag of the Republic of Ireland. For his involvement in an Irish uprising that was, in part, a protest against the removal of the Irish harvest to market in the midst of a starving population, he was sentenced to death for high treason and was transported to Van Diemen's Land, today's Tasmania, with four other leaders of what was called the Young Ireland movement.

In 1852 Meagher made a celebrated escape from Van Diemen's Land aboard an American vessel and, upon arrival in New York, was subsumed at once, like many a humbler immigrant, into the Democratic Party apparatus named Tammany Hall. Meagher would have an exceptional career as orator, lawyer, Civil War general, and political activist before he perished, possibly at the hands of vigilantes, in the Missouri

River while serving as governor of Montana. I outlined his career, and that of other Irish agitators, comprehensively in a recent book, *The Great Shame*. But one aspect of Meagher's friendships that I did not have room to explore in *The Great Shame* was his relationship with a notable Tammany figure named Dan Sickles, and his association as a lawyer in the tragedy of Dan Sickles, his wife, Teresa, and Philip Barton Key, the federal district attorney of Washington, D.C., and son of Francis Scott Key, creator of "The Star-Spangled Banner." It seemed that this calamity and the careers of Dan and Teresa served as a mirror of the marital, political, and even military morality of the day, at a time when the most notable political experiment of the new world was under its severest test. In these pages the story of the Sickleses is examined in, the author hopes, some of the piquant detail it deserves.

# AMERICAN
# SCOUNDREL

# I

IN 1853, AT THE AGE OF THIRTY-THREE,
Daniel Edgar Sickles was appointed first secretary
to the United States legation in London, at a time
when there was much dispute between Britain and
the United States. Sickles, known as an eloquent yet
tough-minded figure in the politics of New York,
had been chosen by the new minister to the Court of
St. James's, a crotchety Democrat elder named James
Buchanan. Dan Sickles was to work with Buchanan
in London on a number of important American objectives, not least of which was convincing the British
government that it was in everyone's interest to let
the United States acquire Cuba, either by purchase or
force of arms.

Those who met, knew, trusted, and loved Dan
Sickles swore by his loyalty, discretion, and effective-
ness. He was urbane, intellectually gifted, a skillful

lawyer. He had already served a political apprenticeship as a New York State assemblyman, and no one doubted that a seat in Congress lay ahead. For the moment, he had given up the choice post of attorney to the New York Corporation to serve his nation at Buchanan's side in Britain. Some said he was escaping debts in New York, but they were predictably Republicans. A trim-waisted, neatly made fellow of just under average height, he carried in his luggage excellent suits and, for use at the British court, the uniform of a colonel of New York militia. He was a promising Yankee, a man with a future, on his way to show the British a thing or two. Yet there was in this stylish New Yorker a tendency to embrace poles of behavior, to go from coolness to delirium in a second, and from statesmanship to excess. His tendency toward berserk and full-blooded risk was partly characteristic of the city he had grown up in, the age he lived in, and his own soul.

Thus, on August 6, 1853, in the presidency of Franklin Pierce, the elderly bachelor Buchanan and the married Dan boarded one of the relatively new and splendidly fitted paddle steamers of the U.S. Mail Steamship Company. But Dan's young wife, Teresa, and his infant daughter were not to join him in London until the following spring, when the child would be considered old enough to face the Atlantic crossing. Instead of Teresa, Dan had invited with him to London a young and successful Mercer Street prostitute named Fanny White. He had been a lover of the succulent, worldly Fanny for some years, since well before his marriage, and now he had invited her to see the sights of London with him over the next six months. She jumped at the chance, left her New York brothel under the management of a friend, and bought her steamer ticket. Dan intended to set her up in rooms where he could visit her, and he was willing to have her accompany him to the West End theaters and operas, for he loved both.

In early 1854 news reached New York, and would ultimately be printed in certain sections of the New York press, that Fanny White had expressed to the indulgent Dan an interest in meeting the woman who would give her name to the era—Queen Victoria. And Dan had been rash enough to take Fanny to a royal reception at Buckingham Palace, at which he passed her off to the Queen and Prince Albert as Miss Julia Bennett of New York. Thus, the proprietor of a fashionable New York bordello took the hand of, and executed a curtsy toward, the monarch of Great Britain and the arbiter of strenuous moral ambitions for an entire empire, even for those lost sections now incorporated in the United States.

Years later, when Dan was involved in murder, military slaughters, and Washington politics, the tale of his association with Fanny White would be repeated by those hostile to him as a clear model of the sort of fellow he was and of the faults and outrages inherent in him. As for his friends, including Mr. Buchanan and, later, Mr. Lincoln, they seemed, like many others, to forgive him everything.[1]

Only some sixteen years earlier, Dan had been considered by his parents, George Garret Sickles and Susan Marsh Sickles, to be sufficiently unsettled and in need of special tutoring that they arranged for him to live in the scholarly house of the Da Ponte family on Spring Street, New York. It was a household like few others in that hardhanded, mercantile city, at a time when New York had little of the Italian character it would later take on.

Dan was already an admirer of Professor Lorenzo Da Ponte the younger, an engaging man in his late thirties who held a chair at the institution that would soon acquire the name New York University. Dan's father, George, had introduced Professor Da Ponte to his son as an improving influence. The junior Da Ponte may have been an impressive fellow, but the head of the household was an astonishing old man, Lorenzo Da Ponte the elder, who held the chair of Italian at Columbia University. By the time Dan came to live in the household, Professor Lorenzo Da Ponte the elder, nearly ninety years old, had lived a life of dazzling personal, amorous, and artistic adventures. Dan provided him with a young American ear into which to relate, in German, Italian, French, and English, his vivid tales of having been a priest, an associate of Casanova, an employee of Holy Roman Emperor Joseph II, a colleague of Salieri and Mozart (for whom he had written librettos), a friend to the French poet and president Lamartine and to the great actor-manager of the Drury Lane Michael Kelly. For reasons impossible to discern, Da Ponte, at a time when other men would be nestling into patriarchy and grandfatherhood, had emigrated to the United States, established a house at 91 Spring Street, and successfully applied, at the age of eighty, for the job of first professor of Italian at Columbia.

Another member of the family was an admirable American girl, Maria Cooke, a splendid young woman from Croton Falls in Westchester. The elder Da Ponte had adopted her, and it was widely believed that she was his "natural child," his daughter from an American liaison conducted when he was near the age of seventy. Maria Cooke was thus barely older than Dan himself, but she was already married and had a child. Her husband was another fascinating Italian, Antonio Bagioli. Born in Bologna, Bagioli had come to the United States in 1832 as *gran maestro* of the Montressor Opera Company, and had, of course, called at Spring Street to pay respects to the renowned Da Ponte. There he had fallen in love with Da Ponte's adolescent ward, Maria, and stayed in New York for love's sake even after the rest of the opera company continued on to Havana. Bagioli married Maria and moved into a house already buzzing with music, discussion, and a highly non-Protestant and non-Yankee brio.

Bagioli had by now established himself in New York as a voice teacher. His American students became eminent performers, and to Bagioli was attributed the spreading popularity of Italian song throughout America. He still worked as an orchestral conductor and, while courting Maria Cooke, had set to music Da Ponte's "Hymn to America," with which he always opened and closed concerts.

His daughter, Teresa, born when Maria Cooke Bagioli was seventeen, was about three years old when Dan began living and studying in the extraordinary Da Ponte Spring Street ménage.[2]

Contact with the Da Pontes nourished Dan's taste for the theater and for the operas performed at, if not the finest, the largest opera house on earth, the New York Academy of Music. But the boy was also congenitally political, a person to whom political associations were the most important of relations, and was already a gifted member of the Democratic machine located in Tammany Hall. Some of his strongest relationships were with the men he met at the Tammany Hall, or Wigwam, on the corner of Frankfort and Nassau Streets. When not yet seventeen, in the summer of 1836 he had given a speech at a rally in Brooklyn in favor of the Democratic presidential candidate Martin Van Buren. As a friend later recorded, an old man who heard Dan turned to one of the party leaders, Captain Brownell, and said, "Captain, who is that young man? God bless him; if he lives he will be great." That idea, released into the air of Brooklyn, would be maintained and reinforced over a quarter of a century, repeated by supporters at high levels, and come to be accepted by Dan himself as self-definition.[3]

But in another and more generic sense, Dan Sickles loved women and was sexually precocious. There would later be a persistent rumor that he had seduced Maria Cooke Bagioli. But he was enthusiastic for prostitutes, and well aware that he lived in a racy port of limitless erotic opportunity. Lorenzo Da Ponte the elder's tales of women in northern Italy and Austria did little to encourage Dan to a life of scrupulous chastity. He had got to know that young and unpolluted girls, many of whom were not professional street women, could be picked up on the corner of Dwayne and Broadway. Relatively elegant prostitutes could be met at the Broadway Theatre, in the gallery, above the dress and family circles. When, a little earlier, Dan had worked as a printer in Fulton Street, he had been in reach of the area near City Hall known as Five Points, at the crossroads of Anthony, Leonard, Orange, and Centre Streets, where seventeen brothels operated, quite apart from the prostitutes who worked the streets. These women were often country girls of evangelical upbringing who had fled to the city when they became pregnant in their rural communities. Many of them abandoned their children on doorsteps, and, after that, found prostitution not such a long step to take, particularly when compared with the drudgery and poverty of domestic service and factory work. In the 1830s, when adolescent Dan began to prowl, charm, and spend, seamstresses were paid from six cents to twelve and a half cents per shirt. And $1.12 for such a female worker was considered a good weekly wage. Domestics, who in some senses

5

lived better, worked fifteen or sixteen hours a day, seven days a week, often slept in cramped quarters, and ate leftover food from the family table.

Apart from young prostitutes of Yankee derivation, a third of the whores of Sickles's energetic New York youth were Irish—women who had been born in strictly regulated rural communities in Ireland, but who now had to make whatever way they could in the stewing, ruthless tenements of the Sixth Ward. As well, there were much-favored brothels that catered to interracial sex—the Diving Bell, the Swimming Bar, and the Arcade on Orange Street, for example.

As yet, young Dan lacked the money to attend the fancier bordellos, but he was an energetic "sporting man," as New Yorkers called a frequenter of brothels, and thus wise enough to avoid the lower end of the flesh market, the *bagnios* of Green Street, notorious for disease, where women dismissed from the fancier establishments because of age or infection got work. He understood too that Water Street, a trap laid for hayseeds coming to the city for a first, dangerous visit, was one of the lowest rungs of the demimonde, where a customer stood an excellent chance of being drugged and robbed, even of being thrown unconscious into the river.[4]

To his dealings with men and women, he brought an air of promise and cultivation, a demeanor that was noticed and appreciated in his fledgling speeches for Tammany Hall. He was a man who could convey an intense feeling of tribalism, of inclusion, of the rightness of the factional argument. Those who knew him always were attracted to him; those who disapproved of him had the record of his fallibility as their guide. Despite all, however, he was extravagantly loved by his parents, his friends in Tammany, the Da Pontes, and the Bagiolis. He was attentive to, and much adored by, the infant Teresa.

Dan had been born at the end of the torrid summer of 1819, during which mosquito infestations brought a yellow fever epidemic to the 125,000 inhabitants of New York, killing hundreds a day. At the time of the birth of the only child to George Garret Sickles and Susan Marsh Sickles, the city did not go much past Fourteenth Street. Beyond that point, cottages, immigrant shacks, farms, market gardens, and an occasional splendid country house were scattered northward in increasingly rustic locales. In town, few if any secular buildings rose more than five stories; church spires dominated the skylines, answered only by the worldly spires of the ships at anchor or docked in the Hudson and the East River. Yet within its narrow limits, the city already possessed an acute sense of its self-worth, a sense that Dan inherited.

The factors that ensured the growth and splendor of young Dan's town were already in place. A series of the first regularly scheduled packets, or steamers, were operating from the docks of Lower Manhattan. Until now, those who sent products from America to the mills of Europe had had to wait on the convenience of ships' masters. But the regular departures of the Black Ball Line, already popular with the cotton planters of the South, would become even more popular with the expansion of north-south railroads. The connection with Southern interests meant that many of the business and political figures of New York, including Dan's father, considered themselves honorary Southerners, and Democratic families like the Sickleses looked upon the Democrats of the South as allies and brothers.[5]

George Sickles had passed on to his son a pride in being a congenital New Yorker, being a Knickerbocker—a descendant, through six generations, of the Van Sickelns, Dutch settlers of New Amsterdam. And, in the Knickerbocker tradition, George Sickles would always be a devout speculator in whom hardheadedness and impulsiveness were combined. He was, like his boy, an intensely charming man, verbally vivacious, canny, but ardent and even poetic. Dan found his mother, Susan Marsh Sickles, a gentler, more timid soul. She was generous but also neurotically pietistic, which made her adolescent son something of a stranger to her. She was a parishioner of Trinity Church, the oldest and most richly endowed church of Lower Manhattan.

The young Dan, neat-boned and wiry, with blue eyes and brown hair, delighted his parents with cleverness but confused them with a turbulence that the father was better equipped to understand than the mother. Though always open to the force of reason or persuasion, "the moment the rod was raised," as *Harper's Weekly* said, "he became a rebel." George Sickles sent his adolescent son upstate to tranquil Glens Falls. But reacting to a thrashing from the school's preceptor, Dan walked out and took a job in the office of the *Glens Falls Messenger*. When his parents visited him at Glens Falls, they suggested that he study with a glamorous don whom George Sickles had recently met, Dr. Lorenzo Da Ponte, professor of philosophy and *belles lettres* at the recently founded New York University. Lorenzo, popular with young men of college age because of his combination of drollness and brilliance, would prepare Dan for entry into NYU. Dan responded to the professor with the total devotion he would always accord to male friends.

George Sickles, then in the real estate market, purchased, in the second half of 1835, 2 Abingdon Square, off Hudson Street, and opened an office in Wall Street from which to trade and to administer his property. George accurately understood his son's temperament, its power to attract faith and friendship from others, and its disordered hungers too. For that reason, he bought a beautiful farm across the Hudson, in Livingston, New Jersey, west of Newark. He had decided after all that Dan, though still young, did not have the academic grounding for NYU but might pursue agricultural science in Livingston, and become, perhaps, a scholar-agriculturist, like Thomas Jefferson.

From the start, however, Dan did not make a good rustic, and agriculture and the seasons—whether as a study or as rural drudgery—did not answer the needs of his lively intellect or his urban nature. As a child, he had already developed a pattern of registering his unhappiness by means of more extreme gestures than most, and a journalist later wrote, "He manifested a resolution which amounted to sternness." Early one morning he simply walked off the farm, went to Princeton, and took a job in a printing office. He thought of joining the navy when, in the last days of 1837, an American steamer, the *Caroline*, was set on fire by the Royal Navy and sent over the falls of Niagara wrapped in a shroud of flames. Raised on memories of the War of 1812, Dan was anxious to have at the British. Happily, his employer dissuaded him.

Dan was much later accused of having at this time embezzled $100 belonging to a Mr. Peter Cooper, a venerable man who had taken a liking to him and had proposed to send him to Princeton University so that he could prepare to become a Presbyterian minister, another unlikely vocation for the young man. Cooper had apparently entrusted Dan with money to carry out a business transaction, and some went missing. We don't know if the story is true, but accusations that he was at best inexact with money would follow him all his life.

Moving on from Princeton, Dan walked to Philadelphia, arriving late at night, and knocked at the door of a fashionable boardinghouse near the Exchange. His manner and appearance so impressed one of the gentlemen boarders that he took Dan into his elegant suite of rooms, rent-free. Dan got work as a printer at *Burton's Magazine*, a humorous weekly, but George Sickles had him located and wrote to him, pleading that he come home, since his mother was pining, and offering him every help with a liberal education. And so the boy returned to New York and to the comprehensive education offered by the Da Ponte household.[6]

The senior Lorenzo, who took time to converse with Dan, had been born of Jewish parents in 1749 in Ceneda in northern Italy. The bishop of Ceneda converted Lorenzo's parents to Catholicism and became a patron to the two bright sons of the marriage. Ordained a priest after an academically brilliant seminary career, Father Lorenzo Da Ponte embarked on a three-year affair with a young woman of Venice. She was not his only love. He liked to amuse listeners with such tales as how he had once been mistakenly invited aboard a gondola—he was not the man the girl aboard was expecting—and how this had led to such an intense *amour* that the woman in question had to be locked away in a convent by order of the Venetian Inquisitori di Stato. Lorenzo himself took a post in the seminary at Traviso as the professor of Italian literature, with a notable interest in erotic poetry. This time he was reported to the Reformatori, the Venetian Ministry of Culture and Theology, for his own erotic verse, and in 1776 was expelled from the seminary. He remained in Venice, however, and met a man who was not designed to improve his behavior, the libertine Giacomo Casanova, with whom he attended the theaters and still less salutary places. The fact that there were but two degrees of separation between Sickles, the young student of New York, and Casanova, the fabled prince of Priapus, did nothing to quell Dan's adolescent sexual appetite.

Da Ponte's movements through Europe, the details of which he later relayed to fascinated students at Columbia and visitors to Spring Street, were often recoils from catastrophic affairs. His Venetian patron, Signor Memmo, expelled him from his house over a girl named Teresa, Memmo's mistress. He went to Padua and was denounced again for public concubinage and adultery. Driven from Italy, he traveled to Vienna, to Dresden, and back to Vienna, earning his keep as poet and writer of melodramas, and achieving sufficient renown that in 1782, when Emperor Joseph II established an Italian theater in Vienna, he appointed Da Ponte as its poet, giving him the task of writing Italian melodramas to the music of Salieri. His first play was a complete fiasco, but his next, *The Barber of Good Heart*, was a grand success.

Yet the story as Da Ponte told it to Dan had just begun. Da Ponte met Salieri's young rival, Wolfgang Amadeus Mozart, in early 1783, and was given the job of translating Beaumarchais's play *Mariage de Figaro* into a libretto for an opera, which was performed in Vienna three years later to stupendous acclaim. Da Ponte then began work on the libretto of Mozart's *Don Giovanni*, performed the following year. *Così fan Tutte* was the third success for Mozart and Da Ponte. But without warning, Da Ponte was asked to leave Vienna because of an offense to Emperor Joseph. His mistress, Nancy, a German girl he had met in Trieste, accompanied him to London, where he married her and worked as a writer for the Drury Lane Theatre. After nearly two decades of successful productions, and for unspecified reasons, he moved to New York in 1805. It was from Da Ponte's stories of European intrigues and imperial artistic projects that Dan went forth to classes at NYU and to Democratic politics.

At the age of ninety, on August 17, 1838, Da Ponte the elder died and was buried in an unmarked grave—a form of homage to Mozart— in the Catholic cemetery at Second Avenue near Eleventh Street. Maestro Bagioli now became the head of the household on Spring Street. Da

Ponte's son, Dan's beloved mentor, Lorenzo the younger, was himself in bad health, suffering from a rare form of tuberculosis. In the winter months of early 1840, when Dan was a few years into his NYU studies, Lorenzo caught pneumonia and was himself buried before a crowd of mourners who included many students from the university.

One of Dan's fellow undergraduates, Charles Bulkley, was typical of the friends Dan attracted from the polite community. Bulkley noted how, as Da Ponte's coffin was lowered, a spasm of grief racked Dan and he became hysterical. "He raved, and tore up and down the graveyard shrieking . . . so much so that it was impossible for us who were his friends to mollify him in any measure by words; we were obliged to take hold of him and by friendly force restrain him, and thus ultimately we took him out of the cemetery." Meeting Dan a few days later, Bulkley found him displaying a lightheartedness that seemed unnatural "in contrast with the grief he had exhibited two days before." Bulkley concluded that Dan was subject to sudden emotions and frenzied displays.[7]

And now that scholarship incarnate had been laid beneath the soil, Dan decided that he was done with academia. After two years of residence in the Da Ponte household, he took rooms in a Broadway boardinghouse. He wanted to become a lawyer and, with his usual luck at making influential connections, began his studies for the bar at the offices of Benjamin F. Butler, a Democrat who had been the law partner of President Martin Van Buren, had served as U.S. Attorney General in Andrew Jackson's administration, and had also briefly been Secretary of War. In placing Dan in Butler's offices, two influences were at work: that of his wealthy Wall Street father, and that of the leaders of Tammany, who wished to groom the talented boy. For those with connections, admission to the New York bar could be, after the passage of enough time and the reading of a certain amount of case law, a formality, exempt from any intense or stringent examination.

Dan's energetic father, a man of confident robustness, decided to read law along with his son, and was, a year after Dan, admitted to the bar, with the proud boast that he was New York's first patent lawyer. Around 1843, Dan opened law offices at 79 Nassau Street, near City

Hall, in a building George Sickles had acquired. There they sat and discussed and studied together, the father memorizing case law from his son's texts. George also made 79 Nassau his headquarters.[8]

Dan was a frequent spokesman for Democratic Party principles, which already included a passionate belief in Manifest Destiny and the right of the United States to acquire and hold Texas, New Mexico, California, perhaps the isthmus of Central America, and certainly Cuba. They embraced a tolerance for immigration, based on the role of the Irish as a continuous stream of New York electoral fodder, every Irishman representing one vote (or, some cynics said, two or three votes) on election day. Democrats also wanted the government to drive a hard bargain with Britain regarding the Oregon-Canada border, and their war cry was "Fifty-four Forty [54 degrees 40 minutes latitude, that is] or Fight!" Another foundation stone of the New York Democrats was the intense commercial relationship between New York and the South, and thus the support, offered sometimes grudgingly but usually with a sort of neutral enthusiasm, of the South's most notable institution: slavery.

By 1844 Dan had written and issued an impressive campaign paper based on these principles, and promoting the election of the Democratic candidates for the presidency and vice presidency, James Polk and George Dallas. He also appeared in a patent case that year, representing two engineers who opposed the renewal of a patent for planing machines lodged by a competitor. One of the U.S. Patent Commissioners hearing the case was Daniel Webster, who gave special praise to young Dan Sickles's advocacy on behalf of his two clients.[9]

Dan still eschewed his parents' home, perhaps because his father understood him too well and his mother's attention cloyed. In 1844 his rooms were only a block and a half from 422 Broome Street, where the Bagiolis now lived, and he called there frequently. The child Teresa was eight years old, conversationally lively, smiling, and uncapricious. Dan was her beau ideal: he dressed superbly, liked to eat at Delmonico's, was an aficionado of the theater. She did not comprehend, of course, that he attended brothels and never had enough money. Nor that he had been accused, rightly or wrongly, of raising $1,000 to produce a political pamphlet that never appeared, and of spending the money instead at a fashionable watering place, probably Saratoga Springs, whose great white hotels and sunny ambience he always loved.[10]

And, in any case, in Dan's New York few could bring you down if you were a friend of Tammany. Tammany, founded by New York Democrats after the American Revolution, had been named in honor of a Delaware chieftain with a reputedly penetrating wisdom. It was initially a benevolent organization, but Aaron Burr used it as a political machine to support the election in 1800 of Thomas Jefferson as President and himself as Vice President. Members of Tammany were called braves, its officeholders sachems and sagamores. A grand sachem of Tammany, Martin Van Buren, had been elected President in 1836, but Tammany most prided itself on its potent influence over municipal elections and the appointment of civic officials. The sundry commissionerships and chiefships of the New York administration were in Tammany's hold, as were the customs and treasury jobs that flowed from Democratic presidencies—the plums with which Tammany rewarded its children.

The chief Wigwam of Tammany, Dan's sacred and tribal site at Frankfort and Nassau Streets, featured at street level a large bar, a venue for factional meetings and less formal power-brokering, and the place in which a lively rank-and-file fueled itself before mass or general committee meetings. Upstairs was the large and ornate Council Hall, which, with the cultivated pretensions of its columns and chandeliers, was not a political environment for the easily cowed.

Having begun as a sturdily Yankee organization, Tammany had become one that sought both to exploit and honor the Irish immigrant as a voter. In their secret hearts, some of the leaders might still despise Catholicism, but they needed the Irish adherents of Tammany to vote as an electoral legion. Many Irishmen of native wit, toughness, and cultivation rose high in Tammany and became close friends with Dan. He liked them for their intensity, their sense of tribalism, and their capacity to play factional politics as a great game, the best and most serious game of all.

During Dan's political career, the minions of Tammany Hall met most immigrant ships and sought to naturalize the newly arrived Irish through tame judges who were party clients. An Irish saloon at Centre Street printed 40,000 certificates to be handed out to its customers for presentation to the clerk of any of New York's courts. These numbered tickets read, "Please naturalize the bearer." And Tammany had other uses for the Irish. It fostered both community service and cohesion among its membership by creating "fire militias," which served voluntarily in the tinderbox of the wooden tenements of Lower Manhattan. The fire militias also sponsored what were called target groups, whose members learned the use of firearms, and chowder clubs, more strictly social but designed to create an intensely loyal set of political paramilitaries for Tammany. These groups could operate without too much fear of the law, for the police force was also under Tammany's thumb and patronage; to be a Tammany man was to stand a good chance of being admitted to the force.[11]

The gangs of Tammany were notorious, whether fire militias or some less formal groupings. One gang leader, Captain Isaiah Rynders, a former New Orleans gambler and skipper of a Hudson River sloop, was a good friend and admirer of Dan's and leader of the Empire Club, which New Yorkers commonly referred to as the Dead Rabbits. Rynders was the type of fellow who was present with his gang when votes were taken in Tammany for nominating conventions in favor of certain candidates. If necessary, he could arrange for extra voters to be brought in from Brooklyn or for ballot boxes favoring other candidates to be confiscated.[12]

The friendships between Rynders and Dan and between Dan and more senior figures of politics and the legal profession were cemented by Dan's lively wit and his quick intellect, but also by something more primal and male. These were the most important and closest connections of his life, perhaps surpassed only by his relationship with his father. He would support his network of friends within Tammany even to his own disadvantage, with a ferocious, uncritical fidelity.

The fraternity of Tammany was, however, under stress as Dan established his new law practice, and the chief fault line was the same as that at the base of all American politics. The question was whether territories captured in the Mexican War should be free of the institution of slavery and involuntary servitude. The Democratic Party split into two factions over this issue. The Hunkers, including Dan and, at least by shared opinion, his father, wanted the new territories opening to the west to have the choice of being slave or free. The Barnburners wished to see slavery restricted to its present limits, and the West to be free of it.[13]

Nowhere, not even in Congress, was the Hunker-Barnburner split more furiously fought out than in Tammany. Bloodshed between the factions was common; even for an intellectual like Dan, the bowie knife and the knuckle-duster became necessary accessories for any visit to the Tammany Wigwam bar.

A commentator of the day said Dan possessed many natural qualifications for leadership—"a handsome face, a plausible address, quick wit and undaunting courage." By 1846, because the Hunkers had the numbers, Dan had been elected as the youngest member of Tammany's general committee, with the help of such potent allies as Captain Rynders, Captain William Wiley, leader of another handy Tammany horde, and a saloon-keeping demagogue named Fernando Wood, who would serve a number of terms as mayor of New York. Dan now became Tammany's nominee for state assemblyman.[14]

Late that same year, a matter appeared on the record that enabled certain newspaper editors to denounce Dan then and later, when he became a more public political figure. He was charged with grand larceny for having stolen from Mr. W. Kemble a deed on the premises at 79 Nassau Street. The property actually belonged to Dan's father, and Dan, always short of cash, raised an $800 loan from Mr. Kemble, giving him the document as security. When Mr. Kemble brought the deed back to Dan's office one day to have the debt recorded upon it by the registrar, Dan said he would return it to Kemble as soon as that was done. According to the charges, when Kemble next asked about it, Dan said that the deed had been accidentally left at the registrar's office. Kemble would claim that the foreman of the grand jury before which Dan was to appear had warned him beforehand that "strong political influence would doubtless be exerted to get the accused clear." When the mortgage was produced at trial, it was indeed seen to be registered in names other than that of Kemble, so the jury was directed to acquit Dan on technical grounds. Some years later, his lawyer, John Graham of the Graham clan of Tammany, declared it as his firm belief, when the story was raised again, "that in this case you were entirely innocent of the offense imputed to you." Kemble had, inappropriately, used the criminal court for a civil case, because he had already failed in the civil case on the matter.[15]

Just the same, an air of financial corner-cutting, not wholly uncharacteristic of young New Yorkers, attached to Dan. One cause of his need of money was the infatuation he developed in his twenties for the clever brown-haired prostitute Fanny White, who worked at that time from a house on Leonard Street. Fanny was young, lively, someone in whose company Dan could be unreservedly himself. She was both beautiful and crafty, and lacked the air of victimhood that marked the hapless fallen girls of popular literature. Unlike a more conventional girl, she did not seek Dan's fidelity and had no impulse to improve him; she sought only that he express his gratitude with gifts. She had, in fact, a talent for eliciting gifts of jewelry and real estate from exuberantly grateful clients. Dan was so taken with what she offered him— enthusiastic sex without complications—that he developed ambitions of exclusive access to her. It could be argued that Fanny was the object of the longest and most intense erotic concentration he would ever offer to a woman. But in Fanny's case, exclusivity was not a cheap objective. By the summer of 1847 he shared her bed, and when Fanny's servant was arrested for stealing money from Miss White's rooms, the charge was that the servant had entered the room where White and her "man" were sleeping and had stolen the money from the man's pocket. When the servant was tried in the police court, she cried, "You know, Miss White, that all I took was a bundle of keys from Daniel Sickles's pocket while both of you were asleep, and you know that I took nothing else." At this public announcement of Dan's status as Fanny's "man," there was great laughter in the body of the court, and the story made the press. But Dan did not appear embarrassed, because he had already proved willing to be seen in public with Fanny. It was a fascinating side of his nature that, as in London later, he would have his affair with Fanny publicly noted in a way he would never have permitted in his associations with married women or widows, or with young women who expected to achieve marriage.[16]

Neither the Kemble affair nor his love of Fanny prevented Dan from being elected to the New York State assembly in 1847. Going to Albany, he trailed behind him the further racy rumor that Fanny White had helped him with the expenses of his candidacy, by providing money earned in her Leonard Street rooms. Whether that was true or not, he did invite Fanny to visit him in Albany, and introduced her around the dining-room table at the hotel where he and other assemblymen stayed. He also arranged for her to tour the assembly chamber. Even for Albany this was too much. Though he may have asked his fellow assemblymen how they knew of Fanny's profession—for though she generated occasional press notice, there was nothing about her appearance to distinguish her from, say, a successful actress—he was censured by the speaker of the assembly as a result of motion passed by the straitlaced Whig members.[17]

But this was a minor blemish on his career. He was elected a delegate to the Democratic convention of 1848, and acquired a further array of powerful friends, among whom were the Van Buren family and August Belmont, the representative of the House of Rothschild in America, and a renowned and cultivated German-Jewish entrepreneur. At the time of Dan's attention to Fanny White, Belmont was himself courting the daughter of Matthew "Japan" Perry, the American naval officer who had opened up trade with Japan. In 1849, with Dan as a wedding guest, Belmont would marry her, and he remained a friend to Dan and a reassuring and stabilizing presence in the Democratic Party. Dan was wise enough, however, not to presume on his friendship with Belmont as a means of raising credit to finance his expensive tastes.[18]

Among the men he frequently met at Delmonico's famous establishment downtown was the great Shakespearean actor Edwin Forrest, who long remained a friend, and toward whom Dan directed the adulation reserved in modern times for cinema stars. An assiduous theatergoer, Dan's interest sometimes ran to Shakespeare and sometimes took him to Wallack's Theatre, at Broadway and Thirteenth, called by one commentator "the best theatre in which the English language is spoken," though it was devoted almost entirely to comedy. Dan still enjoyed grand opera greatly, and went on attending performances at the Academy of Music.[19]

The second half of the nineteenth century came in with expectations of technological, industrial, and political beneficence. For Assemblyman Sickles, it was a matter of making larger borrowings, and to pay them back he exempted himself from standing for reelection to the assembly and set to work again as a lawyer. A great deal of his correspondence received and sent would be concerned with balancing the settlement of one promissory note against the extension of another. Not all those who lent him money were indulgent.[20] Fanny White, on the other hand, was less desperate for cash than Dan, and was able in 1851 to buy a property at 119 Mercer Street and run it as one of the city's most prosperous, reputable, and well-appointed brothels. Her personal tax record of 1851 lists, along with herself, a certain Bagioli as the payer of taxes on the property. So was the father of the now-adolescent Teresa also involved with Fanny White, or had Dan used Bagioli's name as a cover when helping White? There was a sniff of the tribal about Fanny's brothel, anyhow, since she had bought her house from a lawyer of Dan's, John Graham. These transactions were themselves an index of the dense, fibrous quality of relations between Tammany and New York's vigorous unofficial life. George Templeton Strong, the New York lawyer and diarist, whose reminiscences are to his age as significant as those of Samuel Pepys to the Jacobean era, would say that Dan was blackmailing Antonio Bagioli, but there is no evidence of it, and Bagioli's surviving letters to Dan were always unresentful and warm.[21]

In the early 1850s, Teresa Bagioli was a beautiful young woman being trained for the role of wife and cultivated hostess at the Manhattanville Convent of the Sacred Heart, the school for the daughters of the

Catholic elite of New York. Her complexion was transparent, and her soul also; she was blithe, an affectionate friend to her younger sister, Blanchy, and a good if sometimes naive conversationalist. Her openness and lack of malice, the lack of the vanity and self-indulgence that might have gone with beauty, earned her a wide circle of friends. One observer wrote, "Beautiful, brilliant, and highly educated, she mingled with the most garrulous simplicity of manner a firmness which, without sacrifice of feminine grace, exempted her from many foibles which spring from weak nerves."

Though attracted to men by way of the sensuality she had inherited from Grandfather Da Ponte, she expected to enjoy the years of maidenly socializing that lay ahead of most of her fellow students and intimate friends before marriage. Their names and the innocuous, enthusiastic, chatty letters Teresa wrote to them evoke a dewy, privileged American wholesomeness: Jane McCarren of Westchester, Molly Coggin, Mary Hill, Sarah Shevell, Ann Hendrickson, Eliza and Sarah Sanford, and a special friend of unknown surname, Florence. Many of these letters would survive.[22]

But Teresa was besotted with Dan Sickles, who visited the Bagioli house regularly. Although Antonio had for a time done so well as a voice teacher that he had maintained a "country seat" at Hastings-on-Hudson, he too was a man doomed to economic uncertainty, and now he was back in the demi-squalor of town. George Templeton Strong implied that at one stage Dan's frequent visits to the Bagioli household, at 34 East Fifteenth Street, were entirely predatory, and that, again, he was black-mailing Antonio. It was the sort of accusation Dan's repute induced such folk as Strong to make. Unless Dan was extremely perverse and Teresa thoroughly alienated from her parents—and there is no sign that she was—an atmosphere of threat would not have encouraged her infatuation with this mature lawyer and politician who did her the notable honor in all conversation of considering her more than a mere girl. Dan was enchanted by her. He courted her with a sensibility of being a friend of her parents, and he must have suspected that he loved her with a fated and exclusive love.[23]

His passion for Teresa did not diminish his hectic devotion to the tribe of Tammany. It betrayed him into behavior that in other political jurisdictions would have led to his arrest and disbarment, but that was much admired by Democrats in New York. He was engaged in supporting a friend, Robert J. Dillon, for the elective office of corporation counsel, when the supporters of the opposing candidate prepared a circular against Dillon and enclosed it with a ballot in envelopes addressed to all the voters on the electoral rolls. Thousands of these circulars were taken to the Broadway post office for delivery. Informed of this, Dan gathered the cohorts of Captain Wiley's and Captain Rynders's gangs and drove with them in several carriages to the post office. There, in the words of one newspaper, the Tammany legionnaires "captured" the building, ripped open the mailbags, gathered all the offending letters into a pile under Dan's supervision, and set fire to them on the post office floor.

Dan was, of course, prosecuted for robbing and interfering with the mails, but John Graham was able to delay indefinitely his appearance before Justice Osborne in federal court. Indeed, one of his rewards was to be elected a delegate to the Democratic Convention of 1852 in Baltimore, where he supported the ultimate victor, a handsome Mexican War hero from New Hampshire named General Franklin Pierce. And though the *Sun* would six months later urge President Pierce to give Dan short shrift in Washington, "and then forward the gentleman by the first train to the disconsolate and despairing justice," Dan was correctly confident that he would never come to trial for his act of electoral enthusiasm.[24]

Though living so far north, in New Hampshire, Pierce was a pro-Southern Hard Hunker or, as people now said, Hardshell Democrat of the variety Dan liked. Many other Americans liked him too, and Pierce would sweep the country in the coming November, 254 electoral votes to 42. For the first time Dan had the heady experience of looking up to a President who acknowledged a measure of obligation to the young delegate from New York. Dan would, with a mixture of grace and directness, trade on this debt. He had a New York friend, a fire commissioner named Gus Schell, and Dan wrote to the new President to petition for the appointment of Schell, "the fireman's man in New York," as collector of the Port of New York, a position that had always carried with it the most handsome fees and rewards. "I would venture to comprise all that I am permitted to ask from the present administration in one desire—that Augustus Schell may be appointed Collector of the Port of New York."[25]

Now the story gets beyond its most significant element. A month or so before Pierce's election, Dan had proposed marriage to Teresa Bagioli. It was not uncommon in that age for a fifteen-year-old girl to marry, though it was not particularly the practice of the world Dan and Teresa moved in. But Teresa was, in her way and for someone her age, uniquely qualified. Dan believed she possessed the gravity to be a successful lawyer's wife, and her education and rearing in an exceptional family, as well as her frankness of feeling, better equipped her for marriage than were most American women in their twenties. She would always like older, apparently sager, and accomplished men, and was bedazzled by this mature, worldly, sympathetic New Yorker. We do not know the scene of her seduction—his rooms, a hotel, or a house of assignation, that is, one of the special hotels where polite women could go, wearing a veil, to meet their lovers. It may have been a tumult at home while her parents were away—although since Antonio had his studio at home, his absences were not frequent. Wherever the seduction occurred, it signified more to Dan than any of his past liaisons, and was a world-consuming and all-encompassing event for Teresa. As for Dan, with a sudden impulse of innocence, he sought a redemptive, wholesome presence. His life was complex to the point of chaos, and he looked to a girl who was less than half his nearly thirty-three years for a limpid center. It was a task Teresa was ambitious to take on. The date of the civil wedding at City Hall before Mayor Kingsland of New York was September 27, 1852. It was rumored that both sets of parents were against the union, and that Dan had exacted Teresa from Bagioli as a price for silence about an alleged earlier, Italian marriage of Antonio's. But there is no evidence of that, and Teresa's demeanor from the beginning was that of a blithe and beloved bride, rather than of one bartered. Dan and Teresa lived with the Bagioli parents at Fifteenth Street, and if there was any residual *frisson* between handsome Maria Cooke Bagioli and Dan, it was something both of them committed to the past.

There were stories, perhaps more reliable, that Teresa was in the early stages of pregnancy. Given that the coming child's birth was not officially recorded, that is not certain. What is certain is that her pregnancy was not the chief reason for the marriage, for Dan was not a man to be dragooned into marriage by such things, and the truth of Dan's character is that he would have been ruthless enough to arrange his way around an unwanted pregnancy. Though he might marry ill-advisedly, he did not marry lightly. After all, marriage in the Victorian world was an institution from which only tragedy—an epidemic or the death of a mother in childbirth—could liberate a man.

In March 1853, a church marriage took place in the house of Archbishop Hughes, the powerful Catholic prelate of New York. Teresa's condition was visible, and one Sickles-baiting newspaper claimed the marriage before the archbishop took place only when the pregnancy could no longer be concealed from the two sets of parents. This contradicts all we know of the relationship between Dan and Teresa and their parents.[26]

The more serious issue was that whatever pieties may have attended Dan's vows before Mayor Kingsland, and the church marriage the following March, it did not take him long to conclude that the keeping of his marriage vows was beyond him. The problem was not splendid Teresa or her pregnancy; he was simply not designed for conventional marriage and consecrated love. His appetites, whether larger than those of other men or not, were certainly never hedged in by fear of social odium.

In the Bagiolis' view, however, he was a generous husband, unstinting with gifts of jewelry. The Bagioli parents discounted any gossip about him and accepted his frequent absences as inevitable for a man who ran a law practice and had a frantic political life. Teresa, as she and Dan moved to their rented house a little uptown from the Bagiolis, did become aware, with some bafflement, that he was meeting other, older women, and she heard occasional rumors of his not having given up Fanny White. She did not possess the meek gift of denial that got other wives through such crises of knowledge, and she questioned him about the matter more than once, along the normal wifely lines of what these other women gave him that was lacking in her. Since he was her all, and since he possessed the gift to make her feel yet again whenever he came home that she was the one lovely and sensible woman on earth, she could not understand the imperatives that drove him on to his infidelities. But the sole authority she could bring to the question was that of a bewildered adolescent. To her credit, she did not become a wronged and wounded harpy; she employed no stridency. Perhaps had she done so, Dan might have behaved marginally better.

And as if there were rewards for acquiring such a presentable and accomplished young wife, Dan had been married barely three months before it became his turn to receive one of the prime fruits of the Tammany system, the appointed post of corporation attorney of New York City. The corporation attorney was the lawyer who went to court on the instructions of the corporation counsel, an elective post held by Dan's friend Dillon, for whom he had raided the Broadway post office. Dan's new eminence carried with it a handsome retainer, augmented by generous fees for whatever law work he undertook on behalf of the city. But he was also free to take up any other briefs he chose to.[27]

Even with his political opportunism, Dan possessed a civic imagination, and one of his pet projects was to enable the New York Corporation to go ahead with creating a great central park. Though Dan would get very little or no mention in most histories of that huge endeavor, he would always argue that he had been one of the prime facilitators. At the time he became attorney to the corporation, there were pending before the assembly in Albany a number of bills appropriating plots of land in the upper part of the island of Manhattan to be used as a series of parks. Conflicts between the opponents and advocates of these projects, based on the desire of various people to develop the land privately, became so violent that all the park bills were doomed to failure. Dan was among the few enthusiasts who argued that this huge public park should reach as low as Twenty-third Street and stretch all the way up the island to the Harlem River. But the central park, he found, was a scheme that everyone liked in principle but lost interest in because of its difficulties.

With some credibility, Dan depicted himself, in a long document now among his papers in the Library of Congress, as catching the train to Albany in the spring of 1853 to argue with politicians he knew for a revival of the scheme. "On my arrival," he wrote, "I found the Capitol strewn with the remains of defeated Park Bills. . . . The warring champions of each of the old measures were invited to meet me in conference, over a good dinner. The banquet lasted well into the night, and before we separated the Senators interested . . . all agreed to support my consolidated plan for a park." This was a characteristic Sickles manner of doing business.

The result of the dinner meeting was that a bill was quickly passed in the assembly to authorize the city to proceed with the project, leaving the choice of ground to the municipal authorities of New York. Unfortunately, one senator with whom Dan would later quarrel over other matters in a national war, Edwin P. Morgan, managed to insert an amendment that he knew would cause Governor Horatio Seymour to refuse to sign the bill. When the governor did refuse, Dan promised to get that clause eliminated, even though this was the last day of the session, and there were only three hours left of it. But with the same degree of frenetic energy that had fueled the Broadway post office raid, Dan went off to the Senate chamber and was able to persuade Morgan to yield. Then he called on his personal friendship with a number of state senators to ensure consideration of his park bill that evening. "Unhappily, so many senators were absent during the call of the roll, that the affirmative vote was one or two short of the required constitutional number, but I was able to hurry from the lobby two or three friendly absentees." So the bill was passed, and hurrying along to the assembly chamber with it, "I obtained the ear of the Speaker and got a hearing for my Bill in the Lower House, where the amendment was promptly concurred in." It remained only to get the bill once more before the governor, and with the help of the clerks of both houses, this was achieved only half an hour before the final adjournment. The document was sent at once to the office of the secretary of state. Dan wrote that "going there myself soon after, I was enabled to obtain from my friend, Mr. Randall, a certified copy of the Park Bill before taking the seven o'clock train to New York."

By eleven o'clock on the night of the triumph, he was in Union Square, New York, aglow with excitement, in front of the house of the corporation counsel, his friend Dillon. Dillon answered Dan's ringing of the front doorbell by appearing at a third-floor window in nightcap and dressing gown to hear the great news, and descended to the ground floor to accept a copy of the enacted bill.

As authorized by the act, Dan hoped, the municipal authorities would include within the park an area named Jones' Woods, "a considerable tract of native forest, covered by large trees, with contiguous land extending to the East River." His relations with the Common Council of New York, both professional and personal, led him to expect a favorable reaction. An old friend, the Democratic leader in the Board of Aldermen, however, told him frankly that although the boys on the council wanted to do all they could for his plan, "you know it is formidable and you must let up on Jones' Woods and the East River frontage. The boys were offered $50,000 to strike out those plots and I can't control them. The big purse is too tempting to resist."

Having been raised in Tammany, Dan was not at all outraged by these blatantly venal motives, but possibly regretted that he had no equivalent purse at his command. Still, he was able to arrange a characteristic New York deal for an extra hundred acres, through an understanding with Alfred Craven, "then chief engineer of the Croton Aqueduct, who desired his salary raised to $7,500 per annum. This I agreed to arrange for him, provided he would locate the new Aqueduct just then authorized within the limits of the proposed park."

Dan knew that Judge Robert Barnwell Roosevelt of the New York Supreme Court, in common with other large landholders, was opposed to the park. So even though the court had appointed commissioners to produce a report on the project, it let it be forgotten. Events prevented

Dan for the time being from pursuing the vision of a park through the maze of New York City's special interests, but it was a matter to which he would return.[28]

Dan the civic-minded attorney was simultaneously fascinated by the problems of New York public transportation. Conscientiously trying to create a better city for his soon-to-be-born child, he applied his rambunctious intelligence to establishing a crosstown system of horse-drawn omnibuses in Manhattan, noting the receipts from similar services in Brooklyn, and devising equations for traffic. Certainly, by the start of the Civil War, eight years later, New York was full of the stubby, roofed, bathtub-style omnibuses that moved New Yorkers along the tracks and contributed to its traffic jams. But in 1853, Dan was in a position of being their advocate. "Omnibuses do not choke up the streets," he boldly declared for the sake of doubters in the Common Council, and he backed up the assertion with mathematical formulae based on the speed, mass, and carrying capacity of the vehicles.[29]

In view of Dan's notable political gifts, Robert Dillon offered some advice, almost certainly on the matter of his continued association with Fanny White, among other indiscretions. Dan was quick to plead in reply, "I cannot play the courtier to the multitude, much less to individuals." He had never done it and never would, he said. Indeed, his approaches to President Pierce contained no note of sycophancy. So as for Dillon's hope for his reform, he sternly rebuffed the idea: "You waste your own time and pain me by requesting it. . . . I know all the consequences of yielding to this idiosyncrasy, and have many a long year since resolved to enjoy it even at the price which must be inevitably paid. I have said to you before that I do not deem it a wise course, nor approve it, nor recommend it to any friend; but I've adopted it: it is mine, and I will follow it come what may." He concluded with a Latin saw: *"Video melior protoque, deteriora sequor"* ("Though I see what the better things are, even so I follow the worse").[30]

He was dutiful to his father, to whom he wrote regularly, even while he was in Washington pursuing his objectives within the presidential ambience. He had been taken to the Congressional Gardens by a friend, and found that the outing, and a dinner he had eaten, redeemed Washington from being "dull and wearisome—and as hot as ever." He said he would rather be with "the female child and her child." For by now Teresa, "the female child," had joyfully come to term and given birth to a daughter, Laura, to the vast excitement of the Bagiolis and their Italian-American friends. Given his busy-ness, Dan was not present for the birth, but he sent Teresa a poem, which she cherished. "As I entered the room," wrote an Italian friend to Dan, "Teresa was calmly sleeping, the worst was all over. . . . I then looked at your babe. Oh, what a delight! . . . To find it so perfect—although not a boy."

His frank father did his best to get Dan to come back from his lobbying in Washington, regretting that he was still there "in neglect of every matter in which you have an interest." Dan's relationship with George would survive many such hearty statements of disapproval. Two of Dan's notes were due that week, George warned, one for $475 and another for $250. "Now it is hardly fair you should entirely neglect your personal affairs to help out others—and to ask me to fill the breach." George reminded him that as generous as it was to help out Gus Schell, his friend who wanted to be appointed collector of the Port of New York, this should not be achieved at the cost of sacrificing his own name and that of his father.[31]

President Pierce may have been lucky to have such busy importunings as those of Dan to distract him. For on January 5 that year, before the inauguration, he had been traveling with his wife and his thirteen-year-old son, Benny, on the Boston & Maine Railroad, going home to Concord, New Hampshire, when the axle of their passenger car broke. The carriage fell down an embankment, dragging other coaches with it, and although President-elect Pierce and Mrs. Pierce suffered only bad bruising, they saw as they picked themselves up in the splintered and chaotic wreckage that part of the superstructure of the car had crushed Benny's head. Mrs. Jane Pierce had thus come to the White House as a ghostly, inconsolable figure, and although she dutifully fulfilled the official functions of a President's wife, she did so with a smile that contained all the dolorous weight of bereavement. The death weighed obviously but less visibly on the President himself, but he had the duties of office to absorb his conscious mind.[32]

This charming but desolate President, Franklin Pierce, was indirectly about to involve the Sickleses in international diplomacy.

# II

IN MAY 1853, PIERCE CAST ABOUT FOR
someone to represent the United States in Great
Britain, and approached that Democratic notable
from Pennsylvania Senator James Buchanan, known
affectionately in the party as Old Buck. Buchanan
had enjoyed an august career as Secretary of State for
four years under Presidents Jackson and Polk, and
before that as a representative and a senator, as well
as the minister of the United States at the Court of St.
Petersburg. He had sought the presidential nomination in 1852, but it had gone to Pierce. Most people
thought it was his last chance. Though Buchanan
was in many ways still impressive—he had a clear
complexion and large blue eyes, and stood over six
feet—he might prove to be too old for that ultimate
prize, which he had sought for a quarter of a century.
Some physical defects had already begun to assert

themselves: he had a nervous twitch that caused his head to jerk more visibly and frequently the older he got, and he was crotchety.

James Buchanan's lack of a spouse had been, since his early manhood, a source of gossip. His closest relationship had been with Senator William Rufus King, a courtly Democrat from Alabama who was in the Senate when Buchanan arrived there in 1834. Buchanan the Pennsylvanian and King the Southerner roomed together and for over twenty years attended Washington events as a team, until Senator King's death. People referred to King as "Old Buck's wife" and "Mrs. Buchanan," and to the two of them as "the Siamese twins." In 1852, King had been offered the chance to serve as Vice President with Pierce, but, afflicted with tuberculosis, lacked the strength to do so.

It could certainly be said that James Buchanan had had a lot of bad luck with women. The fiancée of his Pennsylvania youth had suddenly called off their engagement, separated herself from him, and soon thereafter died. For such a solid and levelheaded man, he grieved excessively then and later, and perhaps in some way he thought he had provoked her grief and the death that followed it. The conclusion some came to was that the fiancée had discovered or been fed information about Buchanan's liking for other men, and that the news had undermined her. Then, in the 1830s, he was confidently expecting to marry Mary Kittera Snyder, a prominent Philadelphia woman who spent much time in Washington, but when he went to Philadelphia to pay court to her, she snubbed him by going to Baltimore.

Rufus King had died just a few months before Pierce offered Buchanan the State Department's most senior diplomatic post, minister to the Court of St. James's.[1]

Accepting the post, Buchanan asked a famous journalist friend, Colonel John W. Forney, whether he could recruit a suitable Democrat to serve as first secretary to the American legation in London. On the lookout, Forney had to go to New York, and at a dinner, as he described it, "met a gentleman whose talents and address seemed to fit him for the post." The gentleman, of course, was Dan Sickles, a so-called Hardshell Democrat like James Buchanan, and a man of great promise within the

New York party machine. But a problem had arisen. When Dan asked Forney what his pay would be, Forney answered that the post paid $2,500 a year. At this, Dan explained that his annual income was more than fifteen times that amount. "I could not think of such a sacrifice," he told the illustrious Forney.

Later in the day, Dan thought again. Perhaps his income was not really the sumptuous $37,500 or more per annum of which he had boasted. Perhaps various friends also pointed out how well this federal appointment would look on his *curriculum vitae*, and what an enriching and vigorous new challenge it might be to convey to the British government the policy of the United States on the freedom of the seas and on American claims to Central America and the Caribbean. Under the previous President, the Whig Millard Fillmore, the foreign policy of the United States had become, in both Dan's and Buchanan's eyes, too lenient toward Britain. So Buchanan and his secretary of legation would have a new agenda to pursue in London. If Dan went, he would be serving under a minister who in 1812 had worn the uniform of the United States, and the prospect of overcoming British diplomatic suspicions of American ambitions toward Cuba in the same spirit as the British had been militarily overcome by Andrew Jackson at New Orleans was something Dan savored.

The day after meeting Forney, Dan boarded a train to Lancaster, Pennsylvania, and took a carriage out to Buchanan's country estate, Wheatland. Buchanan was delighted to have the energetic young New Yorker come to his house. Forney said Buchanan knew of Dan as a brilliant lawyer and politician, a man of the world who had an army of friends and a counterbalancing army of enemies, "like all men of force and originality." During the meeting at the large though austere house at Wheatland, Dan's imagination was no doubt inflamed by Buchanan's plans for the mission they would run in London, and, with a typically sudden shift of ardor, Dan now wanted the post of first secretary as he wanted few other things. Buchanan sent Dan's name to the Department of State for confirmation. Though Pierce's Secretary of State, William Marcy, a Barnburner New Yorker, objected to Dan's appointment,

President Pierce intervened at Buchanan's request to make sure that it went through.[2]

Not everyone in his circle thought that Dan was doing the right thing. He would have to surrender his work as corporation attorney, and a friend from Tammany advised him, "You'd better think well over it before you surrender up that which would give you *a competency* for life." But Dan was set on the project. Teresa, "the female child," was more ambivalent. There was an immediate problem in that Baby Laura was as yet too young, according to conventional wisdom, to make an autumn journey across the Atlantic. In that era, there were great dangers for mother and child in the event of bad weather or an outbreak of fever. Also, Teresa wanted to stay close to her mother, Maria Bagioli, for a time, even though her letters showed that she loved Dan thoroughly and had a forthright hunger to see him more than his busy life as an instrument of Tammany and attorney to the New York Corporation allowed. In her pleas to him, sometimes written on official corporation paper Dan had brought home with him, she never struck a dismal pose; she did not chide or harangue. One cannot but wish that the generosity of her tone had evoked an answering generosity in charming Dan. In a typically unreproving letter of August 1853, she wrote simply because she longed for his company, though she said she had not a great deal to report. She filled up the letter by telling him frankly and in explicit detail about the buying of a new dress—"it's white silk to be trimmed up with ribbon." Obviously Dan did not stint her on clothing, a saving grace, since he certainly did not stint Fanny White. The occasion for the dress was that she was going in a day or so to August Belmont's house for dinner. It is not hard to imagine the lushness and air of Italian-American wholesomeness with which she must have emerged from her carriage outside Belmont's splendid house on Fifth Avenue, near Fourteenth Street, and entered a mansion opulent enough to possess a picture gallery of masters that some considered one of the finest private collections in the world.

As for the sun-filled August day on which she wrote this letter about longing, a dress, and August Belmont, she had many visitors at home. A Mrs. Phillips had called in, a Mrs. McClenehan, a Ginger Clark, and Ma,

Mrs. Bagioli. Teresa loved to fill her house with friends who fussed over the infant Laura and conversed with her. But nothing compensated for Dan's absence, and she pleaded with him to come home to dinner and stay the night. "I want to be as much with you as possible . . . should you go [to England] without me. Come, do. I wish to be near and with you." The imminent separation haunted her. "I hate the idea of your going away without me, and know that I would not have you [do so] if it were in my power. You know what is best—and I shall act as you wish me to however much I may dislike it. God only knows how I can get along without you—and still I think it would be cruel to leave Ma entirely alone. She seems wrapped up in the baby. . . . Come home as early as you can. God bless you my own dear darling pet. May God bless you is my prayer."[3]

Dan had meanwhile been busy at his offices in Nassau Street in organizing cash flow and credit, both for himself and for others. To note the scale of his indebtedness, one has only to look at the loans he took in a period of less than a year, from December 3, 1852, to August 4, 1853, amounting to more than $3,500. Not only that, but he had claims upon his own generosity. A note written on August 18, 1853, and inscribed "To the aid of A.B.," Antonio Bagioli, was for $750 at six months. Perhaps the scale of these borrowings can be put against the reality that a skilled shoemaker earned $7 a week in 1853, a factory laborer earned $5 to $6, and three-quarters of female workers earned less than $3. The claims on Dan were broader than those of family and Fanny White, and he had his own supplicants. Mrs. Mary Ellwill wrote to him pleading that George Ellwill, her husband or son, be permitted to do secretarial work for Dan to pay off a family debt. Dan also made a loan of $150 to Daniel E. McClenehan, no doubt the husband of the Mrs. McClenehan who was, about the same time, visiting Teresa. In an attached note, McClenehan offered Dan "many thanks for the very kind and warm interest you have taken in my case."[4]

An amusing friend to Dan and Teresa as the date of Dan's departure for London neared was an extraordinary American adventurer named Henry Wikoff, often referred to as the Chevalier Wikoff. He was a man in his mid-forties, fashionable, elegant, and young in spirit. Although tending toward the Democratic Party, he seems to have enchanted most social and political leaders and their womenfolk, and he made himself comfortable with a succession of White House families. It was a coup to have him at a dinner table in Washington or in New York, and people spoke of his "captivating manners" and of there being no other American who knew so many European notables. He always turned up at the tables of the great as an unattached male, which added to his air of worldly mystery. Wikoff's origins were suitably mysterious; he had no identified parents, although he was commonly said to be the son of a Dr. Henry Wikoff of Philadelphia. In 1836, he had served in the same position in the United States mission in London that Dan was now about to take up, and during his time there he had traveled to Paris and secured some of the personal effects of Napoleon to return to Joseph Bonaparte in his exile in London. For some obscure service to the Spanish government he was made a knight—hence, the Chevalier Wikoff. But after his stint as a diplomat, in 1840 he had turned entrepreneur and brought the most famous exotic dancer of the era, Fanny Elssler, for a U.S. tour. The tours he managed for the lusty Miss Elssler were famously turbulent, and his relationship with her was complicated by the extremely volatile affair they embarked on. He not only refused to marry Elssler; for whatever reason, he published a number of her letters.

Then, in the late 1840s, Wikoff published a biography of his exiled friend in London: *Napoleon Louis Bonaparte, First President of France*. In England in 1850 he was approached by Lord Palmerston to become a British agent with the particular objectives of persuading the French papers to moderate their tone toward Britain and of promoting an alliance between the United States and Britain. But he was so indiscreet in the approaches he made that Palmerston gave up on him.

At that time, Dan and Teresa were getting to know the Chevalier Wikoff well, after his recent imprisonment in Italy, where he had served time on the accusation of abducting an American heiress, Jane C. Gamble. He was to have married her in London, but she fled to Italy to avoid him, and he pursued her and was accused of abducting her in Genoa.

The fifteen months he had spent imprisoned were still fresh in his memory when he met the Sickleses, and they enriched his anecdotal liveliness.

The case leading to his imprisonment had indeed achieved international notoriety, and had at first subjected Wikoff to considerable social odium. But he was a close friend of the owner of the *New York Herald*, James Gordon Bennett, who had reported on his movements and adventures extensively and flatteringly, and made him a national figure.[5]

Teresa delighted in Wikoff's company, his capacity as a raconteur, and the added bonus that she could speak Italian with him. As can happen with any child of immigrants who has not beheld the land that served as background for the stories of her immigrant father and grandparents, Italy, in Teresa's imagination and as Wikoff portrayed it in the tales he told her, was a place of baroque extremes—elegance and repressive barbarity; high art and extreme squalor; fragrance and evil airs; coruscating democracy and crude tyranny.

Wikoff's attitude toward Teresa was that of a loyal friend, but he may have felt a chivalric sexual enchantment as well. He became one of Teresa's chief consolers when Dan sailed off in September with the understanding that the following spring Teresa and Laura would follow. Buchanan and Dan left for London on August 6, 1853, and Buchanan, who had spent an hour with Teresa the night before, swelled the chorus of those who praised her. "She is both handsome and agreeable," he wrote to his niece Harriet Lane.[6]

Having accepted Dan's invitation to visit London, Fanny White had talked a friend, Kate Hastings, into moving into and managing the brothel at 119 Mercer Street. Like Fanny, Kate was an entrepreneurial prostitute of spirited disposition.[7]

The grievous possibility is that Fanny traveled on the same ship that Teresa waved off from the port of New York. It was the sort of arrangement that made even a worldling like the Chevalier Wikoff shake his head, but those who knew Dan always found forgiving fatally easy.

In the American legation in London's West End, the elderly and dour Buchanan and the youthful and sometimes flamboyant Dan got on surprisingly well. Dan had his own suite within the embassy, and though he probably visited Fanny's lodgings rather than she his, at some point Buchanan must have found out about her. But contrary to the pontifications of late-twentieth-century demagogues on "traditional values," gentlemen tended to consider the sexual arrangements of their fellows as private business, unless political capital could be made of it. Buchanan reported to John Forney that Dan was "a very agreeable and able man, possessed of much energy of character, and likely to make a favorable impression here. . . . I am warmly and strongly attached to him." Buchanan believed that Teresa, "only a child," would soon arrive.

He did tell Forney that Dan "spends a great deal of money . . . but I find him a very able lawyer, and of great use to me." Yet the two men had sharply different styles. James Buchanan lived and dressed with a republican austerity. Secretary of State Marcy had told all diplomats to do so—to wear and be proud of the plain suit of a citizen. The problem was that at one diplomatic levee, an English guest mistook the elderly, slightly trembling Buchanan for a footman and handed him a hat, coat, and cane for cloaking. From then on, to distinguish himself from servants, Buchanan took to wearing a plain dress sword. Dan by contrast always wore to civil events the uniform of the 12th New York State Militia, of which he had been a studious member, absorbing many military manuals and achieving the rank of major. For the purposes of his English sojourn, Dan had the permission of the colonel of the regiment to assume the informal rank of colonel himself. The 12th was one of Tammany Hall's militia regiments, but its uniform had not been designed with republican austerity, it was based on the uniform of the Austrian Imperial Guard, to the extent that while Buchanan might be mistaken for a servant, Dan was sometimes mistaken for a military attaché from Vienna.

When Buchanan visited the palace to present his credentials to the Queen, one Englishwoman, the Honorable Alice Jenkyns, a lady-in-waiting to Her Majesty, reported that Dan was "both elegant and faintly savage. . . . Rather high and mighty for an American, I should say! . . . Really, deerskins would be more becoming, don't you think?"[8]

Buchanan later told a story that made clear the disparity of style between him and Sickles. He went with Dan and his military attaché and a party of other Americans to visit a duchess at her country estate. After they arrived, Dan took charge of diverting their coachmen off to a nearby inn for refreshments. At the end of the visit, the coachmen returned to take Buchanan, Sickles, and other members of the party back to London, but on their way called at the inn to allow the ambassador to settle the coachmen's bill. Buchanan's Presbyterian rectitude was appalled by the account the men had run up—£5 sterling or $20. He made a typical speech about economy and providence, and Dan good-humoredly offered to meet the bill.

"No, sir," said Buchanan. "I will pay it myself and will keep it as a souvenir of English extortion and your economy. Why, my dear sir, do you know I could have got just as good a dinner for twenty-five cents apiece at John Michael's sign of 'The Grapes,' in my own town of Lancaster, as this man has charged a pound a head for? No, sir; I will keep this bill as a curiosity of its kind, an autograph worthy of historical mention." But even here, in conflict with Dan, Buchanan's tone was one of amused exasperation rather than of condemnation.[9]

The new U.S. legation began to work at reconciling British opinion to the impossibility of the United States surviving as a union without the peculiar institution of slavery, no matter how strongly Britain disapproved of it. Indeed, there were irradicable British and United States commercial interests, particularly those of the enormous British textile industry, which made the continuation of the institution essential. At the same time an ambassador appointed by a Democratic government was required to make representations on behalf of the Irish. Handsome Thomas Francis Meagher had recently arrived in New York to a prodigious welcome after his escape from the British penal colony of Van Diemen's Land, and had held talks with President Pierce about the fate of other renowned political prisoners still detained there. Buchanan was instructed by Pierce to urge the British to pardon Meagher's prominent colleagues as a prelude to reform of the British administration of post-Famine Ireland.[10]

There were also sundry trade matters to negotiate, again involving British preferences for goods shipped on British vessels. But the overriding issue, the grand ambition of Buchanan and Dan's mission to London, was to convince Britain that the United States should be permitted to acquire Cuba by negotiation with Spain, and to advance the reasons for Britain to be calm about such an outcome. Europe by now harbored a phalanx of American officials who saw it as their prime mission to have Cuba for the United States. In Spain, America had as ambassador the French-born Louisiana slaveholder Pierre Soulé, who would be involved most directly in negotiations with Cuba, since the island was a Spanish colony. The U.S. ambassador in Paris was another former legislator and Southerner, John Mason, of Virginia. And acting as chargé at the embassy at The Hague was August Belmont, Dan's banker friend from New York. He had represented the Rothschilds in Havana before he moved to New York, and passionately wanted to facilitate the acquisition of Cuba. Dan was impressed that Belmont was capable of running his New York bank from the legation in The Hague.

Dan Sickles's task in the objective of acquiring Cuba was to serve as liaison among these scattered forces, traveling between London, Paris, the Netherlands, and Madrid, keeping all four missions up to date and working in a concerted manner toward the great objective.

He had time, however, to show Fanny White the sights and to attend the West End theaters. London was the center of the English-speaking world and possessed stars of such magnitude that they did not often consider tours of the United States. Dan's tastes were broad—Shakespeare, Sheridan, grand opera, opéra bouffe, music hall. He was not inhibited from dining publicly with Fanny, or from even more perilous behavior for a diplomat. For though he liked the British well enough, he despised the monarchy. His presentation of Fanny White at one of the Queen's receptions at Buckingham Palace, and his introduction of her to the monarch as a Miss Julia Bennett of New York, did not become news in the United Kingdom, but it certainly reached his old enemy, James Gordon Bennett of the *New York Herald*. Perhaps Dan had the satiric intention that it should. Bennett already had sufficient grievances against Sickles and his friends. Three years before, Dan's comrades John Graham and his brothers—two lawyers and an engineer—had waylaid Bennett on a New York street over an article he had published excoriating them, and horsewhipped him savagely while his frail spiritualist wife stood by screaming. The little Scots editor had been caused considerable physical harm then, and he now believed implicitly that the widely reported incident had taken place and was not a mischievous fiction. It was an unconscionably reckless act for a diplomat, one involved in such a big game as the acquisition of Cuba. Yet it was consonant with Dan Sickles's outrageous form of courage, and with his flaunting of Fanny in Albany. It is easy to believe that if Fanny had asked him frequently enough to take her to see the Queen, he would have acceded, and been further tempted by the possibility of making fun of two hated institutions, the *New York Herald* and the British monarchy. If so, he later drew back from the first part of the insult, and would claim that the name Julia Bennett was not designed to offend James Gordon Bennett, but was a regular alias of Fanny White's.

It was fortunate that Teresa, accompanied by Laura and Maria Bagioli, arrived in Grosvenor Square in the spring of 1854, before the controversy over Fanny White reached the pages of the *Herald*. She no doubt heard its echoes in correspondence with American friends, yet she was saved some of the ornate malice and some of the inventions with which Bennett embellished the story. And by the spring of 1854, Fanny had vanished from the scene, having returned to New York to resume management of the Mercer Street establishment. Teresa had Dan to herself in the great city of the British Empire, the city to which even New York made its obeisance.

Teresa was quickly a great London success. Her multilingual gifts were rare among American diplomats' wives. She became very friendly with Buchanan's niece and ward, Harriet Lane, five years older than the eighteen-year-old Mrs. Sickles, but perhaps less worldly and less experienced in life's disappointments. Teresa continued utterly to enchant Buchanan himself. Tidy Dan, spectacular Teresa, and Buchanan, tall in his saddle, rode together companionably and regularly in Rotten Row, where elegant riders went to watch other elegant riders. When Harriet Lane returned to Pennsylvania early in the summer to attend to some family business, Buchanan appointed shining Teresa, despite her extreme youth, as legation hostess. So, with Dan's willing consent, she stood in the reception line with stooping Old Buck as the great of the empire were received to dinner or levees or balls. Among the women she made friends with and was applauded by were Lady Clarendon and Lady Palmerston. Mrs. Lawrence, the wife of the military attaché, together with Harriet Lane and Teresa, were referred to as the "Three American Graces."[11]

An incident that showed how firm was Buchanan's friendship— some even went so far as to say infatuation—with Teresa was the arrival of Assistant Secretary of State John A. Thomas. Thomas's wife asked Buchanan to arrange for her to be presented at court, and Buchanan organized a time and appointed Teresa, as first lady of the legation, to escort and present Mrs. Thomas. Mrs. Thomas declined, however, to be escorted by one so young. There may have been other reasons that she did not want to state to Buchanan. She was a New Yorker, and had no doubt read of Sickles and Fanny White, and now observed that one rumor was right—that Buchanan *was* under the enchantment of Sickles's young wife. When Mrs. Thomas asked for a more suitable sponsor, saying that she "decidedly declined to go to court with Teresa," it caused a quarrel, and Mrs. Thomas was never presented at court.[12]

Throughout these squabbles, Dan continued his shuttle diplomacy. He particularly liked the French-American Soulé. Soulé believed not only that Cuba should be liberated from a decadent and cruel Spanish regime, but that it could be divided into two slave states to counterbalance the ever-expanding free states of the North. The Democrats of Louisiana, including and perhaps particularly Soulé and the governor of the state, John Quitman, had willingly supported a number of unofficial military expeditions to Cuba. With their backing, and in one of many foreshadowings of the twentieth-century Bay of Pigs, a Cuban refugee named Narcisso Lopez recruited an army of Cuban exiles, adventurers, and Mexican War veterans for an invasion of the island in 1849. Lopez's troops acquired the name "filibuster" from the Spanish *filibustero*, meaning freebooter or pirate. Lopez had established a briefly held beachhead on Cuba before being driven out by Spanish troops. Escaping to Key West on his expeditionary ship, Lopez was greeted by Southerners as a hero, and the port officials of New Orleans conspired in mounting a further expedition, which departed in the late summer of 1851. This time Spanish troops were waiting for Lopez and his filibusters. They shot down some hundreds of them, sent 160 off to dungeons in Spain, garroted Lopez publicly in Havana, and lined up fifty American nationals, including the nephew of U.S. Attorney General John J. Crittenden of Kentucky, and executed them.

Soulé had thus brought a number of intense grievances to his appointment to Spain, and to it was added another. In May 1854 the Spanish administration in Cuba seized the American merchant vessel *Black Warrior*. Americans were enraged, and Democrats called for the seizure of what their newspapers called "the Pearl of the Antilles," Cuba. Soulé actively but surreptitiously offered bribes to the Spanish royal household and supported both Spanish republican activists and Cuban subversives with cash. Dan supported Soulé in his confidence that a little diplomatic cunning and bravery would bring Cuba into American hands, even over the desires of England and France, who had their own interests and ambitions in Central America and the Caribbean.[13]

After his visits to Paris and Madrid, Dan was back in London to be involved in a further scandal that July 4. He was put on the job of negotiating arrangements, with the expatriate Bostonian banker George Peabody, for the celebration of the national day. At initial meetings, Dan found that Peabody, a Boston Brahmin and an Anglophile, sought to improve strained Anglo-American relations by inviting the leaders of British business and community to dinner at the Crystal Palace. Buchanan and Sickles both considered the idea repulsive. July Fourth was, after all, a day of republican observance, not an occasion to improve commerce between the two nations. With lack of support from the American legation for the Crystal Palace idea, Peabody planned, with Sickles's help, a smaller event at the Star and Garter Hotel in Richmond on the Thames.

When Sickles arrived at the celebratory lunch that day in his 12th Regiment uniform, he was outraged to see that a majority of the guests were British and that, at the head of the dining room, a small portrait of Washington was hemmed in between two massive portraits, one of Queen Victoria, the other of the Prince Consort, Albert. According to Dan, Peabody debased himself by asking the Queen to lend these two portraits for a private dinner given at a tavern, and she was foolish enough to comply. On top of that, Dan noticed that, according to the program, the toast to the Queen was to precede the toast to the President, and that the toast to George Washington had been allotted to a Briton, Sir Arthur Tennant. "The Star-Spangled Banner" and "Hail Columbia" had been printed in the menu, but with all reference to the "British foe" excluded.

When Peabody arose at the appointed time and uttered an exuberant toast to Queen Victoria, praising her generosity for lending her portraits from the palace, everyone stood, even crusty old Buchanan. Sickles, in his splendid uniform, remained seated. That act would be described by Mr. Bennett in the *Herald* as "a sly display of democratic jealousy of royalty." Perhaps, said Bennett, Dan daydreamed that the Queen would demand that he return home, where he would become the object of "patriotic ovation, leading him straight to the door of the next Presidency." But other papers applauded him for refusing "to play the fawning minion to Royalty." In London itself, unlike the presentation of Fanny White at court, Dan's failure to stand for the royal toast created a great deal of talk and denunciations from Peabody, and put Buchanan to the difficulty of explaining the behavior of his legation secretary. Buchanan argued that Dan had sought not to insult the Queen, but to distance himself from Peabody.[14]

By September 2, Teresa could tell that Dan was working himself up toward a duel, but Peabody appealed to Buchanan, and the matter, fortunately for Peabody, ended.

It is hard to envisage that Teresa did not try to moderate Dan's tendency to pick fights that summer, but he remained edgy and combative. While he worked to make Cuba American, smaller men were concerned only in gossiping about his sins. One of the conflicts he had that season involved Teresa indirectly, since it had to do with Fanny White. Dan had been outraged by a speech given in New York by an old friend, John Van Buren, the former President's son, now a leader of the Softshell Democrats—those who opposed the extension of slavery to new territories and states. At the Young Men's Democratic Club, Van Buren made some remarks about James Gordon Bennett's attempt, in revenge for not getting the ambassadorship to France, to destroy the union between Hardshell and Softshell Democrats. Then, in whatever context, he mentioned Dan Sickles, and immediately, from the floor, came the question "Where is Fanny White?" This was followed by general laughter, and John Van Buren himself was laughing as he replied, "I did not inquire." At this there was more laughter, but Van Buren moved on to say that in 1849 those who tried to make a coalition between Hardshell and Softshell had lost not only Sickles "but some respectable black men, who quitted us on the ground that we united with Sickles." At this there were roars of laughter. Sickles had never consented to any such reconciliation, but Van Buren had quoted "a respectable colored man, a restaurateur, George T. Downey, as saying, 'No party ever degraded themselves as they did by uniting with Sickles. . . . He was lower than the beasts; and nothing, surely, was lower than that.'" There were reported to be gales of hilarity at this. Dan, eventually reading the press reports in London, was not as amused. He saw his accusers as causing unnecessary pain to Teresa and debasing his family honor.

A few weeks after the July Fourth Peabody incident, John Van Buren, called by his friends "the Prince" because of the courtly epicurean habits he had acquired from Martin Van Buren, came to London on the way to visit his father in Italy. A remorseless Dan tracked him to the Queen's Hotel in the West End and sent around a Californian friend as a second to present a letter demanding an explanation and apology, or else recourse to the instruments of honor, that is, to a duel. Van Buren hurriedly explained himself and stated, in writing, that he had had no intention of using the language emanating from the Negro, Mr. Downey, as applicable to Dan Sickles.[15]

Always publicly buoyant, Teresa was privately bewildered by the Van Buren affair and its references to Fanny White. Despite the frankness with which she sometimes questioned Dan, it was true that in her eyes her husband was an older and important man, with reasons to seek women who supplied some mysterious element she was not able to. And then, both her parents and the nuns had raised her to obey the authority of her husband. He could always claim, at the threat of discussing personal matters, that he was engaged and distracted by the huge game he and the others were playing for Cuba.[16]

Before Dan's challenge to the Anglophile banker Peabody, he made a quick visit to Washington to inform President Pierce and Secretary of State Marcy of the strategy devised by the U.S. ministers in Europe for acquiring Cuba. He also told the President that in the Spain of Isabella II, a revolutionary republican party was forming, some members working within the Spanish constitution and some devoted to violent overthrow. Both sets of radicals, he suggested, should be supported with American funds, not least because sufficient trouble at home would keep the Spanish army too stretched to hang on to Cuba. Spain would then sell the island, but perhaps a $5 million bribe to the Queen Mother, Maria Christina, would help smooth the way. Pierce asked Dan to stay on at the White House and produce a report, which was ultimately entitled *On the State of Europe: Its Bearing upon the Policy of the United States*.

Pierce was impressed by the energy and speed with which this considerable report was produced. Dan was able to return to Europe by the same steamer that had brought him. He carried approval from both Marcy and Pierce for the American ministers in London, Paris, and Madrid to meet at a central and neutral point in Europe with a view to releasing a statement on the future of Cuba and the proposed role of the United States.[17]

When Dan went off to Madrid, almost immediately after his arrival in London, he left behind a surmising London and a rumor that would acquire credit in New York. Unprovable in itself, and perhaps started or implied by the embittered Mrs. Thomas, it cast a belittling stain over Teresa's future and Dan's. The imputation was that, with Dan's consent, Teresa was engaged in an affair with the entranced Buchanan, despite his supposed homosexuality. But if there was any truth to the matter, the experience must have induced in Teresa a cynicism about the value her husband placed on her. Her later actions would be thereby colored.[18]

A meeting place for Buchanan, Mason, and Soulé was at last chosen in Ostend, the Belgian port city. This was a supreme and exciting moment for Dan. When the three ministers and their aides convened in a grand Ostend hotel that autumn, hostile antislavery papers reported that Dan drove the agenda—to the ultimate embarrassment of Buchanan— but it was the slaveholder Soulé who dominated the proceedings. He was such a fire-eater when it came to acquiring Cuba that he did not need any assistance in folly from Dan, and his vivid personality swamped the sobriety of Mason the Virginian and Buchanan the Pennsylvanian. Soulé argued throughout the meeting that the best way to shake Cuba free from Spanish domination was to let all Europe know that, as an established principle, the United States was ready to invade Cuba if Spain would not agree to a deal. If Europe became alarmed, to hell with Europe and all its hypocrisies! If not, consent would be implied.

Talking at great length and with great eloquence in the meeting room, Soulé persuaded Buchanan and Mason to help him in preparing and signing a memorandum which would gain notoriety as the Ostend Manifesto. It is believed that Dan had a large role in drafting it. The manifesto declared that if the United States decided that its security depended on acquiring Cuba, and if Spain would not pass on sovereignty in the island to the United States by peaceful means, including sale, then, "by every law, human and Divine, we shall be justified in wresting it from Spain." Soulé and Dan had made sure that a large contingent of the European press was waiting in a lounge at the conference hotel to receive copies of the startling manifesto and to send them out to London, Paris, and Madrid.

There was an instant and hostile reaction to the document not only in Europe but in many sections of America. One newspaper called it "the Manifesto of the Brigands." Antislavery and abolitionist opinion saw the acquisition of Cuba as an extension of Southern power, not as a liberation of an enslaved province. President Pierce had already been punished for supporting legislation that effectively made Kansas a slave territory; he lost nearly two-thirds of Democratic representation in the Congress in the 1854 elections. Now, for the sake of winning back the North, he was under pressure to denounce the work of his three most senior diplomats, and he did so, distancing himself from the manifesto, as much as he would have supported it had the reaction and the times been different.[19]

Dan was personally disappointed at this failure to seize the grail of Cuba. He never lost faith in the idea, but in the autumn of 1854, with the wrapping-up of the matter for the present, he completed his contracted two years as legation secretary. Again, reports on Dan in the New York press were split. Some journalists claimed that Buchanan was pleased to see the back of his embarrassing legation secretary. A less hostile section of the press gave a more credible reason for Dan's return to the United States; it was "in order to prepare the way for the subsequent nomination of his warm personal friend, Mr. Buchanan, for the Presidency." The same newspapers suggested that in Dan, Buchanan had a most competent electoral aide.

In truth, Dan was eager to start on Buchanan's candidacy. Even if it failed, the process itself would challenge, vivify, and reward him. Not that Old Buck would be easy to promote. Given his white hair, the aged and crooked way he hung his head, and the tremors of his face, he would obviously be having his last tilt at the highest American post. There were a number of younger and more attractive men seeking the nomination—Franklin Pierce himself, and Stephen Douglas of Illinois, as well as Marcy, the aged Secretary of State.[20]

Back in New York, the Sickleses took a house in Lower Manhattan, to which Teresa welcomed her multitude of friends and had much to tell them about the Court of St. James's. She must have wondered whether

Dan's relationship with Fanny White would resume, and may not have known, except through gossip, that Fanny had found a new man-in-chief, a wealthy, older fellow named Jake LeRoy, who appeared with her at the theater and drove up Broadway with her in his "flashy carriage." Jake had greater resources than Dan, but he also had venereal disease, which he would in the end pass on to both his young wife and Fanny, rendering her no longer "a clean girl."[21]

Economic difficulties began to bite soon after the return to New York. Dan had passed on to the U.S. Treasury many of his outstanding British bills, which Secretary of the Treasury James Guthrie refused to pay. This left Dan's London creditors howling. But Dan did not mind so much; he was beyond their reach. His future was an American one. Slotting back into Tammany politics and into his law offices at Nassau Street, he found "my park scheme dead and all my illusions vanished." He was anxious to get the report of the park commissioners confirmed by the New York Superior Court. Although Dillon, the corporation counsel, told him he must know it was impossible, and that all the leading members of the bar would be retained to oppose the confirmation, Dan was determined to get both the park and Buchanan on New York's agenda.

In a characteristic stratagem, he drafted a letter to the governor, pointing out that the calendars of the courts were seriously over-crowded. He asked for an additional judge from rural New York to be detailed to the city for a few months to clear up the backlog. He managed to get his letter signed by thirty or forty leading members of the bar, and the governor indicated that he would designate an additional judge with pleasure, if one could be found. Dan already had one, a friend and future Democratic senator, Ira Harris, judge of the Superior Court in the Albany District. Calling at his house, Dan found him away from home, but Mrs. Harris and the daughters of the family received Dan and were charmed by "the suggestion that the judge might be detailed to sit in New York." He then chased Judge Harris to the small rustic court-house in Monticello, in Sullivan County. After the court rose, at the village tavern Dan presented the judge with the proposal, and rushed to

Albany with the judge's letter of consent. Within a day, Harris was formally designated an additional justice of the court in the City of New York.

Dillon was delighted at Dan's achievement and said, "Before an impartial judge it is worth while to attempt a hearing." Dillon gave notice to the city bench that a motion would be made for the confirmation of the commissioners' report in the matter of the central park. On the day named for hearing the motion, Judge Roosevelt, the senior judge, an opponent of the park, was seated in the largest courtroom in the building, usually occupied by the Superior Court, on the second floor of the western wing of City Hall, ready to hear and dismiss the motion. A great array of counsel, "the most distinguished members of our bar," were in their places to oppose it. Judge Roosevelt, Dan noticed, looked serenely happy. "I could fancy I saw his blade, freshly sharpened," wrote Dan with his usual vividness of imagery, "ready to cut out the vitals of the Central Park report and redden the carpets of the sanctuary of justice with the blood of the victims."

But a crier mounted the bench and, "in the stereotype twang of those officials," announced, "All persons interested in the matter of the application of the Mayor, Aldermen, and Commonalty of the City of New York for the confirmation of the report of the Commissioners of the Central Park, draw near before Mr. Judge Harris of the Supreme Court in Room One, in the City Hall, and be heard."

The company rose as one man and found their way downstairs into Room One, the smallest courtroom in City Hall. Judge Harris sat for a month on the commissioners' report, with Dillon and Dan arguing in its favor, and in that time Mrs. Harris and her daughters were courted with invitations to parties, receptions, theaters, balls, in the hope that they would influence Judge Harris to reject the report. But after a month, he confirmed it. "Then for the first time," wrote Dan, "New York was assured of a great public park within its boundaries."

But Dan encountered a further bar to his plans. The city itself lacked the authority to appropriate money to improve the site of the park, which was "one of the roughest and most forbidding spots on the face of the globe. It was a vast mass of rocks and boulders, variegated here and there by an irredeemable swamp." The New York State legislature would have to grant approval for the city to make the necessary appropriations.[22]

In the meantime Dan was driven by his own shortage of money to take private briefs. One client was a Dr. David Jobson, a Scots dentist, formerly surgeon dentist to the royal family of England and author of a well-known textbook on teeth. Dr. Jobson had met in New York an American dentist named John Allan, who had sued yet another dentist for infringement of a patent for artificial teeth. Allan had employed Jobson as a consultant and put him on a retainer of $100 a week to serve as an expert at the trial. Having disastrously lost his trial against his rival, Dr. Allan had not paid Jobson, who employed Dan to retrieve the sum of $1,500 owed to him.

But shortly afterward, when visiting Dan's law offices, Jobson found the defendant, Dr. Allan, privately closeted with Sickles's clerk and, later, with Sickles's father. Jobson sued both Allan and Dan Sickles, saying that Dan Sickles's conduct was "so extraordinary, to say the least of it," that he felt constrained both to institute the legal proceedings against him and to appeal to the Supreme Court of New York for his disbarment.

Jobson told the court that "as a foreigner and a stranger," he was well aware of the risk of Tammany vengeance for making this appeal— "a blow from the cowardly sling-shot or the nocturnal knife." Fortunately for Dan, neither the legal proceedings nor the disbarment hearing came to anything. Jobson always maintained that he did not pursue his case against Dan Sickles because his new lawyer was also bribed by Allan and Sickles! Poor Dr. Jobson got a sound education in the ethics in power of the New York bar, particularly the side associated with Tammany.[23]

But the Jobson incident barely delayed Dan in his organizing of rallies, Democratic orators, and speeches to support Buchanan's candidacy, and in the autumn of 1855, the dominant Hardshell wing of Tammany nominated Dan for the state senate. They and Dan knew that his candidacy would serve as a litmus test in New York for Buchanan's candidacy. During Dan's service to two campaigns, his own and Buchanan's, Teresa and Laura received less than his already limited attentions to domesticity. In his efforts to be elected he was helped out by all the old gang—by the Grahams; by the charming and universally loved Irish-American lawyer James Topham Brady; by the Irish icon and escaped political prisoner handsome and oratorical Thomas Francis Meagher; by a handsome friend named Sam Butterworth, who had every reason to hope for a profitable post out of a Democratic victory; by the best-selling Chevalier Wikoff, who had now written a book on his courtship and Italian imprisonment; and by perhaps Dan's most reliable friend and ally, Emmanuel (Manny) Hart, a former New York alderman and U.S. congressman. Dan was pleased to see that his much-publicized tweakings of Britannic dignity during his stay in London had done him no harm with passionate Irishmen like Judge Charles Daly and Meagher and those who shared their attitudes. And he was elected to the senate in Albany. He did not choose to take Teresa with him; indeed, she may not have wanted to go to the capital, since the railroad offered Dan the chance of adequate access to his wife and daughter and his friends in New York.[24]

During that spring, Teresa wrote to her confidante Florence about the familiar problem: the way the national scene took Dan away from her. "Dan is going to Washington this evening," she said. After Washington he was going to Richmond, then back to Washington, and then home. He would be gone for a week or ten days. "He said last evening (rather late) I might go with him." That "rather late" may have meant too late for her to do anything about it. But she cast a deliberately blithe light on her not accompanying him. She had much to look after at home; "what with dressmakers, seamstresses, shoemakers, etc. etc. I have my poor hands full." Deprived of a place in his councils and at his side, she made what she could of shopping. But she was looking forward to the summer, when Dan would be free to spend time with her, and they might go to see Florence in the White Mountains. Dan, however, was trying to find a summer house "this side of the Hudson," and if he succeeded, that would be the end of the White Mountains for that year.

As in the old days, before London, Teresa received numerous visits from her friends. Molly Coggins, the Sanford girls, Ann Hendrickson, all visited her in that spring of Dan's state senatorship. And as Teresa had said to Florence, Dan liked to rent substantial houses. Those who disapproved of him assumed he achieved this with the sweeteners he received while serving in office. Dan spoke out against the Albany bridge bill on behalf of interests that would be damaged by it, and also against the Trinity Church bill, brought forward at the behest of less well-off Episcopal churches with which Trinity shared none of its extensive real estate revenues. It was claimed in one newspaper that the interests behind Trinity paid Dan $10,000 to block the bill. But, as open as he may have been to such a fee, his continuing need to borrow makes that an unlikely sum, and the people who made the accusations often distorted other details of his behavior and may have done so again. Not that it would have been contrary to the political traditions of Tammany for a politician to accept cash to espouse a cause of whose rightness he was more or less convinced. As George Washington Plunkett of Tammany Hall later said, this sort of practice was "honest graft," and was to be distinguished from the other kind of graft non-Tammany people, such as Republicans, were involved in.

Sweetened or not, Dan was active on the floor, marshaling opposition to the bill that would have dispersed Trinity's income and canceled its privileges. When it came to his turn to speak, he was all eloquent and nostalgic piety: "I was born and reared within the bosom of this church and in this parish. The graves of my humble ancestors lie within its sacred enclosures. The marriage vow, the baptismal blessing, were pronounced upon those from whom I sprang, by the side of its altars. It is the only church which now remains within my district to take care of the poor."[25]

Dan now found another chance to bring forward an act to establish a plan for the central park while providing the city with the appropriation to begin its improvement. The first $1,500,000 was thus authorized, though even this inadequate sum raised the ire of taxpayers and property owners, who swarmed into the lobby of the capitol at Albany in opposition. Surprisingly, the newspaper that most approved of Dan's efforts was the *Herald*. Mr. Bennett lived near where Dan and Teresa now did, on the outskirts of New York, "in the suburbs," as Dan said, "and allowed me the hospitality of his column for an occasional advocacy of the park. This was our only support in the press."

Dan had gained considerable backing from the rural members of the two houses by such occasional courtesies as drafting bills for them and assisting them in matters of parliamentary procedure, yet he found that opposition to the park "was slowly and surely decimating my forces." Men would come to him and say, "Mr. Sickles, we were disposed, as you know, to favor this hobby of yours, but we are told that no city in the world has ever gone to the expense of establishing such a park as you propose in New York." They had been told that all the great parks in other countries had been paid for by the national governments. Hyde Park, Regent's Park, and Richmond Park in England were owned by the Crown. The Bois de Boulogne was maintained by the French imperial treasury. Dan was asking, they complained, "that the city alone should undertake this job."

So the legislators in Albany believed that their voters and their colleagues would put increasing pressure on them to vote against the bill. His opponents went home, wrote Sickles, loudly expectant of his defeat. But Dan sent for a friend, Charles K. Graham, a young engineer of great promise, and offered him $500 to make two panoramic pictures on a large scale. One was to represent the present topography of the territory within the proposed central park, the rocks and swamps. The other was to be of a Garden of Eden. "One must see in it beautiful lawns of emerald green," said Dan, "soft as velvet, and groves of tall, graceful trees; rambling brooks with musical voices, expanding into lakes that mirror the swans floating on their surfaces; gondoliers filled with happy groups of maidens and cavaliers; bridges of graceful design; broad avenues filled with gay equipages and thousands of happy men, women and children filling the landscape . . . and this we will call The Park, Charlie, when you have finished this Garden of Eden."

In the end, Graham undertook the work as a labor of love, and Dan had the two panoramas placed on the wall of the anteroom of the senate chamber in Albany. He brought members of both houses in small groups to inspect them—on one wall, the forbidding ground that presently existed; on the other, the paradise he promised to create. Some of the critics of the project particularly ridiculed the flowers in the second picture. "Every bud would require police protection, night and day. Bah!"

Dan also brought together three members of the senate and three members of the assembly, all of whom opposed the project, and set aside $300 of his own money to allow this panel of six to visit the city, go over the ground of the proposed Central Park, and report to their associates whether or not the first picture faithfully portrayed the existing topography. Their report, made within the next ten days, was favorable, and as a result of this conversion of the formerly hostile legislators, the tide of opinion turned. A member of the senate told Dan, "You might as well go home. The park bill will pass."

This tale, admittedly related chiefly from Dan's point of view, is nonetheless an indication of his creative powers as a parliamentary manipulator, and an explanation of the devotion many people in the Democratic Party felt for him. It helps explain why Dan had been elected chairman of the executive committee of Tammany Hall, the dominant organizational post in the Democratic Party of New York. His consultative committee of twenty-four Democrats stood by him. He was able to marshal those twenty-four behind him through the entire park process, and thus was able to write, "In the fifties . . . I saw the rocks in Central Park covered with soil . . . filled with earth; great basins for lakes excavated . . . countless trees planted . . . long bridle paths made; bridges of many graceful forms erected . . . and nowadays, as I drive through these charming pleasure grounds and see thousands enjoying them, I sometimes feel a complacent pride in the recollection that I helped to create this park."[26]

While in Albany, Dan was equally, democratically, and splendidly eloquent in the matter of a bill to prevent illegal voting in the City of New York—the registry bill. He needed no prompting to attack this legislation and protect Tammany's strong hold on New York City elections, and he was appalled that the "whole framework of this bill presupposes that election frauds in New York consist in illegal voting by electors." It was electoral inspectors who were corrupt, he claimed, yet the bill sought to give electoral inspectors in New York even greater power! He argued that every voter of what he called the American Party, that is, the Know Nothings, would be duly registered without any inconvenience to himself, while other political parties "would be obliged to depend wholly on the willingness of individuals to attend at the office of the inspectors and undergo the species of examination or trial which the inspectors are authorized by this Bill to institute." A stranger sitting in the senate chamber in Albany and listening to the debates would have supposed that illegal voting was limited to New York, that Buffalo, Utica, Rochester, Albany contained no persons wicked enough to violate the electoral law! They would be amazed, Dan said, that the City of Brooklyn, the second city in the state, "has no occasion for the purifying provisions of this Bill!"

He was pleased to defend the Irish who had helped elect him. He attacked an opposing senator who had spoken of violations of the election laws by the O'Callaghans and the Murphys, names used glibly to represent the Irish clans of Tammany, whereas in ninety-nine cases out of a hundred, said Dan, the Irishman considered election-rigging "a treason to his land of adoption."

This claim must have provoked guffaws among some of the opponents, but the speech was not designed for them. It was designed to be read, cherished, and applauded by the legions of New York Democrats, perhaps specifically by the "O'Callaghans and the Murphys."[27]

Dan now lived in "the suburbs," in a worthy residence uptown, since a larger house in Lower Manhattan was beyond his means. The country house he bought—or, as some said, his father bought for him but kept title to—was a big, foursquare structure that had been built in the first decade of the century on what would later be Ninety-first Street. Though Dan's city had grown in population nearly sevenfold since his birth thirty-seven years before, it had not yet devoured this remote area of Manhattan, known as Bloomingdale. Though a suburb, it had the look of a picturesque village and took its name from the Knickerbockers, an old Dutch East India Company family. Bloomingdale was also the original name of the street later known as Broadway, which connected the township to the city. A regularly scheduled coach could transport the Sickles family down seven miles of increasingly serviceable road to New York proper and its delights, to the corporation attorney's office in City Hall, and to Dan Sickles's law office on Nassau Street. Their house stood on the Hudson—part of its grounds are now Riverside Park. The road into it, a country lane from the direction of Broadway, came down a rocky but verdant escarpment. The area was well wooded, the terrain graced by oak trees, and, a few streets to the north, a picturesque rivulet ran through a ravine into the Hudson at Striker's Bay. Dan's young, admired wife, nineteen-year-old Teresa, and her lovely child, Laura, were adornments to its arcadian air.[28]

The acquisition of the Bloomingdale house, Teresa had hoped, indicated that Dan needed a retreat, a nest; that he harbored a wish to take his wife and daughter rowing on the Hudson on still days in summer. She hoped to put behind her all the gossip in the formerly vicious *Herald* over Dan's association with the dreadful Fanny White. Teresa loved the large, pleasant, but drafty and demanding house, and for the sake of Dan's success, and as a token of her love, became its true and effective administrator. She supervised the moving in and placement of the furniture—the ornate and solid chairs of the Rococo Revival, the ottoman sofas, the Belgian tapestry mats and oriental rugs, the iron and brass beds, including the marriage bed she shared with Dan, which, appropriate for a couple of their standing at that time, was a high, assertive, curtained Renaissance Revival structure. She attended to the complex business of curtaining and valancing the windows.

Similarly, she managed the house's servants, the maid-cook, the gardener, the groom (she had a passion for horses), and she oversaw the domestic animals, hens, dogs, some cows that roamed the verdant reaches of this property by the river, and horses. She would always cherish this house, even after it became her prison.[29]

In her early occupation of Bloomingdale, Teresa told her old school friends, she amused and occupied herself by walking and riding about the rustic location "chased by five dogs and two cats." She had been lent a horse for the time being, till she settled to acquiring one of her own, by a local man, one of the Strykers who gave their name, Anglicized, to a nearby bay of the Hudson and who had lived in the area from before the Revolution. But since Dan was always absent on politics, she confessed, "I found it rather stupid riding on horseback every day alone," and she sent it back to Mr. Stryker, with her thanks.

She went to town occasionally, once to sit for a photograph by the renowned Mathew Brady, whose name would soon become irrevocably attached to photographs of the Civil War. "I dread having to stand for the photograph Brady is taking—still more do I dread the dressing," she confessed. But Brady had taken a portrait of Dan's mother, so Teresa was filially bound to submit. She thought the miniature, now sadly lost, acceptable, but worried that the larger one was too coarse-looking. It was an era in which a certain fleshiness was considered essential to womanly beauty. Childbirth and fevers were great killers of women, and were considered more likely, in an age without antibiotics, to kill the slim, the anorexic, the narrow-hipped. But although it was taken for granted that all beauties were of ample, curved body, as was the young Teresa, that quality had to be combined with a certain maidenly delicacy of feature. Flesh and spirit must effectively combine in true measure, in a way that spoke as authentically of heaven as of desire. A sketch that was based on the Brady photograph, and published in an illustrated paper of the day, shows that Teresa had an exquisite face, heart-shaped, full-lipped, with enormous and arresting dark eyes.

She was delighted that Dan, despite the demands of politics this hectic year, was occasionally with her; on an evening that fall she had been to Wallack's Theatre with him and two of their friends. She loved the theater, as did Dan. She had been perfectly delighted with the pieces, especially the first play, "Don Caesar de Balzar which old Wallack played." On another evening, Manny Hart, Gus Schell, Teresa's mother, Dan, and a friend from Bloomingdale and Tammany, Tom Field, all went to a fair at the Crystal Palace to raise funds for a hospital. Teresa met a number of schoolmates from the convent, and chatted away enjoyably to them, a girl who, in company, "enjoyed myself to my heart's content. If Dan would only come home tonight, I would like to go to Laura Keene's—they say it is a beautiful house, and besides, they are playing a comedy at it now that was written by 'Mr. Wilkins,' one of the editors of the *Herald*—as I know the man, I would like to see if his play is as stupid and disagreeable as the author." We do not know whether Dan got home that evening to take Teresa to Laura Keene's, but clearly she refused to forgive the *Herald* long after Dan found it half expedient to do so.[30]

It is interesting to note how much, apart from Dan's absences, Teresa found pleasure in the semirustic life. After all, she had entertained notables at the heart of the British Empire, and here she was among the oak trees on the Hudson. But she was an adaptable young woman, and would soon adapt yet again to a more public existence. She did not convey in her letters, and certainly did not brag about, how hectic a year it had proved to be. When James Buchanan returned from England, in April 1856, his friend and aide Dan had a resonating welcome ready for him in New York, where he intended to present his old friend with the combined resources of Tammany. Buchanan's ship having docked, he was met by a splendid carriage and driven up Fifth Avenue to the Everett House on Union Square. There, waiting for him, was one Senator John Slidell of Louisiana, an enormously powerful Democratic kingmaker from Louisiana and a great advocate of acquiring Cuba. Senator Slidell had raised a considerable amount of money for Buchanan's campaign from his contacts in Wall Street, to whom Slidell held out the prospect of the ruin of American commerce if the Republican candidate, John Charles Frémont, was elected.[31]

But Dan himself was persuaded by Tammany to run for the United States Congress in those elections of 1856. If he won, together with Old Buck, they would be a team reunited in Washington. Old Buck went into the Democratic convention in Cincinnati with a powerful number of Democrats in his camp. Given the temper of the times, he had an important advantage over Stephen Douglas, the hugely talented, diminutive powerhouse from Illinois, and over President Pierce and Secretary of State Marcy. He carried no blame for the bloody territory of Kansas a thousand miles to the west, a region for control of which pro- and antislavery forces were competing. The national imagination was unsettled and fevered by Kansas. The previous year a posse of eight hundred proslavery men had poured into Lawrence, Kansas, the antislavery Free-Soilers' chief town, demolishing newspaper offices, burning public buildings, including the home of its antislavery governor, shooting males, and looting shops. In response, in the spring of 1856, the abolitionist zealot John Brown had kidnapped five proslavery settlers from their homesteads near Pottawatomie Creek, Kansas, and, in God's name, hacked them to death with broadswords. The nation believed that the conflict in Kansas was a form of civil war, begun at the peril of American society, its culture, its commerce, and its remarkable Constitution. People yearned for an unspectacular but wise figure who bore no responsibility for bleeding Kansas, someone who seemed safer than sparkling Douglas and less fallible than the charming incumbent, Franklin Pierce.

In the North, Buchanan was up against Frémont, but in the South, he was opposed by the Know-Nothing anti-immigrant, and anti-Catholic candidate Millard Fillmore, a former President. Here too he was helped by events, for Fillmore's warnings about the threat to American culture from the Irish did not measure up in most Americans' minds to the central issue: the question of preservation or abolition of slavery, and the capacity of either to break the nation asunder. Though young

Republicans marched in vast torchlit processions, chanting, "Free Soil, Free Speech, Free Men, Frémont," many former Whig voters, the party from which the Republicans had grown, chose Buchanan for the sake of the peace his gravity of manner seemed to offer. Frémont's own father-in-law decided that Buchanan was the safer bet.

On the day, Buchanan carried Pennsylvania, New Jersey, Indiana, Illinois, and California, and nearly the entire South. He was a minority President, achieving only 45 percent of the vote. It was undeniable, though, that the majority of Americans felt relief at patriarchal Buchanan's success, a return to a platform on which the national debate might proceed to a peaceful rather than a rancorous, radical conclusion.[32]

Dan Sickles was not only the political prodigy who brought the New York vote to the Democratic presidential candidate James Buchanan. The same day, he himself was elected as representative for the Third Congressional District of New York, as easily as, the previous year, he had been elected to the state senate. The Third District covered much of the older section of Manhattan south of Houston Street and was bounded on the east by Broadway. It embraced the city's financial center and a long stretch of wharves with a population of just under 100,000, almost half of whom were foreign-born, either German or Irish, though predominantly Irish; it was an area in which hard-line Tammany Democrats could not lose. Dan Sickles was one of fifty-three Northern Democrats elected to the House, where he joined seventy-five Southern Democrats and ninety-two Republicans.[33]

And so it was now Representative Sickles who returned to Teresa in Bloomingdale. At the age of barely twenty, she had achieved the considerable eminence of being a federal legislator's wife. By contrast, the energetically political Mary Todd Lincoln had to wait until she was twice that age to see her husband serve one unsuccessful term as an unimpressive congressman from Illinois. But the price of being Mrs. Congressman Sickles would be severe. To her friend Florence, Teresa confessed herself so distressed by the growing periods of separation from Dan that she begged Florence not to show anyone her letters about being alone. She did not want to give others license for gossip or gratification.

And, in any case, there was the promise of a better and more pleasurable time. Dan proposed taking Teresa and Laura with him to Washington, where they would live under one roof during the sessions of Congress.[34]

# III

EARLY THAT WINTER, ELATED BY COM-
ing to Washington as a legislator and lieutenant,
Dan took up residence in a suite at the National,
where a number of other congressmen, either well
heeled or well funded, stayed. Dan's hotel, together
with Willard's and Brown's, and sundry respectable
boardinghouses, provided accommodation for representatives and senators. The less-than-wealthy Abraham Lincoln and his wife had, during Lincoln's stint
in Congress, stayed at Mrs. Spriggs's boardinghouse
on the present site of one of the Library of Congress
buildings and had occupied rooms so small that the
indulged youngster Robert Lincoln disturbed other
guests with his rowdiness. Often, representatives and
senators of the same party or faction lodged together
in what were called Messes. The F Street Mess of
Southern Democrats was a feared coalition who sat at

one table and talked politics all through dinner. Willard's and the National were used temporarily by congressmen trying to find more permanent domiciles in the capital. As the inauguration of James Buchanan neared, many of the guests at the National were stricken with gastroenteritis, a disease typical in the experience of legislators, Washington having an unsavory reputation.[1]

Washington in the mid to late 1850s still had some of the character Charles Dickens had seen in the 1840s. The parkland of Washington was "a melancholy piece of waste ground with flowsy grass, which looks like a small piece of country which is taken to drinking, and has quite lost itself," Dickens wrote. It was a place of "spacious avenues that begin in nothing and lead nowhere: streets, miles long, that only want houses, roads and inhabitants; and ornaments of great thoroughfares which only need thoroughfares to ornament." Washington was, to Dickens's and other folks' jaundiced eyes, despicable for its lack of elegance, the epicenter of that abhorrent American habit of spitting. It was, as the great English novelist said, "the head-quarters of tobacco-tinctured saliva." Congressmen spat on the steps of the Capitol and on its internal surfaces. The carpets of Willard's did not inhibit the tobacco-chewing spitters; they were splotched with stains. Dan himself had the more urbane, metropolitan manner of chewing on a cheroot, but one met all kinds, from Californians to Appalachian farmers, in the Congress of the United States, and the spittoons were placed in abundance even in Dan's day.[2]

Of course, Dickens brought to his descriptions of Washington the hubris of a native of the great city of London, but many of Dan's contemporaries agreed with him. One Yankee legislator's wife described the capital as a third-rate Southern city of some 61,000 souls. "Everything worth looking at seemed unfinished. Everything finished looked as if it should have been destroyed generations ago." But although the capital was so rustic that the eminent Senator Henry Clay was attacked by a large goat in Pennsylvania Avenue, to young congressional wives it was, in its spaciousness and its social opportunities, what the young Southern bride and friend of Teresa's Mrs. Roger Pryor found it to be: "a garden of delights."[3]

With Laura and an Irish maid, Teresa made the rail trip to Washington for the first time late that winter. She was in a heightened state of anticipation. She would be with Dan at the heart of a national festival; she had an invitation to the inauguration of her friend James Buchanan and to the accompanying parties and balls. She, like other travelers, left New York at eight o'clock in the morning and got to Washington's sooty, inadequate station about seven in the evening, after changing trains in both Philadelphia and Baltimore because of the lack of bridges and a standard railroad gauge. The Southerners had it even harder; some came north by steamer from Charleston, Savannah, Mobile, New Orleans, and Galveston. Congressmen of the Virginia aristocracy caught the Richmond, Fredericksburg & Potomac Railroad to Acquia Landing, from where they had to take the steamer, with all their luggage and their black slave servants, to the capital.[4]

For newcomers like Teresa and Dan, the Southern Democratic gentry constituted the old hands of the Washington scene. Though there were isolated wealthy Northerners among the legislators, the Southerners on average had the higher wealth. They certainly also possessed the higher level of style and self-esteem. To Dan, it was the Southerners who, despite the unfinished dome on the Capitol, the unfinished steps of the Treasury, the still-lacking pillars of the White House, infused Washington with social self-importance. To do well in Democratic Washington, Teresa would need to impress the Southern Democratic brethren.

As Buchanan's inauguration approached, Dan and his wife and child moved out of the National Hotel, for the guests fled when many, including the President-elect, fell ill with the gastroenteric infection. There was a rumor that the illness derived from poisoned rats that had fallen into the hotel well. The hotel blamed the outbreak on the city sewers, a regular and well-deserving target of blame. The Sickles family found accommodation and hospitality in the home of Jonah Hoover, the federal marshal for the District of Columbia. It was there that Dan and Teresa dressed for the inauguration.

On March 4, 1857, the day appointed, Dan shared an open carriage in the presidential procession of Washington notables with Representative John B. Haskin from upstate New York. The parade was headed by the Marine Band, which regularly played at the White House receptions, and by eight companies of regulars and militia. The Washington militia's Montgomery Guard was led by a man who would become a principal figure in the history of Dan and Teresa. It was the popular district attorney of the District of Columbia, Philip Barton Key, wearing a uniform nearly as splendid as the one Dan had worn in London— blue and gold. Barton Key's favorite mount of the moment was an iron-gray horse named Lucifer, which he rode ahead of his colorful detachment.

A little way along Philadelphia Avenue, the carriage of President Pierce and President-elect Buchanan, having come from the White House by a back way, slotted into the procession behind the militia and a float carrying a dazzling, full-bodied young woman swathed in satin and representing the Goddess of Liberty. Buchanan was pale and thin from the infection he had caught at the National. He had had to dose himself with tonics and anti-diarrhea medicine to be able to get into the presidential barouche and be cheered by the citizenry.

The Capitol, toward which the procession made its way, was in the process of being rebuilt, and the House of Representatives was being enlarged. Here, President Pierce, in the last day of his administration, entered with the new chief executive between the muskets of the honor guard, and the two men took their places by the Speaker's chair before the Chief Justice of the Supreme Court, Roger B. Taney. Congressmen from both houses entered and crowded into the desks of the chamber. In the gallery, Teresa had a reserved seat beside a friend from London days, Mr. Buchanan's niece Harriet Lane. Harriet knew that her uncle intended to invite her to be the First Lady—to welcome and entertain guests at the White House, to stand at his side, smiling, and to be the social moderator and focus of the capital. Much of the conversation between the two young women may well have centered on that exciting prospect.

Teresa, looking more a schoolchild than a politician's wife, clearly attracted the curiosity of other congressional wives in the gallery, who probably had read about Dan Sickles and his waywardness, and to whom the fragrant Teresa offered such a contrast. Innumerable people remarked that she looked girlish and unsullied, as she sat beside Harriet Lane, in a dress of ruffled crinoline and with bare shoulders, which, once outside, she would cover with a shawl. On her head was a hat decorated with jonquils as a symbol of coming spring and of the promise of the era. She seemed to incarnate health, beauty, and virtue, and to reflect the substance of Buchanan's reassuringly poetic inaugural speech. "The night is departing, and the roseate and propitious dawn now breaking upon us promises a long day of peace and prosperity for our country. To secure this, all we of the North have to do is to permit our southern neighbors to manage their own domestic affairs, as they permit us to manage ours." At the rostrum, Buchanan was sworn in by Justice Taney, and the Southerners in the gallery and on the floor of the chamber were delighted—a Southern Chief Justice swearing in a southward-leaning chief executive.[5]

The following evening, a huge inaugural ball was held in a vast temporary structure in Judiciary Square. Among the guests were many of Dan's campaign supporters, who had fought for both him and the President. One of them, Sam Butterworth, was not dancing. He had been shot in the foot during a carouse, when, like an omen, a pistol carried by New York's postmaster, Isaac Fowler, dropped out of Fowler's pocket and accidentally fired. Considering that Dan was a novice congressman, one commentator noticed how many experienced men approached him for a word: Jeremiah Black, soon to be Buchanan's Attorney General; Senator Slidell of Louisiana, the Buchanan and Cuba man, and his beautiful Creole wife; the new Vice President, John Breckinridge; wiry Senator Stephen Douglas of Illinois; and Colonel Forney of Pennsylvania, who had recruited Dan for the London job. Chevalier Wikoff was there too, still a good friend to Teresa, as he would be to many a woman bearing secret or not-so-secret woes.

When the gray-haired, avuncular President entered, with his awkward gait and crookedly held head, at about eleven o'clock, followed by

Miss Harriet Lane on the arm of a senator, "Hail to the Chief" resonated through the wooden structure.[6]

A welcome figure at the inaugural ball, District Attorney Philip Barton Key, who had led the Montgomery Guards in the inauguration procession, was already entrenched as a capital favorite by the time Teresa and Dan arrived in Washington. The powerful Mrs. Virginia Clay of Alabama, queen of the Southern Democrats and right-minded people, wife of Senator Clement C. Clay, said that Mr. Key was foremost among the popular men in the capital and that his sister, Mrs. George Pendleton, possessed a classic beauty. Key, wrote Mrs. Clay, "was a widower during my acquaintance with him, and I recall him as the handsomest man in all Washington society." In appearance he was an Apollo, said Mrs. Clay, and prominent "at all the principal functions; a graceful dancer, he was the favorite of every hostess of the day. Clever at repartee, a generous and pleasing man, who was even more popular with other men than with women." Whether everyone saw him as an Apollo, out of his militia uniform, Key was a sandy-haired, tall, languid fellow of thirty-nine whom people tended to call by his second name, Barton. In the recent years of his widowerhood, before his meeting that night with Teresa Sickles reinvigorated his life, he had sometimes been careless with dress, occasionally coming to dinner with a riding whip under his arm, or appearing at formal occasions still dressed in the top boots and leather leggings he had worn when riding.

Barton could get away with all that, since he came from an old and enormously renowned Maryland family. His late father, Francis Scott Key, writer of "The Star-Spangled Banner," had himself held the post his son now occupied. Barton's uncle was another iconic figure, the elderly and fearsome Chief Justice Roger Taney. But Barton Key attended the inaugural ball not purely for social reasons. He was uneasy about his job. Recently he had argued a difficult court case. A Californian congressman named Philemon P. Herbert, breakfasting in Willard's dining room, had made an insulting remark about the Irish waiters. One of them, Thomas Keating, objected to the affront, at which Herbert drew a pistol and shot Keating dead. The ambassador from the Netherlands, who had been eating breakfast at Willard's at the time, could have been useful to District Attorney Key, but would not permit himself, as a diplomat, to be summoned as a witness. Ultimately, to the disgust of Washington's Irish community, Herbert was acquitted. To Key's distress, the question of Herbert's assumption that Keating himself was armed, in a city where so many were armed, was a factor in the successful defense. Nonetheless, Key had been widely criticized for failing to bring about a guilty verdict, and he feared that Buchanan might share the view. Since the position of federal district attorney was in the granting of the new President, Key was eager to speak to as many intimates of Buchanan as he could, seeking their influence on his behalf. So at some stage in the evening, the tall, elegant Key was seen bowing slightly toward the shorter, dapper, energetic Sickles. And on that night, Key met Teresa.[7]

Teresa, an enthusiastic horsewoman, admired Key not least for his being an accomplished horseman. She felt enlarged and fortunate in his presence. She may have been informed by other young Washington women about Key's tragic loss. Barton had grieved intensely for his wife, and had thereby attracted the attention of many sympathetic people, especially young widows and spinsters. He met many of them regularly, since he liked Washington society and attended daytime receptions. Teresa, who admired Dan's energy, was willing to overlook Barton's apparent indolence; he had never been the most energetic DA, but in a way his bloodlines and class discouraged too much effort. Besides, he had for some time suffered from a heart condition, or, as one commentator said, imagined he did, "which gave him a soured and discontented look." Those who knew him best said that his eccentricities of manner covered a kind heart.[8]

"There was," said another laudatory commentator on Teresa, "something inexpressibly fascinating and delightful about her fresh girlish face, and her sweet amiable manner. She was as kind to a raw boy just let loose on society as to its Secretary of State; great and small, rich and poor, Democrat and Republican—she treated all with the same unvary-ing gentleness and lady-like amiability." And unlike many Northerners, Teresa had cultivated tastes in music and could speak well at least three languages—Italian, French, and English—and make her way in Span-ish and German. No wonder, this commentator added, that she became such a favorite in Washington. And little wonder Key found her a re-freshing presence.[9]

In the first days of his presidency, Buchanan received an astonishing gift from the Supreme Court. The same eminent Southerners who had helped ensure Buchanan's election, and had danced with Teresa at the inaugural ball, were bringing pressure to bear on the Supreme Court and on Key's uncle, old Roger Taney. In the face of abolitionist fervor, they were zealous about establishing as a matter of law that Southern slavery had legal force anywhere, in any state, and that if, for example, in the new western territories of the United States, there was a property holder who owned a slave, his right retained full legal force. The status of an aging slave named Dred Scott was then being fought before the Supreme Court, in a case being financed by Missouri abolitionists.

Dred Scott and his wife had been owned by an army surgeon, who had taken them from the slave state of Missouri to a military post in Illi-nois, and then to the northern section of the Louisiana Purchase that be-came Minnesota. The two slaves had lived for such a long period in free territory that they now claimed freedom. Abolitionists had helped them get the case as far as the Missouri High Court, where it had been de-feated, and then encouraged them to take an appeal to the United States Supreme Court to confirm their condition as free people.

Unhappily for Scott and his supporters, there were five Southern justices on the Court. If Dred Scott lost his case, as expected, along re-gional lines, it would mean that Congress had no power to ban slavery from new territories, including Kansas. The Southern institution would be triumphant and unassailable. According to the grand Southern strat-egy, the Supreme Court did find against Dred Scott, by a vote of seven to two. Taney and his fellow justices thus decided that Scott's sojourn for many years in Illinois and for a similar period at Fort Snelling did not make him free once he returned to Missouri, or wherever he went. For the federal government to try to regulate slavery, ruled Justice Taney, was unconstitutional, since it denied the property rights granted citizens under the Fifth Amendment. In addition, seven of the justices found against Dred Scott because, they averred, no slave or descendant of a slave could be or ever had been a U.S. citizen.

Though Dan approved the general tenor of the findings, he must have found some aspects offensive. He did not practice the peculiar institution of slavery, had no desire to do so, but, in a way, he had grown up with it; legal slavery had existed in New York until 1827, when he was eight. Many of his congressional associates practiced slavery, and he was at ease with that as, at worst, a necessary evil. Most of his Southern friends possessed apparently contented, well-disciplined, and well-fed slaves, and some, like the Clays and Slidells, owned plantations based on the labor of supposedly smiling hundreds of African slaves. Slavery was a normal institution in Washington, too; slave sales occurred functionally and without fuss in the capital.

As most American schoolchildren are taught, the Dred Scott decision would achieve a reputation for judicial infamy in American history, but at the time it gave Buchanan massive temporary aid. It denied the right of Congress to decide on the very issue—slavery in the West—that had created so much argument and division in the Democratic Party and the nation. President Buchanan saw himself, at the beginning of his incumbency, as liberated by the Supreme Court to get on with other business. But the implications of the Dred Scott case, instead of putting the North in its place, terrified many reasonable people. Abe Lincoln, a purely local and previously obscure political figure in rural Illinois, would soon delineate the crisis with what would become a famous prophetic image: "A house divided against itself cannot stand." He would, even more accurately, say that advocates of slavery were trying to push the institution forward "until it shall become lawful in *all* the States . . . North as well as South."[10]

A few weeks after the first meeting between Sickles and Key at the inaugural ball, Marshal Jonah Hoover held a stag whist party for sensible and sportive Democratic gentlemen. Teresa and Mrs. Hoover absented themselves and were accompanied by one of Dan's many friends to the theater while a number of congressmen, journalists, and eminent Washingtonians convened in Hoover's house on Pennsylvania Avenue, east of the White House. During the evening of cards and brandy, a number of men overheard genial Dan mention to Key that he had spoken to the President about Key's likelihood of being reconfirmed in his post, and that the President sounded positive that Key would be asked to continue as federal DA. Key expressed his gratitude, but this favor was characteristic of Dan's generosity to men he liked. He had no outstanding service to expect back from Key, unless it was some entrée to the Southern aristocracy. But Dan already had that, by way of his pro-Southern stance in the House. Most of those who witnessed the event, including Congressman John Haskin, considered Dan's advocacy of Key an act of gratuitous generosity.

Willing as Dan was to intercede for a stranger, Philip Barton Key, he had been doubly willing to intervene for his faithful friends from Tammany. A number of those who had helped him and Buchanan to office were now in profitable situations Dan had effortlessly arranged for them. Manny Hart had become surveyor of the Port of New York, and the recuperated Sam Butterworth, who had attended the inaugural ball with a wounded foot, was head of the federal subtreasury in New York. Loyal Captain Isaiah Rynders of the Dead Rabbits was given the post of U.S. marshal for the Southern District of New York, and, at a humbler level, a young man named Beekman, who had done legwork for Dan in the Third District (and who had met and been smitten with Teresa), was rewarded with a clerkship in the Department of the Interior. Finally, the maimed, intelligent George Wooldridge of Albany, who had been a lieutenant of Dan's during his time in the New York State legislature, became a clerk at the Capitol. George Wooldridge was a particularly loyal, reliable, and doughty younger friend of the Sickleses. He dealt bravely with a disability—he had suffered infantile paralysis and could move only on crutches—and his intellectual alertness made him a respected official around the Capitol. Dan trusted him absolutely.

Dan was seeking to set up another friend, Charles K. Graham, the young New York civil engineer who had helped with the park proposal, as engineer at the Brooklyn Navy Yard. This would prove to be a dangerous favor. The man Graham was trying to replace, a man named Murphy, was aggrieved enough to believe that Sickles had spread negative stories about him at the Department of the Navy and elsewhere to smooth the path for Graham.[11]

Meanwhile, Teresa was setting up her own base. The older and more established women of Washington were intensely interested in her, not least because she needed to be fitted by Mrs. Clay, Mrs. Pryor, Mrs. Slidell, Mrs. Postmaster Brown, Mrs. Rose Greenhow, and Mrs. Senator Gwinn into the unofficial seedings of beauty and wit that members of Washington society carried about in their heads.

Harriet Lane, First Lady and a few years older than Teresa, had been given a respectable but lower ranking on this list. Virginia Clay thought that Harriet possessed a no-nonsense, firm-faced, straight-parted directness, but beauty was made of more complex equations than this. According to Mrs. Roger Pryor, Harriet Lane, though "universally admired . . . lacked magnetism . . . a very handsome, fair, blue-eyed, self-centered young woman."

One high-ranked beauty who would become a close friend of Teresa's was Rose O'Neal Greenhow, a woman from a Southern-leaning family in Maryland. Rose was eminently amusing and had what people thought of as a Dixie kind of openness, masking a craftiness more profound than that of Mrs. Clay. She was the widow of a State Department official, and it was believed that some of her income came from keeping foreign embassies abreast of what was said by senior officials and politicians at social events in Washington. She was in her way practicing for what would become a significant and tragic career as a Southern spy. In addition to Rose Greenhow, Mrs. Alicia Pendleton, wife of Ohio congressman George Pendleton and sister of Philip Barton Key, was usually listed among the more beauteous of Washington, as was John Slidell's wife, a Louisiana Creole woman.

But Mrs. Pugh, the wife of Senator George Ellis Pugh from Ohio, topped the rankings, was believed to be the most classically exquisite of Washington women, and had a splendid maiden name, Thérèse Chalfont. Like everyone else, Teresa had heard the tale about the night the Austrian ambassador, Chevalier Hulseman, first saw Thérèse Chalfont Pugh and fell to his knees in front of her, declaring to the company that she was not only the most adorable woman in Washington, not only the most adorable in the Americas, but the most adorable in the world. Though perhaps lacking in the reserved self-confidence of the others, Teresa joined Mrs. Pugh and Mrs. Slidell to become one of a triad of Washington's splendors. Mrs. Clay told people that Teresa was a double for the renowned, luscious diva of her age, Maria Piccolomini. In all these matters, Virginia Clay was certainly the chief social arbiter. People often called the group of Southern congressmen who lodged at Brown's Hotel the Clay mess, and it was not entirely to honor the powerful Alabama husband, Senator Clement Claiborne Clay, but also to give credit to the resolute, lively, accomplished, and clever wife.[12]

Having thus made a splendid range of new friends during the Thirty-fourth Congress, Teresa took Laura back to Bloomingdale, and after Dan concluded his business, he too returned to his law practice, his Tammany haunts, and his retreat at Bloomingdale. But, according to pattern, he was frequently back in Washington, making representations on behalf of New York shipping companies and financial houses to the cabinet and sundry committees on trade and fiscal policy. That spring he could be found quartered again in a suite at Willard's. There, one morning while he was at breakfast, he received an angry note from a representative of the threatened Brooklyn Navy Yard engineer Murphy, accusing him of having assailed Murphy's character. Dan wrote an angry note in reply, denouncing Murphy's letter as "apparently intended to deter me from duty as a representative."

At Willard's early on the morning of May 6 occurred one of those

Sicklesesque incidents which Bennett of the *New York Herald* still recorded with derision and other sections of the press were delighted to grab on to as a means of showing that Dan, though he had achieved the gravity of a seat in Congress, was the same old Dan. He had been sleeping when an urgent knocking at the door roused him. Murphy, bearing a cowhide whip, hurled himself into the room, where Dan struggled with him, backed him into a corner, and began throttling him. When he asked Murphy whether he was satisfied yet, Murphy nodded, and Dan let him depart but kept the whip to show that he had won the encounter. He had, however acquired a black eye, and he immediately wrote an account of Murphy's behavior to the Secretary of the Navy, Isaac Toucey, who dismissed Murphy for his "unwarranted assault on Congressman Sickles." Two days later, Charles K. Graham was appointed civil engineer of the Brooklyn Navy Yard in Murphy's place. Murphy's only vengeance was to write a stinging passage on Dan in the *Evening Post*. "Graduating from the worst sinks of iniquity in the city," wrote Murphy, "he has led the life of a professional vagabond. In debt to everybody, a fashionable roué with a degree of acquired smartness that belongs to men who are only 'bold and bad' enough to challenge the laws of morality, and to fight the easy virtue of frail women, he stands before the public . . . a disgraced and vanquished man, and as such I take my leave of him."[13]

In the saner zone of Bloomingdale, Teresa and Laura enjoyed their first full summer by the river. The banks of the Hudson were a splendid playground where handsome and fond Maria Cooke Bagioli spent time with Teresa and the strong-willed five-year-old girl, who reminded Teresa of Dan. Frequently the two women, the child, and an accompanying maid made a coach or carriage journey down Broadway to shop and visit Laura's grandfather, Antonio Bagioli, conducting his renowned voice and music classes in the Bagioli house. Teresa may have thought somewhat of her pleasant friend Barton and wished he would visit New York and take her riding, since the Sickles family could not go to the mountains or the country that year, Dan being engaged in a fascinating case. His client was one Charles Devlin, who had been appointed street commissioner by the mayor and aldermen. The state authorities in Albany, however, had already promised the job to a man named Conover. When Conover arrived at City Hall and demanded that Devlin vacate his office and leave behind all the relevant documents and maps, Devlin refused. The state attorney general had Devlin arrested and confined in the Lower Manhattan prison known as the Tombs, whose sinister Egyptian-style façade gave onto a dismal interior. Dan, with his abhorrence of what he saw as Albany tyranny, was employed to get Devlin out of the Tombs and back to his office at City Hall.

His opening statement to the court had an elegance and, in its finer arguments, a scholarship that showed quite clearly why, despite his sins, he was a figure worthy of serious attention. Devlin "is imprisoned, I will take the liberty of saying . . . for a political offense, as the result of a conflict between the state and the city authorities, as to which of them has the right to fill a certain office." He took the trouble to refer the judge to the case of James II, before the Revolution of 1688, when the King attempted to appoint the president of Magdalen College, Oxford, and backed up his appointment with bayonets, "to enforce his mandate by violence. . . . And the history of that time tells us that no Crown lawyer could be found so recreant to the teachings of his profession, and the first principles of public liberty, as to defend this usurpation of the King in the court of justice." A string of similar case histories would stretch his defense out to forty-two printed pages. "We invoke for Mr. Devlin all the powers of this great writ of liberty—the writ of habeas corpus—a writ which arose in an age when these acts of tyranny were common and frequent. . . . Let us not, in this enlightened age, imitate those follies which history has recorded as the parent of revolutions." But even with so strong an advocate, Devlin lost, and Dan's former baiter Bennett fully reverted to enmity by claiming that Dan had stooped to "betray the cause of Devlin, and . . . play the spy on behalf of the Conover party." George Sickles was outraged for Dan's sake and urged his son to take legal action. So Dan started a time-consuming civil libel case, claiming $150,000 in damages, and persuaded the district attorney to let him sue Bennett for criminal libel. For this enterprise, Dan's lawyer was John Graham, who seven years earlier, in the company of his brothers, had participated in the horsewhipping of Bennett.

For whatever reason, neither case reached a conclusion, and within a short time, a truce was reached between the acid-penned Bennett and roguish Dan, and in the future, Mrs. Bennett, between her attempts to talk to the dead at séances, would be a guest at the Sickleses' table in Washington.[14]

Fall brought a close to what had been a turbulent New York summer, and Dan returned to Washington for the new congressional session. He was looking for a house in the capital this time, so that he could accommodate his family and avoid the tedium of living in hotels, boardinghouses, and rooms borrowed from friends. Previously, Dan had visited a house in Lafayette Square often referred to as the Stockton Mansion. "Mansion" was perhaps an overstatement. It was a white stucco residence, with basement windows almost on street level, two stories above that, and attic dormer windows protruding from the roof. A sweeping iron-railed staircase ran down to the street from the front door. It was less than a hundred paces from Pennsylvania Avenue, and from its windows one could look out diagonally across the young trees of Lafayette Square to the White House. The same ailanthus trees that grew along Pennsylvania Avenue in front of the presidential mansion and the Treasury, each tree set in a whitewashed little pen reminding some people of a sentry box, were planted on the pavements around Lafayette Square. The rent of the Stockton Mansion was high, $3,000 a year, the entirety of Dan's congressional salary. Nor would his domestic establishment come cheaply; the house was to have a nursemaid-cummaid for Laura and Teresa, a coachman for the expensive carriage Dan ran, a footman, and a cook. But Dan pursued the lease on this property and asked his new friend District Attorney Barton Key to act for him in the matter. A powerful and unnamed set of financial, manufacturing, and transport interests in New York wanted Dan to have a house of this nature—one commentator believed the entire costs were absorbed by a New York steamship company whose executives frequently visited.

One gets a view of the sort of people eager to see Dan situated close to the White House from a friend of his named Samuel Mitchell Barlow. Barlow, a lawyer and the brother-in-law of Dan's dear friend the Irish patriot Thomas Francis Meagher, had married into a steel-manufacturing family named Townsend. He served on the board of a number of north-south rail companies, and thus had the normal New York Democratic interest in preserving the Union, and a respect for Buchanan for having seemed to achieve that goal. Barlow's father-in-law, Peter Townsend, at one stage asked him to approach Dan Sickles and plead with him to use his good influence to ensure that U.S. steelmakers would not have to compete with foreign steelworks for navy contracts. Whether Barlow and Townsend directly supported Sickles with cash subscriptions is not clear, but they certainly stood for the interests that had the resources to make Dan's life in Lafayette Square a sumptuous one.

Again, the late-twentieth-century idea that there was ever a capital in which special interests lacked leverage is at odds with the complex net of interests in Washington during the 1850s.[15]

Here, in his rented house, Dan could entertain and charm Cabinet members and even the President. The Stockton Mansion had spacious downstairs rooms; the parlor or drawing room on the ground floor ran for some eighty or eighty-five feet. The square as Dan prepared to live there boasted many renowned and wealthy householders. Speaker James Orr found it adequate to his needs to occupy one floor of the Decatur House, barely a hundred steps up the square. The wealthy retired grocery millionaire John McBlair occupied another apartment in the Decatur House. St. John's Episcopal, virtually the parish church of the White House, was just across H Street from the square. At the corner farther from the White House, Captain Charles Wilkes, who would leave his name on a huge slice of Antarctica, had the old Dolley Madison house. In the years in which President Madison was survived by his august wife, her home had been such a center of Washington social life that people claimed it more important for the wives of congressmen to be presented to Dolley here than to the President on Pennsylvania Avenue. Hard up for cash but not for social credit, Dolley had died eight years past, in 1849—hence the presence of the famous explorer in her old house. Partway along that block, and closer to the White House, was the Washington Club, also known as the National Club or Clubhouse. From the windows of the Clubhouse there was less intervening foliage than in modern times, and one could have a direct view of the Stockton Mansion, the Sickleses' new home. This line of vision would have an extreme impact on the Sickles family, and the most fundamental one possible on Barton Key.[16]

Here, in Lafayette Square, the Sickleses established their social pattern—Teresa held receptions on Tuesday afternoons, and the couple staged weekly dinners for invited guests on Thursday nights. To Teresa's at-homes came the eminent women of Washington, together with sundry officials and bureaucrats. Though young, she spoke to them as a peer, and they were impressed that she possessed the complex gifts required to maintain a fine house, a corps of servants, and a good dinner table. Some of the younger male visitors became moonstruck over her superior gifts of body and temperament. They included a sickly young man, Henry Watterson, who lived at Brown's Hotel with his parents, and Samuel Beekman, the young clerk of the Interior Department who had been an election aide to Dan. Later, when he was a renowned newspaperman, Henry Watterson would say significantly that he both admired Teresa and sympathized with her on the matter of "her husband's neglect." To a young man who saw Teresa as all that was wholesome and exquisite, Dan's absences must have seemed willful and inexplicable. In any case, Teresa's much-praised ease of manner and general charm led Beekman and Watterson to hope that she would accommodate them romantically. They might have been well advised to take account of her already obvious interest in men twice her age.[17]

Often the women of the capital would be back at the Stockton Mansion on Thursday nights, bringing their famous husbands with them. "The President," said one who was in Washington at that time, "was always fond of Mr. Sickles and his wife and was a frequent visitor at their house." Their dinners and parties were "irreproachable." Even Dan's old enemies at the *Herald* acknowledged that Dan, whether at home in

Bloomingdale or in Washington at the Stockton Mansion, was distinguished "for an agreeable and pleasant social manner. . . . The hospitalities common to society were elegantly dispensed by himself and Mrs. Sickles. There were all the surroundings of wealth, taste and fashion." The *Herald* too confirmed the universal view that Teresa was a great social favorite. "She dispensed the hospitalities of Mr. Sickles's house with a charming grace which lent them a double attraction." Nor was anything deficient in Teresa herself. "Mrs. Sickles," wrote an occasional visitor to the Stockton Mansion, "was famous for her jewelry and toilettes."

Young Mrs. Stanton, for example, brought to these dinners her husband, Edwin Stanton, cherubic-faced but skilled in constitutional law and civil law; Mrs. Gwinn of Texas came with her prodigiously wealthy husband, Senator William Gwinn. It was reported that the Gwinns spent $75,000 a year on their annual Washington sojourn; that is, twenty-five times a congressional salary. Marshal Hoover was often at the Stockton Mansion, as were Representative Haskin and his wife, Representative Pendleton and his. And frequently one or two cabinet members would add an air of august statesmanship to the table of this tyro congressman and his young wife.[18]

Across the road from the Stockton Mansion, in the White House, Dan knew the President was trying to hold the line for the Southerners, on matters of tariffs (they didn't want any), a national bank (they objected to it), a homestead act (they were afraid it would fill the West with abolitionist settlers), and Kansas (which they wanted to be a slave territory). It is necessary, to understand the way the tide ran during Dan's term in Congress, to emphasize the status of Kansas. Discourse there had continued to run along bloody lines during Buchanan's presidency. In an incident in 1858, nine Kansas Free-Soilers had been shot by proslavery firing squads. And again John Brown had replied! He invaded Missouri, killed a slaveholder, and spirited eleven of his slaves away to Canada.[19]

In Kansas, the antislavery settlers were the majority, and had vetoed the minority proslavery legislature at Lecompton, Kansas, refusing to vote for it or serve in it. Buchanan decided on advice to hold a referendum of the people in the territory of Kansas, which would demonstrate the true intentions of the majority. The South could surely not argue with such a democratic process.

But so many Southern senators such as Clay and Slidell denounced the decision that, as Southern newspapers grew thick with long editorials threatening secession, Buchanan gave way. A proslavery convention meeting in Lecompton devised a citizen referendum question crafted so as to produce a Kansas in which present slaveholders were allowed to retain their slaves. Stephen Douglas, the famous Democratic senator from Illinois, denounced this grossly skewed referendum question and warned Old Buck that if he insisted on this version, he, Douglas, would oppose the issue on the floor of the House. "Mr. Douglas," Buchanan told the little senator from Illinois, "I desire you to remember that no Democrat ever differed from an administration of his own choice without being crushed."

The two men represented the schism in the Democratic Party between those who wanted to placate the South, and save the Union that way—men such as Buchanan and his young acolyte Dan Sickles—and those who, like Douglas, while not seeking to abolish slavery in the South, could not stomach its extension, by stealth, threat, or the sort of chicanery resorted to in Lecompton.

The proslavery referendum question was put forth in Kansas and was passed, because antislavery men refused to participate in it. Again the thunder of Southern fury and secessionist threat was heard from the Southern legislators, aimed at getting Kansas admitted on their terms. "If Kansas is driven out of the Union for being a slave state," asked South Carolina's Senator Hammond, "can any slave state remain in it with honor?" This style of rhetoric always worked with James Buchanan, whose chief dread was that he might be remembered as the President under whose administration the Union was destroyed. Responding to graphic Southern warnings, he sent over to the Capitol for ratification by Congress the proposal that Kansas be admitted to the Union as the sixteenth slave state.

On the floor of the House, Dan Sickles gave his voice and vote to

Buchanan, that is, to the admission of a slave Kansas, as a means of—in his eyes—preventing a constitutional and economic calamity for the United States and of putting bloody Kansas to rest.

In the Senate, Stephen Douglas was the chief Democratic denouncer of the admission of Kansas. By this brave show of principle, he sacrificed the support of Southern Democrats and their Northern allies in his bid for the presidency. He was praised hugely in the North for his principled stand, and denounced eloquently in the South for the "filth of his defiant recreancy." During an all-night session of the House, a Republican named Grow of Pennsylvania crossed to the Democratic side to talk with a few Northern Democrat allies. A friend of Dan's, Lawrence Keitt of South Carolina, shouted at Grow, "Go back to your side of the House, you black Republican puppy!" Grow answered with a jibe about slave drivers, and then began wrestling with Keitt and knocked him down. Now men from both sides joined the mêlée. "There was some fifty middle-aged and elderly gentlemen pitching into each other like so many Tipperary savages," said one observer, "most of them incapable, from want of wind and muscle, of doing each other any serious harm." But it was fortunate that no weapons were produced, for the fury was such that they might have been used. Dan, with his augmented sense of statesmanship, did not figure in this fracas.

Then, in the Southern-dominated Senate, the admission of Kansas was approved, but in the House, twenty-two Northern Democrats voted with the Republicans to defeat it.[20]

Through that acrimonious winter of 1857–58, Dan and Teresa had established themselves thoroughly in Washington, finding a place on the roster of notables who opened their houses on a regular basis to visitors. Teresa was delighted to be an active partner in Dan's political ascent. In preparation for her at-homes and dinners, she shopped in the D.C. markets, accompanied by her servant to do the toting, for brant and canvasback duck and sora (marsh birds), oysters from the Maryland and Virginia seashore, and terrapin. She kept vats of salt water in her pantry for the storage of oysters and the terrapin used for turtle soup. Between buying fine produce at the market and delicacies at Charles Gautier's famous salon of French fancy goods on Pennsylvania Avenue, and applying oneself to the demands of high fashion, life was extremely crowded for women like Teresa. Some of the plainest dinners were served in the White House, where "Mr. Buchanan set an example of republican simplicity." But Teresa had to try harder than the eccentric Buchanan, and preparing for such dinners as she offered visitors each Thursday evening was a demanding process, to which Dan contributed nothing but his company.[21]

Tending her personal appearance and hairstyle—the toilette, as people called it—took a woman hours, whether she was going out or entertaining at home. Virginia Clay gave in detail a typical process she had herself either endured or enjoyed. The hair in the front was stiffened with a beltlike device, called the bandolier, and formed into a sleek, smooth bandeau, framing the face. Behind, all the hair was tightly tied, low at the nape, and then divided into two parts, each woven with many strands into a single braid. Simple fashion, said Mrs. Clay, such as wearing one's hair with apparent informality, *à la grecque,* with flowers wreathed over it, or a golden dagger or arrow to secure it, gave way to far more ornate and demanding hairstyles as the decade neared an end, with heavy braids wound like a coronet over the head, often topped with a tiara of velvet and pearls. As for dresses, ornate "basques with postilion backs became the order of the day." The dressing done, and the coach brought around to the sweeping stairs at the front of the house, Teresa was ready to go forth to enchant and, in some cases, ravish the sensibilities of the people of Washington.[22]

For when not preparing for her own Stockton Mansion events, Teresa was on most weekday afternoons driven in her enclosed carriage by the Sickleses' Scots coachman, John Thompson, to the receptions held by the wives of other legislators. There she would hear further details of the history of Philip Barton Key, who himself frequently visited these at-homes. The consensus in the drawing rooms was that he had been very much in love with his wife, Ellen, who had died in 1855 of unspecified causes. Since the time of her death came not long after the birth of the Keys' youngest child, Lizzie, it may have been caused by some lasting postpartum malaise. Though he was a large muscular man, a good horseman, a militia captain, and a public official with a relatively demanding job, Key behaved as if his health were frail. He would often excuse himself from the office, and some of his work fell onto his deputy and his chief clerk. But he was rarely absent from the social rounds, which, his friends indulgently agreed, he needed in view of the grievous loss of his beloved Ellen. On many occasions, Mr. Barton Key would arrive at the same reception as Teresa. Some of the older women began to ask one another, amusedly, whether Barton was following Teresa around. They thought it, at first, a harmless and gallant way for a gentleman to behave. At the time Key began to feel a potent attraction to Mrs. Sickles, the same feeling as had been observed in a number of younger men, his eldest child, Alice, was nearing twelve years. The two middle children were Mary and James, and Lizzie was nearly four. The sentimental liked to say that Key lived separately from his children— they in K Street, Washington, near the courts, under the care of a genteel former relative; he in Georgetown—because they reminded him too acutely of his lost Ellen. This made him a suitable escort for the wives of legislators who were too busy with daytime and evening sessions to attend receptions and balls, or who were forced to arrive at them late.[23]

Early that winter, before Teresa's association with Key became a habitual matter, the eighteen-year-old Henry Watterson, whose father was a newspaperman in Washington, and a friend of the Clays, would be called on to escort Teresa to dinners and dances. Later in the season, when he was ill, Teresa became one of his nurses, visiting Willard's, to which his parents had moved, to sit with the boy at the cost of social engagements. As a child, Henry had been a playmate of President Pierce's ill-fated son, Benny, and the Watterson parents feared that Henry might follow Benny into the shades. They need not have done so—he would live until 1921, and at the end of his life claimed to have had close personal contact with every President from Andrew Jackson to Warren G. Harding. Teresa also had her place in his memoirs, as the nurse and the exquisite wronged presence. But then, to the savage disappointment of Henry Watterson and the young clerk Sam Beekman, Key took over the role of squiring Mrs. Sickles as a permanent task. Chevalier Wikoff had occasionally escorted Teresa to social events, and accepted Teresa's predilection for Key with a greater composure than did the younger men.[24]

Commentators would later say that it was treacherous of Key to take advantage of the task of escort to Teresa which Dan entrusted to him, but many, including Virginia Clay, thought that Sickles, by design or neglect, "forced his wife into Barton's company." There may have been some justice in this observation. A later letter of Teresa's to her friend Florence mentioned wistfully that a second Sickles baby was unlikely. In any case, Barton and Teresa began spending a great deal of time with each other that winter of 1857–58. People often noticed Key's gray horse, Lucifer, tethered outside the Stockton Mansion and were aware that, since Key generally mixed with Southern Democrats, this was the most intense friendship he had ever developed with Northern ones.[25]

Unlike Key, who gave many visible indications of his affection for Teresa, Dan, except for his follies with Fanny White, did not so egregiously wear his heart on his sleeve. Despite his capacity for tears at the loss of friends and his fervid loyalty to his brothers-in-faction, he was careful in his love affairs. He conveniently caught the train and met one of his lovers at Barnum's Hotel in Baltimore, neutral ground, since the woman he met was perceived as being married and had herself probably traveled south from Philadelphia for the assignations.

Dan was capable of evoking the same intense and dedicated affection in his women friends as he had in Teresa, and that accounted for his capacity to attract women of respectable background, only a few of whose names we know. Fixing a woman with his intense, glittering eye, he would utter all the requisite imagery of desperate love. As with other such men, his ultimate failure was that there was never one of them, not even Teresa, to whom he rendered the degree of enduring devotion that the imagery promised. But that each of his lovers believed him to be her own dear Dan (or Edgar, his second name) is shown by an unsigned, undated letter from a married woman with whom he was engaged in an affair.

The scene the letter evokes is clear. A married woman has just come home to her affluent and tedious household to find a note from Dan. Seated in the same parlor as her husband, who has arrived back from his office, she replies to Dan's (Edgar's) note while a servant woman waits by, anxious to go back to her tenement but having the task, on the way, of dropping the letter to Dan's office or house.

> *I have just come home and have your dear note, many many thanks, for it has made me very happy to hear you still think of me. It is now six o'clock and too late to meet you. It is best for I might sin. . . . Ginnie is waiting to go home it is so dark. My hand can hardly hold the pen. My husband is sitting looking strait at me. Love me still, dear Edgar, it is so sweet to be loved by one so dear to my sad heart. I am afraid I shall always be so, God forgive me, and bless you my so dearly loved one.* [26]

People began to notice that Key and Teresa were now together not merely in the locations demanded by a busy social life but in unexpected places. One of the earliest of these observations was made by Dan's congressional colleague John B. Haskin, of Westchester County. In late March 1858, Dan was going away on business in New York, and he asked John Haskin to "drop up occasionally and see Teresa and inquire if she wanted anything." The day after this request, Haskin, passing the White House in a carriage with his wife and children on the way to Georgetown to get some shoes, remembered Sickles's request. (Very likely, too, he saw Lucifer tethered by the house.) Although Haskin was in a hurry, he drove up to the Stockton Mansion, helped Mrs. Haskin down, rushed up the stairs, opened the front door, and, hearing a noise in the little study, opened the door into it without knocking. He found Mrs. Sickles and Mr. Key seated at a round table that held a large bowl of salad, which Teresa was mixing. To compound the compromising aspect of Key and Teresa's being together here, a bottle of champagne and two partly consumed glasses sat on the table. Haskin knew that Key and Mrs. Sickles were friends—he had seen them together once or twice at the theater, once or twice riding on Pennsylvania Avenue—but their presence here looked improper enough to cause Haskin and Mrs. Haskin sharp embarrassment.

Haskin excused his abrupt entrance, and Teresa rose, blushed, and invited Mr. and Mrs. Haskin to take a glass of wine with her. The two couples sat together, forcing conversation, until Haskin pleaded that the shoes must be bought, and he and Mrs. Haskin left. On entering the carriage, Mrs. Haskin said to her husband, "Mrs. Sickles is a bad woman."

Shortly after that, Haskin met the two again, once more in a situation likely to cause comment. Taking a short cut through the old cemetery on the edge of Georgetown, he saw Key and Teresa riding together. Key, either there at the cemetery or at another time, approached Haskin for the purposes of defending Teresa's honor and girlish innocence and of emphasizing the propriety of his paternal feelings toward her. Men like Haskin would never forgive Barton's lies on that matter. They lived in a world where their fellows might be guilty of folly but, once discovered, were expected to have too much gentlemanly honor to dissemble.[27]

The obsessed young Interior Department bureaucrat Samuel Beekman appeared to have observed contacts between Key and Teresa more systematically than anyone else. One night in March 1858, shortly before Haskin surprised Teresa with Key, Beekman met up with another New Yorker and junior official of the Interior department, a man named Bacon, at Willard's for drinks. The two young public servants, who had often met each other at Dan's, were devoted to the congressman and looked upon him as a patron. According to Beekman, it was Bacon who raised the question of Mr. Key's attentions to Mrs. Sickles "in the most confidential tone, making several very indelicate remarks about Mrs. Sickles."

In reality it was probable that the besotted and tipsy Beekman broached the subject that was dearest to his heart. He said that he had been in an inn in Bladensburg, Maryland, northeast of the city, when a storm came on, and Mrs. Sickles and Mr. Key tumbled into the tavern in their drenched riding habits. Mr. Key took a room in which Mrs. Sickles could warm and dry herself until the storm passed, and until her clothes, hung by the fire downstairs, could be put on again. Key pretended that he had stayed in the kitchen, his clothes steaming, but Beekman believed that to be a mere subterfuge, and that Key spent most of the time at the Bladensburg tavern in the same room as Mrs. Sickles.

Beekman's tale was a prime item of scandalous material, and the next morning Bacon relayed it to Dan's devoted friend the House clerk George Wooldridge. Naturally, he swore Wooldridge to silence, but Wooldridge was much more than a friend to Dan during those early months of 1858—he was also a private secretary, going to the Stockton Mansion three days a week to deal with Dan's considerable correspondence. So he took Dan aside the next day in the Capitol and warned him of what was being said about Key and Teresa.

At once, Dan sent a note to Beekman, summoning him to the Stockton Mansion at seven o'clock that night. When Beekman arrived and was shown into the parlor, he was met by Teresa's mother, in Washington visiting Teresa and Laura, and by a friend of Dan's, John J. McElhone, a reporter for the *Congressional Globe* and another Sickles acolyte. Mrs. Bagioli knew why Beekman had been called there; clearly, Dan had confided in her. It was an astonishing aspect of Dan's character that he always dealt with his most intimate problems by enlisting advice, by assembling friends, by summoning in sympathetic opinion. After all, this was the Tammany way of doing business. Mrs. Maria Bagioli had already warned her daughter strongly of the consequences of any folly. Now she informed Beekman of the rumors Dan had heard, supposedly emanating from him.

Dan made his appearance while his mother-in-law was present, and Beekman, challenged by Dan, admitted only that Bacon had made certain unworthy remarks, he himself having unluckily dropped "several trifling jokes about the female sex in general," and only by implication about Teresa. He was guilty of nothing but these trifling remarks, he insisted, having uttered "no charges, no facts, no inferences even, injurious of Mrs. Sickles, but merely generalities without the slightest design of menace." Dan told him that Wooldridge's informant, Bacon, had heard

Beekman speak far more specific calumnies. "Excited and enraged beyond control, I told Mr. Sickles, on the impulse of the moment, that
what I had said I had said, and was personally responsible for, and left
the house, which I never entered afterwards."

It was merely the beginning of Beekman's embarrassment.
Sickles—in what could nearly be called naiveté—organized a meeting
with Key and told him of the gossip attributed to Beekman. Despite his
own notable sins, he knew that gentlemanly honor would forbid him to
seduce the wife of a man who had done him the sort of notable favors he
had done Key! Dan was thus gratified to see that, according to the best
tradition of his haughty, gentrified family and class, Key was outraged
for his own sake and Dan's. He told Dan, "This is the highest affront
that can be offered to me, and whoever asserts it must meet me at the
point of a pistol." He was immensely more at home than Beekman with
the idea of a contest of honor, for about the time of his marriage Key had
been willing to fight a duel with a Colonel May, one of the other suitors
of his betrothed, Ellen Swann. His older brother, Midshipman Daniel
Key, had been killed at the Bladensburg dueling grounds over twenty
years before, and now Bladensburg had again risen to impute the honor
of a Key.

Key assured Dan that he would be in touch directly with the three
young men involved—Wooldridge, Beekman, Bacon. He used his old
friend and coadjutor Marshal Jonah Hoover as his messenger. In answer
to a request for information on the content of the rumors, George
Wooldridge was quite forthcoming in what he had heard from Bacon:
"that they stopped at a house on the road towards Bladensburg, and that
Mrs. Sickles had a room there and remained one hour and a half; also
that she took off her habit, and that he had no doubt there was an intimacy between Mr. Key and Mrs. Sickles." Another alleged remark of
Beekman's conveyed to Key, and taken exception to, was that Key had
boasted that he asked only thirty-six hours with any woman to make her
do whatever he pleased.

The heat was back on Beekman. He "disavowed" that he was the author of the imputations. He denied that the statements of Mr. Bacon came from him. Philip Barton Key put all the replies—Beekman's, Bacon's, Wooldridge's—in an envelope and sent them by way of Jonah Hoover to Dan Sickles. "My Dear Sir, I send by Jonah Hoover a copy of the correspondence had today, and you will perceive any attempt to fix the ridiculous and disgusting slander on me as the party concerned was unsuccessful."

Key had taken a great deal of trouble to lie to Dan, and it seemed that Dan was willing to attribute the accusations against Teresa and Key to boyish cowardice or malice on Beekman's part. Marshal Jonah Hoover would later remember that Dan said to him, "I like Key. This thing shocked me when I first heard about it, and I am glad to have the scurrilous business cleared up." Key himself went again to Congressman Haskin and declared, "I regard her almost as a child. It is ridiculous to suppose I could have anything but honorable intentions towards her." He asked Haskin please to pass on to Dan what he had said.[28]

A wiser man than Key, or perhaps a man who was merely toying with Teresa Sickles, would from then on have kept his distance from her. It was not as if Key lacked for other female company. There were a number of women he had paid occasional court to, some of whom had ambitions to marry him. He must surely have realized that if one of Teresa's admirers had embarrassed him this time, one of his own might embarrass him next. He and Teresa possibly both engaged in a temporary resolve to end the affair. If so, a more powerful mutual obsession, combined with Teresa's need of intimacy and affection from a mature male, quickly reestablished their relationship as it had been.

This season of Key's temporary embarrassment and renewed passion for Teresa was not marked by any fresh surge of brotherhood between North and South in the legislature. But as much as fraternity had been eroded on the floor of the House, it was still observed in society, and the rich Gwinns of California decided to stage a massive fancy-dress ball, in part to restore amity in the capital. Senator Gwinn, as host, claimed the right not to wear a costume. The President was also unlikely to be a costume wearer. But most of Washington engaged enthusiastically in hunting for fancy apparel.

The night of the ball, April 8, 1858, was a mere week after the House had refused by eight votes to admit Kansas as a slave state. Dan had been in New York on business for a few days, and had brought a buccaneer costume back with him for the ball. But he was ill with flu on the night of the event, so Teresa took the carriage, alone except for the driver, John Thompson, and the footman, McDonald, to the Gwinn house. At that moment she may have wished that she had spent more care on her own costume—she was dressed as Little Red Riding Hood and ran the risk that there might be other Riding Hoods at such a huge ball. She had, however, gone to the trouble of equipping herself with a basketful of good things to distribute among the guests.

The Gwinn mansion, at Nineteenth and I Streets, some three blocks up Pennsylvania Avenue from the White House, sported a ballroom of prodigious scale, comparable with the huge East Room of the White House or the ballroom at Willard's. The evening was so lustrous that one of the guests, Major John von Sonntag de Havilland, wrote a long narrative poem about it, which would be published in book form and serve better as a snapshot of the Washington community than as literature. Both Key and Teresa were mentioned in widely separated sections of the work, but they were soon together on the large dance floor, talking and engaging in polkas, schottisches, germans, and gallops.

"To that gay Capital, they congregate," wrote Major de Havilland in lines not entirely without resonance for either later events or for modern Washington,

> The worst and wisest of this mighty State;
> Where patriot politicians yearly wend,
> The Nation's fortunes, and their own, to mend;
> Where snobbish scribblers eke the scanty dole
> By telegraphing lies from pole to pole;
> Where bad hotels impose their onerous tax,

And countless Jehus sport untiring hacks;
Where Murder boldly stalks, nor cares a straw
For useless police, or unused Law;
Where shrieking Kansas whirls her frantic arms
To fright the country with her false alarms . . .
Thither, O Muse of Fashion, wing thy flight,
And shed the radiance of thy varied light. . . .

There were two other Little Red Riding Hoods on the floor—a Mrs. Hughes of Virginia and Mrs. John Floyd, whose husband was Buchanan's Secretary of War and a future Confederate general. It was Teresa, however, who attracted the poet's attention.

Lo, little "Riding Hood" with artless grace
Reveals the sweetness of her childish face;
And if the wolf's not driven from the door
She knows precisely how to treat a bore;
And they who "pull the bobbin, lift the latch,"
Will find a hostess very hard to match.

The key to de Havilland's long poem shows that other women also duplicated costumes. There were five Peasant Girls, and Barton Key had chosen the same costume as two other men. Long after, Mrs. Clay would remember handsome Barton "as an English hunter, clad in white satin breeches, cherry-velvet jacket and jaunty cap, with lemon-colored high-top boots, and a silver bugle (upon which he blew from time to time) hung across his breast . . . a conspicuous figure in that splendid, happy assemblage." There is something poignant in the image of Key, the widower, the transparent lover, the recklessly innocent liar, the hypochondriac, the Maryland aristocrat, so exuberantly blowing his hunting horn.

"Here, 'English hunters' run their prey to earth," as de Havilland wrote, "And strike the 'Key' note of their jovial mirth."

Like all the men here, like the laid-up Dan, Key wore his hair elegantly uncropped but well groomed and had a full mustache. His sandy hair suited his strong features. Mrs. Clay said that when she had first come to Washington with her husband six years before, mustaches had not been seen on fashionable men—they were decorations for Tennessee hog drivers and brigands. But this was the way fashion had recently shifted.

Key's sister, Mrs. Pendleton, expressed the transsectarian spirit of the evening by appearing as the Star-Spangled Banner, thus honoring her father's memory, and Major de Havilland also celebrated the political spaciousness of the evening.

> No Slavery, but to Beauty, here is seen,
> Nor Abolition, save of Discord's mien.
> Chivalric sway all hearts and minds maintain
> From sunny Texas up to snowy Maine.

Virginia Clay, dressed as fictional Mrs. Partington, "the loquacious malapropos dame of American theatre," had taken the trouble to engage the son of a senator to accompany her and impersonate Mrs. Partington's simple-witted son. Mrs. Clay had also learned by heart the theatrical lines of Mrs. Partington and intended to amuse the President with them when he arrived. Already she was the hit of the ball, "and was followed everywhere by a crowd of eager listeners, drinking in her instant repartee."

At last the aged, embattled, stooping, owllike chief executive entered, dressed plainly in a dark suit.

> Behold, in the centre, he who calmly bears,
> Upon that snowy head, the nation's cares,
> The people's chosen "Chieftain," simply great,
> In that proud name, beyond imperial state!

Years later, witnesses would remind Mrs. Clay "how you vexed and tortured dear old President Buchanan at Doctor and Mrs. Gwinn's famous fancy party!"

The evening was, in its way, an extraordinary encapsulation of the time. Mrs. Jefferson Davis, who would one day be First Lady of the Rebel states, appeared as Madame de Staël. Mrs. Stephen Douglas was Aurora, and Mrs. Bayor of Louisiana impersonated a whittling Yankee. Mr. Mathew Brady, who would photograph the battlefields of the coming conflict, appeared appropriately as the painter Van Dyck, and James Gordon Bennett came down from his newspaper in New York and cannily made do for fancy dress with his kilts. Rose Greenhow, Confederate spy-in-waiting, appeared plainly as a housekeeper whose beauty contradicted the dustiness of her clothing. Senator William H. Seward, Republican and abolitionist, managed, like many of the older men in high office, to retain his dignity by wearing a suit, but was seen chatting with Virginia Clay, even though she had once said that "not even to save the nation could I be induced to . . . speak with him."[29] A number of people noticed Key and Teresa leave together about two in the morning. Some were titillated by the sight; others more gravely assessed the peril to the girl and the district attorney.

Before she entered the carriage with Key, Teresa told Thompson, the coachman, to drive for a while around the streets of Washington. As he drove, he had no doubt that Mrs. Sickles and Mr. Key enjoyed a fumbling, semi-intoxicated sexual episode on the upholstered seat within. After a time, Thompson heard a voice within the carriage tell him to drive to the National Hotel, and there he waited a considerable time until the English huntsman got down with his hunting horn and disappeared inside.

For whatever reason, Teresa did not see this love affair as tragic and dangerous. She lived within it as in a secret fantasy, as in a virtual and time-consuming experience that lacked any power to inflict damage on other areas of her life. Both she and Barton thought they were taking more care, and being less observed by people, than they were. It was as if, despite his outrage at any imputation of bad behavior, Barton unconsciously courted a certain visibility for his love of Teresa. Teresa may have similarly and ill-advisedly enjoyed the flaunting side of the relationship, the idea that it must come to Dan's attention eventually, and that he would thereby be chastened and rendered repentant for his previous neglect.

In a time when servants were considered invisible, when a coachman could not speak in a frank manner to the congressman who employed him, Thompson was acquiring a lot of information his master did not possess on the relationship between Key and Teresa. His servant's honor forestalled him from selling the news to the press or betraying anything to people of Teresa's caste. Thompson was a good, earthy Scots Presbyterian, and his attitude to the lovers was one of slightly salacious but definite disapproval. In the end, it would take a subpoena to make him talk, and with that authority, he would talk copiously.

The other servant who knew more than she was yet saying was Bridget Duffy, Teresa's competent maid, who spent considerable time attending to Laura and slept near the child's nursery. The majority of American maids, ninety-two out of every hundred, were, like Bridget, Irish. Though depicted by the anti-Irish Know-Nothing lodges as brutish and suffused with superstition, they often picked up the routines of fine houses in quick order and, for $4 to $7 a month plus board, proved energetic and loyal. When it was taken into account—as it rarely was—that many came from Europe's rawest hovels in the west of Ireland, their adaptability was astonishing. Their habits were normally what was called "regular," because most loyally remitted much of their earnings back home to post-Famine Ireland, for the support of parents or to enable their siblings to leave the hopeless Irish countryside, buy steamer tickets, and join them in America. But in some instances their mores differed from those of the Anglo-Saxon and Protestant majority. Raised in the gossipiness of small Irish villages and clachans, they were unabashed about listening in to what they accidentally overheard, and sometimes they passed on news of domestic scandals to one another.

About lunchtime on most days, having given Bridget instructions for the afternoon and leaving Laura in her care, Teresa would set out by carriage to visit eminent Washington hostesses. She gave Thompson a "lie-bill" of the houses she wanted to visit, and Thompson would choose the order in which she did so. There was hardly a day, said Thompson, when Key did not meet them, joining Mrs. Sickles either at the destination or, more commonly, beforehand. "He met us at the President's, Mr. McDonalds's, Mr. Gwinn's, and Mr. Slidell's. Sometimes he would get into the carriage and tell us to drive through back streets." At other times Key would encounter the carriage in the street near Lafayette Square, where he saluted Mrs. Sickles and called her madam. Sometimes he would remain on horseback and accompany the carriage; sometimes he would dismount and enter it, leaving his mount to be tethered to the back of the carriage. He never got in at the Sickleses' door, and always but once got out before they returned to the house, generally at the Clubhouse across the square. On only one occasion, when Dan was away from Washington, did he enter the house directly from the carriage. But that did not mean he was not frequently there by other means. On his visits during Mr. Sickles's absences, said Thompson, Key and Mrs. Sickles would go into the study. "The door was shut while they were there. There was a sofa in that room with its right foot at the door."

Thompson had known Key to be in the house one night till one o'clock—this was while Dan was out of town in May 1858. Thompson was going to bed when he thought he heard the front doorbell ring, and he met Bridget Duffy emerging from her room in her nightclothes, under the same impression of having heard the doorbell. Perhaps a young clerk on the way home had mischievously rung it. Perhaps one of Teresa's young admirers, fueled with liquor in the Clubhouse and knowing what was happening in the Stockton Mansion, was playing a little trick on the lovers. From above, Duffy and Thompson saw Mr. Key and Teresa come into the hall, unlock the inner front door, and look out through the front window to see whether anyone was outside on the step. They obviously saw nobody, and locked up again, reentered the study, shut the door into the hall and locked it, and locked as well the door that led from the study to the parlor.

"I stood a little while and heard them making this noise on the sofa for about two or three minutes," the coachman said. He remarked to

Bridget that they were making a mysterious noise, and Bridget ran away. "She would not hearken to me—as it was not language suitable for her to hear. I heard them for about two or three minutes. I then went to bed; I knew they wasn't at no good work."

Sometimes Thompson drove Teresa to the old congressional cemetery on the eastern fringe of the city. Mr. Barton Key either joined the carriage on the way or was waiting on his horse among the trees of the graveyard. He would dismount and greet Teresa, and the two of them would vanish for an hour or an hour and a half. They also met a number of times in the Georgetown cemetery.

On one of those visits to the congressional burying ground, Thompson saw Barton elegantly emerge from the trees on his horse, Lucifer, dismount, tie the horse to a railing, help Mrs. Sickles out of the carriage, and walk away with her "down the burying ground." Another day only Mr. Key's tethered horse was visible, and a colored man appeared and handed Mrs. Sickles a note. She took it and walked away among the graves, and Mr. Key arrived afterward in a carriage and told the man to take the same carriage home. Then he followed Teresa's tracks down through the burial monuments toward a supposedly joyous meeting.[30]

At least the burial ground meetings were discreet to a certain degree, and the afternoon meetings at polite homes had a reasonable seemliness to them, but in combination with the meetings in the Sickleses' home, they formed a pattern of recklessness, as if Key and Teresa felt they were pursuing a literary or theatrical version of hopeless yet admirable love. We do not know if Teresa saw Key as a potential partner for life or had fantasies of fleeing with him to California, Cuba, or Central America. There is no evidence. But Key must have been a wonderful lover, with his excellent physique, with—behind his actions—all the energy of his somber temperament, of his desperate, neurotic soul, of his hypochondriacal fear of death and his frenzy to be confirmed as one of the living.

As the affair became habitual, Dan was operating as one of the more effective Buchanan supporters on the floor of the House. In June he had made what his side considered an able speech in defense of the President's stand against a recent stint of British "visitation and search" activities against American ships in the Gulf of Mexico. He was pleased that the Secretary of the Navy had sent a fleet into the Gulf strong enough to drive the British squadron from those waters. Dan's outrage, however, was not as purely republican as it might first have seemed; the British excuse was that the Royal Navy was trying to intercept American ships engaged illegally in the slave trade.

The Sickleses closed up their Washington house and left for New York on July 1. Key saw Teresa and Dan off and promised to visit them during the summer. Dan would lack Barton's degree of leisure, because he had a hard reelection contest ahead of him. Fernando Wood had formed his own Democratic machine, called Mozart Hall, and would put up a candidate against Dan. So would the anti-immigrant Know-Nothings, more effective on a local level than ever they were on the national scale.

That summer, while Dan campaigned, Philip Barton Key arrived from Washington to visit the Sickleses at their residence on the Hudson. Barton was on his way to the great watering place at Saratoga Springs, where he intended for the sake of his health to imbibe the waters from the local springs and to enjoy the languorous rest the fine white hotels of Saratoga offered. He saw Dan and Teresa before he left and on his return trip. In fact, he was back in Manhattan at an exciting time. On September 1, the successful laying of the telegraph cable between New York and London was greeted with popular enthusiasm as the wedding of Europe and America. Broadway was alive with people, and Daniel Dougherty of Philadelphia, a friend of Dan's who was in town for the celebration of the event, saw Teresa Sickles sitting in a carriage that had been stopped by traffic. He asked her to give him a lift to the Metropolitan Hotel, where he knew that Dan had gone for a better view of the celebratory procession. Dougherty found Dan and Barton Key in one of the reception rooms of the Metropolitan, from whose window they had a prime view of the parade. The cable would break within three days, but of course no one knew that at the moment, and Dan was one of the laudatory speakers at a banquet to greet the phenomenon. Dougherty would meet Key again as a guest at Bloomingdale.[31]

Barton was already making plans for the fall when Teresa would return to Washington, but for the present, he and Teresa managed to have assignations in New York. The people of the hotel where Key stayed noticed that "he left . . . at exactly the same time every day, as if for an appointment." It was later "conjectured what his regular appointment was." But though his movements and intentions were so obvious, his vanity permitted him to see himself as an accomplished and worldly lover. He told a friend, "French intrigue! A fig for common license! French intrigue and romance, with a good spice of danger in it."[32]

Dan's reelection headquarters were in Gardner's Hotel. Here, during a busy summer, he received intelligence that Fernando Wood's Democratic wing had met at Room 49 in the Astor House with Republicans, including Horace Greeley, and with Know-Nothing General Walbridge, to devise ways to beat Dan Sickles. When, on election day, he triumphed, with the help of Tammany's Captain Wiley and his electoral cohorts, his supporters celebrated by sending up a balloon from whose passenger basket hung effigies of Mr. Fernando Wood and General Walbridge in a most precarious position, "one depending from it by his arms and the other by his legs." A satin banner, decorated with gold fringe and tassels, hung from the balloon and bore the inscription "The Honorable D. E. Sickles—triumphant over a base combination of moral and political depravity and corruption. . . ."[33]

By the time this exuberant celebration took place, Dan and Teresa had organized the return of their household to the Stockton Mansion. A new set of congressmen were impressed by the way Dan was able to live. One of the Sickleses' friends, the North Carolina representative and future Confederate general Lawrence O'Brien Branch, could not afford anything like Lafayette Square, so he rented rooms in a not entirely comfortable boardinghouse. "Board is bad," he wrote, "but the House sits nearly all day and I make my dinner on ham and tongue at the Capitol." When he did return to his room, he was kept awake by the endless conversation of "two old maids" who occupied the room next door.

Thus, he was delighted to attend a dinner at the Sickleses' house that winter, a party of about twenty ladies and gentlemen, and to accompany Mrs. Sickles, "young, pretty, and very stylish," to the table. The aristocratic Branch was astounded that Dan lived "in great style keeping one of the finest carriages etc. etc. in the city."[34]

After one dinner, Teresa wrote to her friend Florence that, in the pattern of the social life of the previous congressional session, the entire dinner group went off to a party at Postmaster General Aaron V. Brown's, where they danced the lancers till three in the morning. "Tomorrow at Mrs. Douglas' party will be a perfect crush," but a breathing space was afforded, because a dinner at the Gwinns' was postponed because of the illness of the Gwinn daughter. All Teresa's letters to friends spoke with naive excitement about the social pace of Washington, but none of them mentioned or hinted at the existence of a lover. It was Key's asides to friends, and his boyish carelessness even when he thought he was being cautious, that would most attract the attention of bystanders to the existence of the affair.[35]

In October, Barton had ridden up Fifteenth Street in his usual white riding cap, which, oddly, he sometimes wore even to social events, dismounted, and stepped onto the porch of a house that belonged to a White House gardener named Thomas Brown and his wife, Nancy. Key asked Nancy Brown whether the house two doors along the street, Number 383, was occupied. Mrs. Brown said it wasn't. Key asked whether she knew to whom it belonged. A colored man named John Gray, she told him, who lived somewhere on Capitol Hill. The colored people around there, she said, could give him all the information about Gray.

Mrs. Brown saw him again about three weeks later. He tied his horse, the gray, to her tree and knocked on her door. Mrs. Brown, a forthright woman, asked whether he was aware that it was against the law to tie horses to people's trees in Washington. Key obligingly said he would no longer tie it there, and told her that he had rented Number 383 for a friend, implying that the friend was a member of the Senate. He then untied his horse and rode away. John Gray would later say that he rented the house to Mr. Key on November 25, 1858, for occupation by a gentleman from Massachusetts named Wright.

Mrs. Brown did not see all the arrivals and departures of Key and Teresa, but she observed a number of them. Indeed, an increasingly excited group of both white and black people in the neighborhood observed the parties to the affair. Key would often turn up first, let himself in through the front door, and reappear in the yard at the back of the house to get armfuls of wood. The thread of smoke from the chimney would unleash knowing and risqué comments from the observant neighbors. Sometimes Teresa would enter the house by the back way, down the alley and through the muddy yard. Perhaps an hour later, Key would let her out the front door, though occasionally she would both arrive and leave via the back door and the muddy side lane to the street.

For one of the assignations, said Mrs. Brown, the woman she would come to learn was Teresa Sickles wore a little plaid silk dress, a black raglan cloak fringed with bugles, and a black velvet shawl with lace. On another occasion she wore a brown robe, like a traveling dress. She was always well cloaked and shawled. Her observations of Teresa accorded with those of a freed colored woman named Mrs. Baylis and her son, Crittenden, from across the street. Once, passing Mrs. Brown's house, Mrs. Sickles, the congressman's wife, looked with darksome unease at the gardener's wife. Mrs. Brown noticed that generally Mr. Key would hang a ribbon or string from one of the upstairs shutters as a signal to his lover that he was there and that it was safe for her to come on. One day, however, as Mr. Key and Mrs. Sickles arrived simultaneously, they saw two policemen speaking together on the corner of K and Fifteenth Streets, and were so inhibited by the police presence that they walked right past the house and continued up the street, as if on their way to somewhere else.

Other observers, apart from the Baylis mother and son, were Mr. Seeley, a housepainter, his wife, and their sixteen-year-old daughter, Matilda. All the Seeleys admitted to being engrossed in, and voyeuristic about, the appearances of Key and Mrs. Sickles. Having lived in George-town, they recognized Key, though they depended on local gossip from such people as Nancy Brown to let them know who the young woman was.[36]

Perhaps Key's greatest achievement was his capacity to retain the loyalty and respect of his staff at City Hall when his desk went unoccupied on most afternoons. He assigned much of his work to an earnest young assistant district attorney, Robert Ould, and spent nearly every weekday afternoon, when he was not actually meeting with Teresa in an intimate setting, trailing her around Washington. John Cooney, who succeeded John Thompson as coachman, first met Key the second day he went to work for the Sickleses. "I met him on the avenue, on the coach; I was on the box, driving Mrs. Sickles in the coach; Mrs. Sickles rang the coach bell; I drew up, and Mr. Key got in; I drove them to Douglas' green-house, and from there down the avenue."

Like John Thompson before him, Cooney saw Mr. Key nearly every day. The carriage would meet up with him in the back streets, and he would get in. "He never went from Mrs. Sickles's house in the coach, or returned with her; he would join her on some part of the journey; he met her pretty much at Douglas' green-house or at Taylor and Maury's Bookstore; she was generally there before he was, and then he would enter her coach." Cooney remembered taking Teresa to the house of Secretary of the Interior Jacob Thompson, whose wife was receiving visitors. Within a few minutes, Key also appeared at Mrs. Thompson's reception. A half hour passed, and Teresa emerged, asking Cooney to drive her to the next stop, Mrs. Postmaster General Brown's. Within ten minutes Key was at the Browns' as well. The next stop for Teresa was Rose Greenhow's, and Key turned up there and, later, rolled on as far as Fifteenth Street in the Sickleses' carriage, alighting before it covered the last few blocks to the home in Lafayette Square. It is more than likely that the polite people whom Key and Teresa visited knew well enough that an affair was in full progress. They may have thought, given Key's lack of discretion, that Dan had given at least an implied consent, for surely a husband of average attentiveness, one who took even a benign interest in his wife's movements, must have had certain suspicions.[37]

Barton had by now developed the strategy of signaling from the direction of the Clubhouse toward Teresa's window in the Stockton Mansion. Bridget Duffy, seeing him one day, remarked, with a pithiness that betrayed that in another life she might have been a wordsmith, "There is Disgrace, waiting to meet Disgust."

A Washington contractor named Albert Megaffey, who had warned Key the previous summer about his indiscreet mode of proceeding with Mrs. Sickles, met him again at the ball to send off the British ambassador, Lord Napier, held at Willard's on February 17, 1859. Key used his normal lines on Megaffey: that he had a great friendship for Teresa, that he considered her a child, that he had paternal feelings toward her. He repelled angrily the idea of having anything but kind and fatherly feelings, said Megaffey. But Megaffey raised the matter again a few days after the Napier ball, suggesting to Key that he might be in danger or difficulty. Key raised his hand to the left breast of his coat and said, "I am prepared for any emergencies."

On the Tuesday of Key's last week, Teresa gave what would prove to be her final daytime reception as a congressional wife, and the Washington correspondent of the *New York Times* was a guest. The rooms were full of company, including Mr. Key, his familiar horse tethered outside the house. Soft spring sunlight poured in through the windows, and Mrs. Sickles displayed to wonderful effect "her almost girlish beauty, wearing a bouquet of crocuses, the firstlings of the season; [she] seemed the very incarnation of Spring and youth, and the beautiful promise of life."[38]

Dan, distracted by the affair he was conducting with the unknown married woman who met him occasionally in Baltimore, had returned to Washington from a Baltimore assignation on the morning of the Napier ball and was also absorbed by the business of the Thirty-sixth Congress. He was serving on the House Foreign Affairs Committee, but domestic American issues engrossed him and all his colleagues. That winter, on the floor of the House, some of the matters of conflict had included the question of a Northern versus a Southern route for the Pacific railroad. Rather than authorize a Northern route, the Senate voted down yet another transcontinental railroad bill. Southern opposition to pressure for tariffs to protect Northern industries from foreign competition was a severe test for Dan, but he stuck faithfully with Southern and with transportation interests—with the President, too—in opposing tariffs. The South still expected its Northern supporters to oppose a western homestead act, which would open up new territory above the slavery line. This vote divided the Democratic Party along the same lines as the question of the admission of Kansas. And then, in what was a last flutter of interest in acquiring Cuba, Dan supported, with the rest of his party, the annexation of the island. Buchanan had pushed for renewed negotiations with Spain to purchase Cuba, and Dan voted for the bill of Senator Slidell of Louisiana for an appropriation of $30 million as a down payment. Dan's committee had already approved the idea earlier that February. But Senate Republicans delayed the bill, as revenge for the Democrats' delay of the homestead bill. Abolitionist Senator Ben Wade of Ohio asked, "Shall we give niggers to the nigger-less, or land to the landless?" Ultimately both parties decided to take the issue of Cuba to the voters in 1860, but internal American peril would rob it of any visibility.[39]

These were the preoccupying issues for Dan as Teresa and Key made love in the Sickleses' carriage and in the house on Fifteenth Street. On the last Wednesday night of February, the Washington correspondent for the *New York Times* saw Teresa, Barton, and Henry Wikoff at the theater together. The story told after the coming tragedy was that a man closely muffled in a shawl questioned a colored woman on Fifteenth Street about Number 383, and then waited for Key to emerge, when, muffling his face still closer, he spoke to Key. It was not Dan, for Dan had not yet been informed about Number 383. To the man from the *Times*, Key did not appear to be burdened by any worries as he, Teresa, and the chevalier laughed and applauded at the theater.

Somewhere else in Washington, a person using the initials R.P.G. was preparing a letter designed to inform the Honorable Daniel Sickles of the treachery of his wife and of his friend Mr. Key.[40]

# IV

THIS WAS THE LAST SUNDAY OF FEBRU-
ary, and the parishioners of Washington's most fashionable church, St. John's Episcopal, on H Street
across from Lafayette Square, had on entering remarked that, after the ice storm of Friday and a
frigid Saturday, this was the warmest Sunday of the
year thus far. By noon, some said, given the stillness of the air, people on the street would not need
their overcoats. The Reverend Smith Pyne, rector of
this national parish, was a considerable pulpit orator,
whom the President nonetheless thought talked at
too great a length. Invoking the prayers for fraternity
and the health of the President, he looked out on his
divided congregation in the pews.[1]

Here sat many of the potent Southern legislators
and their spouses. Their confident, vivacious features
seemed to need little help from the humble Nazarene

who had died for their sins. They prayed to an august God that he might prevent abolitionist fervor from splitting asunder the Republic, which represented the highest political achievement of humankind. But directing their prayers to the same deity were antislavery and abolitionist members of the newborn Republican Party, and some antislavery Democrats as well. All these pleas rose as a confusing incense within this white pure space—twined up its columns, wreathed its galleries. Smith Pyne knew these were plaints that God would indeed need to be omniscient to untangle.

It was thus that, with perhaps more emphasis than realism, Pyne told his congregation to depart in peace, out into the variable light of this Washington morning. Farewelling his parishioners on the steps, he could see, across Lafayette Square, the front of the White House on Pennsylvania Avenue.

From his position on the steps, Pyne could also see the site of closer problems. Nearby on Lafayette Square stood the house occupied by an amiable if worldly congressman representing the Third District of New York, the Honorable Daniel Edgar Sickles, and his extremely young and accomplished wife, Teresa. Only two weeks earlier, the St. John's rector had been ready to christen their five-year-old daughter. It would have been a splendid event, for the President had agreed to be the godfather, and the beautiful Mrs. Slidell, wife of the senator from Louisiana, was to have been the godmother. Pyne had been willing to conduct the baptismal ceremony not least because he presumed that Teresa Sickles, being an Italian Catholic by upbringing, had probably, already and secretly, had the little girl baptized into that heathenish religion, and it would be a pleasant thing to induct the child into the civilized Episcopal faith, thus saving her from popery.

The child had, however, caught whooping cough, so the christening had been delayed. If Dan Sickles had been at church, Pyne could have inquired after his daughter's health. But Dan Sickles was only occasionally observant of the rites at this or any church.[2]

Pyne had a more recent reason to think of Congressman Sickles. Just yesterday he had seen him, a small but striking and expensively dressed man, a man normally possessed of considerable social presence, walking in Lafayette Square. The rector and his son were returning home past the White House, and the boy pointed out to his father Congressman Sickles, striding rapidly in the opposite direction. His posture at the time was not appropriate for one considered a darling of Washington society, at least as far as Democrats defined it. His head was thrown back. Pyne saw a wildness and an air of great trouble about him. He would say, "There was a kind of mingled defiant air about him; a desolate air." Pyne knew all the rumors of a certain New York Tammany unruliness and lawlessness attached to Dan Sickles, but there was usually no trace of that in the urbane and cultivated demeanor Dan brought with him to Washington.[3]

Now, less than a hundred yards from where Pyne had made his congenial farewells to his worshipers, something far more dismal than the aftereffects of whooping cough dominated the Stockton Mansion. It was three days since the last sound of joy had been heard there; Thursday had proved to be the last tolerable day. That evening, though the House was in session, Dan Sickles came home for the customary Thursday-night dinner. The distinguished guests that night included Virginia Clay, wife of Senator Clement Claiborne Clay of Alabama, who went there in a threesome with Thérèse Chalfont Pugh, the beautiful Cajun wife of Senator George Ellis Pugh of Ohio, and a Miss Acklin. The two senators' wives had been liberated from their extremely busy husbands for the evening. Waspish and amusing Mrs. Clay would always remember how young and fragrant Teresa Sickles seemed that evening; so naive and unspoiled that, said Mrs. Clay, "none of the party of which I was one was willing to harbor a belief in the rumors which were then in circulation." The hostess was more unaffectedly dazzling than usual. She was obviously happy that her daughter, Laura, had recovered from the recent illness, and on that Thursday evening she wore a filmy muslin gown, decorated with the outline of the crocus, and a broad sash of brocaded ribbon about her waist. Her dark hair was dressed with yellow crocus blooms—the crocus being a favorite flower in Washington. "I never saw her again," said Mrs. Clay, "but the picture of which she formed the center was so fair and innocent, it fixed itself permanently in my mind."[4]

The chief guest that evening was Mrs. Bennett of New York, the plain little Scots wife of James Gordon Bennett, the powerful editor of the *New York Herald*. Mrs. Bennett was, among other things, a spiritualist; she had attended séances in Washington and didn't mind telling people about them. She was the guest Dan Sickles would take to dinner on his elbow. But much of the duty of entertaining the table that night would fall on that exceptionally amusing fellow the Chevalier Henry Wikoff. Other guests were the Philadelphia lawyer and Democrat Daniel Dougherty and his wife, and a young woman Teresa Sickles had met on New Year's Eve and befriended as a fellow spirit, Miss Octavia Ridgeley, who was to stay overnight.[5]

The meat served that evening came from a Mr. Emerson, at whose stall in the Washington market house Mrs. Sickles had appeared surprisingly early, between eight and nine o'clock. She had been there with the district attorney of the District of Columbia, Philip Barton Key, who was also abroad early, given that he had been to the theater the night before. Emerson the butcher knew the Sickleses well—he had been dealing with them for two Congresses. Teresa gave Mr. Emerson her order that morning, asked him how much it came to, and handed Mr. Key her purse, saying, "Pay Mr. Emerson." The district attorney had taken out of the purse a ten-dollar goldpiece to complete the transaction. But though he had his part in acquiring the meat, Key was not at dinner at the Stockton Mansion that night.[6]

The excellent dinner now eaten, the guests sat for a while in the drawing room, and at about ten o'clock began to leave for the Thursday-night hop at Willard's Hotel. Teresa Sickles pretended to be casual about Willard's. In fact, she was sick with anticipation. If Dan let her go, she would see Key. At last Dan suggested she go off in a carriage with courtly Henry Wikoff and Miss Ridgeley. He would follow after his last guests left the house. It was only a few blocks from the Stockton Mansion, past the White House and the elegant Treasury Building, to

Willard's, but a carriage was *de rigueur*, not least because the roads of Washington were notoriously mucky in winter.

In Willard's splendid ballroom, with its moldings and ceiling and chandeliers worthy of the Astor House in New York, young Octavia Ridgeley saw Teresa meet up with Philip Barton Key. Though he was an expert dancing partner, Barton did not dance with Teresa that night. Couples engaged in the gallops, the lancers, the germans, but throughout, Teresa and Philip Barton Key were locked in absorbed conversation. They did not have much time. Indeed, as soon as Congressman Sickles entered the room, Barton rose and abruptly left Teresa's side.

Scanning the ballroom for Teresa, Dan saw nothing strange and was still in the final hours of his contentment. As he was leaving his house, he had received from a messenger boy a letter in a yellow envelope, which he thrust, unopened, into his pocket, meaning to read it on his return home. It sat in his pocket throughout the rest of the evening

After dancing for more than three hours, the Sickleses and Octavia Ridgeley went outside, bestirred their carriage driver, John Cooney, and rolled home, back to the Stockton Mansion. It was two o'clock when they entered the door, and Teresa Sickles and Octavia Ridgeley began to prepare for bed. But Dan wanted to deal with the day's correspondence, so he went to his study, the small room near the front door, one flight up from the basement and at the front of the house. Among other items he opened was the yellow envelope he had just received.[7]

In an elegant and, many would believe, feminine hand, it read:

*Washington February 24th, 1859*
*Hon Daniel Sickles*

*Dear Sir,*
*    With deep regret I enclose to your address the few lines but an indispensable duty compels me so to do seeing that you are greatly imposed upon.*
*    There is a fellow I may say for he is not a gentleman by any*

*means by the [name] of Philip Barton Key and I believe the District*
*Attorney who rents the house of a negro man by the name of Jno. A.*
*Gray situated on 15th Street b'twn K and L streets for no other pur-*
*pose than to meet your wife Mrs. Sickles. He hangs a string out of the*
*window as a signal to her that he is in and leaves the door unfastened*
*and she walks in and sir I do assure you he has as much the use of*
*your wife as you have.*

*With these few hints I leave the rest of you to imagine.*

*Most Respfly*
*Your friend R.P.G.[8]*


The idea that his viperous friend Key had presumed to possess his treasure, his sublime Teresa, penetrated Dan like physical agony. His pain took no account of his own sexual behavior. Teresa was his, and he sheltered her as best he could from the viciousness of the larger world. Had she, of her own will and without his knowledge, embraced the parlous, venal world of Washington in the form of a supposed Maryland aristocrat named Key?

The R.P.G. note must have been the first letter he read, for he quickly emerged briefly from the study. Octavia Ridgeley saw him and was aware of a new distance in Dan's demeanor, of what she would call a wild and distracted look.[9]

The next morning Dan was up early and dressed and shaved in his usual exacting manner. He was not yet frenzied—he remembered the crazed things said out of malice about Teresa and Barton Key in the past. But that Friday Dan was distressed enough to try to gather his allies around him. Manny Hart, the former congressman who had been rewarded at Sickles's urging with the post of surveyor of the Port of New York, was sent a wire: would he come to Washington as soon as he could? Hart was considered a reliable friend by Teresa and Dan both.

Sickles then walked a few blocks north, reached Fifteenth Street, and began to talk to residents between K and L. Though so close to Lafayette Square, this was a nondescript neighborhood, filled with the families of white craftsmen and slightly better-off liberated slaves. The letter had not named an address, but the people he questioned, asking whether they had observed a tall man with a blond mustache and a young woman visiting a house around here, pointed with instant conviction to a modest two-story house, Number 383.

Dan withdrew. He had reason not to want to be remembered as the chief inquirer into this matter. It was a demeaning role for a husband, and he had agents who could fill it for him. He caught a carriage eastward to the Capitol, where he sought out his young friend John J. McElhone, reporter for the *Congressional Globe*. This was the journal that gave a complete record of proceedings in the House and the Senate, and McElhone was on the floor of the chamber delivering proofs of the previous day's speeches to the men who had made them and might want to correct errors. Dan, who had an extraordinary capacity to attract the loyalty of young, ambitious men, signaled the reporter over. He asked McElhone to visit the offices of two Washington newspapers, the *Daily States* and the *Evening Star*, and insert the following notice:

> R.P.G., who recently addressed a letter to a gentleman in this city, will confer a great favor upon the gentleman to whom the letter was addressed by granting him an early, immediate, and confidential interview.[10]

Dan was slated that day to speak in the House on the navy yard appropriations bill, particularly about the Brooklyn and Philadelphia navy yards. As the case of Dan's friend Charles K. Graham had proved, all posts at the Brooklyn navy yard, from chief engineer and navy agents down to the lowliest shipyard laborer, were in Tammany's keeping. The Democratic machine in Philadelphia possessed the same power over its navy yard. The Democrats believed, for various reasons—above all, the frequent interference of the British Royal Navy with American shipping—in a strong United States Navy. Besides that, Dan, as a member of the Foreign Affairs Committee, had an interest in such matters. Thus, patriotism and political expedience intersected at the navy yards.

But the R.P.G. note distracted Congressman Sickles, and he sent for another friend, the House clerk George Wooldridge, who was now working in the Capitol map room.

When summoned by the distinguished Dan Sickles, Wooldridge came immediately on his crutches to a small anteroom behind the Speaker's chair in the House. Dan sat Wooldridge down on a sofa, told him that he must speak to him about a painful matter, and handed him the letter he had received the night before. But before Wooldridge could scan it, Dan took it back and read it to Wooldridge. Wooldridge knew enough by now of Dan's ardent temperament—which could swing from calm reserve to turbulence in an instant—not to be surprised when Dan burst into tears and passed the letter back to the clerk. As Wooldridge finished reading it, Dan regained his composure. He told George Wooldridge that he had always had a policy of throwing out unsigned and anonymous letters. But this was a matter that could be easily proved true or false. He had gone up to Fifteenth Street that morning, he explained, and had been told that a man and woman seemed to be using Number 383 for assignations. The house had been, according to the neighbors, rented by a tall gentleman from a Negro man named Gray, as the letter claimed. Dan explained to Wooldridge that he hoped further investigation would prove that the woman the neighbors had seen was not Teresa, but then he asked or instructed Wooldridge, "As my friend, you will go there, and see whether it is or not."

Still seated on the sofa in the anteroom, Dan began to sob again, his head in his hands. Then he gathered himself, jumped up, and rushed to another anteroom, where a number of congressmen were waiting to see him on the bill before the House. Wooldridge followed on his crutches. Before entering the other room, however, Dan turned to him and ordered him to get a carriage. "We'll go," said Dan, "and I'll show you the house." And, the navy yards appropriations bill forgotten, they left the Capitol, the agile Wooldridge preceding Dan down the long outer stairs and hailing them a hack, which traveled down Pennsylvania Avenue, past the White House and Lafayette Square, and turned left into the neighborhood in question. At Fifteenth Street, Dan pointed out Number 383, and, before turning to go back to the Capitol, let Wooldridge out of the carriage to continue the investigation.[11]

Pursuing his task, Wooldridge knocked on some of the doors across the street from Number 383. Sometime during that cold afternoon, after the gaslamps in the street were lit, he spoke to a woman named Mrs. Baylis, and to her son, Crittenden Baylis. Crittenden had lighter skin than his mother and so expressed in his features the ironic fact that the national capital, a city rather Southern in character, where slave markets still operated and in which freed black Americans were at best tolerated and patronized, nonetheless harbored instances of secret congress between black and white. Crittenden had certainly seen the man and woman coming to Number 383. He knew who the man was, too; it was the esteemed Mr. Key, the DA. The woman, said Mrs. Baylis, often wore a black raglan cloak and a black shawl fringed with bugles. When had they last seen the man and woman? Both Mrs. Baylis and Crittenden said it was the afternoon before, Thursday. If that was so, George Wooldridge knew it might make cheery news for Dan Sickles, for Teresa would have been engaged that afternoon in preparing for her regular Thursday-evening dinner party.

Wooldridge then asked Mrs. Baylis whether he could rent a room from her, from which he could observe Number 383. Mrs. Baylis agreed, so Wooldridge was further emboldened to ask whether Crittenden would accompany him to the Capitol. He obviously intended to give Dan Sickles a chance to question Crittenden in person. Again, Mrs. Baylis consented. Snow clouds hung over Washington, and a keen wind was at work as Wooldridge crouched into a carriage and asked Crittenden aboard.

At the Capitol, Dan, just after six o'clock, had moved that the House adjourn. He had to sit at his desk in the House, in uncertainty of soul, as the Speaker ordered the sergeant-at-arms to gather up absentee members for a vote on an adjournment, and an argument went on for two more hours about who would be excused from the debate. As Wooldridge led Crittenden up the steps of the Capitol at about eight-thirty, the members were briskly deciding to adjourn after all and get home before ice made the pavements dangerous. Wooldridge left Crittenden in the entrance hall and went to signal his presence to Dan. On seeing him, Dan immediately abandoned his seat and again met with him in one of the anterooms, but he did not want to talk to Crittenden—it might involve too intense an exposure of his vulnerability, and to a mulatto boy. Just the same, he was vastly relieved when Wooldridge told him that both Crittenden and his mother had insisted that the man and woman had met at Number 383 the afternoon before.

Wooldridge would later remember that, grasping him joyously by the shoulder, Dan had exclaimed, "Then it can't be Teresa! She was at home all yesterday afternoon preparing for the dinner party; he's got some other woman on the string." He knew, too, that during Thursday afternoon, as Cooney the coachman could tell him, Teresa had visited the afternoon receptions of a number of friends, including Mrs. Brown, wife of the Postmaster General, Mrs. Thompson, wife of the Secretary of the Interior, and the lively Rose Greenhow.[12]

Nonetheless, Dan took home with him a certain solemnity and doubt that Friday night. Even the servants felt that the air in the Stockton Mansion had turned glacial as a skirling wind combed the city and ice settled on trees.

The next morning, without risking an acrimonious scene with Teresa, Dan spoke to his new coachman, John Cooney, who had been working for the Sickleses a mere few weeks. He seemed reliable and confirmed that he had taken Mrs. Sickles to all her social rounds on Thursday afternoon. Fluctuating between suspecting Teresa and the fear that he suspected her unjustly, Dan wrote an urgent note to Wooldridge, telling him not to use Teresa's name in his investigations, "as suspicion, if not proven or not true, is worse than the dreadful reality." He also told Wooldridge that he had made his inquiries of his coachman and found that it could not have been his wife who was at Number 383 on Thursday.

That Saturday morning, attending to his duty as a legislator, Dan turned toward the Capitol, catching an omnibus along a Pennsylvania Avenue whose pavements were marked by snow and whose linden trees were blighted by ice. As Dan went to his desk, Daniel Dougherty, a guest at the Sickleses' house the previous Thursday night, had just left Marshal Jonah Hoover's house and was walking down Pennsylvania Avenue toward Lafayette Square to say goodbye to Teresa. He met up with Barton Key, who should have been at his desk in City Hall at this time, and they strolled on toward the White House and the square. Dougherty presumed that Key was also visiting the Sickleses, but he peeled away in an awkward manner, Dougherty would remember, to the Clubhouse on the other side of the square. He had, after all, received a few days past a letter in a not too difficult code warning him that Washington knew of his passion for Teresa and that he should be careful. Obsession nonetheless dragged him to Lafayette Square as if it contained the only air he could breathe.[13]

In the House, debate continued on a number of appropriation bills. Dan voted on a post office bill and was listed to speak in a continuation of debate on the navy yards appropriations bill and the claims of the Brooklyn Navy Yard. He hoped that by late afternoon he would hear from R.P.G., for the appeal for R.P.G. to get in touch had been published in that morning's *Daily States*. Meanwhile, Wooldridge was keeping watch in his rented room in Mrs. Baylis's house across from Number 383. He waited there through the forenoon, but saw no one approach the assignation house. He was pleased when the boy, Crittenden, shortly after three, came upstairs and relieved the ennui of surveillance by beginning to chat. Crittenden described the woman again; it was a description that, Wooldridge noticed, fitted Teresa. More crucially, the boy let slip that his mother and he had been wrong about the man and woman having visited Number 383 on Thursday. It was in fact Wednesday afternoon that they had turned up!

At three o'clock, a hungry and depressed Wooldridge got up, took his crutches, and returned on foot through icy streets to his boardinghouse on Twelfth Street for a meal. He clearly thought that in what was left of this bitter day no assignation was likely to occur in unlit and unwarmed Number 383, but he did not look forward to telling Dan that it was Wednesday afternoon, not Thursday, when the Fifteenth Street lovers had last met at Number 383. At some stage that day, Wooldridge went to Lafayette Square and spoke to the Sickleses' servants, and may have attracted Teresa's vague suspicion by doing so. Teresa did not like Wooldridge as much as Dan did, and considered him something of a busybody. But he did not want too lightly to pass on to Dan the correction the Baylis mother and son had made. He learned by questioning the coachman Cooney, the footman McDonald, and the maid Duffy that they had often seen Mr. Key across the square, signaling with a white handkerchief from the direction of the Clubhouse. So at last Wooldridge had no choice but to catch an omnibus to the Capitol and face Dan.

He stood on his crutches in the hall outside the House of Representatives and sent a message in to Sickles, who had just finished arguing in favor of an expansion of the Brooklyn Navy Yard, The *Congressional Globe* proofs of his speech were strewn on his desk on the floor of the House, where he willingly left them to go to Wooldridge. The clerk would later say that at that moment Dan seemed different from the way he had the day before—more like himself, less haunted. But Wooldridge had the sorry task of telling him that Thursday had been a mistake; Wednesday was the day. He described the clothing the woman had worn that day and said that the Baylises had kept track of the assignations and asserted the meetings took place two or three times a week. The man, Mr. Key, would arrive first, go into the house, leave the door ajar, and place a ribbon or towel or anything white in the shutters of the upstairs window as a signal.

The news consumed Dan. This friend! This wife! So much for Dan's admiration of stylish Southerners! His political calm was swept away, and he wept freely and without apology. His tears were copious enough that Wooldridge went with him to a "retiring" room, where Dan took a considerable time to compose himself to a degree that Wooldridge felt it safe to leave him.

Dan did not have the patience or peace of mind to wait for a hack at the Capitol; he strode homeward in the early darkness. Francis Mohun, a building contractor and Washington alderman who lived on Pennsylvania Avenue, saw him pass, "in a very excited condition. . . . His whole appearance, though I cannot exactly describe how it affected me, did affect me very seriously at the time."[14]

In the Sickles household, both the maid, Bridget Duffy, and the guest, Octavia Ridgeley, could tell that this would be an uncomfortable night. Mr. Sickles's gloom and suppressed anger seemed of a more distressful order tonight. He did not want to speak to Teresa, did not want to eat downstairs. He asked Bridget Duffy to bring him a tray of food in his bedroom upstairs, and she noticed tears when she delivered it to him. Octavia Ridgeley's mother was out of town, so she was stuck at the Stockton Mansion, with some terrible domestic explosion likely to occur at any minute. Finding her normally lively friend Teresa pale and distracted, Octavia settled in the downstairs parlor and tried to entertain herself. Like Dan, Teresa wished Manny Hart, from New York, had been there, but he had sent a telegram saying he could not get away from the city. So Teresa inevitably went up to the bedroom at the front of the house to talk to Dan. Along the corridor, the convalescent child, Laura, was playing in the nursery room that she shared with Bridget, and when Bridget went up to see the child, she found the Sickleses' bedroom door ajar. She heard loud conversation, and listened a moment, for even though she came from the stringently regulated sexual atmosphere of rural Ireland, she could have told Congressman Sickles a thing or two about Key and Teresa.

Dan was giving it to her now! She had begun by denying all but had then broken down and seemed to be fainting. Bridget moved on but came back twenty minutes later and knocked on the door to take Dan's tray away. As she described it, there was "some unhappy feeling between Mr. and Mrs. Sickles." Octavia Ridgeley could also hear the conflict. Dan's noises of grief were, in her opinion, fearful; his groans seemed to come from his very feet.[15]

The evening ached away on this grim and freezing Saturday night. Some time after eight-thirty, Sickles emerged and called to both Octavia and Bridget to join him and his wife in the front bedroom. If today such a scene of domestic confusion would borrow its tone and even its lines from cinema, in the Victorian era it was a combination of the Bible,

Shakespeare, and contemporary theater that influenced the speech and gestures of such crises of love, marriage, infidelity as were to be played here. Dan took into this confrontation with his wife the vivid memory of Edwin Forrest's portrayal of Othello the Moor, and Othello's torment at the idea of Desdemona's infidelity. Though Dan was certainly desolated by all aspects of this business, it was simply not within the code either of the time or of a man like Dan Sickles to be rendered more sad than angry at his wife's sins. Sadly for Teresa, he was required both by culture and by temperament to rage inordinately, to howl with reproach. At a time like this, as the two summoned women, the guest and the servant, entered, he was required by the conventions of the day to be ruthlessly severe.

Octavia and Bridget, on entering the room, saw a pallid Teresa, with tear-stained, lowered eyes, sitting at her desk in the process of writing or adding to a letter. Bridget was appropriately left standing while Dan pointed Octavia to a sofa by the window. There was silence in the room and a pregnant air of outrage. Teresa finished writing a little before nine, and Dan took the pages from her, scanned them, and laid them down with all but the bottom of the last page covered. He asked the two women to sign as witnesses the last, partly exposed page of the document. They had little idea of its contents, although Bridget knew better than Octavia that this was probably a form of confession of adultery.

Both women signed at once, anxious to be dismissed from the charged air of this bedroom. Dan thanked them and said they could go. What they had put their names to, a document in Teresa's handwriting, which tonight had been rendered irregular by the pressures of guilt and recrimination, read as follows:

I have been in a house in Fifteenth Street, with Mr. Key. How many times, I don't know. I believe the house belongs to a colored man. . . . Commenced going there the latter part of January. Have been in alone and with Mr. Key. Usually stayed an hour. There was a bed in the second story. I did what is usual for a wicked woman to do. The intimacy commenced this winter, when I came from New York, in that house—an intimacy of an improper kind. Have met a dozen times or more, at different hours of the day. On Monday of this week, and Wednesday also. . . .

Teresa went on to admit that she and Key would arrange assignations when they met in the street and at parties. "Never would speak to him when Mr. Sickles was at home, because I knew he [Sickles] did not like me to speak to him [Key]." Indeed, she said, she had not seen Mr. Key for some days after arriving in the city for the winter session of Congress. But when Key approached her and said he had rented the house, she agreed to meet him there. They did not eat and drink in the house, she declared, obviously in response to a question from Dan. The room was warmed by a wood fire. Key would go first, though sometimes they walked there together—"four times—I do not think more." She had gone on her own the Wednesday before, between two and three, to meet Key, who was inside.

A detail that would in some eyes make Teresa appear more culpable was that Laura, recently ill but in perfectly renewed health, had been minded at the house of a friend, Mrs. Hoover, wife of the recently retired federal marshal, while Teresa was with Key. Teresa admitted—a detail that rankled with Dan—that it was Mr. Key who had dropped Laura off there, "at my request." After Barton left Laura at the Hoovers', he went to meet Teresa at a reception at the house of Senator Stephen Douglas, where Teresa had been communing with Mrs. Douglas and others while waiting for Barton. From this apparently chance meeting, Teresa and Key left separately. Key went first to light the fire in the house on Fifteenth Street, and Teresa followed. "Went in by the back gate. Went in the same bedroom, and there an improper interview was had. I undressed myself. Mr. Key undressed also. This occurred on Wednesday, 23rd February, 1859."

What Dan had elicited from her were the sort of appalling details that no woman of Teresa's class would voluntarily surrender except when overwhelmed by the savage disappointment of a wronged husband. And obviously she did not intend that this document should become public, though it might end up in the hands of a divorce lawyer. Even that prospect left her stupefied with humiliation.

One question Dan must have asked was something like "Did anything happen here, in Lafayette Square?" Teresa admitted Key had been in the Stockton Mansion not merely as Dan's friend, but for erotic purposes. "Mr. Key has kissed me in this house a number of times. I do not deny that we have had connection in this house, last spring, a year ago, in the parlor, on the sofa. Mr. Sickles was sometimes out of town, and sometimes in." But Teresa said she had not thought it right to go on meeting there, "because there are servants who might suspect something." Then, under further pressure, she confessed that the affair had started long before the beginning of this congressional session. "I think the intimacy commenced in April or May, 1858."

Generally, for her meetings at the house in Fifteenth Street, she further admitted, she had worn a black-and-white woolen plaid dress and a beaver hat trimmed with black velvet. But then she remembered that she had also worn a black silk dress, also a plaid silk dress, a black velvet cloak trimmed with lace, and a black velvet shawl trimmed, as the Baylises of Fifteenth Street had said, with a fringe.

Had Key ridden in the Sickleses' carriage? Dan asked. Yes, he had, the written confession admitted. Had he called at the house recently, without my knowledge? asked remorseless Dan. Yes, said Teresa. "And after my being told not to invite him to do so, and against Mr. Sickles' repeated requests."

This part of the document, like other sections of the confession, was signed "Teresa Bagioli," not "Teresa Sickles."

For there were two postscripts to the main body of the document. The lawyer in Dan foresaw that in the case of a divorce, which in his present state he believed to be the sole course open to him, a lawyer for Teresa might say the confession had been forced from her. Thus, she had appended, at Dan's demand, the assertion: "This is a true statement, written by myself, without any inducement held out by Mr. Sickles of forgiveness or reward, and without any menace from him. This I have written with my bed-room door open, and my maid and child in the adjoining room, at half past eight in the evening. Miss Ridgeley is in the house, within call."

Again, she signed herself Teresa Bagioli, but there was still a last scatter of questions that had occurred to Dan. Yes, agreed Teresa, Key's sister, wife of Representative Pendleton of Ohio, had dined in the Sickleses' house "two weeks ago last Thursday with a large party. Mr. Key was also here . . . and at my suggestion he was invited, because he lived in the same house, and also because he'd invited Mr. Sickles to dine with him."[16]

That night Dan tried to find sleep in the bedroom, in the bed he considered shamefully dishonored by Key. Teresa shared Octavia's room, and, in the spirit of Catholic penitence, insisted on sleeping on the floor, her head resting on a stool. Whenever Bridget Duffy woke during the hours of dark, in the same room as young Laura, she heard "exclamations and sobbing" from both Dan's room and Octavia's room. Little Laura, bewildered by her parents' sobs, had at last gone to her father's room and spent the rest of the night with him. And so a night of polar cold gave way to the temperate morning so praised by the Reverend Smith Pyne's Sabbath parishioners.

Octavia ate breakfast downstairs with Laura. Even when moving tentatively about the house, she could hear Dan's grief wherever she was. His groans were unearthly. They would not have astounded his father. Had George Sickles been in Washington, he might have settled his son down. At the same time, Dan, knowing he needed a range of advice, turned, according to his long-held custom, to Tammany friends. He had heard that Sam Butterworth, a lawyer and supporter of his from New York and Tammany, who had worked with Sickles to help James Buchanan win the crucial state of New York, was visiting Washington that weekend, staying at the house of Senator Gwinn. Butterworth, taller than Dan and floridly good-looking, had as a reward for his work on the 1856 ballot been appointed head of the federal subtreasury in New York. He was a hardheaded opportunist and, unlike Manny Hart, was not well respected by Teresa. Nonetheless, Dan sent a message by servant to him: "Dear B. Come to me right away!" Butterworth showed the note to Gwinn, who knew Sickles well, and then to another guest in the house, Robert J. Walker, who had been for a time appointed governor of Kansas by Old Buck. "Sickles wants to see me immediately," Butterworth told Walker. "What can this mean?"

Dan had also summoned Wooldridge to provide the comfort of familiar companionship and to be on hand for sensitive errands. But to use a term of a later century, it was Butterworth who was to act as his "spin doctor." Wooldridge was the first to arrive, tired after having been out till midnight. He saw that Dan, in the study at the front of the house, was not himself in a good state. His eyes were bloodshot, and he was pacing up and down in acute distress. He could not even stay in the room for long. He would go upstairs, return down to the study, talk to Wooldridge, drift out again, and go upstairs. Every time he came back into the study, said Wooldridge, "he pressed his hands to his temples and would go over to the secretary and sob," using the desk to prop himself upright. Because Dan was obviously in need of relief, Wooldridge told him to give vent to his tears.

Butterworth arrived about noon, while Dan was again upstairs. Wooldridge briefed him in the study, because he knew that any recital of the situation by Dan himself would bring on further bouts of tears. Wooldridge had permission to show Teresa's confession, now on Dan's desk, to Butterworth. In Dan's world, a shame shared with a reliable brother was a shame halved. A desolated Teresa no doubt felt otherwise. When Butterworth had finished reading the confession and mounted the steps to the bedroom, he found Dan facedown on his pillow. Having followed on his crutches, Wooldridge witnessed the conversation. "I am a dishonored and ruined man," Dan told his friend, "and cannot look you in the face!"

That combination of adjectives—"dishonored" and "ruined"—showed that Dan had ceased to think exclusively of what he saw as the wrong done him and had also begun to contemplate what the affair of Key and Teresa might do to him as a public man and as a man of honor.

Despite what we would consider his melodramatic line, the fact was that Dan's friends were profoundly touched by the depth of his feeling, and were convinced that he needed to be saved from a severe derangement of his senses; from lunacy, that is. Sam Butterworth at last persuaded him to come down to the study for a calmer conversation. Dan held an unlighted cigar clamped between his teeth as they descended. Butterworth advised him to send his wife to her mother's house in New York. Such a departure was close enough to the end of the session not to excite any remark. Then, "for the honor of his little daughter," when the season ended and before Congress convened the following December, Dan should take a trip to Europe, distancing himself from a frequently vicious New York press, and his lawyers could arrange a separation in the meantime. This was the advice of Butterworth the lawyer, and it was good counsel.

Dan told him, "My friend, I would gladly pursue this course, but so abandoned, so reckless have Key and my wife been, that all the Negroes in that neighborhood, and I dare not say how many other persons, know all about the circumstances."[17]

He had, in the language of the time, been cuckolded in an era when only those radical women known as Bloomers believed marriages to be equal partnerships, when men, even in splendid and contented marriages, were considered to own wives, when marriage was spoken of by most respectable men and women in terms of the husband's proprietorship and governance of his wife, while women were seen to have been redeemed from degradation by possession of a husband. So Dan's rights and his kindliness—of which there were many examples—had been violated in a most visible manner. It seemed, too, that Teresa Bagioli Sickles represented for him a zone of luscious, Italianate inviolability, an innocence to which he could return from his political wars, even from his sins. That sanctuary had now been multiply plundered. It was characteristic of Dan that he did not mind Butterworth's and Wooldridge's knowing; he would tell them anything, for they were his men. But the knowledge of men not bound to him in Democratic fraternity appalled him. To a greater or lesser extent, Washington knew about the

Teresa–Key affair. Even the President must suspect. The Republicans knew! That public shame compounded Dan's intimate sense of betrayal. In the Congress, he had loyally defended the world for which Barton Key stood, the world of Southern good sense and *noblesse oblige*. Barton had done much to prove that world an opportunistic stunt, a set of rehearsed manners hiding viciousness at the heart.

Dan did not yet know that Barton Key was that afternoon within a short distance of the place where he sought Butterworth's counsel. During his affair with Teresa, Key had fluctuated between despair, fatalism, neurosis, and exaltation. But he was dependent on the sight of her, and that bright morning, with the streets turning to a morass from the melt of last night's storm, and the temperature heading above a pleasant fifty degrees Fahrenheit, Key meant to spend in anticipatory joy of a signal from Teresa, and of a meeting that might be arranged and even achieved by midafternoon. He had come in to Willard's Hotel from the Pendletons' house in Georgetown. He must have taken the omnibus or a carriage, since his gray mount, Lucifer, was not to be seen in town that day. A mile or so across the town from Willard's, in K Street near the courts, his four children—Alice, James, Mary, Lizzie—lived in the house he had once shared with them and their mother. Today, he had no apparent desire to visit them. Nor did any fear of imminent sickness, which had sometimes delayed him in attending to his duties as district attorney, and had sent him last summer to the spas of Saratoga Springs and, before that, on a recuperative journey to Cuba, influence him today.

Key arrived at Willard's relatively early and in the hotel barbershop had a shave and a hair trim. Then he walked up the hill to Pennsylvania, past the unfinished classic facade of the Treasury, and into Lafayette Square. He was dressed well, though not flamboyantly, in a gray-striped vest and trousers and a jacket of brown tweed and, since it was still cold this early, a brown overcoat. In his pocket, along with other things, he carried two brass keys, both of them crafted for the front door of 383 Fifteenth Street. In the side pocket of his jacket, he had a pair of opera glasses. He had also a coded anonymous letter he had received a few days ago, warning him that people knew about Mrs. Sickles and him. It was not enough to keep him away from Lafayette Square.

Given the existence of this letter, it is a wonder that, even with the sense of invincibility he derived from his love, he was not carrying a pistol in his pocket, for many gentlemen went armed in a city that was both politically and socially turbulent. Within a few days, a New York newspaper would comment, "Washington has for years been a bear-garden, in which most travelers have ventured armed."[18]

Outside the barbershop at Willard's, Key ran into two acquaintances, Washington's mayor, James G. Berret, and a fellow lawyer, Southey Parker, who was also a friend of the Sickleses. Key showed yet again that he was not an accomplished manager of affairs with married women. He went so far as to joke that he might be killed by Mr. Sickles. Berret had himself heard rumors about Key and Mrs. Sickles, but he believed that Mr. Key's remark was hyperbole.

Bridget Duffy returned about now from the Catholic church some blocks north. Going into the Stockton Mansion and taking off her shawl, she found her master still given to sobs, "calling on God to witness his troubles." She went to her upstairs room to put away her hat and shawl, and from the window saw Barton Key walking on Pennsylvania Avenue, seemingly headed toward Georgetown, though she suspected that was just a feint. Downstairs, in the study, Wooldridge also saw Key and watched him cross Pennsylvania Avenue. One of the Reverend Smith Pyne's homeward-bound parishioners saw Barton stop on the edge of the pavement and look toward the Sickleses' house. On top of that, a Treasury Department architect walking in the square saw Key, too. And twenty minutes later, from the kitchen window, Bridget saw him yet again, as he crossed the park toward the Clubhouse.

This building, until recently operating as the National Club, still housed a restaurant and bar and rooms for rent. It had at one time been the home of Chief Justice Roger Brook Taney, Key's frail, venerable pro-Southern uncle. Obviously Key thought that the position of the Clubhouse, where he was not unknown, gave some credibility to his loitering in the square, yet, hungry for Teresa, he was no better than a schoolboy at hiding his real purpose. So by the time Butterworth was counseling Dan Sickles, Key had been sighted at least eight times in the Sickleses' neighborhood, including twice by Bridget Duffy and once by Mayor Berret.

Having given his advice and partially soothed Dan, Butterworth, keeping an arranged appointment, went to meet a friend at the Clubhouse and drink a glass of ale with him. While Butterworth was gone, Barton appeared again in Lafayette Square; among those who saw him were the coachman John Cooney and the groom McDonald. A lawyer from Buffalo, New York, who knew him, spotted him as he walked back and forth near the statue of Andrew Jackson, a memorial made from the metal of British guns captured at the Battle of New Orleans. The man approached him, "passed the time of day with him," and went off to eat his Sunday dinner at Willard's, as Barton left the square by its southwest gate, "whirling a handkerchief as he went along."

These sightings suggested that Barton Key may have been desperate for a glimpse of Teresa in an upper window or a reciprocating signal from her. He had been reconnoitering the house and prowling into the square, retreating occasionally to the Clubhouse, for well over two hours and had not received any sign. Was she ill? Had her husband given her warnings? An exasperated and yet grimly gratified Bridget observed him a third time. He had run into a young couple he knew, who were crossing the square on their way from an unspecified church. By now Barton was depressed, and he told the young woman, when she asked him how he was, "I am despondent about my health and very desperate. Indeed, I have half a mind to go out on the prairie and try buffalo hunting. The excursion would either cure me or kill me, and, really, I don't care much which."

Now the Sickleses' dog, an Italian greyhound named Dandy, spotted Barton and ran out into the street to greet him, or, as Bridget Duffy said, "to fawn on him." As if playing with the dog, Barton again extracted his white handkerchief and whirled it three or four times. Though he may have seen himself as a heroic lover, he had become a figure of bathos. He continued to wave the handkerchief in "a slow, rotary motion," even after the dog had given up and departed. From the study by the front door, above the kitchen, Wooldridge also saw Barton with the young couple, waving his handkerchief while averting his eyes from his friends and hoping for a signal from Mrs. Sickles.[19]

Teresa's feelings and movements that day would always remain less scrupulously examined by others than those of Sickles and Key. She would not ever be asked, for example, "Did you wish to go to the window and warn Barton away by gesture? Or did you, even this early, curse him as the source of your present misery? Did Octavia Ridgeley urge you not to make any signal, assuring you that Key would in the end go away?" The sad case was that the subtler mixture of feelings of a shamed woman like Teresa would not be considered relevant, and she would never be consulted on them.

Dan was upstairs again as Butterworth strolled back to the Sickleses' house from the Clubhouse. Somehow he missed seeing Barton Key in the square, but when he went up the outer stairs and through the front door and into the study, Wooldridge told him in a lowered voice that Key had been backward and forward a number of times. Wooldridge then turned in distress to a set of stereoscopic views with which he had been relieving the pressure and lost himself in three-dimensional images of the White House, the Capitol, the Treasury building, the Washington Memorial.

About then, Dan Sickles, glancing from his window upstairs, also happened to see Key. It was preposterous that the man who had sullied Teresa while denying he was doing so should be so provocative as to present himself openly in Lafayette Square. In a frenzy, Dan rushed downstairs into the library. "That villain has just passed my house," he cried. "My God, this is horrible!"

Both Butterworth and Wooldridge knew from the look of Dan's enraged face, his blood-engorged blue eyes, that he was at his most dangerous. Sam Butterworth said, "Mr. Sickles, you must be calm, and look this matter square in the face. If there be a possibility of keeping a certain knowledge of this crime from the public, you must do nothing to destroy that possibility. You may be mistaken in your belief that it is known to the whole city."

But Dan reiterated, "It's the town talk. The whole world knows it."

Butterworth declared that if it was the town talk, "there is but one course left to you as a man of honor. You need no advice." Sam was proposing a duel between Sickles and Barton Key.

On the edge of reacting, Dan fell into a dark reflectiveness. He said he was sure that Key had been in the habit of using a room at the Clubhouse from which to signal Teresa. But Teresa had denied it, and he wondered why, since she'd admitted so much else. Without trying to resolve this puzzle, Dan now walked into the hallway. There, according to Butterworth, he suggested that they go to the room of a mutual friend, Stuart, at the Clubhouse, to ask him whether Key had a room there. A little implausibly, Butterworth claimed that he then walked out of the Stockton Mansion, down its sweep of iron stairs, and off toward the Clubhouse, thinking that Sickles was following him.

In view of coming events, Sam Butterworth had every reason to claim that when he left Dan in the hall he was satisfied that the congressman had no weapons on his person, and that he was without his overcoat. Finding himself alone on the pavement, Sam, instead of returning to the house, claimed to have walked slowly down Pennsylvania Avenue on the south side, the side on which the White House stood, and then crossed to encounter Barton Key from the flank by the railings of the park. His movements would to many bespeak a man partaking in an ambush, for according to his own account, he walked 120 yards or more wrongly thinking Sickles was with or just behind him.

Since Butterworth was the type of New York Democrat who had strong associations in the capital and with its Southern gentry, Key recognized him as he approached, and greeted him by name. "What a fine day we have!" said Key.

Butterworth asked in reply whether Key had come from the Clubhouse, and Key said he had. Butterfield then asked whether his friend Mr. Stuart was in his room.

"Yes; and he is quite well."

Butterworth said he was on his way to see Stuart and bade Key goodbye, but now saw Sickles, wearing an overcoat despite the warmth of the day, coming rapidly toward them around the square and down Madison Place to cut off Key's line of retreat to the Clubhouse. Dan must have ultimately left his house by the basement door, for the stereoscopically engaged Wooldridge did not see him leave by the front door. Now, even at this extremity of feeling, Dan took his lines from contemporary drama. He called, "Key, you scoundrel, you have dishonored my house—you must die!"

It happened that at that second of threat there were many people in the environs of Lafayette Square, but Dan's fury transcended that reality. Most of these witnesses would say later that Dan mentioned a dishonored bed. Butterworth claimed that before anything else happened, Barton Key's hand flashed into his vest or side coat pocket, and that he took a step in the direction of Dan Sickles. As Barton stepped forward, Dan produced a gun from his overcoat pocket and fired from close range. That first shot produced little more than a contusion on one of Barton Key's hands. When Dan raised his arm to fire again, Barton jumped at him, seizing him by the collar of his coat with his left hand. Dan backed from the sidewalk into the street and dropped the gun he held, a derringer, onto the sidewalk. Some said he jettisoned it deliberately; others, accidentally. Barton grabbed him from behind when Dan turned as if to leave, though that was not his intention. All this untoward grappling between two eminent servants of the Republic was occurring on the corner of Pennsylvania Avenue, the corner of the square and of the little pathway called Madison Place, connecting Pennsylvania and H Street. Had the President been at any of the front windows of the White House, he would have had a clear view of the untoward struggle between Key and Sickles. But he was in his office on the south side, looking—if he had time to—over the unseemly swamp that is now the Ellipse, toward the Washington Monument and the Potomac.

At last, Dan pulled himself from Barton's hold, swung around, and hauled another gun from his overcoat pocket. Barton backed a few steps up Madison Place toward the Clubhouse, crying, "Don't murder me!" He reached inside his own coat, took out the opera glasses, and threw them at Dan. They hit the congressman, who thought the gesture contemptible, and fell to the ground. Butterworth said that at this moment he was still sure Key was armed, and that Dan must have believed it too. In any case, this show of ineffectual aggression from Barton occurred just before Dan fired again, from a distance of a few feet.

The second bullet struck Barton in the upper leg. Perhaps the wound which resulted reflected the fact that Key was taller than Dan, though Dan was accustomed to using a pistol. His friends in the Tammany target clubs said his eye was accurate. So it may have been that the wound was also a near-miss symbolic injury, for the bullet entered Key's trousers just two inches below his groin, high enough that it exited in the fold between buttocks and upper leg. The inflicting of this wound was witnessed by at least seven people, one of them a young White House page from South Carolina, J. H. W. Bonitz, who had just left the staff quarters of the White House and was emerging through its gateway on to the avenue. Behind Barton as he backed into Madison Place, Thomas Martin, a Treasury Department clerk, was leaving the Clubhouse, where he had been chatting with three colleagues. On top of that, a Mr. McCormack, of the corner house—the Maynard house—on Pennsylvania Avenue and Madison Place, saw the whole thing from his seat at a second-floor window.

"I'm shot," Barton announced and staggered toward the sidewalk. He asked Dan not to fire again. Dan still shouted, calling him a villain, ranting about his dishonored marriage. Barton leaned against a tree outside the Maynard house, but he could not hold on to it and slid to the pavement, where he lay on his right side, with his hand over the hole near his groin.

Had Dan stopped, with a nonfatal blood debt having been paid—the coroner would find that the bullet missed the main artery of the thigh—he would have been easily vindicated. The presumption that Key was carrying a gun would have been considered reasonable not only in terms of the culture of Washington, but from assertions Key had made to other people. But Dan's nature required the extreme sacrifice. The witnesses heard Barton cry, "Don't shoot me. Murder! Murder!" When Dan pulled the trigger again, the gun merely made a snapping noise, and did not fire. He cocked the weapon again, placed the barrel close to Key, and fired.

This time the bullet entered beneath Barton's heart, passing between the eleventh and twelfth ribs. The bullet entered the large lobe of the liver, punctured the right cavity of the chest, and hit the ribs at Barton's back, lodging under the skin. Immediately, the left side of his chest began to fill with blood.

Either because they were too far away or because they were stunned, the witnesses had not intervened. Even Sam Butterworth, who would be depicted in the illustrated papers as either standing coolly by or leaning easefully on the railings of Lafayette Square, did not step in. The young Treasury man, Thomas Martin, who had just come from the Clubhouse, was the most active witness, and rushed back inside the building to mobilize his three friends.

Dan now moved close to Key's body for the *coup de grâce*. The gun, its barrel close to Key's head, again misfired. Thomas Martin, back on the street, was able to get between the two men. Dan asked him, "Is the scoundrel dead?" Martin took Barton Key in his arms and looked up at Dan. "He has violated my bed," Dan said as justification for what had just happened. One of Martin's friends, who put his hand on Dan's shoulder and begged him not to fire again, was offered the same justification.

Butterworth, who some would believe was pleased to stand by while Key was punished, stepped up, took Dan by the arm, and led him away toward the corner of H Street and Madison Place. As he walked, Dan put the gun in his overcoat pocket. Dr. Coolidge, an army surgeon who lived on H Street and who had heard the unmistakable and successive sound of gunshots, was on his way, running to Lafayette Square with his surgeon's bag. Martin and his fellow federal employees were engaged in carrying Barton Key into the Clubhouse. They placed him on the floor in one of the first rooms inside the door, and someone tilted a chair upside down so that Key could lean his head and shoulders against its legs and rungs. When Martin felt for the pulse and found it thin, he asked Barton if there were any messages he would like passed on to his children, but Key, drowning in his own blood, did not seem to grasp the question. Dr. Coolidge, entering the scene, found Key "pulseless." Key "partially breathed twice," but when Dr. Coolidge opened Barton's shirt and trousers, looking for his wounds, he decided that nothing could be done. His initial assessment was that the chest wound would prove fatal, and even as he inspected it, Barton died.[20]

Young Bonitz, the White House page, ran back to the White House at once. In the informal presidential household of the day, he was able to get immediate access to the office and tell the President that Congressman Sickles had just shot District Attorney Key. Bonitz knew, from the tremors of Old Buck's head, that the news had nearly felled the gray and aged President. "I was afraid it would happen!" said the President. "I must see Sickles—I must see him at once!" As the page detailed for the President the sequence of events he had just witnessed, it became apparent to Buchanan that Dan, who, according to Bonitz, had vanished across Lafayette Square, could be in great peril. Even apart from personal affections and sadness, the President believed that such a serviceable and promising Democrat needed to be saved. Clearly there would be a trial, and that meant a risk that certain details of his own connection with the Sickleses would emerge.

The President did not spend much time considering the law-enforcement aspect of Dan's act. No message was sent from the White House to the federal marshal. No message went to Attorney General Jeremiah Black. President Buchanan had other priorities. Quite inaccurately, he warned the relatively unworldly Bonitz, a young man from rural South Carolina, that as an eyewitness he was in a difficult situation; he could be held in jail without bail pending his being called as a witness. He should leave Washington straightaway, and return home on indefinite leave. Hence an American President, often referred to as the Chief Magistrate of the Republic, urged a witness—for all he knew the only witness to the murder—to flee from his legal responsibility. The President searched around to give Bonitz a personal memento, and came up with a new razor, handing it and some money to the young man. Bonitz packed his valise and rushed off to the Potomac to cross to the far side and take the Wilmington train homeward. In an age when the press believed it impolite to keep watch on a Sabbath, or any other day, on the White House lawn, the description went utterly unobserved.[21]

As Barton Key breathed his last in the Clubhouse, Dan, still accompanied by Butterworth, was walking resolutely toward the house of Attorney General Black, a few blocks northeast on Franklin Park. Once there, he went inside alone, for he had decided on reflection to send Butterworth doubling back to Lafayette Square to collect any helpful evidence, especially the opera glasses, which could credibly have been mistaken for an instant for a drawn pistol or something else of danger. At the Attorney General's door, Dan spoke to a servant, who led him to a back parlor, where two other gentlemen were waiting to see Mr. Black. One was a man named Haldemar, editor of a Democratic paper in Harrisburg, Pennsylvania, and the other a former senator named Richard Brodhead. With surreal politeness, Dan began to discuss Pennsylvania politics with Haldemar. Brodhead mentioned that Dan had some mud on his boots, which he might want to remove. Dan got up without a protest and left the room to attend to the problem, the mud on his boots being the only clue to the disorder that now claimed his life. Returning from outside, he ran into Attorney General Black in the hall, calmly explained his situation, and surrendered his gun. To his visitors, Black appeared to be far more distraught than Congressman Sickles as he came into the parlor and informed the editor and the former senator. Then Dan strolled in and joined them. Both visitors offered to go with Dan to a magistrate, and one of them surmised that the offense might be a bailable one. Dan said, "If all the facts were known, it would be. For God knows I would be justified."

Butterworth, returned from Lafayette Square, was admitted to the house by Black's servant and presented to Dan and the company the opera glasses with mud on their rims. One of the men asked what was the news of Barton. Was he dead? Butterworth said that he was. Dan muttered, "One wretch less in the world."

The news of the shooting spread exponentially through the capital during the remainder of the afternoon. At Brown's Hotel, where Senator Clement Claiborne Clay of Alabama and lively Virginia Clay lived, the senator burst in on his wife and cried, "A horrible, horrible thing has happened, Virginia! Sickles has killed Key; killed him most brutally, while he was unarmed!" Through all the nearby hotels and boarding-houses where legislators lived during their service in Washington, the astonishing information ran, and a large crowd moved up from Willard's to Lafayette Square. The journalists of the national and capital newspapers arrived and began to interview any witness or servant from the houses around the square, and pressed their way into the over-crowded Clubhouse. All the inquiry and surmise centered on Dan and on the murdered Key. Teresa was more the material of the crime, and no journalist wondered whether, drawn by the sound of gunfire, she had inadvertently seen her lover's killing, or what state this had left her in. The questions were never answered. Teresa had placed herself beyond inquiry.

One witness to all the excitement, a friend of Dan's named McClusky, said that a suddenly assembled trail of people, including himself, had followed Dan and Butterworth to the Attorney General's house and joined the crowd there. First Butterworth left the house, to go back to the Stockton Mansion. Two Washington police officers, summoned by Attorney General Black, went inside, and there was fevered wonderment as Dan came out, accompanied by the police, and got into a carriage with them. Such a press of citizens blocked the carriage that McClusky got back to the Sickleses' house first and told Wooldridge what had happened. Somehow Wooldridge had escaped seeing the events on the far side of the park, had continued to ease the intensity of the afternoon by looking at his stereoscopic views, sitting by the library window with the westering afternoon light to help augment his enjoyment. He must have seen crowds assembling in the area, but had preferred not to inquire about them. This orderly, intelligent, maimed young man had retreated from the pace of events. Perhaps, after all, the greensward of Lafayette Square and the trees around its margins had absorbed the shots and screams. Teresa herself was still mercifully unaware. When Wooldridge heard the news, he was overwhelmed. "I never want to see such another day," he cried, turning his face.[22]

Crowds saw Dan enter the Stockton Mansion's front door. Others of Dan's friends turned up, flooding the lower floors. Some may have had a fleeting voyeur impulse to lay eyes on the exquisite Teresa. Two of Dan's neighbors, the retired grocer John McBlair and Senator John Slidell of Louisiana, arrived. Like everyone else that afternoon, Slidell was taken by the way in which Dan fluctuated between calmness and desperation. The man from whose house Butterworth had come this morning, Senator William Gwinn, a habitual gun-toter himself, brought another friend of Dan's, former Kansas governor Robert J. Walker. Dan told them all, "A thousand thanks for coming to see me under these circumstances." Then he threw himself on a sofa, covered his face, and emitted "an agony of unnatural and unearthly sounds."

On the arrival of Mayor James Berret, who had spoken to Key that morning, and of Chief of Police Goddard, Dan handed over the opera glasses. He then turned to go upstairs, but the two police officers at the door did not know whether to let him, for fear of any vengeance he might take against Teresa. At last they agreed that he could mount the stairs if he promised not to harm his wife. Dan declared he had no such intention.

He found Teresa in Octavia Ridgeley's room, still lying on the floor, her dress disheveled. Laura was being entertained in the kitchen by Bridget Duffy and Octavia. She was affected by the tumult in the house and the extreme misery of her parents. Yet this day was one that would define her unwitting life. Teresa, having stayed all day in Octavia's room, stupefied, in a torpor of grief, rose as Dan arrived at the door. Whether she feared for her life, as the men downstairs had, is unlikely, but this was a confrontation editors and presumably readers of the illustrated papers wished to see reproduced. The scene would, reliably or otherwise, be depicted as a *tableau vivant*, a scene from a play, in the papers, Dan with clenched fists, Teresa looking over her shoulder with her hand to her heart. A New York newspaper report said that Dan uttered merely one sentence: "I've killed him." If there was any accuracy to this, it must have come from friends on the stairs, following him for the purpose of intervening if necessary. Again, given that Teresa herself was beyond the pale, no one bothered passing on any information about her reaction. She had cherished and succored Key as recently as Wednesday afternoon. Was she edified, vindicated, appalled, grief-stricken to hear that her seducer—or was it her truest love?—had been fatally punished?

Either now, or on the evening before, when the confession was signed, Dan had asked for her wedding ring and a few gifts of jewelry associated with the marriage. He would take them in his pockets to prison with him, since she was no longer entitled to them. He would also take the signed confession.[23]

When he went downstairs again, Mayor Berret told him to compose himself, because he had to go to jail for a preliminary examination. Dan agreed but, suggesting he needed a drink first, offered spirits to everyone in the room. Only Butterworth accepted. Dan poured both himself and his associate brandies from the sideboard.

As Dan drank, the police chief and his officers conferred on how to handle the transfer. Key had many friends and relatives in Georgetown and Washington. Mr. Sickles might be shot as he got into the carriage. The police officers pledged themselves to protect him, and decided to keep their hands inside their jackets on the handles of their pistols as they walked in the dwindling afternoon light down the stairs from the front door to the crowded pavement of Lafayette Square. Hedged in by policemen, by the mayor, by Robert Walker, and by the eminent Senator Gwinn, Dan came down to the carriage and recklessly waved to some of the crowd. Mayor Berret told him it was best not to signal to anyone, and helped him into the carriage. Thus, the crowd saw, there were eminent men on a local and national level, Gwinn and Walker, who were willing to protect Dan with their presence. The route to the prison was along

H Street, and a large crowd of shouting men and boys followed the carriage all the way.

The jail to which Dan was taken was usually referred to as the Washington Jail or county jail. Due east of the Lafayette Square and the White House and near City Hall, it was a Gothic Revival building, and its facade was august, but all else about it had been done on the cheap. It was ill-lit, ill-drained. One journalist who would visit it to interview Dan said that it combined "all the disadvantages which have been gradually removed from every other place of confinement in Christendom." It had plentiful vermin, more than white lime and insecticide could deal with. It had no sewerage and thus only the most primitive privies, no bath, no running water, and poor ventilation, and it often contained twelve prisoners in each of its close, narrow cells.

The warden led Dan to a white-limed cell in which the late-afternoon cold and damp of a winter Sabbath had dismally pooled. Though he had it to himself, it was a severe space, with a semicircular ceiling, one of the walls being entirely a set of bars letting in every draft and giving Dan no privacy. According to one of the illustrated papers, Dan asked the warden whether there was a chance of anything better. "This is the best place you members of Congress have afforded us," the warden told him.[24]

Dan was examined by a magistrate in the prison office, the fact of the killing was established, and Dan was committed to his cell. Locked in now with his clean linen and toiletries, he would fall into tears, but they were not tears of remorse. He had no sense of guilt for what he had done to Key. Dan, like the gentlemen who accompanied him to his cell, was a child of armed America, a society in which men habitually carried pistols, swordsticks, and canes and felt an unquestioning right to deploy them at any dishonorable word uttered against them. A few years past, a young congressman from South Carolina named Preston Brooks had walked into the Senate with his gold-topped cane and attacked the abolitionist Senator Charles Sumner, who had spoken about South Carolina's "shameful imbecility from slavery." Brooks told Sumner that his recent speech had been a libel on South Carolina and on Brooks's relatives. He had then beaten Sumner fifty times over the head and shoulders with the cane, seriously injuring him, but he was lionized in the South as a hero and never faced discipline. South Carolinians sent Brooks dozens of new canes, inscribed with such mottoes as "Hit Him Again!" and "Use Knock-Down Arguments."

And early in 1859 there had been the supreme example of the capital's bloody tendency—the public murder at Willard's Hotel by Congressman Philemon P. Herbert of Thomas Keating, the Irish waiter. Herbert had not, however, shot Keating three times, nor attempted to deliver a *coup de grâce*.[25]

Even so, the phantoms that afflicted Dan during the night in his cell at the Washington Jail did not arise from any sense of legal culpability; they arose from the loss of Teresa, and intimate, public, and political humiliation. Even in his hour of death, Key had contributed to the humiliation. Had Key been armed, and been good enough to draw a pistol, all propositions would now be different. But Key had drawn something more treacherous, something that trivialized, condemned, and caricatured Dan's righteous anger: a dainty pair of opera glasses.

Dan was not bereft of friends and sympathetic presences for a large part of that first night. One was the reporter from the *New York Times*, who could see from Dan's haggard countenance that he was laboring under strong mental anguish. But the man from the *Times* also noted that Dan's nerves were steady, that even when he wept there was no whining. Dan himself offered a clinical summary of his motivation: "Satisfied as I was of his guilt, we could not live together on the same planet." He spent the time alternately sobbing and exhibiting a steely composure, and neglected a good meal brought to him from the kitchens of the National Hotel.[26]

During the period it had taken to get Dan to prison, Barton Key's corpse had lain on the Clubhouse floor, awaiting the arrival of the District of Columbia coroner, Thomas Woodward. By the time he turned up, Woodward discovered more than a hundred people crowding the Clubhouse itself and nearly twenty in the room where Barton's corpse lay. He swore in a panel on the spot and began hearing testimony from witnesses of the killing; on being informed that Butterworth was at the Stockton Mansion, he sent for him. The man who had picked up the derringer Dan had thrown into the street now handed it to Woodward. Then Barton's clothing was searched. A handkerchief, two house keys, the case for the opera glasses, fourteen one-dollar bills, and some coins were found.

But several items had already been removed. Before the coroner arrived, while the site was under the cavalier supervision of one constable, a Treasury Department clerk who knew the Key family was permitted to take from the body a small knife, a memorandum book, a purse, and a card case, and from the fob pocket of the trousers a wad of papers, among them one that might have been of great interest to the coroner, the enciphered letter. These papers were pilfered by the clerk with the intention of passing them on to Barton's brother-in-law, Representative George Pendleton. The body had also been visited by a wealthy relative, Benjamin Ogle Tayloe, who lived on the square next door to the Clubhouse. Tayloe removed a ring and a pair of cuff links—no doubt to be given to Barton's children as keepsakes of their father. The coroner thus found Barton's corpse with the cuffs of its shirt aflap.

Sam Butterworth arrived but refused to answer questions without legal representation. He argued that it was adequate for the coroner's purpose to say that Mr. Sickles shot Mr. Key, resulting in death. With Barton's body still present, Coroner Woodward wrote down the finding of his impromptu panel of gentlemen: "That the said Philip Barton Key came to his death from the effect of pistol balls fired at him by the hand of Daniel E. Sickles while standing near the south-east corner of Lafayette Square . . . said wounds causing his death in a few moments."

The news of the murder traveled on the telegraph and galvanized the newspapers of Dan and Teresa's home city, the Empire City, New York. It went like a knife through George and Susan Sickles and the Bagiolis, who did not squabble about blame but arranged to leave for Washington and their children as soon as possible. Though Dan was well known and Teresa somewhat celebrated in New York, Teresa's background was overshadowed to a degree by great figures of European culture. Teams of journalists were put on the job of searching into the childhood of each of the Sickleses for omens, while the duty editors of the dailies gratefully set in print the first dispatches on the murder from their correspondents in Washington, who had expected to spend Sunday evening as languidly as the day merited but instead passed it writing exhaustively of the behavior of Sickles and of the victim, of the Stockton Mansion and the Clubhouse, and the transaction that filled the space between them.[27]

# V

As Dan went to the county jail, his Washington lawyers decided to appeal to Judge Crawford by way of a writ of habeas corpus for Dan to be released on bail. But when they informed Dan of this, he told them to desist. If he was a murderer, he said, he did not deserve bail. If justified in his act, he did not want to descend to little legal tricks. Behind the tears, stern logic still worked in him, but his decision against seeking bail would also ensure that the case went to the grand jury as soon as possible. A man from the *New York Times* who saw Dan that first night wondered in print whether in the end the grand jury would ever indict Sickles. This was a view that other papers lined up to condemn. Certainly, it did not prove a reliable prediction.[1]

As, in that unspacious cell, friends pressed close, as lawyers muttered to one another, across the city in

Lafayette Square Teresa still hid and wept in Octavia's room. In three days her world, her repute as mother, the innocent sportiveness she took even to her encounters with Key, had all collapsed on her and she was in hell. But also under siege. The crowds still milled and stared with fever-ish surmise at the facade of the Stockton Mansion. The press strove for exact definition of Dan's mental and spiritual balance on the evening of the killing, but none sought to ask what proportion of Teresa's feelings was loss and what was shame. She had become, in the words of Bridget Duffy, Disgust Incarnate, a breathing cautionary statue. Isolated in the Stockton Mansion, she may have glimpsed the fuss outside the Club-house, where, amid a crowd in the early dark, Key's body, whose inti-mate contours she knew, was brought out on a litter to an undertaker's cart and taken to his home on C Street, the house he had occupied in the days of his marriage, where he was cleansed of his blood and laid out.[2]

That first night in prison, Dan's cell was filled with chairs so that he could be comforted by the presence of Mayor James Berret, Attorney General Black, an edgy Sam Butterworth, and a local clergyman. They intended to stay with him until they were assured that he could be safely left by himself; that he wished to stand trial. The minister, Mr. Haley, was a Unitarian Presbyterian whose church, near City Hall, was the closest to the jail, and who had early in the evening taken it upon him-self to visit the prisoner. In the spirit of Dan's religious eclecticism, or perhaps indifference, the prisoner took to Haley. At Dan's request, or because he thought it his duty to achieve reconciliation, Haley went the ten blocks between the jail and the Stockton Mansion on the very night of the killing, and was one of the few callers allowed to see Teresa. He kept shuttling back and forth on foot—since he wore out his coachman and horses by midevening—between Dan and Teresa.

Haley saw that Teresa was most upset and distracted by the same is-sue that upset Dan: the shame she had brought upon her daughter, Laura. Until last Thursday, Teresa had considered her dalliance with Key something nearly harmless; an adventure in high feeling, tender-ness, and sensuality. Now she and her daughter were defined by it for-ever. Haley spotted at once that she was trying in her way to achieve either lunacy or death. Only her physical strength and her previously robust soul held her back for the moment from the abyss. She pleaded with the minister to ask Dan to give her wedding ring back as a confirmation of forgiveness, and as a guarantee of her daughter's social protection. From his interviews with her, Haley had no doubt that the return of the ring had taken on a crucial meaning for the balance of her mind.

Back at the prison some time after midnight, Haley begged Sickles to give back the wedding ring he had brought with him in his pocket. Dan asserted, respectfully, that he was "unalterably determined" never to see Teresa again, but that he would send her back the ring. The ring he sent, however, and which Teresa received, had its band broken. Some said he had broken it at the time of Teresa's confession; others, that he broke it in prison before passing it on to the Reverend Haley. At least some hoped for Teresa's sake that it was the former, committed in fury rather than in that state of calm outrage that was one of Dan's competing phases in prison.[3]

All this done, as the warden later told the journalists camped in front of the prison, Dan washed himself with water brought inside and settled to sleep as naturally as if he were settling in a room at Willard's. During the night, however, he discovered that prison was a serious discipline to undertake and was hostile to all gentlemanly routine. In other cells around him, raucous prisoners were crowded together and spent their time playing cards. Since, according to one commentator, "any smart mechanic could cut his way out with a jackknife," armed guards patrolled the corridor between the cells to prevent escapes. To deal with the dankness of the place, tin ventilators had been inserted in some of the windows, and night and day made a "merry rattling, which would almost lead one to the belief that the dungeon is part of an immense train jogging uncomfortably along at the rate of twenty miles an hour." Then, in the small hours, Dan woke to find his body covered with bedbugs, literally black with them. In the morning the jailer, Mr. Jacob King, was apologetic, but even the press would defend the warden, arguing that all the lime in the world and all the vigilance could not prevent the forays of the pests.[4]

Five-year-old Laura's wants were briskly looked after by Bridget, who told the child that her father had gone away on business. Laura was a spirited but vulnerable little girl, and asked again and again, but in the end Bridget's answer made sense to her, since it fitted the established pattern. Teresa had spent such a desolate night that Octavia Ridgeley feared she would die at any second, which might have been a merciful thing, since today she would need to face the indignity of appearing downstairs in the long parlor for identification by such Fifteenth Street witnesses as Mrs. Brown, Mr. and Mrs. Seeley and their daughter Matilda, and Mrs. Baylis, mother of the precocious Crittenden, who were brought to the Stockton Mansion by law officers. As these folk arrived downstairs, Teresa was summoned to descend and show herself to them, one by one. She was the meat in the market, the ogre at the carnival. A little way across the square, souvenir hunters were cutting fragments of wood out of the tree by which Key had fallen, and artists from the illustrated papers set up their easels and began sketching every aspect of the area—the railings, the Stockton Mansion, the Clubhouse.

On that Monday, Dan's reliable friend and Teresa's most favored counselor, Manny Hart, appalled at the morning's news, which all the papers exultantly carried, was on his way from New York's Pennsylvania Station. Mr. George Sickles boarded the same train with his wife and Teresa's parents. George had received a telegram from one of Dan's friends during the night, and broke the awful news to frail Susan Sickles and then to the Bagiolis. To their credit, through their grief, they traveled and worked as a team under George's leadership. They had already telegraphed their intentions to arrive and help with the management of the affairs of the Stockton Mansion, of demented Mrs. Sickles, of Laura, and of imprisoned Dan. By that evening, Teresa's mother would tell the solicitous Mr. Haley that Teresa had for a long time been afflicted with a functional disorder of the heart, which was normally no problem, but which under this degree of distress and excitement "became very alarming in its effects." It was uncertain whether she was speaking of a disorder of the body or of the soul.

As for Dan's day, he still had the distraction of plentiful visits, but some of those who emerged from seeing him to speak to the press said he was in a state of mental prostration, and for long exercise periods paced the corridor in silent grief pressing his head between his hands, sorrowing for his disgraced marriage, his child, his loss of a political future. Chevalier Wikoff stopped in to press Dan's hand and speak earnestly to him. Speaker Orr, Vice President Breckinridge, and many cabinet members visited. So many dignitaries arrived at the jail that everyone outside expected to see the President come through the door soon, and some newspapers reported that Mr. Buchanan had visited Dan. It was not the truth, but the President, while wanting to place a certain distance between himself and the sexual imbroglios of the Sickleses, had still sent Dan a hearty letter of condolence.[5]

Though some of his visitors reassured Dan that a jury would understand his attack on Key, at least one informed friend hurrying down from New York, the most renowned Irish-American lawyer James Topham Brady, thought Dan was in severe peril. He would need an acutely crafted defense to save him from hanging as a result of a judge-directed verdict. Over a stellar legal career, Brady himself had achieved murder acquittals in all his cases except one, but much of the press agreed with him as to the danger Dan was in. One newspaper pointed out that at the time of Key's death, as the prayer from the litany of the Episcopal church—"From battle and murder and sudden death, Good Lord, deliver us!"—still hung in the air of Lafayette Square, Sickles had shot down an unarmed man, and had fired not once but many times at a victim who had implored his adversary not to kill him. Dan had been able to do this because "Key had been detained by a friend in conversation at a convenient spot, until the assassin could have time to arm himself and prepare for putting Key to death."

Who was to say a jury would not reach the same conclusion, particularly if presented with a catalog of Dan's own crimes of carnality? That energetic diarist of American events George Templeton Strong of New York wrote that Dan Sickles, after all his other sins, "has attained the dignity of homicide. . . . Were he not an unmitigated blackguard and profligate, one could pardon any act of violence committed on such

143

provocation. But Sickles is not the man to take the law into his own hands and constitute himself the avenger of sin." Butterworth, with no wrong to avenge and no passion to cloud his sense of right and wrong, had set forth and engaged Key in conversation "till Sickles could get his pistols and come up and use them." This sort of argument could be lethal to Dan's chances.

In some of the press, there was a tendency to be lenient toward young Mrs. Sickles, ruined as she was. "The character of the husband too often corrupts that of the wife, particularly at the impressible period of early youth." And on his way to Washington, James Topham Brady must have read with a particular concern the passage in one hostile New York paper: "The manslayer does not seem to have acted on the promptings of any sudden impulse, but to have perpetrated the deed with entire premeditation." Brady knew that that would be the central question of the trial, and if the jury agreed that "the manslayer does not seem to have acted on the promptings of any sudden impulse," Sickles would be hanged. Brady knew too that for every Old Testament–style husband who defended Dan there were an equal number of modern men who would condemn him for excessive force.[6]

In the Stockton Mansion, once Manny Hart and the senior Sickleses and Bagiolis arrived in the cold early dark, much discussion and planning was under way. Laura thought it a considerable holiday to have four grandparents present, but was confused—as so often recently—by their solemnity. They spent their days and nights guarding Teresa from doing herself damage, and reminding her of her daughter's need of her. At the moment, though, even the sight of Laura caused Teresa acute sorrow. She did not have a self-pitying temperament and thus lacked the normal solace of such people—that their sins were caused by others. She was skewered on self-blame. Manny, the Sickleses, and the Bagiolis all agreed they should get Teresa away from the scene as soon as possible. She was done with Washington, and staying there merely imperiled her health.

When the Bagiolis visited Dan the next morning, Mrs. Bagioli, "a fine-looking woman, rather well advanced in years," came out leaning on the arm of Mr. Charles K. Graham, engineer of the Brooklyn Navy Yard, and sobbing in a most violent manner. The sorrow had been mutual—Dan had seen in his mother-in-law's face the shadow of his long-taken-for-granted and now lost Teresa. An observer mentioned that Mr. Sickles was unable to control his feelings for some time after the party had left the prison. The same day, Manny Hart brought Susan Sickles to visit Dan, and she was so overcome at seeing her son that she fainted. Among her other desperate feelings, his indelible gesture against Key had brought an unaccustomed sense to her, the meekest and most observant of women, of being marked in an exceptional and guilty way. The grim condition of those close to Dan made a strong impact upon journalists waiting in the prison lobby. It was also partly the reason why, by midweek, Dan became depressed and lost any appetite for food.

On the Tuesday after the killing, Jacob King, the warden, had made an attempt to cheer Dan by kindly giving up his capacious office for the prisoner's use. This change afforded Dan privacy, a desk at which to write, and a little bookshelf. He was permitted to exercise more freely in the narrow corridor outside the office. His meals came from the kitchen at home. As for spiritual counsel, it abounded. Apart from Haley, Dan was also visited by the Methodist Reverend F. C. Grandberry and Father Charles J. White of St. Matthew's Roman Catholic Church.

Washington did not have a city morgue, so the autopsy on Key had been held on the Monday morning at Barton's house at C Street. Then, at one o'clock in the afternoon on Tuesday, the members of the bar and officers of the court met at City Hall and marched in a group to Key's house, where the last rites were pronounced over the remains. A "motley crowd, boy and man, rich and poor, black and white, free and slave," poured through the parlor to have a glimpse of the corpse. Numerous friends also pushed in through the crowd for a last look at an admired friend. The coffin in which Barton lay was of mahogany, and the corpse was dressed in black coat and pants, white vest, and white kid gloves. In the hands a bouquet of fragrant flowers had been placed, and Mrs. Pendleton, Key's sister, had seen to it that the inside of the coffin was strewn with japonicas and geranium leaves.

The four children were not at the funeral service; they had been moved to Barton's mother's home in Baltimore. As a younger son, Barton left no property, but his family connections were equipped to look after the children. The Episcopal funeral service having been read over the remains, the coffin was placed in a hearse, which took it to the railroad depot for transport to Baltimore. Among the pallbearers were James M. Carlisle, an eminent Washington lawyer, and Senator Joseph H. Bradley, and they and a number of other friends traveled to Baltimore on the three-o'clock train with the remains. A few hours later Key was buried in the Presbyterian cemetery on Green Street, in the same grave as his wife. At a somber gathering at his parents' Baltimore home, Key's mother, the widow of the great anthem's creator, mourned the violent death of the third of her sons. Friends discussed his eccentricities and the nervous condition caused by his wife's death; spoke of his drinking, which had increased during his affair with Teresa, though he had recently cut back; canvassed the fact that he might have been a leading lawyer but for his easy ways; and decided with justice that he was still a "first-rate fellow," ready for a joke or a frolic, and an excellent storyteller. He had always been lavish with money, spent a good deal on horseflesh, and would often hire a carriage to carry him a single square. He was, in a word, a former young man of fashion who dared to be unconventional, and was able to be something more than a man about town.[7]

As Teresa languished in her room or emerged to mystify her daughter with tears of contrition, Antonio and George, the two fathers, were brokering between them the terms of the inevitable separation. Antonio felt that his daughter, however much he retained a love for her, had dishonored the Bagioli name, and made no bones about that when writing to Dan. "You have heaped on my child affection, kindness, devotion, generosity. You have been a good son, a true friend, and a devoted, kind, loving husband and father." But Teresa was young, and if her normally robust spirits returned, she would live a long time and need a civilized haven. George Sickles was reported to have made a conditional offer that one of the country homes, among which it seemed he had title to the one in Bloomingdale, should be at the disposal of Antonio Bagioli as a haven for his daughter, provided he would live with her and supervise her. Bloomingdale would obviously be Teresa's ultimate harbor, but an essential part of the pact about Teresa's returning to New York under her father's care was that if she fulfilled these terms, she could keep her daughter, Laura.[8] There may have been both compassion and practicality in this. In an age when servants were readily employable, Dan could have—in an acceptable sense of the time—raised the child without too much inconvenience to himself. But it was obvious that Teresa was the better parent for Laura, given that the poor child, blithe and vocal in the company of her two indulgent grannies, was socially blighted to begin with.

A number of poor Teresa's former guests were suddenly ashamed of her. Rumors flew throughout the town. Mrs. Sickles was pregnant, but by whom? Mrs. Sickles had actually visited Dan in prison! George Templeton Strong heard people commenting on the Sickles business everywhere, giving conflicting stories and conflicting views. "By gracious, you may depend upon it," said a prominent New Yorker. "Poor Key's great mistake was mixing himself up with a low set like the Sickleses." The distinguished historian, politician, and diplomat George Bancroft was one of the few who had a sense of Teresa's pain: "Poor child, what a cruel thing to deprive her of her sole stay and support. Key was the only man she could look to for sympathy and protection."[9]

Indeed, though the Sickleses and Bagiolis would have been for a time capable of shielding her from the knowledge, the general details of Teresa's confession were somehow known within a week of the killing, since George Templeton Strong discussed them at dinner in New York on March 5. James Topham Brady—whom one could call a reliable source—would later deny that Dan was involved in releasing either the fact of a confession or news of the existence of the tip-off letter signed R.P.G. Perhaps it was the work of some other friend or counsel of Dan's. Though both documents certainly helped build a case that Key had offered Dan Sickles intolerable provocation, their release would be a calamity for Teresa and Laura, Teresa providing the focus for the prurience of a nation.

The news of the confession caused, as George Templeton Strong gleefully reported, a strong reaction against Sickles himself. People, said Strong, believed that the confession extorted from his wife and put on paper before witnesses "was the dodge of a Tombs' lawyer, and shows the homicide to have been premeditated from the first. That Sickles seduced his mother-in-law and silenced the husband by telling him there was another Mrs. Bagioli in Italy, and also seduced the daughter before their marriage, appears granted." There was a common rumor that since the killing occurred on federal territory, should Dan be found guilty, President Buchanan, "that disgraceful old Chief Magistrate," would intervene to save him, for the relations between the lady and Buchanan had been designed to put "that venerable sinner in Dan's power. . . . There is hardly a kind or degree of baseness that somebody is not quite ready to vouch for." Like many others, Strong overestimated Dan's composure at the time of the confession and of the crime, and the political feasibility of the President's issuing an executive pardon.

It was widely said, too, that the R.P.G. letter had been written by lusty Rose Greenhow, jealous at not having enchanted the widower Key, who was a true Southern gentleman as she was a true Southern lady. Other rumors were that Dan had attempted to commit suicide after shooting Barton; that Barton's younger brother Charles threatened to avenge him by shooting Sickles; that the President had earlier found out about the affair between Teresa and Barton and had set out to dismiss him as district attorney; that at a ball at the Douglas house three weeks before the killing, Key "made love to her in a distant corner of the crowded rooms, while Mr. Sickles was dancing with the widow Mrs. Conrad," though "making love" then meant courting rather than coitus.[10]

By midweek, not all of Dan's friends could gain admission to the prison, and cards were left at the prison gates "to an alarming extent."

One journalist wrote that he doubted he had ever known such friendship exhibited toward a prisoner. Manny Hart had arranged for Dan's dog, Dandy, to be brought to the jail so that Dan could have canine comfort. The hound was ecstatic to see Dan, and would be depicted in the illustrated papers as jumping on its master's knee. For a portfolio-toting artist from *Frank Leslie's Illustrated Newspaper* had visited to make a drawing of the new room in which Mr. Sickles was henceforth to be imprisoned, and engaging Dan, fondling the greyhound, became the fellow's intimate friend for the duration of the sitting.[11]

It took some days before Maria Bagioli saw any improvement in Teresa's condition. But after a week, Teresa began to respond to the reminders of motherly duty toward Laura. When she seemed well enough to make a journey north to New York, Mrs. Bagioli brought Laura in a carriage on a bright late-winter day to say goodbye to her father. Dan had worried that the prison might create terror in the child, but the little girl passed without a qualm from the clear sunlight into the vaulted room with bare whitewashed walls and brick floor. After greeting her father and telling him excitedly that she and her mother were going back to New York, she explored the room and found in one corner a rack containing antiquated muskets, which had been replaced by the new side arms the guards now carried. She could tell, not least from the bars of the window and the whitewashed walls, that this was a strange place, and she asked her father why he did not come home. Dan told her he had a great deal of work to do at the moment and could not leave. She asked a barrage of further questions, her face becoming more troubled, and finally she began to sob. In the end she was taken away by her grandmother, carrying with her a little bunch of flowers Dan had given her. Dan, according to one observer, hid his face in his pillow and wept the most bitter tears he had shed since being in prison.[12]

Dan having waived a formal hearing before a magistrate, his hope of soon being in front of the grand jury was thwarted by the sudden death of Postmaster General Aaron Brown. The grand jury could not sit until March 12, after the funeral. Once Mr. Brown had been buried, the municipal officials summoned a grand jury as quickly as possible rather than let the press frenzy and berserk speculation have an even longer period in which to grow.[13] Among the members of the jury was Barton's relative Benjamin Ogle Tayloe, whose splendid house still stands beside the location of the Clubhouse. Dan's lawyers decided not to challenge his right to be on the panel.

The grand jury began hearing testimony at City Hall on March 14, two jurors to a desk, placed in an oval around a table at which officials and lawyers sat. The illustration in *Frank Leslie's* showed a freed black man, probably Mr. Gray, from whom Barton had rented the Fifteenth Street house, in spectacular plaid pants and holding a top hat, sitting in the witness's chair. Dan was not summoned before this tribunal during its ten days of deliberation; that the killing had occurred and Congressman Sickles's responsibility for it, were not in dispute, the only question being whether the bill made out by Acting District Attorney Robert Ould would be returned as a true bill of murder. The attendance of the two established Washington attorneys who represented Dan before the grand jury, Daniel Ratcliffe and Allen Bowie Magruder, was little but a necessary formality.

Dan was now given his trial date—Monday, April 4—and his legal team was assembled. In addition to Allen Magruder and Daniel Ratcliffe, considered keen lawyers by D.C. standards, Dan had employed the services of a former Alabama congressman, a Jewish Southerner named Philip Phillips, who had stayed on in Washington after his term in Congress to open a law office and who enjoyed great repute at the Washington bar. Magruder's elderly but respected partner, Sam Chilton, promised to help with case law and occasional advocacy. Even more eminent a lawyer was Edwin Stanton, who would achieve wide renown as Secretary of War in the coming conflict but who was already well regarded as a jurist and had just returned to Washington from California, where he had successfully settled land claims resulting from the war against Mexico. Like that of the late Mr. Key, Edwin Stanton's house was on C Street, but unlike Ratcliffe and Magruder, he and his young wife had been intimates of the Sickleses and had attended dinners at the

Stockton Mansion. Stanton was, in an unconventional way, impressive physically, for although he was chubby about the face, his head was titanic, and his eye and his manner piercing. His legal forte had always been civil and constitutional matters, and there were some potential constitutional matters in this trial, since the District of Columbia borrowed much of its statutes and case law on homicide, marriage, and adultery from such states as Virginia and Maryland. Stanton's very face on the team gave Dan's defense a seriousness it might not otherwise have possessed.

When it came to counsel from New York, Dan had had no reason to go beyond his concerned friend James Topham Brady. Unlike many Tammany men, Brady was admired and even loved by society in general, but on top of that, though his legal repertoire was wide, he had been involved successfully in more than fifty murder cases. His parents had emigrated from Ireland, and his father had been a progressive schoolmaster in Lower Manhattan who had then studied law. Brady was born in New York, in 1815, but many sentimentally assumed his eloquence came from his Irish inheritance. As soon as he was admitted to the bar, in 1836, people became aware of his unusual forensic ability. He was a tireless student of the briefs he received and left nothing to chance, but he combined this exacting professional attitude with the greatest urbanity and an almost manic politeness to opposing counsel and witnesses. "His addresses to jury and court," wrote an observer, "flattered the listener by many classical illusions and were extremely seductive." He had a much gentler demeanor than did Stanton, and, as one commentator said, "What Mr. Brady lavishes in the *suaviter* [gentle methods], Mr. Stanton makes up for in the *fortiter* [strong methods]." In 1843, he became at the age of twenty-eight the district attorney for New York City, and two years later was rewarded with the post of corporation counsel. He had been offered the cabinet post of Attorney General in the government of Van Buren, but declined. As a civil lawyer, he had achieved in one case an award that long remained a record: $300,000.[14]

More germane in this case was Brady's record in murder trials, as a result of which he made a special study of pleas of insanity. He had raised the matter of insanity in two famous will cases. And in the murder trial of a man named Cole, he had invoked the defense of "moral insanity," permanent insanity induced by extreme moral outrage. He had not yet attempted to have a client acquitted on a plea of *temporary* insanity, nor had any other lawyer in America. But he saw it as the only way to deal with Dan's case.

Another New York member of Dan's team was his old friend John Graham, of the Tammany Hall Graham family. The Graham brothers combined, in the same New York manner as Sickles, toughness and urbanity, and John Graham had already represented Dan in the libel case against Bennett of the *New York Herald*.

The last of Dan's lawyers was something of a darling of Irish and Democratic America, Thomas Francis Meagher, the former Irish convict who had escaped from Australia. He brought Dan's legal team to eight. Meagher was in his mid-thirties, good-looking, animated, as fashionable a dresser as Dan Sickles—in fact, more of a dandy—and one of the foremost orators of his day. Handsome Tom Meagher was considered the most genial-looking of the lawyers in Dan's defense, but he may also have been the least experienced, since he divided his time between speaking tours around the United States, Tammany politics, Irish activism, contributing to newspapers and editing one of his own, and sharing the company of his steel heiress wife, Libby Townsend, whose family had the proud claim of having forged the enormous chain the Continental Congress had ordered slung across the Hudson to impede armed British vessels during the Revolutionary War. Smiling Meagher was hopeful that the Key murder case would both save his friend Dan and revive his own intermittent law career, for some potential clients suspected that his earlier admission to the bar had been more a reward for his services to the Irish cause than a recognition of legal scholarship.

During meetings in the home of Edwin Stanton, and in the National, where Brady wanted the defense team to dwell, Dan's lawyers devised a defense strategy based on the plea of temporary insanity. Brady had certain problems of personal principle to sort out, as well. Deprived of his parents when still a boy, he had become the head of his family and had never married, yet for a celibate, he had spoken a great deal about women's affairs. In a case involving marital rights, he was interpreted as justifying the husband's absolute bodily control of his wife. A number of newspapers and the women's rights movement had denounced him. So he accepted an invitation to give an address on the issue, along with the famous preacher Henry Ward Beecher, brother of Harriet Beecher Stowe. Like Beecher, Brady attacked much apparent gallantry toward women as "enlightened selfishness" on the part of men. And, like Beecher, he expressed the view of the era that woman was either noble, "in her own sphere . . . a wife, a mother and a companion," or else "the most wretched thing that ever was expressed on earth this side of per-dition." In an age in which syphilis, tuberculosis, and other horrifying diseases commonly struck underfed, underpaid, and underprotected women, it was true that the woman who lost or spurned her marriage did tend to express in her body the physical signs of perdition. So, a pro-gressive male for his era, Brady believed that the true chivalry of man-hood consisted in genuine help to women. This help was most needed by a woman when "the world has pronounced against her a dreadful sentence of outlawry." It was at that stage that a man should step from the "common ranks of his fellows, though this step might subject him to suspicion and censure," and, taking the fallen woman by the hand, raise her "from the degradation to which she has been assigned, and restore her to humble comforts, if not indeed to happiness." It was presumed that his lecture had had no small effect on the state legislature in Albany, which had, at the time of the trial, just passed measures acknowledging women's right of ownership to property even within marriage.

In the prison, when Brady sat with Dan and acquainted him with the defense he intended to run, he may have been tentative, expecting that Dan would consider a plea of momentary insanity vaguely insulting and dishonorable. But either by persuasion or as a result of Dan's belief that he had been reduced to an Othello-like temporary madness by Key's behavior, Dan accepted Brady's strategy. Brady could thus give practical form to his beliefs concerning temporary insanity in the trial of Dan Sickles, his friend and client, but he would need to violate his tender feelings toward so-called fallen women. For though Dan no longer had vengeful feelings toward Teresa, the more of a pariah Brady could make her out to be, the more likely he could prove deranging provocation of his client.[15]

Tasks were allocated around the legal team. Mr. Phillips, the former Southern congressman, was to be in charge of jury selection. Thomas Francis Meagher would be the creator of imagery and oratory, especially for use in the speeches of John Graham and James Topham Brady, who much admired his eloquence. Graham, as friend and counsel, would address the jury to open Dan's defense, but not until the prosecution had completed its initial examination of witnesses. Brady would then lead the examination and cross-examination of witnesses. But Stanton's job would be to argue matters of law with elderly Judge Crawford, who was considered his intellectual inferior, and would summarize the case toward the end of the trial, before Brady made the address-in-chief to the jury. Ratcliffe and Magruder would serve in a junior capacity on matters of both fact and law.[16]

As the opening day of the trial neared, Barton's brother-in-law George Pendleton gave the enciphered letter found on Key's body to another brother-in-law, Charles Howard, who took it home to Baltimore and tried to decode it. Pendleton had already searched the house on Fifteenth Street with the owner, John Gray. According to Pendleton, they found nothing belonging to Barton, but Dan's lawyers would suspect, or pretend to suspect, that some evidence had been removed, just as items had been removed from Key's body.

Barton's family was distressed by the official appointment of Barton's deputy, Robert Ould, to the post left vacant by Key's death. Ould was a younger, florid man of straightforward industry and intellect who had studied in a theological seminary and had something of a clerical air still. He had been a member of the commission that codified the laws of the District of Columbia, but he was a friend of Buchanan's—indeed, he owed his post to him—and therefore might be less assiduous in searching out matters that could embarrass the White House. He also lacked prosecutorial experience. The Key family went to the White House to appeal to President Buchanan, and asked him to appoint a special prosecutor to work with Ould and give him guidance. But Buchanan had his reasons for not complying, one of them being that he considered that Key had been a fool and had courted a bullet.

As foreshadowed by Laura's visit to Dan, ten days after the murder Teresa rose early in the cold dark of March 10 to dress for departure for New York and the new order of her life. She had reachieved an air of dignity, though her confident youthfulness was not as evident as it had been. She knew her task now was to be the limited but crucial one of contrite shelterer of her exuberant five-year-old daughter. Polite people did not rise to see her leave for the train at an hour when the sleepy servants of Lafayette Square had just begun sweeping the front steps of neighboring houses. One artist from an illustrated paper had arrived at his post early and was near the railings of the square, sketching the house. He was rewarded with the visual scoop of Mrs. Sickles's departure from the Stockton Mansion to catch the six-o'clock train north. She was dressed darkly, wore a veil, looked neither to the right nor left. The wider scene as depicted by the artist is a tragic one—Manny Hart beckoning Mrs. Bagioli, Teresa, Bridget Duffy, and the child, Laura, down the curved steps to a carriage. The women are heavily cloaked, and the only apparently happy personage in the scene is a black servant, sweeping the pavement beneath the steps and pausing for a minute to see the white women go on their way in grief. Teresa walked as she ever would from this point on, guardedly in her cone of shame, with always the proximate risk of someone shouting an insult.

To define her condition, a poet contributed a better than average verse to the pages of *Harper's Weekly*. Entitled "Judge Not," it advised women:

> Bridle your virtue,
> Tether the tongue;
> Pity the fair vine
> Blighted so young!
> Why not the tomb?

Sad, shattered life;
Think of her doom—
Widow yet wife![17]

As the carriage set off, Teresa had a chance for last glimpses of the capital, as they turned away from the White House in its misty gardens, past the familiar houses and stores where Teresa was so well known; past Marshal Hoover's, where Laura liked to go; past the famous Gautier's; past the Capitol, where Teresa had sat with the First Lady for the most sacred American secular moment: the inauguration of a President. Every scene between Washington and New York, all she had passed with a glad heart last fall, she now saw again, this gloomy day, through reaches of air from which all promise had been sucked.

In New York by evening, Teresa would live for the time being in her parents' house. Even the humblest residents of a neighborhood not considered to be of the first order looked askance at her. If she went out of the house by day, she faced the sneers of delivery boys, the coolness of grocers and butchers, the turned shoulder of the respectable. She was also a figure of lubricious sexuality to many solitary males whom she would encounter if she dared go walking. She could not therefore consider going riding in the park, the recreation she loved best of all. She was a prisoner of her parents, of a father given to fulsome and baroque moral attitudes, of a mother understandably susceptible to fits of weeping and lamentation. For the Bagiolis and Teresa could all see the future. Ultimately, when she achieved equilibrium, Teresa would move uptown to Bloomingdale, where she would live out the residue of her life, first as a figure of futile and violated beauty, and then as a cracked and spurned village crone. The account of her indelible crimes would be passed from one generation of townspeople to another.

One day later in March, Tom Field of Bloomingdale, having recently returned from visiting Dan in Washington, came to her door with something which for the moment softened the picture. It was an envelope with Dan's writing on it.

Dan's behavior in the weeks leading up to the trial is difficult to make sense of. On the one hand, there was the shameful public fact that, for legal reasons, he or someone near him would choose to leak to the nation's press both the R.P.G. letter and the details of the confession written by his wife. On the other, there was the secret reality that he began writing dangerously forgiving letters to Teresa. His lawyers, if they knew, must have despaired. For the question would be asked, "If the wife can be forgiven, why did Mr. Key need to be shot?" We do not have the text of the letter Dan sent from prison by his friend Tom Field, but it arrived in time for the desperately excluded Teresa to answer, more or less one month after the killing of Key, with considerable gratitude and pithiness.

> *Good morning, dear Dan, Mr. Field has just left. He brought me a kind, good letter from you. Thank you many times for all your kind expressions and God bless you for the mercy and prayers you offer up for me. Do not ask if I never think about the events of the past month. Yesterday, at each hour by the clock I thought "one month ago this day, at this hour, such and such things were going on in our once happy home." That fearful Saturday night! . . . If I could have foreseen the scenes of the following day I would have braved all dangers, all things, to have prevented them. Oh that Manny Hart could have been with us! . . . I have been out of the house but three times since I came home; and you know how much exercise I have been in the habit of taking. . . . One night I walked with Manny Hart; but my body trembled, my legs seemed to give way under me and my heart beat violently.*

Dan had enclosed some verses that she thought were very beautiful. She would always keep them, she said. Perhaps, she wrote, she had spoken hastily of George Wooldridge, whom she had dubbed a scandal-monger and a busybody. She promised not to mention again his name, or Wiley's or Butterworth's, in any of her letters. But she was not yet beaten to dust, and she could answer frankly some charges made by Dan's friends. "One thing I will assure you of, and that is that I did *not* tell Mr. Butterworth to mind his own business or something to that effect. Mr. Butterworth, I think, only needed encouragement from me to flirt. I may be mistaken, but I doubt it. But let all suspicions be forgotten and unthought of—the reality is bad enough without suspecting or supposing things."

Answering what was obviously a question of Dan's, as to whether he'd ever denied her anything, she replied that he had not, that "you gave me many things I did not deserve—everyone knows this." So, as a small gesture of recompense, she would soon begin working on a pair of slippers for him, and she would not stop until they were finished. "Will you wear them for me? Or would you dislike to wear again anything that I have made? God bless you for the two kisses you sent me—and with God's help and my own determination to be good, true, and faithful to you and myself hereafter, those kisses shall never leave my lips while *I* am called wife and you *husband*. I swear it by Laura." She resolved to write to a Washington nursery to have flowers sent to the prison for Dan.[18]

This letter, despite its chastened tone, lacked self-pity. But clearly she had been encouraged to foresee a future as a wife. If her protestations are to be believed, she had utterly repented of Key. But surely he came to her in dreams, and surely his caresses were involuntarily remembered with either revulsion or longing.

As the date of the trial neared, Barton Key's relatives and friends decided to employ John Carlisle, a prominent Washington lawyer and a friend of Key's who had spoken at his memorial service. Carlisle would work with Ould and represent the family's interests at the trial.

It was undeniable that, though Dan could weep like a child, his morale was high, and that he found the resources to behave with dignity and energy in prison. Dan had become his old practical and improving self. He sent the jail gardener to the Patent Office for some seeds, and set him to work in the prison yard making flower beds. Unlike other prisoners, on Sundays he often went walking in the stone yard next to the jail, where during the week masons worked on the marble columns for the Treasury building and the Post Office. He was not accompanied by a guard, and could have walked out to the street and into Pennsylvania Avenue had he chosen. Instead, since there was but one true escape for him, he contemplated the august carved stones and the oncoming spring. He knew he might be executed before the summer was out, and he was aware of the hard facts of that, of the degrading idea of the noose, of how an ill-tied one might cause minutes of anguish for the hanged man, of how a desperate, dangling man whose neck had not been broken in the fall through the trapdoor might soil himself, of how his blood—in a last attempt to avert the deadly effects of strangulation—would rush to his penis and produce an erection, which the surgeons primly called priapism. None of that seemed to weigh on him or influence his mental state. If it did, it was when others were not present.

The journalist from the *Herald* who visited Dan the evening before the trial began found three gentlemen sitting quietly with the prisoner, one of them, of course, his fond father, George. Dan conversed in a pleasantly natural manner on politics and foreign affairs. He was still what he had been, a man who sought to save the Union by appeasing the South. Abolitionists were still, to him, fanatics, and George and others were pleased to pass on to Dan tales of their latest follies. Dan's relations with George were open and manly, and smacked more of fraternity than of the more conventional filial quality. With Dandy sitting on his knee, he looked so easeful "that no one would imagine that he bore a great and abiding grief in his heart." The *Herald* writer might have been fascinated to know that Dan was corresponding warmly with Teresa, to the great and reckless peril of his own neck.

The opening of the trial was attended by representatives of both the American and the foreign press. One journalist reflected on the reason the British were taking so much notice of the case. It was, he concluded, because the elements of the murder—the openness of the killing, the prisoner's immediate surrender, the intolerable provocation, the beauty of Mrs. Sickles—"combined to take it out of the ordinary catalogue of criminal crimes and to render it one of the *causes célèbres* of history."[19]

The venue for the trial was City Hall, where Barton had had his offices; it was barely more than a block from where, a little more than a month before, his body had lain in state. The room in which elderly Judge Thomas Hartley Crawford was to hear the murder case had high, arched windows with louvered blinds and candelabra lacking candles. Because the weather had turned cold again, the furnaces were fired up. From his seat on the bench, the bespectacled Judge Crawford peered down through a fog of uncomfortably humid air at a court to whose atmosphere those gentlemen who were not as fastidious with their washing as Dan Sickles added their malodor. The temperature within the chamber would indeed become so stifling one afternoon that the judge adjourned the trial.[20]

When the doors of the court were opened at nine-thirty that first day, gentlemen of the public, including diplomats and members of the Washington bar not directly involved in the trial, came rushing in, and some were forced to invade the courtroom through a window and stand on tiptoe against the wall to witness events. The only women to attend during the course of the trial would be women witnesses. Because of the numbers of accredited journalists, the court attempted to accommodate them on stools and at a long bench brought in from the lobby, but some complained that they had no surface on which to write, and more seats and desks were needed. Near the defense table, Dan's father sat beside Antonio Bagioli. People considered George youthful-looking despite his gray beard, and he had in his hand the copy of *Harper's Weekly* that contained an illustration of Dan, which he showed to people nearby. Touchingly, he seemed gratified when they said it was a good likeness.[21]

Judge Crawford entered the courtroom at 10:15 a.m., had the case—Docket Number 124—called, and asked both teams of lawyers if they were ready to proceed. When the lawyers said they were, Crawford had the law clerk, Erasmus Middleton, a young man to whom Barton had given a gold pen at New Year's, call out the names of the witnesses for the prosecution.

For the lawyers at Dan's table there was the excitement of being involved in the most notable murder case of the era, even for those—Edwin Stanton, James Topham Brady, Philip Phillips, Sam Chilton, and John Graham—who already had established legal reputations. But the eminent Edwin Stanton did not charm the journalists as Brady and Meagher did. Stanton was hard-bitten; he was sour-faced. But he was estimable. As for the younger lawyers, it was perhaps the most exciting trial they had been involved in, the one exception being Thomas Francis Meagher. For, after all, Meagher had been famously charged in Tipperary with the capital offense of high treason for his involvement in the Irish uprising of 1848, and been condemned to be hanged, drawn, and quartered, a sentence later commuted by act of the British Parliament to transportation to Australia for life.[22]

As the names of prosecution witnesses were read that morning, Dan, scrupulously washed and shaven, and soberly dressed in a dark coat and vest, light pants, a frock coat over the lot, and a top hat, left the district jail to walk the three blocks to City Hall. He was led by Marshal Seldon and accompanied by a police guard and by the warden, Jacob King. King was by now a friend and had every reason to be grateful to Dan. Because of his presence the jail was newly provided with water closets and primitive sewerage.

One Washington child who would live well into the twentieth century remembered Dan being escorted to and from the jail on most of the days of the trial, for Dan's route lay near Washington's public school on Fifth and F Streets. Dan, this child remembered, marched with head erect, glancing neither to the left nor right, and did not play to the "rabble crowding and running in the streets."

He was received at the court and, accompanied by guards and several supporters not yet inside, entered the hubbub and the hot air of the court. He was placed in the dock, a cagelike yard a little over waist high and, in the view of some of his friends and counsel, abhorrent to his dignity. They described it variously as a "cattle crate" or as a "chicken coop with a chair placed inside it." In this demeaning enclosure, its limits jostled by an avid crowd, Dan stood upright and with fixed expression throughout the reading of the curiously worded indictment. It was specifically the second shot that Dan would stand trial for: ". . . and that the said Daniel E. Sickles, with the leaden bullet aforesaid, out of the pistol aforesaid . . . then and there feloniously, willfully and of his malice aforethought, did strike, penetrate and wound him, the said Philip Barton Key, in and upon the left side of him . . . [giving him] one mortal wound of the depth of ten inches and of the breadth of half an inch; of which said mortal wound, he, the said Philip Barton Key, then and there instantly died." In response to the question of how he pleaded, Dan declared, "Not guilty."[23]

Thirty talesmen, or potential jurors, were waiting to be called and examined, chiefly by Mr. Ould and Mr. Phillips. The issues cast up by the questioning of the first talesman, Mr. Joseph B. Bryan, were ones that would cover the whole jury selection. The new district attorney put the question to Bryan: "Have you at any time expressed an opinion in relation to the guilt or innocence of the accused?" The juror said that he had. Phillips, for Dan's defense, suspecting that this juror might have voiced an opinion in Dan's favor, argued that the question was not whether the juror had formed or expressed an opinion based upon rumor or newspaper reports or things said by neighbors and friends who had witnessed the killing. The salient question was whether, if the facts made known through the trial turned out to be different from those the juror had expected, he would be able to render an impartial verdict. But Mr. Bryan, the potential juror, said he could not render such a verdict anyhow. "I form my opinion merely upon rumor . . . my mind is biased in favor of the prisoner." The judge ruled for the prosecution. Mr. Bryan was thanked and discharged. Through all this, Dan maintained his stoic demeanor.

The reality, however, as Dan's lawyers saw, was that only those Christian souls who believed the slaughter of the lover to be inappropriate behavior for a wronged husband would be selected. Mr. Ould threw in the added complication that he insisted upon property qualifications in jurors, as did the State of Maryland, and ruled out jurors who did not meet the requirement of owning property valued at $800. Since this $800 property limit had not been imposed in similar cases, Ould's insistence on it would attract much scorn from Dan's lawyers, especially the scathing Stanton.

A number of talesmen were dismissed for saying they were prejudiced one way or another and did not think they could render a fair and impartial verdict.[24] Early in the afternoon, after only five jurors had been chosen, Clerk Middleton announced that the regular panel of thirty potential jurors was exhausted, and the court ordered the marshal to summon seventy-five citizens to be present the next morning at ten o'clock for selection. But the day's business was not ended. Mr. Stanton rose, with an aggressiveness of manner that thoroughly affronted District Attorney Ould, and stated that he wanted to direct attention to the position of the prisoner's dock. It was situated in such a way that counsel could have no access to him. The place where the prisoner should be, close to his counsel, was occupied by bystanders. Judge Crawford said the dock had always been there, but the officer of the court would, he stated, keep a passage open between the defense table and the dock. Mr. Magruder then presented the second wing of the argument: The gentlemen associated in the defense of Dan were from Virginia, Alabama, Pennsylvania, and New York, and it was a practice in all those states to place the prisoner in such a position that he could readily communicate with his counsel. During the trial of Vice President Aaron Burr for high treason, the accused had been permitted to sit at the table with his legal advisers, and was furnished with pen, ink, and paper.

The judge, who had had a hard day in his unruly, overcrowded, and overheated court, said he had never heard of a man on trial for his life being taken from the dock and allowed to sit on the floor of the courtroom. But, expecting a daily mass of spectators, he wisely ordered that the dock be moved overnight to the rear of the bar, to a place behind Dan's counsel and immediately facing the bench.

When the court adjourned, Dan was marched out of the courthouse, as he would be every day, with a phalanx of friends, consisting today of a chipper and paternally hopeful George C. Sickles, Manny Hart, Antonio Bagioli, Chevalier Wikoff, Sidney Webster (the private secretary of the President), and Thomas Francis Meagher, along with "other gentlemen, distinguished in law and politics, from the city and State of New York."[25] Dan had been reassured when so many potential jurors had expressed a prejudice in his favor and only one had mentioned the gallows.

His friends thought that this helped account for his self-possessed and calm manner.

Judge Crawford took his seat the next morning at ten-thirty, and found that though the crowd had increased, it was better organized and regulated. The first thirty-seven citizens questioned in jury selection that day were excused. Washington being a small city, one man declared he was on the spot a few minutes after the killing, and had expressed his opinion there, at the site of the murder, and it was an opinion strongly in favor of one side.

Edwin Stanton still feared that many potentially favorable jurors were being excused by the court on a questionable point of law. He expressed this belief at a stage of the day when only one new juror, James Kelley, a Washington tinsmith, had been sworn. "There was no intelligent man who did not read newspapers . . . and when those impressions were such as would yield to the superior weight of evidence when introduced to him in the jury box, he was, most assuredly, a qualified juror." But Judge Crawford let Ould continue to apply a narrow test to the selection, and of the seventy-five talesmen summoned to the court that day, only three were selected, and with the five chosen the day before, they were cautioned by the court not to allow anyone to converse with them on the case now pending, and were sent away to an amiable quarantine at the National Hotel. They were generally delighted to be associated with this famous trial, but one, Mr. Arnold, an older man who would be jury foreman, prayed that God would spare him to complete the task.[26]

Even by the third day, when another seventy-five talesmen were available, the less than exciting business of empaneling a jury had not lost its crowd appeal, and again in court there was heat and the press of bodies. An incident that amused the crowd but harrowed Antonio Bagioli occurred when a man named Charles H. Kiltberger declared that, as an indication of his lack of bias, "if the prisoner was guilty, he would say, hang him as high as hell." Though Dan seemed calm, there was what the press always called "a sensation" in the court, and the defense peremptorily challenged Kiltberger. As he left the box, Mr. Bagioli rose and stood in his way. "I heard you just now say something harsh of the prisoner," said the renowned musician and voice teacher, "but let me ask you if you had lost your wife, or had your daughter sacrificed, would you have been able to control your feelings and be governed by your reason?" It was not quite a rational question, but an embarrassed Kiltberger could see that Bagioli was in pain, and he offered apologies for his remark.

That third afternoon, with the jury still not fully selected, Stanton again challenged the $800 property requirement, bamboozling Ould into admitting that he had tried only one other murder case, and in that one the $800 qualification had not been insisted upon. "It was because," admitted Ould, "I was not aware of the existence of the law at that time, and therefore could not put it into practice."

This was a naive and fatal admission to make to such a ferocious jurist as Stanton. He asked Mr. Ould how long he had been practicing law in this district, and Ould replied that it had been since 1844. So Stanton started in: "You have the declaration of the gentleman, who for fifteen years has been engaged in the practice of the criminal law, who has been appointed by the President of the United States as a gentleman in every way qualified to enforce the laws of the United States . . . and yet has declared that until recently he did not know what was the qualification of jurors in this district. . . . Where has this practice been hidden that a man of intelligence didn't know it? Why has it been buried in the oblivion of a hundred years to be dug out for the trial of Daniel E. Sickles?"

Dan, secretly gratified to have Stanton behave in this terrierlike way, showed no emotion in the dock. But he knew that pressing on Stanton was the sense of what he was up against with Ould and the judge. They thought of Washington, for the purposes of this trial, as part of Maryland and thus subject to Maryland law. Ould himself was a states' rights man. He would ultimately become a Rebel officer on that principle, and be given charge of the exchange of Union prisoners for Confederates. And Judge Crawford, like much of the D.C. bench, tended to see the

United States, for which he worked, as a mere pooling of residual jurisdiction not yet claimed by any states. Crawford thus believed that Maryland law prevailed here, and once again upheld Ould.

At the end of the day, twelve jurors had at last been sworn in. Two of them were D.C. farmers, four were grocers, one described himself as a merchant, another as a gents' furnisher. A shoemaker, the tinner Kelley, a coach maker, and a cabinetmaker filled out the roster. Most of them fitted the American ideal of the self-made man, to the extent of a minimum $800. Going back to his cell that night, Dan knew the intimate features of those who would decide whether or not he would hang.[27]

The fourth day of the trial was the subject of public anticipation, since Robert Ould would make his address to the jury, and those wonderfully titillating issues murder and adultery would at last be broached. Dan's assiduous lawyers may have suspected something of their client's contact with Teresa but would have been horrified to know that he had written yet again to his wife, and in such terms as to evoke a response that could have been close to fatal to the defense.

"I cannot tell you, dear, dear Dan," Teresa wrote within a few days of receiving Dan's further correspondence, "how much pleasure your letter written yesterday gave me. I am so glad the flowers were acceptable. You are not wrong in supposing that I am pained by your silence, and equally pained at receiving the letter you sent me." In it, Dan had defended some of his allies, such as Butterworth, Wooldridge, perhaps even Stanton and Meagher, and such value did he put on them that it seemed he wanted her to agree with him that they were all jolly decent fellows. But as dependent on kindness from Dan as she now was, Teresa would not submit and accept that all his friends were seamlessly good men. After all, some had mischievously made known the details of her confession, which he had shown them. It was an index of the weight he put on his friendships with other males that he should have sought to set her such a test. "You know, Dan," she told him, "I never affect to love or dislike a person—and I am, in a certain way, as frank as any breathing creature. You say if I can hate those whom you love and who love you then it is vain for you to appeal to me again on such a subject. Dear Dan, it would be impossible to love those who hate me and have injured me, have called me every foul name, as I believe it would be to have you love me again or even ever wipe out the past." She continued in the same forthright vein. "You say that any object you have loved remains dear to you. Do I now stand upon a footing with the other women I know you have loved? I have long felt like asking you what your love affairs have been—love of the heart, or love of their superior qualities such as you have often informed me I did not possess, or attraction of face and form, or an infatuation? If during the first years we were married my conduct did not keep you true to me, can I suppose for a moment the last year has? Ask your own heart who sinned first, and then tell me, if you will."[28]

Obviously, Dan needed to steel himself to hear Ould's address to the jury, which would attempt to darken him by extolling the right of the eminent Mr. Key to go on living unmolested. Sickles's pernicious act had been committed against Key in the soft gush of Sabbath sunlight. Key, unarmed and defenseless, had used the feeble means that were in his power to save his life. Whereas the prisoner at the bar came fully armed "to this carnival of blood. . . . He was a walking magazine." Ould argued that Dan had selected his weaponry with care, and had provided himself with "the temporary armory" of a "convenient overcoat on an inconveniently warm day." Against this moving battery, said Ould, the victim "interposed nothing, and had nothing to interpose," except his physical strength, his presence of mind, "a poor and feeble opera glass . . . and last of all, the piteous exclamations which, however they might have moved other men, in this case, let me state, fell upon ears of stone."

As chief prosecutor, Ould declared himself ready to prove that not only was the deceased unarmed, but Dan knew him to be so. He knew it when the first shot was fired, and certainly must have known it when he stood over his victim, "revolver in hand, seeking to scatter the brains of one who had already been mortally wounded in three vital parts, and whose eyes were being covered with the film of death." This was not a murder committed on momentary impulse. So deliberate had Dan been that when he was stopped by bystanders, he had been trying "to add mutilation to murder." Murder was the killing of a human being with malice aforethought, manslaughter the killing of a human being without malice aforethought. Obviously, Dan Sickles had malice aforethought. These matters were established in common law, said Ould. No degree of innovation had ever suggested that revenge should be either a justification or a palliation of the crime of murder.

The crowd in court looked to Dan to see how he was standing up to these evocative accusations, but he showed no tremor. He, his lawyers, and faithful George Sickles were no doubt pleased that Ould did not foreshadow evidence that would show the double standards by which Dan lived, and that could have been used to diminish the idea of extreme provocation by Key. Why he did not do so may have been a reflection of nineteenth-century popular moral nicety about matters of male adultery, or may have been the result of pressure, implied or explicit, from powerful Democrats, perhaps even from Mr. Buchanan. Ould simply asked the jurors "to proclaim to the four quarters of the now listening world that there is virtue left yet in a jury, no matter how high the position or lofty the pretensions of the offender."

Thus, as the new DA sat down, there must have been some relief at the defense table. James Topham Brady deferred the defense's opening, and the first prosecution witness was called. James H. Reed, a wood and coal merchant, told a hushed court that, when strolling on Pennsylvania Avenue, he had seen by Lafayette Square the confrontation between Dan and Key, had seen Key running around Reed in his attempt to get away from Sickles and then slowly throwing something through the air. Most damagingly, Mr. Reed said that "no shot was fired when the parties were not facing each other. Their faces were toward each other on the occasion of each shot. . . ." The prosecution was pleased to hear this said, since it meant that at each stage of the killing, Key's stricken and pleading face was visible to Dan. Reed also helped damn Sickles by saying that the shortest distance between him and Mr. Key during the last shot and the final misfire was only about two or two and a half feet. "Key fell on his side and elbow with his face toward Sickles." The district attorney had Mr. Reed repeat and confirm that distance—the lethal two or three feet. Dan's counsel and his father kept a sharp eye on him now, wondering if Reed's memories of the fatal Sunday would unsettle him. But still he gave no sign of being affected. It was obvious that he was not ashamed of the scene in the square.

The second and third witnesses, Mr. Van Wyck, clerk in the Treasury Department, and Mr. Delafield, would confirm Reed's picture of events as reliable in all its fundamentals. Martin, Isaac, Tidball, Usher, the young employees of the federal government who had carried Key's body back into the Clubhouse, also confirmed the prosecution view of events, so Brady turned to another matter: the idea Ould had released in the courtroom that the only reason Dan had worn an overcoat that Sunday was to store his weapons in it. Usher, questioned by Brady, confessed that he too had worn an overcoat that day. Two others of the four admitted donning overcoats that Sunday. "I presume I did," said one. "However, for not being in good health, I usually do." A witness who had claimed that Sickles wore rather a long overcoat confessed on cross-examination that he too had worn one from the National Hotel that day.[29]

Dan had come through a crucial section of the prosecution evidence without embarrassing his defense by any display of emotion. It was the journalists who were in a frenzy, and they fell into yet another fever on the fifth day of the trial, when the coroner, Thomas Woodward, came to the witness stand. First, he produced a derringer pistol, "stocked to the muzzle, plated, and about seven inches long, with a wide rifle bore. Ramrod absent." He had been given it by a witness, he said, who had picked it up from the street when Dan apparently cast it away. The coroner had also supposedly brought to court the clothes of the victim. Before an engrossed public and jury he lifted from the floor of the witness box a large kerchief and untied it. He took from it first two keys and the case for a pair of opera glasses, and then unfolded a bundle of clothing and held up a white bloodstained shirt, which he displayed to the court, and then a pair of gray-striped pantaloons. He pointed to the blood-encrusted hole in the pantaloons where the ball had entered the right thigh. "The place is stiffened and stained with blood," the coroner explained. There was, yet again, "a deep sensation" in court. To some, these blood-soiled clothes represented the relics of a victim. To Dan, they were the rags of a contemptible fellow. From the top to the bottom of his soul, he believed it; he did not have to argue with himself on that issue.

Where were the vest and coat? the coroner was asked. Oh, he casually confessed, he did not have them with him. So he was instructed by the judge to leave the stand to find and produce them. A little later he came back, apologetic. They were somewhere around the building, but he wasn't sure where. The district attorney announced he could get by without the vest or coat, but Edwin Stanton objected, and a search of the building at last turned them up. The coroner pointed out the hole made by the lethal ball on the left side of the vest. The garment was handed around among the jury members, as was the brown tweed coat with its bullet hole.

When Brady interrogated the coroner on the number of pockets in the pantaloons, and their contents, Mr. Woodward did not seem informed at all on these matters. He said he believed there was a small wallet on Mr. Key's person, which he had already delivered up, but the situation at the Clubhouse had been hopeless, with more than a hundred men on the premises. "Knew most of them," he said philosophically. "Some were strangers." But no one in particular had had charge of the body.[30]

The army surgeon who had come running from H Street to the sound of shots that Sunday afternoon, Dr. Coolidge, testified that the clothes were removed from Key by Dr. Stone and him, and that the next day both doctors had performed a more thorough postmortem. When the body was opened, said Coolidge, there proved to be a great quantity of blood in the cavity of the belly. The bullet had entered the left side, under the edge of the spleen, and cut the portion that lay near the backbone. "It did not injure the great blood vessel to the body, but the two of the left kidney." After traversing the whole thickness of the lobe of the liver, it entered the right cavity of the chest, broke the eighth rib, and lodged under the skin. The left side of the chest contained a large quantity of blood—a quart, at least.

Dan sat solemnly through this surgical depiction of the damage he had done Key. What of the man's treacherous heart? Barton had always been concerned about the health of this particular organ. Yet it appeared that his anxiety had been baseless. "There was a somewhat unusual amount of fatty deposit on the left side of it," said the surgeon, "but the structure of the heart itself was healthy." As for the first wound in the thigh, which might have been more easily argued to arise from ungovernable impulses on Dan's part, it had not been fatal. "The vessel wounded was an external vein—flesh wound." As a scientific gentleman, Ould asked, what would the surgeon say had been the position of Key at the time of the fatal shot? Though Dr. Coolidge argued that the course of a pistol ball was very tortuous and difficult to trace, his opinion was that Mr. Key must have been lying on his right side, the body turned a little to the right, and the shoulders somewhat higher than the hips. That is, his face had been toward Mr. Sickles.[31]

From the objects on the prosecution table, Ould was able to pick up the ball taken from Barton Key's body and ask whether it was the lethal bullet fired by Dan. Yes, said Dr. Coolidge; he recognized the mark made on it by Dr. Stone. It was the one he had extracted from the right side, the only ball found in the body. District Attorney Ould tried to fit it to the derringer pistol that was being presented in court, and it did not fit, nor did it conclusively fit the revolver Dan had carried away from the scene and surrendered to the U.S. Attorney General. So Dan must have had a third pistol, the prosecution implied, and could fairly be considered a walking arsenal.

And that, for the moment, was the prosecution case. District Attorney Ould announced that the United States had closed its testimony. Even the defense lawyers were a little surprised. Ratcliffe rose for Dan Sickles and asked His Honor to require the DA to call certain witnesses not yet placed on the stand—among them Samuel F. Butterworth, Governor Robert J. Walker, and George C. Wooldridge, the clerk of the

Congress. Dan Sickles, said Ratcliffe, had been committed to prison on the testimony of Mr. Butterworth, and if his testimony had been good enough to imprison Dan, it was good enough to be presented in court now.

At this, Robert Ould became furious. He had good reasons, he said, not to summon Butterworth before the grand jury; and these reasons he intended to keep within his own breast now and hereafter. "I imagine, however, that these reasons were very well known to the gentlemen for the defense." Some surmised from this mysterious statement that the President may have intervened to keep Butterworth away from the court. Judge Crawford, writhing and sweating in his judicial wool on the bench, declared that it was a fair presumption that the affidavit Butterworth made at the jail was an act friendly to the prisoner, and that it was done to prevent a thorough examination at that time. Thus, the judge ruled there was no need to call Sam Butterworth to the stand. As for Walker and Wooldridge, they were not present in the court at the moment, and that itself was sufficient reason to reject the motion.

It was late at night before the matter was decided, and through a March cold snap that laid ice on the branches of the capital's trees, Dan and his friends walked back to the jail. Laymen at Dan's side, like Chevalier Wikoff, assured him that if this was all the defense had, he was safe. But Dan must have noticed that his legal team offered no such guarantees.[32]

George Sickles was staying at the National with Brady and other counsel. He was tired from the daily emotional attrition of the case, but he shared with Dan the tough cast of the Sickles heart, and he was surprised and delighted that night by a deputation of ladies who arrived to ask whether, to give comfort to the prisoner, they should present themselves with as many others as they could muster at the courthouse. The one at the head of the deputation was a venerable woman of some sixty years who said she and her sisters demanded Dan's discharge "on behalf of our sex. Let him be convicted, and the libertine obtains new license." George Sickles acknowledged the honorable and generous motives of these ladies, and promised to pass their sympathy to his son, but he thought the courthouse too harsh and earthy an environment for them, and that they served the cause best by staying by their hearths and praying for Dan.[33]

Though all knew that in a significant trial this would be a significant day, for whatever reason Dan next morning was late in being brought to court. John Graham was ready to address the jury on behalf of the defense. But it was nearly half past ten before Dan was in his dock and John Graham was able to embark on a spate of oratory that would massively outshine Robert Ould's more cumbersome opening. For one thing, Graham's opening would run the rest of the day and into the next morning.

He began with a Latin adage *Amicos res optimae pariunt adversae probant*—"Good situations generate plenty of friends whom bad times test." "I have been his companion in sunshine," said Graham, "and am now called here to participate in the gloom of his present affliction." It was only a few weeks since the body of a human being was found in the throes of death in one of the streets of the capital; the body of what Graham called "a confirmed and habitual adulterer." All on a day too sacred for Key to profane it by worldly toil; on a day when he should have risen above the grossness of his nature; on a day when he should have "sent his aspirations heavenward." Instead, Key used that day to besiege "that castle where for their security and repose the law had placed the wife and children of his neighbor." What was Dan to do on such a day and under such siege? "The injured father and husband rushes on him in the moment of his guilt, and under the influence of a frenzy executes on him a judgment which was as just as it was summary."

Dan appreciated these arguments all the more because they came not only from an advocate but from a longtime friend, one to whose value as a comrade he had even sought to compel Teresa to assent. Graham told the jurors they were in court "to fix the price of the marriage bed; you are here to say in what estimation that sacred couch is held by an honest and intelligent American jury." In this federal city, consecrated to liberty but not the libertine, it could be construed that the death of Key was to the jurors' personal gain, for they had no guarantee that their wives and daughters had not been "marked by the same eyes that destroyed the marriage relations of the defendant." Shakespeare's Othello, said John Graham, gave a good lesson for the misery of the defendant. Told by a friend of the supposed adultery of Desdemona, Othello cried,

> Had it pleased heaven
> To try me with affliction; had he rais'd
> All kinds of sores, and shames, on my bare head;
> Steep'd me in poverty to the very lips . . .
> I should have found in some part of my soul
> A drop of patience . . .
> But there where I have garner'd up my heart;
> Where either I must live or bear no life . . .
> Ay, there, look grim as hell.

Mr. Ould had used "extraordinary expressions," such as "the prisoner coming to the carnival of blood"; "adding mutilation to murder"; "as though he had a dagger in his hand, ready to plunge it in his bosom." But the learned counsel had not described the weapons in possession of the adulterer. What about the opera glasses and the white handkerchief, just as certain of causing death to the adulterer and moral death to a household as the weapons of the defendant?

In all this, the central issue to which Graham kept returning was the one of temporary insanity, the idea that Dan could not have been in a state of malice aforethought before the killing in the square. "We mean to say not that Mr. Sickles labored under insanity in consequence of an established mental permanent disease, but that the condition of his mind at the time of the commission of the act in question as such would leave him legally unaccountable, as much so as if the state of his mind had been produced by a mental disease."

At least one newspaper later criticized Graham for arguing that on one hand Dan was too frenzied to behave calmly and with reason, and yet in the same breath claiming that the killing of the adulterer was right and just and admirable. "If it be a crime for a husband to defend his humble family altar," Graham had said, "and death is visited on him for defending it, then the highest honor which can be conferred on any man is to compel him to die such a death."

But back to provocation! Mr. Key was not some seducer unknown to the husband. He was a man who had been regularly permitted to enter the house of Mr. Sickles as a close friend. When Mr. Sickles sighted Key in the square that Sunday, all Dan's just rage was inflamed. In these circumstances, Graham boldly argued, the prosecution needed to prove Dan's sanity at the time of the act. And they could not do that, because there was enough in the case "to melt the heart that is not cut from the unwedgeable gnarled oak." Admittedly, the common law of Maryland, derived from Britain, did not consider adultery an offense. But the reason society had not legislated against adultery was that it considered it every man's right to defend himself against the adulterer! In law, said Graham, the personal body of the wife was the property of the husband, and the wife could not give away her own purity. If she did, the husband "has the same right against the adulterer as if he ravished her." Graham quoted authorities who had established the principle "that in defending his wife, the husband defends himself."

So the cardinal inquiry was whether the deceased was in the grace of God and of the United States when he was killed; and whether Mr. Sickles was moved and seduced by the Devil when he killed him. That, after all, was the language in the indictment. What an atrocious verdict that would be: "to declare on the oaths of a jury that when Philip Barton Key met his death he was in the peace of his God and this community . . . and that Daniel E. Sickles, the injured and outraged husband, when he slew him under this provocation . . . was tempted and set on by the Devil."

Graham by now had been speaking for hours, but the spectators remained engrossed. Nineteenth-century orators and their audiences possessed heroic attention spans, and oratory was public sport. Instead of groaning each time Graham's prodigious speech entered a new phase, the crowd leaned forward more eagerly. Veering between legal scholarship and moralism, Graham confessed that he had called on Mr. Haley, the Presbyterian clergyman who had visited Dan on the first night of his imprisonment, to find instances of retribution for adultery in Scripture. Mr. Haley had obliged not only with Old Testament tales of pestilence and death arising from adultery, but with the injunctions of Christ himself. Did then the jury suppose that society really meant that adultery should go unpunished? "No; it throws you on the law of your heart—there is the repository of your instincts; go by them and you affect the will of heaven, and when you execute them you execute the judgment of Heaven."

A year earlier, a case had been tried in this very court against a man named Jarboe, indicted for the murder of his sister's seducer. The judge, Judge Crawford himself, had told the jury that the status of the prisoner's mind was a matter entirely for them, and in that case the jury had acquitted the brother after fifteen minutes of deliberation. Because, said Graham, "to stab an adulterer was not to draw a weapon within the meaning of the statute of James I, even though the adulterer had no weapon, because the statute was never meant for the protection of the adulterer." In the prosecution's mind, the killing of an adulterer seemed reducible to manslaughter only if the husband discovered "the actual coition. . . . But if the husband has never the right to stay the adulterer until he catches him in coition with his wife, he will never have the right at all."

As in the Jarboe case, the issue was the degree of provocation. At the second when Mr. Sickles sighted Key that Sunday, Mr. Sickles already knew about the house on Fifteenth Street, and he knew that Key used the Clubhouse for refuge. And Key should have known he knew. Dan had not invited him to the square that fatal afternoon. Key had arrived of his own cold deliberation. Lord Erskine, the renowned British jurist, had divided insanity into intellectual and moral, and on the fatal Sunday Sickles was acting under the influence of moral mania, said Graham.

Deane's *Medical Jurisprudence*, to which Graham referred the learned judge, explained the condition.[34]

Judge Crawford would need to consult that tome overnight, since, sadly, the day was consumed, with Graham still not finished delivering his blazing defense speech. Throughout, the elegantly but neutrally dressed Dan had remained in the dock near Graham, looking exactly like a man who did in fact need the most extreme provocations to act beyond reason. He was exhilarated to know that his friend Graham, though a sinner himself who maintained a colored mistress in New York, had overpowered the defense, at least for the moment. And now there was a rest in prospect, because the Sabbath would intervene before Graham again took up the thread of his potent argument.

Visits to Dan by Haley and other clergymen occupied a large portion of that Sunday, and he met his counsel, spiritual and legal, at a cramped table, fourteen by twenty inches. He took it well when nonexperts, clergymen, the Chevalier Wikoff, his father, tried too hard to assure him he would be found not guilty. For though his Tammany brother was arguing brilliantly, there was no certainty that he could make palatable to judge and jury the fact that this defense plea had never been used before. Old Crawford might find it too dangerous a defense to condone and release into the judicial system, and might therefore direct a guilty verdict.

By this Sunday, Dan's letters had given Teresa purpose, and she was enough recovered to be in the process of moving up to Bloomingdale and resuming her role as head of that house. At the Bagioli house at East Fifteenth Street, in the sometimes raw, sometimes charming April weather, Mrs. Bagioli minded the forthright child Laura, who pleaded with her grandmother to be taken for a walk along Fifth Avenue and uptown toward the fringes of the work-in-progress park her father had told her about. Possessing her father's relentlessness, Laura could not be put off by excuses. Mrs. Bagioli had to sally forth with her, and on the street Laura became aware, on a different level from that of an adult, of the whispers behind hands, of the women with expressionless faces who snubbed her grandmother.

That Sabbath, John Graham enjoyed dinner with other members of the legal team at the National Hotel. Visitors came by continually to congratulate Graham on his magnificent address to the jury. His spellbinding day-long speech would be reprinted the next day in all the major newspapers of the nation.[35]

On Monday morning, a little after ten, when he rose again in court, having exchanged compliments with his client, Graham promised that he was close to concluding. He said that if no other reason admonished him to finish, his own exhaustion would serve. Yet the truth was that he took hours more to come to an end. In Britain, he told the jury, in one of the founding common law cases in the area of moral insanity, a man named Fisher killed the sodomizer of his son, and since the father deliberately committed the killing, the judge charged the jurors that they must convict him of murder. But the jury convicted him only of manslaughter. Fisher had spent all night pursuing the offender before killing him, an indication that in such a crime, a night was insufficient cooling period—indeed, a lifetime was.

Graham was not done yet with heaping blame on Key either. Key, as prosecuting officer of the District of Columbia, had been selected to conserve the cause of public morality and decency. In this court he had hunted down "the mere worms that crawl upon the face of the earth," while he himself, "a full-grown man of crime," walked through the community unpunished. Dan Sickles had interceded to have Mr. Key appointed to the very position that Key's private life disgraced. Mr. Sickles had even sent Key private clients, and at one time, when Mr. Sickles had occasion himself to employ professional services, "he secured those of this Mr. Key."

The adultery Key had committed involved a woman young enough to be his daughter. Now for the first time, Teresa was subjected to extensive comment by an officer of the court, and although it was comment normal for its time, it had a demeaning ring. "Reasoning from her years, and from our knowledge of the mental structure of woman, it is not too much to suppose that all the frivolity that surrounds a woman at that age environed her . . . that she was susceptible to the attentions of men, and looked upon them as so many offerings passed upon the shrine of her beauty. At her period of life, the marriage vow had not impressed itself with all its gravity upon her mind." By contrast with Teresa and Key, Dan was the accredited member "of the councils of the nation," and "in bringing within the precincts of the city of the national capital his wife and his child, he threw them and himself upon you and the laws of this district for protection."

In Graham's scenario, even Key's illness was a pretense. After all, "he had the strength enough to carry out his designs in reference to the wife of his neighbor." Why was Mr. Key constantly in the vicinity of the Sickleses' home when he lived so far away? Why was he in the habit of riding by on horseback, "practicing all those blandishments which adulterers cultivate for the purpose of reaching the target which they have set before them"? He took advantage of Sickles's house, yes, but not only of Sickles's. If he encountered Mrs. Sickles in the President's mansion, he made an assignation with her there. Similarly, if he met her in the mansion of some senator, "she could scarcely go more than a few hundred feet from her house before he was by her side." What had the servants said? "Here comes Disgrace to see Disgust."

Close to an end at last, Graham warned the jurors of the prosecutor's hint that Sickles might be condemned by the jury but be pardoned by "executive clemency" of the President. It was their task, and no one else's, to decide whether Sickles was "an involuntary instrument in the hands of some controlling and directing power for putting an effective termination to the adulterous career of Mr. Key."

As for those who said that Sickles should have sought monetary compensation to soothe the bleeding wounds he had suffered as a husband, this was a pernicious view. "It opens every house in your city as a brothel. It tells every man that if he will pay the price which the jury may set upon his adultery or his seduction, he can . . . rifle the purest bed . . . of its purest contents. . . . In God's name, repudiate that principle from your bosom!" Graham reminded the jury, last of all, "You are

179

here at the feet of our Federal government; you are overshadowed by the halo of the name of Washington; let the recollection of that name inspire you with fitting and becoming thoughts."

Graham resumed his seat amid cheers and resonating applause, and turned to nod to Dan, who nodded back. He was heartily complimented by other lawyers and supporters of Dan; he was told he had had a triumph. But being hardheaded, he knew that the trial would resume immediately, and on a more banal and technical course.

And almost at once there arose a dreary but significant argument about the admissibility of the letters Key had written to Sickles, Wooldridge, and others, about the accusation by the clerk Beekman of improper behavior between Teresa and Key at the Bladensburg inn. Brady wanted them accepted by the judge as proof of how cordial and trusting was Dan's attitude to Key. But only some of the letters were finally admitted by Judge Crawford.[36]

That settled, Representative John B. Haskin, an early witness for the defense, confirmed that, at a whist party at Marshal Hoover's, Dan had promised to intercede with the President in the matter of Key's appointment as district attorney. The last occasion on which Haskin had seen Sickles and Key together was the night when Piccolomini (who so resembled Teresa) had performed at the capital's opera. Key, Teresa, Miss Badger of Pennsylvania, and Manny Hart had all been at the opera that evening, and—delayed in Congress—Mr. Sickles had come in late.[37]

Dan began to feel a recurrence of profound and panicked anguish at these recitals of Key's betrayal. His father and his lawyers could see, beneath his stillness, that the caldron of feeling had begun to overflow. They watched him closely as Governor Walker, one of the men who had come to comfort Dan after the event of blood in the square, approached the witness stand. Walker spoke of Dan's writhing and convulsions after the killing, and of violent spasms and exclamations during which "he seemed particularly to dwell on the disgrace brought upon his child." As Walker gave his testimony, Dan—feeling the weight of his lost career, his shamed marriage and ruined child—was not capable of preventing sobs from gushing up within him. Many of the predominantly male spectators were themselves moved to tears as well. Stanton asked the judge that the examination be discontinued to allow Dan to retire. As a recess was granted, Dan's dearest sources of comfort, Manny Hart and George Sickles, were permitted to help him from the courtroom to a holding room.

Some minutes later Dan was brought back into court, and a court reporter noted that his countenance still indicated extreme mental suffering, and "the desolateness of his whole appearance" evoked sympathy in a number of the males in court.[38]

The members of the court looked sideways at Dan, hoping that he would not reach such depths now. But his emotional breakdown was not the only point of interest in the argument and testimony that Tuesday. For now appeared the first female witness, the Irish maid, Bridget Duffy. James Topham Brady knew how to interview an Irish domestic. He would have read well her suppressed moral outrage and resentment of the lady she served, and would play upon it subtly to influence the jury. He passed a paper to the witness: the confession of Mrs. Sickles. One of the signatures was certainly her "hand write," said Bridget. She had signed the document at the request of Mrs. Sickles, not of Dan's, she insisted. So Mrs. Sickles's confession was handed by James Topham Brady, New York's universal gentleman, to the prosecution, with the proposition that it be admitted into evidence. This was a task that many of Brady's friends must have known he could not, as a man of sensibility and broad compassion, have enjoyed. Through whatever means, news of this document had already reached the press and public, but not its precise text, and now Brady was trying to enter into the least erasable of records an account, from Teresa's own pen, of her shame. He believed his profession demanded this sacrifice: that he should seek to reconfirm her moral death sentence.

There was an immediate objection from the district attorney to the document's being placed in evidence. It was hearsay; it was a communication between husband and wife, who were excluded from being witnesses for or against each other. If the husband was thrown into a state of insanity by this letter of confession, the document itself was not needed. Its impact could be proved by the movements and conduct of the prisoner. While this argument went on, an unnamed member of Dan's counsel had an Associated Press journalist positioned near the defense table. If the judge ruled against admissibility, the journalist would copy out the confession on telegraphic slips and have it transmitted to New York. Even a newspaper that had enmity for Dan said later it was true that he would not have chosen to have his wife's confession published. So one wonders whether Dan was unaware that his lawyers had decided to publish the letter if the judge did not admit it, or chose to be unaware. It was said reasonably enough afterward that Mr. Sickles and his counsel were not remarkably alert in arresting the publication of the document, and yet there was his life at stake to justify it.[39]

Brady argued that only the jury could decide how the confession would act on the prisoner's mind, and they couldn't decide that without having it read to them. Brady warned Judge Crawford that the confession was important because it showed that the time that elapsed between the Saturday night, when Teresa wrote it, and the Sunday afternoon, when Dan shot Key, was irrelevant. Although written in the Stockton Mansion the night before the killing, the document "loaded every breath that came from the defendant from the time he first saw or heard of it, down to the moment when the act was committed. . . . Time in no way took from the freshness of the provocation." If the confession of the night before the killing came too early in the sequence of events to form the basis of any actions, what hour on that Sunday morning would His Honor consider germane to the case? "Will Your Honor, as a matter of law, say that we shall take the hour of ten o'clock on that Sunday morning, that we shall question up to that time, and shall not go beyond it? Why shall we not go to the hour which stood before that . . . and so on until we travel back through the vigil of the night, and come to the very moment when the contents of the document were poured into the ears of that afflicted and distressed husband?"

While Bridget waited, with the disgust of a commonsensical young woman, to resume her testimony, listening to the supposedly learned gentlemen vapor on, the argument of the admissibility of the confession stretched into the next day. She was summoned back for the next morning's sitting, and the judge's ruling was at last made. The confession was indeed testimony from a wife, and since such testimony was excluded, so must be the confession. The document was passed to the AP man instantly, and he began to scribble it out on his forms, transferring Teresa's demented admissions to the most public of mediums. Along the telegraph wires from Washington to New York the confession rushed in a series of electric impulses, presenting respectable editors with a moral dilemma. They had never published as explicit a sexual confession as this. Those editors who did decide to place the text in the next day's papers would cover themselves with palavering editorials about their duty to public morals, and how they had been forced with regret to suppress their delicacy of soul and give the document prominence for the sake of the public interest.[40]

Bridget Duffy was at last recalled. She stood before men who were accustomed to see her type of woman caricatured on the stage and in cartoons in the illustrated papers. They expected Bridget to live up to the stereotype, to be lively, peppery, and unwittingly amusing. Her testimony, the little they had heard so far, had been most engaging, and she now described, even demonstrated with a slow rotary movement, how Mr. Key waved from the direction of the Clubhouse to his beloved at the Stockton Mansion. On that Sunday, when Dandy the greyhound ran to Key and fawned upon him, Key had waved his handkerchief from very close to the house. Mr. Carlisle wanted to know whether Bridget was positive of that. To which Bridget spiritedly answered, "Sure, and you don't think I would lie?" There was universal laughter, and an indulgent smile from Mr. Carlisle. He said, "Don't fire up so, Bridget—there is no occasion for it." Brady helped soothe her.

It was not the last clash Carlisle had with the witness, and reporters were delighted to recount his continued exchanges with Bridget. The waving of the handkerchief was a continuous whirl, said the witness, and again demonstrated. Mr. Carlisle asked, "About as fast as you would turn the handle of a coffee mill?" To which the witness answered with rustic passion, "I am not in the habit of turning coffee mills." The court disbanded, chuckling at the prime lines she had given them.

Teresa left no exact record of how in Bloomingdale she passed the next day, the day of publication of her confession. Since the press appeared to consider that the text of the confession spoke adequately for Mrs. Sickles, reporters did not come tumbling up Broadway from town to ask her to elaborate or to inquire how she felt. On such a day, of course, she would have been pleased that she no longer lived in the city, and no doubt her own robust soul and the friends she still had—her parents, Tom Field, a few others—helped her through hours that might have killed other women.

When Dan got to court that morning, he knew that the question of Teresa's confession was still the chief, though unofficial, issue of the morning. Among the lawyers, as among those who were merely spectators, it was rumored that had the confession been received as evidence, evidence would have been offered by the prosecutor that Mr. Sickles had spent nights with a lady not his wife in Barnum's Hotel in Baltimore. The register of the hotel was already in court, under the prosecution's care. It showed Dan's signature on a particular line, and then, ten lines down, in an unidentified handwriting, the name Mrs. Daniel E. Sickles. The author of the *De Witt's Special Report*, a transcript of the trial, remarked that had Judge Crawford admitted Mrs. Sickles's confession, a vast quantity of scandal on both sides would have been brought into the trial, involving people not yet mentioned in the affair. Since these included the President, some on the defense side considered it a good thing that the document had been ruled out of court. Through the press, after all, it had more safely done its best work in the tribunal of public opinion.

Mr. Stanton, however, returned to the matter of admissibility of evidence in general. There was a North Carolina case, he said, in which a slave had killed his wife's lover. Evidence on the man's frame of mind was admitted, and Stanton "only demanded for the prisoner of the bar the same right which is accorded to a North Carolina slave." In pleading his point, Stanton went so far as to accuse DA Ould of having fiercely hunted Sickles and of being driven by desire for blood vengeance. In return, Ould said that there seemed to be different parts assigned to the various counsels for the defense—to some high tragedy; to some comedy; to some, the part of walking gentlemen (Brady); and to one the task of theologian (John Graham by way of the Reverend Mr. Haley). But one of the counselors carried out the part of the bully and the bruiser, and that, he implied, was Stanton. This produced yet another of the courtroom furors the press was so pleased to record, and Haley was particularly offended. Stanton himself cried, "I have not the honor of his [Ould's] acquaintance and, after his language just uttered, do not desire it." Many of Dan's friends in court supported this by stamping their feet on the ground, and the racket was so great that the marshal and the officers of the court had to pass down the rows of spectators to reimpose order.[41]

In the oncoming spring, the immutable and unadjustable heating system gave an even more withering feel to the courtroom, but neither this nor all the racket produced by the fights between Stanton and Ould seemed to give Dan discomfort. In the broiling air, more defense witnesses were questioned. It is not recorded how Dan reacted to some of the evidence of Frederick Wilson, who said that he had seen Mr. Key, Mrs. Sickles, and Laura on the Thursday before the killing coming up Pennsylvania Avenue to Green's Furniture Store, and that Mrs. Sickles and the little girl had gone into the store while Key waited on the pavement, reading a letter that had a yellow envelope, about the same hue as the one already presented that held the letter signed R.P.G. With some embarrassment, Wilson admitted that he had virtually stalked Mrs. Sickles, Key, and the child; his curiosity had been piqued by seeing Mr. Key a number of times outside the Sickleses' house—nearly every day, the witness declared, to ribald laughter in the courtroom. With the sensitivity of the prisoner in mind, the judge thought the line of questioning and the general laughter in the court improper, but Dan remained sternly unexcited throughout it, calm enough that, the next morning, the court journalist reported that the prisoner "looked less careworn than hitherto."[42]

Early that day, in an argument about the admissibility of what Nancy Brown, wife of a White House gardener and resident of Fifteenth Street, had to say about the adulterers, Magruder asked Carlisle whether, under the Maryland statute, one punishment for adultery was a fine of a hundred pounds of tobacco. Carlisle said he couldn't say exactly what the punishment was. Brady pursued the matter: "Then the only satisfaction an injured husband could have would be a chew of tobacco." Again, the entire court guffawed, and no one recorded what Dan's reaction was.

The old argument over admissibility continued on through Saturday. With the issue unresolved, the court and its spectators at last scattered in an evening downpour. On Sunday, as Dan's lawyers met at Edwin Stanton's house and as George visited his son in jail, Washington socialized. All the talk was of the trial. "It is the sole topic of conversation wherever men meet," said one observer, "or women either."[43]

Teresa and Mrs. Bagioli and Laura, in a sense the forgotten people of the trial, went strolling that Sunday along the banks of the Hudson, which were miry from spring rain. The breath of the new season washed in on the breeze from New Jersey. Teresa was aware that the prodigiously popular *Harper's Weekly* had promised that its next issue would contain a full facsimile, in huge written script—supposedly a reproduction of her crazed hand that night—of her letter of confession. Those godly sections of America that had not read the document—thanks to the moral inhibitions of local newspaper editors—would now have it massively reproduced for them on the magazine's broadsheet front page. Within the limits of that knowledge, Teresa remained half elated, partly fearful, and wholly hopeful of becoming Dan's openly acknowledged wife again. Laura had always been the chief issue. Certainly Teresa cringed to think of the afternoon she had been willing to have Key drop off Laura at the Hoovers'. Laura had been lost sight of in the heady urgency of getting to Number 383 Fifteenth Street. In view of that lapse,

Teresa was considered not only a scarlet whore but an appalling mother. But she knew herself an essentially decent mother, and knew too that some form of reunion with Dan was essential to her daughter's future happiness. She was cheered by reassuring notes from dear Manny Hart and the Chevalier Wikoff that Dan seemed well, and so—she concluded—less likely to strike attitudes with her. And she was blessedly busy. There were many chickens on the grounds of the house. Eggs had to be searched out in the thickets and the verdant low ground by the Hudson. Horses had to be fed and curried, gardening done, and servants managed. Teresa was content to lose herself in the minutiae of domestic life in a large country house, and those who visited her were impressed by her energy.

In Washington, Mrs. Brown began the week in the witness box still listening to the dreary argument about admissibility, but to the delight of the defense, the judge seemed to be leaning their way. Mrs. Brown had met a man, Key, said the judge, who had claimed to rent a house. She had then seen what he used that house for. The jury needed to know what that house renting signified. Take a simpler example, the judge suggested. "The exhibitions of a handkerchief! What do they mean? Have not the jury a right to understand what they mean? . . . I am of the opinion that the evidence is admissible." There was what one observer called a rare silent expression of satisfaction in the courtroom, as Mrs. Brown was re-sworn. Soon such a level of hilarity was raised by Nancy Brown's evidence on the affair conducted on Fifteenth Street that the judge was concerned that it could be heard beyond the chamber.[44]

The Sickleses' coachmen were called, and John McDonald, "a smart young Irishman" who had been working as footman for the Sickleses only two weeks when the murder occurred, added new material to what was already known. He described how, on that last Thursday, Key had tracked Teresa through the afternoon from one reception to another. Miss Ridgeley, Mrs. Sickles, and Mr. Key left the last house of call, Rose Greenhow's, together, and Mr. Key sat half in and half out of the carriage, conversing softly with Mrs. Sickles. On his perch behind the carriage, McDonald heard most of the conversation. Was she going to the hop at Willard's? Key wanted to know. If Dan would allow her, she said. Key expressed the hope that he would meet her there. He also said that her eyes looked bad, and Teresa told Key she did not feel well. Mr. Key was let down off the coach between Fifteenth and Sixteenth Streets on K, and Mrs. Sickles, the efficient hostess, and Miss Ridgeley went on to Gautier's, the confectioners.[45]

By April 21, the sixteenth day of the trial, counsel were commenting even to friends and acquaintances in court that they were growing weary. They were momentarily revived by a strange letter that had arrived at the courthouse in the morning, care of the lawyers but addressed to Dan, indicating the extent to which the explicit details of the case had fevered the nation's young imaginations. A young woman who signed herself Olympia Aiken, and had used the Greek alphabet to write her name, described herself in the letter as "one of the order of frailty—one of the simple waiters for the wave of some masculine pocket handkerchief." In its combination of longing, febrile hope, and helplessness, this letter so thoroughly reproduced the manner in which society, the court, and the counsel defined womanhood that Dan's lawyers were more amused than abashed, and passed the pathetic missive, postmarked West Randolph, Vermont, around to reporters.

Another, more ominous letter that arrived that day was addressed to one of the jurors, the grocer Jesse Wilson, care of the court. It was passed to Dan and his lawyers, who then returned it to the judge. James Topham Brady thought it similar in handwriting to the R.P.G. letter, and the judge reflected only that it was a matter of extreme regret that the author of the R.P.G. letter was not known. But word got around the court that this new letter, which was kept secret and destroyed, had something to do with the scandalous lives of some of the defense counsel, and that it was aimed at enlisting the juror Jesse Wilson to punish these lawyers through punishing their client.

Of a succession of recalled prosecution witnesses who saw Dan after the shooting and remarked on his apparent calm, Brady now asked whether they had ever been to a lunatic asylum or seen an inmate. None admitted they had. Well, said Brady, he *had* been to asylums, had been extensively to New York's Blackwell's Island, and up to the more rural lunatic asylum to the north of Bloomingdale, and had studied the sometimes "cool and deliberate" demeanor of the certified.[46]

The judge, wearied and feeling his years, reminded the court that this was Holy Thursday, the eve of the most solemn day of the Christian calendar, Good Friday, and the jurors were offered a chance to observe the holy day. But after consulting with one another, they declared themselves to have a solemn duty to fulfill. Hence the court reassembled on Good Friday. Catholics like Thomas Francis Meagher and James Topham Brady were exempt, because of the arduous duty of saving Dan, from the full observance of the Lenten fast, but as true Catholics on this day of days they abstained from liquor, drank black tea, ate only crusts. Fasting, if anything, sharpened the devout Brady's native intelligence.

On this deepest of holy days, with the air darkening beyond the court's dim, tall windows, Carlisle had introduced into court what Brady called "corpulent rolls of print galleys of the *Congressional Globe*." They showed that Dan had made a congressional speech under the five-minute rule on both Friday and Saturday, when, according to such witnesses as Wooldridge, he was supposed to be in agony of spirit. These galleys had handwritten corrections by Dan, and so he obviously had had enough presence of mind to want himself accurately reported in the permanent record of Congress. Dan and his lawyers spent more than half an hour examining the rolls, and also considering something else Carlisle was seeking to introduce —what Carlisle would tell the judge was "an offer of evidence." Everyone in the court, according to one observer, seemed to know what this evidence was. The matter of "his visits with a lady to Barnum's Hotel, Baltimore," was about to achieve visibility—if the prosecution had its way. The manager of Barnum's was waiting in the corridor to be called. As Brady, Graham, and Ould conversed at the bench in a low tone, the judge made a preliminary statement that he did not think the evidence admissible. But Ould took a seat beside His Honor and entered into a deep consultation with him, while the audience was agog at the legal and titillatory possibilities that might be about to be revealed. But as Judge Crawford had ruled the confession out as evidence of provocation to Dan, so now too evidence of Dan's adultery was ruled out. The hotel manager was free to catch the train back to Baltimore.[47]

Rebuffed on the issue of Dan's sins, Carlisle sought to introduce two last witnesses on the question of insanity. They were the two gentlemen who had been waiting in the back parlor of Attorney General Black's house when Dan turned up after the murder to hand himself over: the former senator Richard Brodhead and Mr. Haldemar, editor of a Democratic paper in Pennsylvania. The judge agreed to admit these witnesses if they were in court by the next morning.[48]

Along the broad avenues of Washington, a gale blew, and any hope the jurors might have had of being quit of their responsibilities in time for Easter Sunday dinner were destroyed by the arrival of Brodhead in court on Easter Saturday morning. And though Brodhead recounted the meeting with Dan after the killing, and Dan's ordinary conversation, nothing was added thereby to the prosecution's case. Haldemar himself had not arrived, so District Attorney Ould declared the testimony closed on the part of the United States. The jurors had been separated from their Easters at home for no good purpose.

After examination of the instructions the defense wished the judge to give the jury, Carlisle began his strong final speech, asking whether anything could be more irreconcilable with peace and good government than the doctrine that he who is grievously wronged is to take into his own hands the knife. In the middle of Carlisle's argument, some argumentation developed between prosecution and defense over the famous M'Naghten case in Britain in 1843. M'Naghten was an unstable Scottish woodman who had murdered the secretary of British Prime Minister Sir Robert Peel under the delusion that the secretary was Sir Robert. After his twelve judges referred the question of M'Naghten's mind to the jury, he was acquitted on grounds of insanity, as Brady was pleased to emphasize. Carlisle went on to close his argument by warning the jurors that it was the job of the defense to prove this risky and precedent-setting plea of temporary insanity.[49]

Edwin Stanton, whom Ould and Carlisle least liked, rose first to sum up for the defense. In case the jury had heard intimations of Dan's own philandering, Stanton argued that, by marriage, "the woman is sanctified to the husband, and this bond must be preserved for the evil as well as for the good." His graphic picture of what adultery implied included the extraordinary argument that "when her [the wife's] body has been once surrendered to the adulterer, she longs for the death of her husband, whose life is often sacrificed by the cup of the poisoner, or the dagger or pistol of the assassin." More credibly, he argued that "when an adulterer tears a young wife from her husband, her child is cut off from all kindred fellowship." Young Laura, though she had no siblings, was certainly suffering from a lack of fellowship as this trial proceeded. Only one final shame had not descended upon Teresa herself, Stanton admitted. Often the sinning wife was "plunged into the horrible filth of common prostitution, to which she is rapidly hurrying, and which is already yawning before her." The hapless victim could thus be "swept through a miserable life and a horrible death to the gates of hell, unless her husband's arms shall save her." Who, knowing these facts and these potentialities, would not rush to save the mother of a child? "Although she be lost as a wife, rescue her from the horrid adulterer; and may the Lord who watches over the home and the family, guide the bullet and direct the stroke."

Counsel for the prosecution, Stanton continued, had had the daring to suggest that the killing of the adulterer had first been made illegal in the era of Charles I. Why would it not be, asked Edwin Stanton, when, under the government of Charles, "the palace was filled with harlots, and thronged with adulterers and adulteresses." As for this later and better time, for this capital city and for the District of Columbia, the ethos of the region was a social one, and the habit of officers of the government, and those in public employment, to throw open their doors with wide hospitality was "unprecedentedly common." But if these social occasions were to serve as a platform upon which the adulterer pursued his lust, "then the doors of family shall be swiftly closed." When he ended, Stanton was again greeted with an outburst of acclaim, with which the day concluded. For Easter had arrived, and the example of the tomb doors of Christ opening and releasing death's divine prisoner was not lost on the counsel or on the prisoner.

Dan ate his splendid Easter dinner that Sunday knowing that, with the prosecution done, the correspondence between Teresa and himself was no longer a legal peril. When his counsel called by to see him, Meagher considered him equally and serenely ready for death or resurrection. That was just as well, since Stanton and Brady were uneasy about what the judge's instructions to the jury would be. And though eminent Brady was hopeful, he knew something of the unpredictability of juries. In Bloomingdale, Teresa above all yearned for resurrection as she planted painted Easter eggs, earlier harvested from chickens, about the garden and among the rocks on the Broadway side of the property, above the Hudson. In searching for them later in the morning, Laura would not be troubled with competition, since there were no child visitors. To sour Easter, the large facsimile confession had appeared the day before in *Harper's Weekly*, and Teresa could suppose that it dominated the Easter discourse of the nation's adults.

At the dinner tables of the capital, many wives heard their husbands say they wished to attend court the next day to hear the great advocate James Topham Brady speak for Dan Sickles. And next morning the court was crowded to the limit a quarter of an hour before the judge appeared, and the doors remained besieged all morning by people trying to get in. Soon, Brady was called on by Judge Crawford, and, in his usual honeyed way, hoped for the polite attention of the court, which he was grateful to have hitherto received. "The whole world, Your Honor, has its eye on this case, and although there may seem to be egotism involved in the remark which I make, I cannot help saying, because I am here in the discharge of my duty, that, when all of this shall have passed away, and when each shall have taken his chamber in the silent halls of death . . . the name of everyone associated with this trial, from Your Honor who presides in the first position of dignity, to the humblest witness that shall be called on the stand, will endure as long as the earth shall exist."

At the end of the killing, what remained on the street? He asked. The opera glasses and a derringer pistol. To whom did the pistol belong? No one had asked whether the derringer had been in Key's possession. No witness had been brought into court to say whether Key had such a pistol, not even those servants who attended his domestic affairs and who brushed his clothes, not even his friends and associates had been asked whether this pistol might have belonged to Key. So who was to say it was not Key's? "In this case a revolver was in the hands of Mr. Sickles, and a derringer in those of Mr. Key, and there was no mortal to gainsay it. . . . The bullet which killed Mr. Key came out the revolver. What then became of the bullet from the derringer?" The prosecution must have now realized what a mistake it had made in not pursuing more thoroughly the question of the derringer. Brady declared that there were four shots fired in this case, and from the evidence as it stood, only three were fired from the pistol of Mr. Sickles. As to the fourth shot, "I am not called on to say or know who fired it." On the basis of the evidence, a reasonable doubt arose as to whether Dan had been a walking arsenal.

So what about the provocation offered—that of the white hand-kerchief? Had Key been thoughtful of his father's anthem, had he not chosen his own "foul substitute for its [the flag's] beautiful folds," the white handkerchief, he would never have forgotten two lines in particular:

> And thus be it ever when free men shall stand
> Between their loved homes and the war's desolation!

As it was, he had produced in Dan a condition in which "every drop of his blood carried with it a sense of his shame . . . a realization that . . . the future which opened to him so full of brilliancy, had been enshrouded perhaps in eternal gloom." Insane or not, he was bound to do what he had done, said gentle Brady. "If he had done anything more or less than became a man . . . whatever may have been the intimacy of our past relations, I would have been willing to see him die the most ignominious death before I would venture to raise anything on his be-half but a prayer to Heaven for the salvation which after death might come." Again, the resonating New Yorker drew vigorous applause from the crowd.

Yet as apparently justified as Dan was in what he had done, Brady referred to the last report of the lunatic asylums of Pennsylvania, which showed that one of the inciting causes of insanity was domestic affliction. Well, Dan's friends had such an acute sense of his affliction that many of them had come here voluntarily, and without fee or reward, to offer on his behalf the affection and devotion he had once tendered to them. One in particular, a man from New York, was working as counsel for the de-fense on that basis. At this stage, Brady nodded to the eminent Thomas Francis Meagher, former prisoner of the Queen of Great Britain, who had given the same dignity to the criminal dock of his native country, where he had been charged for his defiance of British policy during the Famine, as Mr. Sickles gave to this American one. Meagher had recently written a manuscript on the Sickles case, from which Brady now quoted rhetorical measures that dampened many a manly cheek in the court. "Then may we well say to the jury," Meagher had written and Brady now intoned, "if your love of home will suffer it—if your genuine sense of justice will consent to it . . . if your pride of manhood will stoop to it—if your instinctive perception of right and wrong will sanction it, stamp 'murder' upon the bursting forehead. . . . Do this, do it if you can, and then, having consigned the prisoner to the scaffold, return to your homes, and there, within those endangered sanctuaries, following your ignoble verdict, set to and teach your imperiled wives a lesson in the vulgar arithmetic of a compromising morality. And let them be inspired with a sense of womanly dignity by a knowledge of the value you attach to the sanctity of the household, to the inviolability of the wife, to the security of the hospitable roof, and last of all, and above all, to the in-herited tradition of an innocent but ruined offspring."

A moment of awe, a burst of applause, followed. Now, to the citi-zens of the District of Columbia, said Brady, Mr. Sickles committed his life, his character, and all that was to elevate and keep him in existence.

Resuming his seat, Brady covered his face and wept as friends of Dan's bayed their approval inside the courtroom. Even Dan, amid his tears of gratitude to Brady and Meagher, must still have wondered whether this meant anything. The courtroom provided spectator sport, and many of the spectators were Southern Democrats or men of Dan's Northern pro-Southern stripe. Republicans had largely stayed away, and as for the jurors themselves, they were sworn before God to dispassion. The defense was particularly worried about one juror, a tinsmith named McDermott, who had not reacted enthusiastically to some of Brady's argumentation; and about another who had proved to be very pious and was believed to be praying for divine guidance on the verdict.

Mr. Ould concluded the prosecution case with fewer pyrotechnics than Brady. No great surging forces of rhetoric formed his case, but he did seek in his way to elevate the status of women. "I thank God that the matrons and maids of our land have a surer protection from the pistol or the bowie knife. Sad, indeed, would be their fate if it were not so." He denied that Key was carrying a pistol at the time. He insisted that he did not need to put to His Honor the argument as to the ease with which insanity could be simulated or feigned, and how wrong it would be to let the party accused escape just punishment. And so, in saying what he would not put, he ended.[50]

For whatever cause, Dan had been absent from the court for much of Ould's speech, and was now summoned back by Judge Crawford. His Honor was remarkably economical, by the standards of both defense and prosecution, in what he told the jury. That there was a legal presumption of malice in every deliberate killing, and the burden of repelling it was on the slayer. That it was for the jury to say what was the state of Mr. Sickles's mind as regards the capacity to decide upon the criminality of the homicide. But he acknowledged that the insanity of which the defense spoke need not exist for a definite period, but only for the moment of the act of which the accused was charged. Indeed, in this novel case, Judge Crawford's neat summation of the instructions of both sides, and his glosses upon them, indicated a mind not yet borne down by age. The marshal was instructed to give the indictment to the

195

chairman of the jury, and at half past one, the jurors got up and retired to their consultation room.[51]

This was the signal for the throwing off of all restraint. Lawyers, officers, spectators, all seemed to think it was time to speak as they pleased. The judge remained at his bench and said that although he could not reduce the audience to silence, he hoped there would be some regard exhibited for the place where they were. But the noise abounded. Many crowded around the dock to cheer and support Mr. Sickles "in this the pregnant moment of his fate." Dan had slept badly the night before but was in a high state of concentration. He lived, as Teresa had, on a particular axis of possibility no one could share with him. In ten, fifteen minutes, or an hour or two, or a day, he would be restored to light or consigned to the dark. He spoke out of his dispassionate isolation to others. One of the three ministers of religion who attended to comfort Dan, the Reverend Dr. Sunderland of the Fourth Presbyterian Church, took Sickles by the hand and said that "if the voice of the people of this city could speak at this moment, your acquittal would be instantaneous." But many of Dan's friends stated their disappointment that the jury had need to retire at all, much less spend so much time in consultation. Just after Sunderland spoke to Dan, a policeman entered the court and took the jury's chairs out to the marshal's room, where the jury was conferring. This increased rumors about a jury split or arguing hard. At the moment, standing close to the dock were John Graham's two brothers, Charles and DeWitt Graham of New York, the Chevalier Wikoff, the Tammany enforcer Captain Wiley, and various other Tammany friends. Mayor Berret was there, with Alderman Francis Mohun, who had seen demented Dan rush past his house the evening before the killing. They had hoped for a sensible fifteen-minute verdict of not guilty. But this was all going on so long that they began to fear a guilty verdict. Dan did not seem oppressed by the thought of his own death by hanging, but his lawyers, staying in or near the court, were taut with anxiety.

After seventy minutes, just as the clock began striking three, the door nearest the jury box opened, and the jury filed in. Men crowded up to have a look at the jurors' faces, some climbing on benches and tables. There were pleas from those whose view was obstructed to "get off the benches!" The judge was able to impose order only by having the clerk read the names of the jury members, and by the time the twelfth had been read and been responded to, there was silence. Dan sat, immobile, in his good suit. The clerk told him to stand up and look to the jury, and, without the blood draining from his face, Dan obeyed. The press men noticed that at this second by contrast, James Topham Brady looked acutely pale. The chairman of the jury, Mr. Arnold, had risen also. The clerk asked him whether his jury had agreed on a verdict. Mr. Arnold said they had. Daniel Edgar Sickles was not guilty.

No doubt Dan's vigorous blood surged in that second he received the jury's permission to live on in some honor. The verdict also confirmed his secular rank; he was still the representative for the Third District of New York. Yet he did not weep with gratitude, any more than he would have wept with fear had the verdict gone otherwise. His expression, people thought, did not convey a sense of triumph, but rather a belief that the trial through which he had passed could have had no other result. The clerk asked the jury, "And so say you all?" The jury assented. Mr. Stanton cried, "I now move that Mr. Sickles be discharged from custody." Though the judge pleaded, "No noise," that prohibition went unheeded. Judge Crawford could barely be heard as he ordered Dan's release, and Dan, in the dock, came under siege from ecstatic friends. Captain Wiley immediately kissed Dan. The normally dour Mr. Stanton cried that he would dance like David before the Ark of the Tabernacle. Scholarly Mr. Phillips gave way and, covering his face with his hands, wept like a child. Meagher clapped people on the back and asked them if it was not glorious. He even extended this courtesy to the district attorney, who turned to Meagher and said, "I thought the verdict would be so." The jailer, Jacob King, was weeping deeply, and looked bemused when Meagher came up, slapped his shoulder, and consoled him for losing a tenant.[52]

It was slow work for a calm, steady Dan and his ecstatic counsel to make their way to the door. He began to feel the shock of the verdict of deliverance. Those near him noticed that there was some tension apparent around his temples. On his way to the door, Dan passed the jury box, where it seemed that all the jurors wanted to congratulate him, although, it was later learned, at least one did not particularly desire to. People in the neighborhood of the court who had heard the news came rushing through the streets and up the steps, expecting a speech as Dan came forth. But Dan was growing faint, and Captain Wiley, the Tammany gang leader, helped him into one of the many carriages waiting. Some enthusiasts for the reprieved congressman tried to take the horses out of the shafts so that they themselves could drag Dan in triumph through the streets, but they were persuaded not to. Dan, dazed yet still dignified, was taken first to the house of John McBlair, the grocery king, who lived at the Decatur House near St. John's Episcopal, and next went to the Stockton Mansion, some fifty yards away, to collect clothing and toiletries for his stay with McBlair.

A crowd was already assembled at McBlair's to cheer Dan, and many people filed through the parlor, shaking his hand. It was this demonstration of warmth that caused Dan now to break into tears. He was touched when a vendor of oranges, a Mr. Scott, rushed into the house and placed a large box of his choicest stock in the drawing room. Several other tradesmen brought gifts. Some of the guests, and the young men in the street, loudly offered to tear down the Fifteenth Street assignation house made so infamous by the trial.

That night a crowd came to the National Hotel to serenade the counsel who were staying there. Brady and the others requested that the serenaders not go on to the McBlair house, since Mr. Sickles was worn out by the trial and wished to retire to rest undisturbed. By invitation, nine or ten of the jurors went up to Brady's suite for refreshments and to receive the thanks of counsel. American jurors were always freer with their jury-room confessions than the British were permitted to be; it came in part from the freedom of speech, from an already robust American interest in celebrities, which the jurors were for the moment, and in circuses, which the trial had to an extent been. The defense counsel were surprised to see, among the jurors who did turn up that night, the tin-smith McDermott, the one they had predicted would be a tough nut. Another juror, Henry Knight, a young grocer, brought with him his fiddle, and entertained Brady and the others. Counsel had regarded him also with suspicion throughout the trial, because it had emerged that he was a member of a Know-Nothing lodge, and thus, *ex officio,* hostile to pro-Irish Democrats like Sickles and to Irish lawyers like Brady and Meagher. "But," Mr. Brady was quoted as saying, "if we had known that he played the fiddle, we might have made our minds easy, for no fiddler was ever known to find a conviction of murder."

The jurors all expressed themselves in an unrestrained manner. They admitted that one of their number had been for a guilty verdict and, in the jury room, had withdrawn into a corner and sought divine guidance. He had got up from his knees, reentered the discussion, again retired to the corner, and finally rose with a divine message in favor of acquittal. Yet another juror, Mr. William Hopkins, the gents' furnisher and something of a wag and mimic, stated himself so far in favor of Mr. Sickles that in a similar situation he himself would not have been satisfied with a derringer or revolver, but would have brought a howitzer to bear on the seducer! It was interesting that he mentioned the derringer in that way; obviously the jurors did not, despite Brady's clever arguments, believe Key had been armed. But they could quite correctly have considered that the prosecution had failed to prove he was unarmed.

At one stage during that overexuberant evening, the Marine Band turned up to serenade the lawyers outside Brady's suite. Serenaders also went to Philip Phillips's home on G Street, and Phillips came to the door and told them, accurately, that with Dan's acquittal and the success of the plea of temporary insanity, a new era had begun in the world of jurisprudence. "An honest, upright, and intelligent American jury," said Phillips, as reported by the press, "had established a precedent which all civilized nations would henceforth recognize and be guided by."

For Robert Ould, however, this was a bitter night. Some morning papers would say he had been outwitted and was "far from being thorough or searching. . . . At no time did he manifest a real lawyer's ardor or ambition." One newspaper claimed that, in private, he had admitted more than once that the case fatigued him or gave him migraines.

In Bloomingdale with her mother, Teresa had received with some joy the telegram announcing Dan's acquittal. Key was perhaps a remote personage in her affections by now, if indeed her early fondness had not been transmuted by suffering into hostility. Again, her primary impulse was to rehabilitate Laura as a normal daughter and herself as a normal wife. There was no chance of this if, as well as killing her lover through her folly, she was to bear blame for the hanging of her husband.

Dan slept soundly at the Decatur House and intended to return to New York in a week's time for the summer. In the interim, one day he passed Lafayette Square with two friends—Captain Wiley and the Chevalier Wikoff—and walked out the scene of the crime with them, recounting how he had struggled with Barton Key. Plainly, he said, he had had every intention to kill Key.[53]

But he would be forever an acquitted killer.

# VI

RETURNED TO NEW YORK, DAN UNDER-
stood too well that, despite Democratic joy over his
acquittal, he was expected to live quietly for a time.
With half his soul, he wanted to. He tried to do so
that summer at the house of his friend Thomas C.
Field, in Bloomingdale. Many would later consider
that by doing that he had put himself in lethal prox-
imity to Teresa. Cynics believed that, in light of his
notorious trial and because many of the respectable women he liked to seduce now looked askance
at him, Teresa was perhaps too sexually available
to a man of such marked appetite. She was still
there, though, the girl his profoundest instincts had
prompted him to marry. Bloomingdale's summer
flush lay on her face, and as she threw herself into her
rustic chores, she looked like someone who inhabited
a better world. As well as that, Laura—who even

as an infant was charmed and dazzled by a father so like herself in nature—and her future standing were now the chief concerns for him.

Dan commuted from Bloomingdale to town, however intermittently, to his father at their Nassau Street law offices, where he was welcome. But in the councils of Tammany he was quiet. Though he was still a congressman, considerable time had to pass before he could be looked at again as a Democratic power.[1]

In semi-idleness, then, which suited him badly, Dan began to visit Teresa. It was not a casual impulse, as his enemies would say it was. In all his relations with Teresa from then on there would be a deliberateness. Appropriate rumors about a reunion of the scandalous couple were heard around New York and caused people in Dan's circle to shake their heads. One version of the tale had the two fathers, George Sickles and Antonio Bagioli, working at the reconciliation, and if that was so, the two older men were stricken by the same delusion as Teresa—that reconciliation would be tolerated by society. The first scornful news of the resumption of "marital relations" appeared in the New York Herald on July 12, three and a half months after the killing of Key. It had been decided by both families for "Mr. Sickles and his wife to live together again in peace and mutual affection, burying the past in the grave of oblivion. Both parties have agreed to this step, and it is said that their love is greater than ever."

Even journals that had in the past supported Dan took a hostile view. There were leading personal and political friends of Mr. Sickles, said the New York Times, who honestly believed him to be a man maddened by intolerable wrong, and who in that belief stood between him "and the hasty rage of public feeling at the time of his trial in Washington," and were not responsible for this step taken entirely on the impulse of Mr. Sickles. In fact, James Topham Brady was said to be outraged.[2]

As for those who had never liked Dan, there was now nothing but scalding contempt. George Templeton Strong declared confidently, "Teresa had a hold upon him and knew of matters he did not desire to be revealed. Some say he had promoted her intrigue with Key; others that our disreputable old Buchanan's interest in his welfare was due to relations with her which her husband had encouraged. He must have been in her power somehow, or he would not have taken this step and sacrificed all his hopes of political advancement, and all his political friends and allies. He can hardly shew himself in Washington again." Horace Greeley's newspaper, the *Tribune*, said it was sure that in taking this remarkable step Mr. Sickles had alienated himself from most if not all of his friends, personal and political. Basically, then, everyone was baffled, and nearly everyone disapproved.

> Hail! Matchless pair! [a newspaper poet wrote]
> United once again
> In newborn bliss forget your bygone pain . . .
> What though the world may say, "with hands all red
> Yon bridegroom steals to a dishonored bed."
> And friends, estranged, exclaim on every side:
> "Behold! Adultery couched with Homicide!"[3]

Dan, flayed by the newspapers, and perhaps surprised by the fury of friends, sat down to write a measured letter of explanation to James Gordon Bennett, the editor he had once parodied in name at the court of Queen Victoria. Bennett's *Herald* was the best-selling paper in New York, and its account of the reconciliation had, Dan said, been "temperate and dignified." As to the idea that had got about that he and Teresa might have reconciled on the advice of his lawyers, that was entirely erroneous, wrote Dan.

> *My reconciliation with my wife was my own act, done without consultation with any relative, connection, friend or adviser. . . . If I ever failed to comprehend the utterly desolate position of the offending though penitent woman—the hopeless future, with its dark possibilities of danger, to which she is doomed when proscribed as an outcast, I can now see plainly enough in the almost universal howl of denunciation with which she is followed to my threshold, the misery and perils from which I have rescued the mother of my*

*child. . . . In conclusion let me ask only one favor of those who, from whatever motive, may deem it necessary or agreeable to comment in public or private on this sad history; and that is, to aim all their arrows at my breast, and for the sake of my innocent child, to spare her yet youthful mother, while she seeks in sorrow and contrition the mercy and pardon of Him to whom, sooner or later, we must all appeal.*[4]

It was a brave letter, but if the world had been divided in response to his murder of Key, the world was universally outraged by his reconciliation with Teresa. Dan told George he was indifferent to public opinion, but he was a politician by nature. Teresa, who knew him better than he knew himself, feared his ambition would separate them again. The public speculation was whether he would dare turn up in Washington for the congressional session in the fall. But he had a rigorous intent to do so, and in the late summer he received a scatter of letters urging him to "stand by your conscience and let no political demagogues influence your own judgment." Another letter congratulated Sickles on his forgiveness, since Teresa was "more sinned against than sinning" and "will yield the 'grateful fragrance of the crushed flower.' "[5]

But, though Captain Wiley, Manny Hart, and Chevalier Wikoff remained Dan's friends, there were few letters of applause from the powerful of Tammany. Dan did turn up in Washington in time for the congressional session, but in spite of the reconciliation, he was without Laura and Teresa, and lived alone in a suite at Willard's and then in plain lodgings on Thirteenth Street. This took courage on Dan's part, but the reunion and Teresa's desperate hopes for its success had somehow not flowered into a genuine marriage of minds. Laura's interests had been served, so perhaps the rest could be neglected.[6]

There was certainly a sense of faded splendor in Dan's new Washington existence. It would have been interesting to see, had Teresa returned with him, what doors if any would have been opened to her by the city's society. Perhaps she was pleased not to have to put her acceptability to the test just yet. A journalist noted that even as regarded Dan, there was very little tendency on the part of any of the representatives to establish intimate relations with him. No matter the tumults of feeling of which he was capable, in this circumstance he showed he had a stoic soul. He maintained, according to his solitary sense of self, a characteristic "ease and coolness," but he was also remarkably retiring and unobtrusive as he turned up in the House each day, about fifteen minutes after twelve. He still dressed in exquisite taste and had grown a large pair of brown whiskers, but he kept his place on one of the benches on the western side of the House, where, resting his head on his gloved hand, he remained seated, taking no part in the discussions, merely voting in a low voice when called upon within a chamber where, if anything, the political furies of the previous year had not been moderated but had grown in scale. In the evenings he ate the plain fare of the congressional dining room, and occasionally dined with a small circle of friends, including Governor Walker. He did not attend many receptions and never went to balls. For the first time in his life, he lived like a reclusive fellow.[7]

One day a young South Carolina woman, Mary Miller Chesnut, the wife of the newly elected Senator James Chesnut of South Carolina, visited the House gallery with some other congressional wives. Looking down, she noticed Dan Sickles seated alone on a bench, and remarked that she had seen two men in all her life who had been sent to Coventry thoroughly and deliberately. One was a young naval officer who played the gigolo to a "rich old harridan." The other was Dan. He was left strictly to himself, she noticed, "as if he had smallpox." Mrs. Chesnut discussed the matter with a friend sitting nearby. The woman explained that though he had killed Philip Barton Key, "that was all right. . . . A fellow could survive such a thing. The real reason he was ostracized was because he condoned his wife's profligacy and took her back."[8]

In the House, at a remove from the other legislators, he listened to debate that would normally have vexed him. John Brown's body was still swinging from a rope in Virginia, the famous abolitionist having been tried and executed for attempting to seize the armory at Harpers Ferry and unleash a slave rebellion. Henry David Thoreau had declared

Brown "a crucified hero," and Ralph Waldo Emerson prophesied that Brown would "make the gallows as glorious as the Cross." This was exactly the sort of abolitionist oratory that, before the murder, was set to outrage Dan and cause him to rise urgently to his feet and attempt to rebuild North-South fraternity. A Baltimore newspaper had asked the question Dan's Southern allies were asking, whether the South could any longer live under a government "the majority of whose subjects or citizens regard John Brown as a martyr and a Christian hero." Every Northern representative and senator who did not explicitly condemn Brown was considered his ally and sympathizer; Senator Stephen Douglas of Illinois said as much in the Senate. Yet Dan was able to keep silent and wait in his isolation, as if he were the one legislator who lay outside the bubble of national frenzy. And when he listed his name with the Speaker and rose in the House on December 13, 1859, he commenced with an air of apology for speaking at all, declaring it would be more agreeable to him if some other gentleman had taken the floor. As it was, he had reluctantly decided to accept "the duty of a just expression of the sentiments of the national men of the North."

By the time Dan gave this, his first speech of the session, many Southern regions had grown so alarmed that they had begun to form militia companies and, in a number of communities, to ride Yankees out of town. Dan was willing to protect the Union, and complained that to listen to some Republicans in the House, one would think "the irrepressible conflict is not in the distant future—it is here. It is no longer a prophecy; it is a fact." But the truth was that in the North there beat millions of hearts devoted not only to the Union but to the Constitution upon which it rested, and thus amenable to peace with the South.

This speech was one of a series Dan would give from within his political isolation, and as a record they would successively mark out the path many Northern Democrats would follow over the next eighteen months, beginning—as Dan did now—with a complete defense of the South's position in the Union on questions of representation, on the fugitive slave law, on taxes, on Southern exports, and on the slave trade itself. Attempts to extinguish the slave trade, argued Dan in this first speech, had run up not against Southern intransigence, but against hypocritical Northern capitalists who invested in ships for the enterprise. There was now in transit in Washington, or had been the day before, a Captain Farnham of the *Wanderer*, arrested in New York City by Marshal Rynders (Dan's old friend) for the violation of the law prohibiting the import of new slaves. The requisition for Farnham came from the authorities of a Southern jurisdiction, Georgia, which meant to try him.

The doctrine of coming irrepressible conflict "encouraged fanatics and traitors to invade homes and communities in our sister States; led to scenes of such excitement and danger as we have witnessed upon the floor of the House; led to Southern citizens having no security at home; led to Virginia—the mother of States—standing at her frontiers to protect herself from the uplifted blade." There was certainly a danger to the Union. That danger arose whenever a Republican proclaimed on this floor "that there is a conflict between the South and the North, that it is 'as deep as the foundation of the mountains and as pervading as the atmosphere.'" Many sensible Northerners, said Dan, knew that the results of disunion for Northern laborers would be catastrophic, because the Southern states were the best customers of the North. "Without the Southern staples, what have we got to sell to Europe?" asked Dan. And without the South, the North would become a nation of traders without customers.

Dan was concerned, however, that the South made too much of the supposed anti-Southern feeling in the North. When John Brown met his fate, a hundred guns were fired in Albany, the capital of New York State, to salute his heroism. "Well, sir, that was a disgraceful, but not an alarming or significant occurrence." It was an old habit of Northern people to fire pieces of artillery an indefinite number of times. Much-heralded sermons had been preached in sacred Northern pulpits, applauding Brown's acts of treason, but in the whole state of New York, said Dan, he had heard of only four or five such sermons. There had been strange meetings held in Syracuse, but it was a city that lacked theaters and made up for it with radical speeches. In reality, "there is not an omnibus load of sane men in the North who would wish Texas out of the Union. . . . I say then to the House and to the people of this country, leave this crisis to public opinion. Leave it to the reason and sense of justice and conscience of the North."[9]

His speech brought some restrained respect, but society remained cold to Dan and Teresa throughout 1860, the last year of peace, and Dan's former second home, the Democratic Party, began to fragment further early in the year, with Southern Democrats and their Northern allies seeking revenge against Senator Stephen Douglas for voting against the admission of Kansas as a slave state. At the Democratic convention at Charleston, not attended by the out-of-favor Dan, fifty delegates from the lower South walked out, leaving Douglas short of the two-thirds majority required for nomination. The delegates met again six weeks later in Baltimore, where another schism occurred. Those who walked out this time, the Southerners and some Northerners, formed their own convention and nominated John C. Breckinridge of Kentucky, Buchanan's Vice President, on a platform that would include a slave code to be extended to all new territories. So now there would be two Democratic candidates to divide the vote.

The Republican convention was held in Chicago, where Senator William H. Seward was expected to be nominated. By the time the convention opened on May 16, the until recently obscure Abraham Lincoln had emerged as Seward's main rival. Lincoln had come to national renown not for any great success in Washington but because of his Illinois debates with Senator Douglas. Ironically, in view of what would befall Dan in the coming upheaval, though Lincoln was considered a moderate and thus less likely than someone like Seward to create disunion, he was exactly the sort of Illinois bumpkin antislavery a worldly New York Democrat like Dan despised. Seward was worth despising and fearing; Lincoln was merely contemptible. But he succeeded on the third ballot, on a platform that pledged support for a homestead act and federal aid for the construction of a transcontinental railroad. The platform also included a tariff plank "to encourage the development of the industrial interests of the whole country." Lincoln mentioned, too, the contemplated treason of the South, which it was "the imperative duty of an indignant people sternly to rebuke and forever silence."[10]

As the Republican campaign commenced, Dan was back in New York, living soberly but with sufficient intellectual and emotional room to be appalled by what had happened to his party and by the shadow that had fallen over his nation. He resided at least part of the time at Bloomingdale with a grateful Teresa, who had entered her second year of purdah and must have been a little bemused that this summer was a repetition of the last, with only the most loyal friends and relatives turning up and life continuing in something of a social vacuum. But perhaps, with his work all located in New York, Dan might become a more regular presence in the house at Bloomingdale. He would not be standing for Congress again in November, and would be lost for a time—if not forever—to national politics.

Not aware how pleasantly and advantageously close he would in time become to the new President, Dan was bewildered when Lincoln was elected as a minority President with 40 percent of the national popular vote but a hundred electoral votes. North of the forty-first parallel, Lincoln won more than 60 percent of the vote.

Back in Washington for his last session in Congress, though feeling depressed at Lincoln's election, Dan was beginning to lose faith in some of his former Southern friends as well. All President Buchanan could think of in the crisis of the moment was to call into being a House committee, consisting of one member from each state, to decide the terms on which lasting peace could be established. At least one congressman, Mr. Hawkins of Florida, refused to serve, and this brought Dan to his feet again on December 10, 1860. He wanted to appeal to Mr. Hawkins, in the name of New York. "No man," Dan promised his Southern friend, "will ever pass the boundaries of the city of New York for the purpose of waging war against any State of this Union. . . . The Union can be made perpetual by justice—it cannot be maintained an instant by force."

He was willing to defend peaceful secession, for after all it was "the last dread alternative of a free state when it has to choose between liberty and justice."

But in the meantime, argued Dan, there were options for maintaining the Union, and one of them was the President's committee. No Republican had refused to serve on the committee Mr. Buchanan had proposed, and this was a cheering sign, said Dan. As for New York, if the Union of the United States was torn asunder by abolitionist zeal, "we [New York City] will not consent to remain the submissive appendage of a puritan province. We will assert our own independence. The North will then see and feel that secession, although it may begin at the South, will not end at the South." And once secession began, "I tell you, that imperial city will throw off the odious government to which she now yields a reluctant allegiance; she will repel the hateful cabal at Albany, which has so long abused its power over her; and with her own flag, sustained by the courage and devotion of her own gallant sons, she will, as a free city, open wide her gates to the civilization and commerce of the world." With that tempting but improbable vision of New York the city-state, the Venetian Republic of the Atlantic Coast, Dan resumed his seat to some applause, and was done for the year.[11]

The Bagiolis and Sickleses visited Bloomingdale for Christmas and watched the solitary child open her presents. They knew that only a gesture of domestic peace had been made in this household. George Sickles took his son aside and urged him to work to achieve a sane, settled life. He knew that there was more potential for a union of souls between Dan and Teresa than between himself and Dan's earnest and tremulous mother. Like others who raised moral issues with Dan, though, George found once again that any advice on Dan's private morality made him take on a waspish, intransigent, and angry tone. Waspish, intransigent, and angry tones were echoed in the larger household of the nation itself. During January, six states seceded, led by South Carolina. New York business was provoked by the declaration of Southern clients that they would not pay their New York bills until they could be paid in Confederate currency.[12]

At a time of emergency on January 16, 1861, the House being in that emergency mode described as "a Committee of the whole of the States of the Union," Dan put his name on the speaking list again, and this time his attitude had moved quite a distance from his pre-Christmas speech about peaceful secession and the fanciful concept of the secession of New York. He had by now become affronted by the way the seceding states were behaving toward federal property. He said that perhaps there was now more alienation of feeling and antagonism between the sections of the United States "than prevailed between the mother country and the colonies in 1774." Still, he chiefly blamed Republican intransigence for this. But he was willing to admit that secession was the least effectual form of protest for the South. "And now of course, it remained to be shown whether in their interference with forts, arsenals, navy yards, and the common property of the Union, they had not committed a fatal error in the development of their own policy." In resolving the national issue, "it will never do, sir, for them to protest against coercion, and, at the same moment seize all the arms and arsenals and forts and navy yards, and ships that may, through our forbearance, fall within their power. This is not peaceful secession. These acts, whensoever or by whomsoever done, are overt acts of war."

Dan was listened to with more interest than during his earlier two speeches. It was apparent that his Southern-leaning philosophy had been rocked by South Carolina's assault on Castle Pinckney and Fort Moultrie in Charleston. "With all the pomp and circumstance of war, the battalions of South Carolina, duly provided with scaling ladders, battle-axes, and pontoons, march in grim array to the assault of these fortifications—the clear and indisputable property and domain of the United States. . . . These are seditious proceedings." And Dan had been particularly surprised by the fact that a small body of federal reinforcements and some supplies, sent on an unarmed merchant vessel called the *Star of the West*, had been fired upon by South Carolina artillery. The American flag was flying at the masthead of the ship when "the authorities of South Carolina, through their military forces, opened fire upon that defenseless ship, and compelled her to retire and abandon

211

the peaceful and legitimate mission in which she was engaged. Now, sir, that was an act of war, unqualified war." As for his earlier prediction that no man would cross the frontier of New York to employ coercion against the people of a Southern state, that was still the truth. "But the men of New York would go in untold thousands anywhere to protect the flag of their country and to maintain its legitimate authority."

Representative Sickles was now doing so well that when the Speaker intervened to say that the gentleman's hour had expired, several members expressed a desire to hear the conclusion of the argument, and an extension of time was unanimously granted. As for the security of the United States, Dan continued, "these fortified places are of a thousand times more importance if secession becomes an accomplished and irreversible fact, than if it had never been contemplated." If France and Britain were inclined to seek any opportunity offered by American weakness to dismember the Union, these forts were essential to the interests of the United States. "In all the partisan issues between the South and the Republican Party, the people of the city of New York are with the South, but when the South makes an untenable issue with our country, when the flag of the Union is insulted, when the fortified places provided for the common defense are assaulted and seized, when the South abandons its Northern friends for English and French alliances, then the loyal and patriotic population of that imperial city are unanimous with the Union."[13]

Dan was moving toward being a Union-dedicated Democrat who had run out of patience with the South, which, after all, had produced the deceiver Key. It was clear that the crisis of the hour had given back to disgraced Dan Sickles some of his voice. After the *Star of the West* was repulsed by gunfire from South Carolina batteries, Dan became passionately concerned that his old friend Buchanan might simply abandon Major Anderson and Fort Sumter to South Carolina. On one of the gloomiest days of the winter, said Dan later, Edwin Stanton, who was now Buchanan's Attorney General, asked the congressman to go on a mission to the chief Northern cities, particularly Philadelphia and New York, to announce that the President was determined to hold on to

Sumter and to encourage the North to applaud this decision. Stanton told Dan to see to it that militia cannon were primed with some celebratory gunpowder. "A thousand bullets and a bale of hemp would save us from a bloody revolution." Stanton believed the President would support the men in Fort Sumter if he saw that the temper of the people demanded resistance. Thus, "go and fire some cannon and let the echoes come to the White House."

On a visit to the White House, Dan got the definite impression that the President was wavering. Hence, Dan visited Philadelphia and asked his friend Daniel Dougherty, who had given evidence at the trial, to muster militia artillery units and fire off a hundred guns in Independence Square to applaud the President's sturdy resistance. Dougherty was also to go to all the leading merchants of Philadelphia and have them send telegrams—"long ones"—applauding the President's sturdiness, and to encourage all Philadelphia newspapers to carry congratulatory headlines. In Trenton, Albany, and New York, Dan Sickles used the same strategy, canvassing Wall Street, the bank presidents, the leading manufacturers, all to send telegrams to the same effect. He went to the editors of the *Herald* and *Sun* and had them print double-headed editorials supporting a strong line on Sumter. This was the sort of work Dan was best at, and the stiffness of resolve in his own power base confirmed Old Buck in brave resistance to South Carolina's demands. The garrison of Sumter would not be withdrawn. Stanton wired, *Victory—we won. Thank you for your kind offices.*[14]

Now, in the Republic's darkest days, Dan was slowly regaining political credit. His next congressional speech was in support of the bills to suspend the postal services to the secessionist states. He spoke on February 5, when already South Carolina, Mississippi, Florida, Alabama, Georgia, Louisiana, and Texas had defected. Many congressmen from the South, however, still sat in the House, as did those from the states that were suspected of having a firm intention to secede soon, such as Virginia and North Carolina. Dan spoke in favor of the suspension of postal services in the South because the government of the United States had no choice—it must either subject the mails to the hazard of every possible trespass and depredation by the insurgent states, or else withhold them altogether. Specifically, because it did not involve federal coercion, he supported the cancellation of postal services.

The new crisis did not bear merely on the mails, Dan announced. There was an issue that funds belonging to the United States, lying in a number of subtreasuries and mints in the South, were no longer safe to the United States. And here again Dan showed his disappointment with his former friends. The magnanimous policy of President Buchanan, who had solemnly announced to the people of the country that he would not adopt the policy of coercion, "has been followed by insults to our flag; by the expulsion of the United States troops and authorities from navy yards and forts and arsenals; by measures to control the vast commerce of the Mississippi River and its tributaries. . . . While we are here deliberating upon measures of honorable and fraternal compromise, envoys have been sent abroad to request the Cabinets of Europe to sit in counsel . . . upon the paralyzed and impotent United States of America.

"Surely the chivalrous men of the South would scorn to receive the benefits of our postal laws," said Dan. "They cannot intend to remain, like Mahomid's coffin, between heaven and earth, neither in nor out of the Union, getting all the benefits that they can secure and subjecting us to all its burdens." Then Dan traced the gradations of attitude through which his kind of Northerner had passed. In December, the cry had been for "peaceable secession." In January, the South had forced "the immediate and forcible expulsion of the United States authorities from even the limits of their exclusive jurisdiction—from their custom houses, post offices, treasuries, navy yards, ships, arsenals, and forts." In February, "secession, despoliation, and war. What next?" He declared, in the presence of this new and latest phase of the revolution, that the action of the South could have no friends or apologists in the North; "and if these aggressive and predatory enterprises are sanctioned by the authorities and the public opinion of the alienated States, it will soon be difficult to find a respectable exception to the general denunciation which they must encounter from the loyal and patriotic citizens of this country."[15]

His very last congressional activity was to propose a resolution in the House calling for the celebration of George Washington's birthday as a national holiday, and to try to organize, through his reopened lines of communication to the White House, a military parade of regular troops on February 22. The dove had become something of a hawk. But the parade did not happen. Abraham and Mary Todd Lincoln were on their way to Washington, and Old Buck yearned for rustic peace at Wheatland. So Dan went home to New York and to political oblivion.

When the guns of South Carolina bombarded Fort Sumter on April 12, Dan was nominally living in Bloomingdale with Teresa. He had adjusted with some success to his new condition. Though no longer a man who could go down to Washington and spend time with the powerful, and though a Nassau Street lawyer of no better than questionable reputation, he still found many reasons to be absent from home. To him, the success of his reconciliation with Teresa was one of the lesser features of the landscape. Teresa herself knew that by now. But she also knew that Fanny White was no longer a part of the Sickles equation. About the time Teresa had begun her secret affair with Barton Key, Fanny was engaged in a highly public affair with wealthy Jake LeRoy, older and richer than Dan. Then she had moved with two of her "boarders" from her industrial-strength brothel on Mercer Street to quieter quarters on Twelfth Street, and she met and married a lawyer, Edmon Blankman. Her retirement from a profitable business had almost certainly been caused by the onset of tuberculosis, a plague in New York, and one not uncommon among prostitutes. But Jake LeRoy had suffered from syphilis, and it was likely that that disease as well made inroads on Fanny's health. Whichever was the cause of her early death, Fanny perished in 1860. She was said to own "three fine city mansions," besides other property. The value of her real estate and jewelry was variously estimated at $50,000 to $100,000. She had flourished by sin. But at least she was no longer a distraction for Dan.[16]

From the day Sumter was shelled and war broke out, Teresa and Laura saw even less of Dan. Someone coming up from the city told Teresa he meant to enlist as a private. She wrote to him, "How true this rumor is you can best tell me. *Please come home dear Dan.* It seems so unsettled [and] so lonely to have you so much away." Her news echoed the banal limits of her life since Key. She had been to a funeral, that of a local woman, of whom there were rumors that the death was suicide. "James T. Brady was one of the pallbearers." Teresa had seen Wikoff only once recently—he was on his way to a masked ball at the Bennetts', precisely the style of event, although she did not say so, she was no longer invited to. As for dear Manny Hart, he was due home from a trip to Europe. Papa Antonio Bagioli, she reported last of all, was going to sell or rent out his house on Fifteenth Street and was thinking of boarding.

This plain letter gave clues to the way she filled her days. She had supervised the setting out of a garden by a gardener named Frederick, whom she also used to fix up the grounds to the easterly, higher part of the property, and the "upper roads," the one that connected the house with Broadway and the north-south one that ran along the higher ground. She thought the gardener was doing a very good job on all scores. "Your friend Quirk came here on Tuesday . . . he was so *tight* [drunk] he told me about it and apologized. His errand however was to say he was going to send me some gravel to fix the roads and he wished me to superintend the work—to order just what I pleased . . . and 'God bless my little soul,' he wanted me to be satisfied and gratified with the work, etc. etc. So a man has been bringing from Manhattanville four loads a day since Quirk was here." She intended to sell a six-week-old calf, and was hard at work packing away winter clothing in the attic and bringing out the "summer articles." The hens were laying a lot of eggs, and the horses never looked better, but poor Dandy the greyhound was "a pitiful object to behold."

Like any picturesque place on the inconvenient edge of a large city, Bloomingdale had a fluctuating population. Dan himself was an indication of this. Dr. Paine, Teresa recorded for Dan's information, wanted to give his place up because it was hard to keep. Their friend Tom Field had just come back to Bloomingdale, but his wife was staying downtown in the Everett House. Dr. Bradford had abandoned his place, and Dr. Williams's family had moved into Fanny Field's house. As for Laura, on the day Teresa asked Dan whether it was true that he intended to enlist as a private, the child was just back from Sunday school "and would like you to answer her letter. She will spend tomorrow with your mother." And if Dan would tell her, Teresa, when he was to come, she would endeavor to have the dining aspects of the house in order, although the rats were so formidable as almost to make it unsafe to go into the lower storeroom.

There had been gossip about Teresa's taking opiates to soothe her unhappy lot, an annoying cough, and a general feeling of malaise, and now she confessed to Dan she had been taking Brandreth's Pills for her biliousness. The contents of such patent medicines were a mystery, but they commonly contained laudanum and other drugs. Indeed, in the case of Brandreth's Pills, she said she had been "going it strong on them." And then there was the final, reiterated plea that he write soon and often, and let her know "when we may expect you home." She signed it as his "sincerely attached wife."[17]

Unlike other women who felt they had a stake in their husbands' attitudes toward the war, she did not mention the national crisis at all—indeed, both before and after the death of Key, there was little politics in her letters. Thus she did not take the time most Democratic wives did to pillory or satirize hapless Abraham Lincoln's new presidency.

The firing upon Fort Sumter, its surrender on April 14, and Mr. Lincoln's call for volunteers on April 15 had all breathed a new spirit into Dan. He was appalled by the cannonades directed at the Union flag over Sumter. Many of Tammany Hall's children were, like Dan, discovering themselves as a new breed named Union Democrats, men ready to fight for Lincoln's Union. There was a sort of consistency in their attitude. They had tolerated the blustering of the South, and its peculiar institutions, to keep the Union in existence. By seceding, the South had relieved them of any further tolerance toward it. Thomas Francis Meagher took only two days to decide that he must fight for the preservation of the Union that had given him and many other Irishmen political asylum. Meagher presented himself to the headquarters of the 69th New York Militia and promised to raise one hundred young Irishmen for the service of the Union. In this military intention, Meagher had the complete support of his wife, Elizabeth, and in years to come, when Meagher was a general, Elizabeth Meagher would become honorary colonel of one of his regiments, the 88th New York, which would style itself "Mrs. Meagher's Own."[18]

It is not hard to see why, in the spring of 1861, at loose ends and with a limit to options, Dan became sufficiently exhilarated by the great national and fraternal fervor to risk obscure death. For the moment, he had joined Colonel Abram Vosburg's 71st Battalion of the National Guard. But one day that April, when he and Captain William Wiley of Tammany Hall were in Lorenzo Delmonico's famous restaurant, at Broadway and Chambers Street, surrounded by men all talking about the war, someone suggested to Wiley that he should get up a company or regiment to aid in the defense of Washington. Sickles declared that if Wiley assembled such a unit, he would enlist as a private. Wiley said he had a better idea. "If you will command a regiment," he told Sickles, "I will raise, arm, and equip it."

In those war-naive days, men thought of a regiment of up to a thousand as a huge number of soldiers. They thought of a brigade, made up of three or, in some cases, five regiments, as a massive military entity. In their imaginings, the three brigades that made up a division seemed an absolute host of men; it had been considered so in the war against the Mexicans. Conflict had not yet educated Dan in the quantities of men who would be committed and lost, and in that spring a colonel seemed an exalted commander, a little below the Deity. Dan could be a colonel, but he had to move quickly, since Vosburg's unit was about to leave New York for the Washington area. Deadlines appealed to Dan, and Wiley and he were able to get quick authorization from Republican governor Edwin Morgan to raise their regiment. The New York Union Defense

Committee seeded the endeavors of Sickles and Wiley with $500, and handbills advertising the new regiment were posted around New York.

Within a fortnight, Wiley and Sickles had raised a regiment of eight companies. Dan was back to working feverishly, which he so loved to do. He was able to recruit through Wiley those robust New Yorkers who made up the muscle of Tammany Hall, the men who, from the waterfront to sanitation to other minor municipal work, owed their initial employment to Dan, Captain Wiley, or their friends. Charles Graham was able to supply four hundred Brooklyn Navy Yard workers. Former assemblyman Dennis Meehan brought in a hundred Tammany men from around the city. Dan looked for some of his officers among the Democratic press of New York, and one of these journalists, the French-born Régis de Trobriand, noted that during the lead-up to Sumter, Dan had been among the conciliatory and the moderate, "but when the sword was drawn, he was one of those most ready to throw away the scabbard." De Trobriand argued that it was specifically because Dan felt the South had put the Democrats of the North in such a false position that he felt duty bound, more perhaps than others, "to carry on war *à outrance*, unto the complete triumph of the national government."[19]

War *à outrance* made the domestic idyll Teresa wanted and George Sickles had suggested to his son more unlikely than ever. And in his period of raising men for the Union, it is interesting that Dan did not appeal to Teresa on the recruiting platform as an incarnation of Northern womanhood, or ask her to attend, as Meagher had asked his wife to do. He failed to ask her to appear before the public as an exemplar of the hearths for which the men of the Union would be fighting.

Governor Morgan was pleased that Dan and Wiley had been able to recruit an entire regiment in a few weeks, but then they received an order from him to raise an entire brigade. Since Dan was a semiofficial colonel of militia at the moment, he might become a brigadier general. Finding four thousand men in five regiments, then, became his most urgent summer work. He lodged downtown to attend to this heady business, and, typically, was distracted only by concern that the climactic battle of the season would be fought without any participation from him and his boys. In May he had seen the 69th New York and Thomas Francis Meagher march to glorious acclaim down Broadway to the steamers at the Battery. The Irish were already in the forts around Washington.

Dan's brigade was raised not only in New York but also, as a result of recruiting excursions, in the country towns of upstate New York, notably Dunkirk and Jamestown, in Boston, in near New Jersey, and in far Pittsburgh. He named his brigade the Excelsior, to honor the Latin motto of the State of New York, a state he had once declared worth seceding from. Among his soldiers one could find old Dutch and Anglo-Saxon names—Degroot, Dutcher, Graham, Arbuthnot, Hollywood, Dalgliesh—as well as Tammany's plenteous Irish—Tracey, Nugent, Carney, Carrigan, Hanrahan, McGovern, Driscoll—and notable numbers of Germans—Grecheneck, Grossinger, Berger, Holst. As the men came in, Wiley and Dan's exuberant headquarters continued to be eccentrically located at Delmonico's, but the problems of supplying men with food and shelter were prodigious. Dan's troops were billeted both in the state militia barracks near the Broadway Post Office Dan had once raided for political purposes and in less savory garrets, lofts, and walk-ups off Broadway.

Perhaps acknowledging his self-redeeming energy on behalf of the Union, a number of chaplains presented themselves to serve with Dan's Excelsior Brigade. One was an urbane young man named Joseph Hopkins Twichell, of Connecticut, who had distinguished himself at Yale as an oarsman. Another was Dan's old school friend from NYU, the Reverend C. H. A. Bulkley, who had been at his side during part of the trial, and a third was a muscular Jesuit, Father Joseph O'Hagen.[20]

With more than three thousand men recruited by mid-May, Dan and Wiley were suddenly punished. Governor Morgan himself was at the time under a peculiar pressure from county officials, who were faced with the imperative to raise their own quota of men, and the Excelsior Brigade had cut into their capacity to do so. Morgan telegraphed Dan to disband all but eight of his forty companies. An astonished Dan saw this as a Republican plot. And the waiting men of the Excelsior, in the lofts and walk-ups he visited off Broadway, indicated that they did not want to be disbanded to return to Pittsburgh or Boston or upstate New York as rejected warriors.

Sickles now made an extraordinary decision, one as interesting from the point of view of ideology as of personality. While a congressman, he had been a defender of states' and even cities' rights. Obviously, Sumter had changed all that. The present emergency—and, the unkind would say, the desire for rank—drove him to a new vision.

He went again to Washington, but with the proposition of meeting that very different being Lincoln. A gulf of politics and nature divided him from the new President. For a start, the President was if anything a conscientious family man; some said a family-dominated and wife-dominated man. Whereas Dan had barely been home for a month. To Lincoln, his emotionally uncomfortable *domus*, including his difficult wife, Mary Todd Lincoln, constituted nonetheless a guide to a national order and a unit of the national fraternity, the great polity of America writ small. The reality of family was thus for President Lincoln not disconnected from the public man he was. Whereas Dan saw little connection between the public and the private.

A man re-creating himself as an acting brigadier general and with something to offer, Dan reached a Willard's full of officers in new blue uniforms and, through appointment, the White House. This was probably managed because of the Union's hunger for personnel, or there may have been an interest in rural Lincoln to see the great urban scalawag who had shot Key dead, just down there on the corner of Lafayette Square. To Dan, and to many other Easterners, Abraham Lincoln was a strange figure, a creature from the frontier, hewn—it seemed—out of the knotty wood of some primeval forest. He pretended to none of Dan's urban polish, but he proved genial and he heard Dan out. Dan's proposition was that since his men were responding to a federal emergency, the federal government should accept them directly, without state intervention, as United States volunteers. This was a heretical idea even for Lincoln. The raising of militias had always been a state matter, and it was peculiar that Lincoln should attempt to negate a proposition to the contrary from a Tammany Hall Hardshell lawyer.

According to what Dan later told his chaplain, Twichell, the Republican Lincoln saw the peril more quickly than Sickles did. "What will the governors say if I raise regiments without their having a hand in it?" he asked. Dan, never without a constitutional reference, urged Lincoln to consider the authority contained under the head of the Power to Raise Armies.

It was a confusing and frantic time for Lincoln, but he was attracted to the worldly little New Yorker who wanted to bring his men into action for the Union. Lincoln called in his Secretary of War, Simon Cameron (a man derisively called the Winnebago Chief because he was alleged to have cheated an Indian tribe in a supply contract). Lincoln and Cameron ordered that Dan keep his men together until they could be inducted by United States officers.[21]

Dan and Wiley both had reason to hope that would occur soon, since the War Department would then pick up the expense of the brigade. The bills already accumulating would take years to settle. Wiley had commandeered cooks for the brigade from among the chefs at Delmonico's, and, working in inadequate kitchens in side streets, they tried to turn out enough food for the men. The pressure on sanitation was enormous; many of the men lacked a change of clothing, or even soap and razors, and became so hairy and bedraggled that the citizenry were frightened of them. Drunkenness was common, since saloons abounded. But Dan made an arrangement with the owner of a bathhouse-cum-barbershop on Crosby Street, who agreed to bathe, shave, and cut the hair of the recruits for ten cents per man.

The state authorities in Albany were angry at Dan for going straight to Lincoln, and gave him notice to vacate the militia armory. He moved his men to the Fashion racetrack, near the present-day La Guardia Airport, where they lived in what tents Wiley had been able to find and in the stables and jockeys' changing rooms. He was next offered a more permanent campsite on Staten Island, near Fort Wadsworth, where he and his men could wait until the issue of mustering-in was settled.[22]

Even by the standards of politics, Dan found it a prodigiously expensive and time-absorbing operation to move three thousand men, their tents, and their cooking equipment from the racetrack, but he and Wiley attended to it with thorough energy and brotherly cooperation. The camp they found themselves in, as the weather warmed, was a low reedy stretch of shoreline facing east, toward Brooklyn, and south, toward the Atlantic. Dan called it Camp Scott. Here, as the summer of 1861 came on, Dan, with his usual resourcefulness, acquired from P. T. Barnum on credit a large circus tent to accommodate some of his men who still lacked canvas to sleep under. There were disadvantages to the location. This was malarial ground, and the dusk was full of the whine of mosquitoes. The men had a mere three hundred rifles, and companies took turns drilling.

Dan showed a daily enthusiasm for commanding and training his mass of young men, and did not fear being intimately bound to them as he feared being bound to women and their homely yearnings and habits of dependence. He was able to exercise strong command without evoking resentment, and the daily routine of reveille, roll call, morning and afternoon drill, surgeon's call, guard mounting, evening parade, and retreat was insisted upon. His men began to notice the beauties of this low shore, the lines of linden trees that divided farm from farm, the green fields at the verge of which their rows of white tents stood. Dan grew to like his camp and would later describe the scene as he remembered it: "the exquisite sunset scene in old Camp Scott, the long lines of Union blue in evening's dress parade, the ever welcome visits of friends."

The visiting friends did not include his wife and daughter. Some observers thought this was a case of Dan's having been given back an active life, one by which he might expiate the mess of 1859, of which he did not care to be reminded. Whereas Teresa was still stuck there, tethered to the scandals like an ancient Greek maiden to a rock. As *Harper's Weekly* had earlier said of Dan, he could show "a resolution which amounted to sternness." That degree of resolution meant that Teresa did not belong in the camp. She was not invited even on the national holiday. George Sickles belonged to this new landscape of promise, however, and often visited and undertook legal and business tasks relating to the Excelsior.[23]

Teresa spent that wartime July Fourth at Bloomingdale. Her father, his friend Mr. Tosticaldi, Mr. Phillips, and a young German gentleman came and remained all day. Teresa entertained them, she told her friend Florence, with walking, "seesawing on the whirligig, pitching, racing, riding." There was a fine display of fireworks over Bloomingdale in the evening, and then a bonfire. Teresa and her mother played an old game: "I slapped Ma (in fun) and she threw water on me." A water fight developed. "Mrs. Nesi [a visitor] and myself were drenched—the hall near my door very much like a small lake." Running to get away, Teresa had slipped near the room they called the Applewood Room, and fallen, and "as for my body it is a mass of black and blue spots."

In her fondness for animals, around that time she had acquired a new bulldog; she had to be content in large part with animal company. She had as well a black-and-tan terrier on order. "I am also to have two peacocks and a monkey, and what after that I do not know—not a 'baby' I promise you." It seemed she did not see Dan sufficiently for that. The war had claimed him.

Chevalier Wikoff had been down to see the new occupants of the White House himself, and during visits to Teresa, for whom he felt what seemed an avuncular affection, he told her about Mr. Lincoln's wife, something of a Tartar, fiery but amusing. Wikoff obviously appealed to Mary Todd Lincoln. Whereas Abraham Lincoln made a virtue out of his gawky, frontier ways, Mrs. Lincoln was somewhat embarrassed by her own unworldliness and looked to cosmopolitan gentlemen like the chevalier to remedy it. There was no question, in the minds of some of the White House staff, such as the President's secretaries John G. Nicolay, John Hay, and William O. Stoddard, that she was putting together a salon of disreputable fellows, whom she met and conversed with in the Blue Room at the White House. They considered Wikoff one of the disreputables.

Yet now, when Wikoff visited Teresa, he brought White House gossip. Teresa might have felt some sympathy for Mary Todd Lincoln, who was also socially vulnerable, but with Mrs. Lincoln it was because many Washington women considered her both unpolished and unconven-

tional. Her husband was afraid of her temperament and was always saying, "Now then, Mother." She was haunted by anxiety about her children's health, having already lost her second son, Eddie, when he was
less than four, to infantile tuberculosis.

Wikoff was always welcome at Bloomingdale, even when he reiterated for Teresa's delight his staple tales as well as his White House impressions. In modern times Wikoff's confessions might have earned him
a reputation as something of a stalker and made him the subject of court
injunctions to keep his distance. But the world had been engrossed by
the melodrama of his obsession for a young American woman named
Miss Jane Gamble, and the places, including the San Andrea prison in
Genoa, to which his dedication to her had led him. His courtship had
taken place between London and Paris, exotic locations for such yearn-
ing American hearts as that of Teresa Sickles and, indeed, that of Mary
Todd Lincoln, whose chief experience of life had been her Lexington,
Kentucky, childhood and her Springfield, Illinois, married life. Hundreds of thousands of Mary Todd Lincolns had similarly found Wikoff's
story engrossing.

One can well imagine the operatic light in which Mrs. Lincoln and
Mrs. Sickles cast the prison and the malign British consul who had persuaded his beloved to give evidence designed to consign Wikoff there.

These were the tales with which the lonely Mrs. Sickles and out-of-
her-depth Mrs. Lincoln were diverted by the chevalier. Of course, they
had both read the book and knew that after fifteen months, Wikoff
emerged, sadder and enriched by wisdom, but there was nothing like
hearing these anecdotes from the mouth of the author. And if such tales
did not suffice, whom did he not know in Europe? Why, King Louis
Phillippe, Lamartine the poet-president, Thiers, Chateaubriand, Victor
Hugo, Louis Napoleon, and Lord Palmerston, all of them his intimates.[24] Dan, of course, could have diverted his wife with enriching
stories of remarkable Americans and even of love, but his anecdotal ex-
pansiveness did not for the moment extend to her.

When he went to see Lincoln a second time, the President cheerfully
remarked, "Your camp has gone all to pieces, I hear." Dan claimed

otherwise. His men wanted to come south; that was all. Lincoln said that if Dan could hold the men together for just a few days, a mustering officer would come "and take you all in out of the cold."

It was mid-July before the quarrel between Washington and Albany over Sickles's men was resolved. Two regular army officers delighted Dan when they arrived at Camp Scott, where they were made strenuously welcome by the men now mustered in as United States volunteers. Dan's rank as a provisional general of brigade, subject to confirmation by the Senate, was further bolstered by this event. The cry "On to Richmond!" resonated over the reed beds and linden trees of Camp Scott. The Excelsior men believed they would be just in time. The daily papers reported how Union troops were harrying General Pierre Beauregard's Rebels south of Centreville, Virginia.

But there was now an economic impediment to their becoming warriors. The total debt of the Excelsior Brigade, to the point where the federal government took it over was, in Wiley's estimate, $283,000, and writs were beginning to pour in from providers, outfitters, produce merchants. A number of merchants secured judgments against Dan, and he was not permitted to leave New York until they were paid. But he was an expert in debt management. With some confidence, he and Wiley went into conference with these creditors; because the members were officially United States volunteers, the brigade's debts were to be handled in part by the War Department. But as late as May 1, 1862, a Chamber Street merchant was still urging Sickles to approach the Secretary of War about paying his "fair and reasonable" bill.

The creditors were helped to accommodate Dan by the events of July 21, when the first, disastrous battle of Bull Run was fought and lost. Edwin Stanton, who would be Secretary of War before the year was out, wrote from Washington, "The capture of Washington now seems to be inevitable—during the whole of Monday and Tuesday it might have been taken without any resistance. The rout, overthrow, and utter demoralization of the whole army is complete."[25]

The day after the battle, the Excelsior Brigade broke camp, caught ferries to Manhattan, and got on the train for Washington. If Teresa had looked forward to a time when the preparation of the Excelsior was complete and Dan might have some free time, this whirlwind departure put paid to it. Wiley was, by some accounts, left disgruntled. He was quoted as declaring, "So he [Sickles] marched off with three regiments, and paraded them before Lincoln, and said he had done all this out of his own pocket. There were piles of judgments against him in the offices. He had no more to do with the brigade than the receiving of the recruits." It would be fifteen months before Wiley could get a final settlement with the creditors, which he did by calling a meeting at the Astor House and again referring the bills to the Secretary of War. "I left him on account of it," Wiley was ultimately reported as saying, "denounced him then, and have done so since."[26]

Camped in meadows outside Washington, General Sickles's men were part of the Third Army Corps, and their divisional commander was a brisk, profane professional named Joe Hooker. Dan observed that Hooker had the customary West Point graduate's attitude toward civilian and, indeed, political generals, an attitude no doubt compounded by what Hooker knew of Dan's notorious murder trial. Yet Dan was not easily depressed by contrary opinion and would always remember this early war period as a golden time. It was delightful to be a leader, and he reflected to his men his joyous sense of being a newborn warrior, while they reflected back their combined sense of their identities as members of the legions of righteousness. He was so happy at the way his men settled down in their encampments that he speculated that had they been available for Bull Run, they might have turned the tide. He was becoming a serious student of military affairs, and in his papers are found pages of memoranda that indicate it. He made notes, for example, that a red over a white light displayed at night meant that friendly troops had occupied this place, whereas a white over a red meant "Prepare to disembark," and a red over a green meant "Move forward to protect the landing." He noted that the signal flags for B and O signified "These batteries are ours!" while F, L, and R signaled "Fire a little to the right of your last shot." The signal numbers for Hooker's headquarters were 1142; for his own, 1132; for the federal balloon that operated in the area, 231.[27]

Washington, which he regularly visited from the encampment, was in some ways the Washington he had known. The West End still threatened to become "one vast slough of impassable mud." The Capitol was still unfinished, with no goddess of liberty atop it—only scaffolding and a crane for lifting building materials. Tiber Creek, which, it had been planned, would be pumped to the top of the Capitol and fall in a cascade from near the dome, "stretched," in the words of one Washingtonian, "in ignominious stagnation across the city, oozing at last through green scum and slime into a still more ignominious canal, the receptacle of all abominations, the pest breeder and disgrace of the city." Especially so now that the city was crammed with soldiers and their sanitary needs. There were forts on every hilltop. Shed hospitals and camps covered acres in every suburb. Soldiers were entrenched at every gateway. Churches, museums, and private mansions were filled with officers—as they would soon be with the wounded and dying of both armies. Bull Run had been merely a foretaste, and even now the streets were full of ambulances, and people hurried by to escape the noise of groans and screams.[28]

Wikoff was eager to introduce his friend Dan to the new family in the White House, whom Wikoff now knew well, particularly the President's wife. Mary Todd Lincoln was, at the time Dan first met her, a volatile woman engaged with varying levels of daring in redecorating the White House. One of Mr. Lincoln's secretaries named Mary Todd Lincoln the Hell-cat. She had, said another, extreme mood swings, one day being considerate, kindly, generous, hopeful, on another unreasonable, irritable, despondent. She possessed the instability that characterized the child she actually was—one who had felt orphaned by the early death of a mother and by a father's marriage to a cold stepmother. She was hungry for the world's approbation, and, like Teresa, she did not have it.

For one thing, she had alienated the capital by failing to buy the refurbishing materials from Washington merchants. She was in a city where she needed tolerant friends when she did absurd things, but her temperament ensured that she did not always have them. When, later in the year, Mr. Lincoln became appalled at the amount she was spending in New York on lamps, carpets, wall hangings, and crystal, she strenuously undertook to economize by selling off old White House furniture. She also sacked White House staff to meet the bills. Driven by a sudden panic over "poverty to come" after the presidency, she decided at one time, in extreme depression, to sell the manure from the executive stables. Throughout 1861, she involved herself in shady financial practices with John Watt, her chief gardener, who controlled the payroll of the outside staff. He padded his expense account and, by kicking back funds to Mary Todd Lincoln, turned her into a co-conspirator. Watt also bought the provisions for the White House, so it was easy for him to sign vouchers for nonexistent purchases, especially after he and the First Lady got away with drawing an inflated $1,000 invoice for buying seeds, fruit trees, and bushes from a Philadelphia nursery. In reality the purchase had cost much less, and Mrs. Lincoln Todd used the spare money to pay for further purchasing expeditions to New York.

Even Mrs. Lincoln's dresses attracted contrary comment. She dressed egregiously—her fashion exemplar was the Empress Eugénie of France—and was as skillful as modern notables are at finding donors for her dresses. In this area as well she built up bills that made Lincoln flinch, but he seemed to avoid more than occasional contrary comment.

To add to her perceived and real improprieties, the gardener Watt was also a Southern sympathizer, as many said the First Lady was. Indeed, a number of her Kentucky brothers and half brothers were fighting for the Confederacy, and her half sister, Emilie, had married a Rebel officer named Helm, who would become a Confederate general.

Such were the domestic realities of the Lincoln White House about the time Dan first became a familiar of Mary Todd's and Abraham's. Mary Todd would receive her visitors on her salon evenings in the oval

Blue Room on the ground floor, and to this chamber, undergoing redecoration, Wikoff took General Sickles to meet her. Mary Todd Lincoln served as a good example of Dan's capacity for social charm. She was at once enchanted by his urbane manner and conversation, his exemplary clothing, his well-tended features, and the possibility of danger that he bespoke. To a woman from Kentucky, the idea of what he had done to his wife's lover was not so great an impediment to friendship—Kentuckians were accustomed to exacting their own justice. And Lincoln was complacent—many believed too much so—about the people Mrs. Lincoln invited to her *soirées*, so long as they made her happy.

Dan noticed early in his conversations with Mrs. Lincoln that she had quite an interest in spiritualism, séances, and spirit-rapping. This was not considered an abnormal enthusiasm for that era. It was surmised that she had had her first experience of these practices through the voodoo of the household slaves in Kentucky, where she grew up. Then, in Illinois, there had been a string of traveling white prophets, telling the future and getting in touch with the dead from the stage of the Masonic Hall. As well, Henry Wikoff had enchanted her with a full-blooded account of being hypnotized by a seer in Romania, and of the visions he had beheld as a result. This special interest and obsession of Mrs. Lincoln's would come to be an embarrassment to the President and to have a significance for Dan Sickles.

Lincoln himself would sometimes look in on the Blue Room *soirées*, entering the parlors of his house somewhat like a lost soul. He made the acquaintance again of General Sickles and took further interest in him and his brigade. The Reverend Joseph Twichell would remember as a golden day the one that summer when the Excelsior marched past the White House to be reviewed by the President and General Sickles.[29]

Dan and the brigade spent nearly three months, July to October, near Washington, but in that time he did not invite his wife to visit him, even though she could easily have been accommodated at Willard's. In the meantime, his relationship with the Lincolns continued well, and his relationship with his divisional commander, General Joe Hooker, poorly. And he had still not been confirmed in the rank of brigadier general. In that regard, he went to see Stanton, who was now working down the street from the White House as special counsel to Secretary of War Simon Cameron, and would soon replace him. Dan also asked Wikoff to have his old enemy James Gordon Bennett of the *New York Herald* write a piece on what a suitable fellow he was for confirmation. Dan knew Wikoff was already passing positive news on Mary Todd Lincoln to the *Herald*, for which the Lincolns were most grateful.

In October, still under veteran Joe Hooker, Dan and his brigade were sent down to the lower Potomac, in Maryland opposite Acquia Creek, Virginia, and on the low shore of the river. Dan got into trouble for having too many ambulance wagons in his line of march, but Hooker resented above all the way Dan could ride up to Washington to see the First Lady. His demeanor always improved when Dan craftily told him that "the President spoke warmly and enthusiastically of you." The presence of Hooker and Dan's troops on the lower Potomac made it less possible for the Confederates to attempt a blockade of the S-bent river between Charles County and Rock Point. But it was a tedious and muddy life down there.

Laura, now aged seven, wrote to her father in late October, somewhat in the adoring mode Teresa herself generally adopted. Teresa may, in fact, have influenced the child's handwriting, which was firm, intelligent, and determined. "I hope dear Papa that you will write just as often as you can, since we are all so happy when your letters are received." The child said that he would be amused by the new dog, Jack; he was so playful and funny, and could not be spared to be sent to Dan. As for the aged dog Nero, said Laura, they hadn't seen him for five days and feared he had died. The child recorded that she and her mama and grandmama had spent the day with Grandma Sickles on Wednesday; Mrs. Sickles and George were very fond grandparents. "How very fine your Soldiers and Horses must appear and how glad I should be to see them. Will you let us all come to see you one of these days? Grandma Sickles says she intends to make you a visit. Oh how happy we shall be if you can come to us at Xmas! Accept an affectionate embrace and 10,000 kisses dear good Papa from your Laura."

His mother, Susan Marsh Sickles, had sent a locket with her miniature in it to serve as his protection and shield, and wished that he would write to his father and persuade him to take both of them to visit him in Washington. Teresa had been amply forgiven by that good Christian and loyal mother Susan Sickles, in part because of grandparental concern for Laura, and in part because of Teresa's own character. "Teresa tells me you have not the shirts, I mean the nightshirts I made for you," his mother accused him. "I think you had better send for them. They will be so warm for the winter."[30]

About the only contacts with the enemy Dan's men experienced were shouted exchanges of insults when on picket duty on the riverbank. Early in November, Hooker's division was ordered a considerable distance upriver nearer to Washington, to an area named Budds Ferry. Dan martially called his brigade's area Camp Stanton, but the men thought they were having less and less to do with the war. To enable New York State to meet its quota, Dan's 1st, 2nd, 3rd, 4th, and 5th United States Volunteers were handed back to Governor Morgan and renamed by the War Department the 70th, 71st, 72nd, 73rd, and 74th New York Regiments.[31]

Dan's camp was enlivened that month by the arrival of the federal balloonist Professor Lowe, aboard a naval tug on which sat his balloon and all its paraphernalia. Dan was absolutely enchanted with this apparatus, and so stimulated that one evening he himself took off in the huge machine with the portrait of George Washington on its side, and observed the mass of enemy campfires on the south bank of the river around Dumfries and Occoquan. In following days he took a number of other flights, and was particularly pleased when the Rebels fruitlessly fired at the craft, having become overexcited at seeing his general's epaulettes through telescopes.[32]

It was cold and misty on this stretch of the Potomac when Dan's friend Edwin Stanton was appointed Secretary of War, replacing Cameron. Dan knew better than most how to handle Stanton's brusqueness, and hoped for good things from it. But he was nervous enough about his coming confirmation to approach his friend Wikoff.

> *My Dear Wikoff:*
> *What is the news? Of course I am exceedingly anxious to know what the Senate is doing. . . . Did Mrs. L. [Lincoln] think of the senators? Remember me to her very cordially.*

As for the soldiers he commanded, Dan assured the chevalier that the Excelsior definitely wanted him for their general. Except for a fraction of his 3rd Regiment, "there is the *sharpest, possible solicitude* from my confirmation, a feeling that is shared by the [Naval] Squadron in the river near me. When the news comes their bunting will be all out for a holiday & my camps will ring with huzzas."

But he was uneasily aware of Republican newspapers that suggested that the troops raised by him and other Democrats would march over to Jefferson Davis in the first battle in which they were engaged. There were certainly senators who agreed with this proposition. He had done his homework and knew, for instance, that the abolitionist Senator Henry Wilson of Massachusetts would probably oppose him because he thought Dan occupied himself and his soldiers in hunting for runaway slaves in Maryland, whereas Senators Kennedy and Pearce of Maryland would probably vote against him because he refused to send his men Negro-catching. To hell with the slaveholders, was his attitude. He agreed with the sentiments of Hooker. "I am a brigadier general of United States Volunteers," Joe Hooker complained about the sullen farmers, the border secessionists whose land surrounded his camp, and who came looking for their contraband slaves, "and no nigger catcher." Dan Sickles's own dislike of slave-owning, pro-secessionist Marylanders made them less willing to supply produce and comforts to the camp. So be it! These days he had no time for the institution or its participants, on either side of the Potomac.

He had Wikoff inquire of Stanton whether Stanton would give him a chance at some action. "My men have been looking at the enemy and living in the mud for three months. I cannot endure it much longer."[33] As, on the Potomac, Dan yearned for validation and for action, in New York Teresa awaited *her* validation, the other form of confirmation which only Dan could give her, perhaps in the form of an invitation to Washington. One day at the general's side would restore her and bring social benefits to Laura. In her rustic lassitude in Bloomingdale, Teresa must have half envied her former Washington friend and hostess Rose O'Neal Greenhow, as a woman who, though considered a traitor by some, had at least had an effect upon events. Even before the war, Mrs. Greenhow had been a Southern secret agent, to the extent of being an intelligence gatherer for an officer named Colonel Thomas Jordan, who was preparing a Southern intelligence network before the conflict began. It was apparent now why, unlike many Southerners such as Mrs. Clay, who had in the last months before the war come to specialize in cutting Northerners dead, Rose had consorted with so many Northern friends. She was believed to be the lover of the antislavery Senator Wilson of Massachusetts (the same man Dan feared would not vote for him), and certainly had the good senator on a string. Early in the war, Colonel Keyes, General Scott's military secretary, was cultivated by Rose Greenhow, as was Senator Joseph Lane of Oregon, and from the very start of the conflict, she used a Southern cipher to communicate intelligence to Colonel Jordan, now General Beauregard's chief of staff.

At the time of Rose Greenhow's arrest, she had been under suspicion by the federal authorities for some time, and General George McClellan had complained, "She knows my plans better than Lincoln or the Cabinet and has four times compelled me to change them." After the Confederate success at Bull Run, she received an official letter of thanks from General Beauregard for her crucial contribution to the Rebel victory. She would later boast of having sent to Richmond the Senate Military Committee's map of the Union Army's proposed route into the South, and her arrest on August 23, 1861, had been due to the capture of a letter of hers with a haul of other papers and maps at Fairfax County Courthouse after a Confederate retreat. Greenhow was detained at the same time as Senator William Gwinn, who had also been something of a recruiting agent on behalf of Southern intelligence, and, after a period of house arrest, was placed with her nine-year-old daughter in the Old Capital Prison. As Teresa waited unregarded in Bloomingdale, Rose Greenhow was a heroine to many and an impressive woman to all, and was now engaged in her much-publicized and defiant ten-month stint in prison. It would enhance her legend but begin to erode her famous beauty. In the end, the government could think of nothing other to do with her than to send her south under a parole. Much later, having visited Europe on a mission for the Confederacy, she would drown when trying to run the Yankee blockade of the South.[34]

To Teresa, all Dan's needs seemed to be encompassed for the moment entirely in his desire for a general's star. And though Wikoff was still a friend and helper in that regard, he was suddenly of less use to Sickles. For Wikoff had embarrassed the Lincolns and was in trouble with the legislators. Late the previous year, James Bennett had been able to publish in the *Herald* embargoed extracts from a speech Abraham Lincoln intended to give before Congress. The House Judiciary Committee gathered evidence that Wikoff had filed segments of the purloined presidential speech at the telegraph office in Washington for transmission to the *Herald*. The committee members summoned him to appear before them on February 10, and Wikoff asked General Dan Sickles to come from Budds Ferry and appear as his legal counsel.

He was also less officially representing the White House, since many suspected Wikoff had acquired the speech by way of the President's wife. Sickles was known to be so popular with Mrs. Lincoln that somehow his appointment as counsel confirmed, in the minds of many, that there was a White House clique around Mrs. Lincoln who would close ranks and protect her from the disgrace some were only too willing to visit on her. Appearing before the committee in the Capitol, Wikoff refused to name his source. He was, he said, "under an obligation of strict secrecy." So the sergeant-at-arms of the Congress was ordered to arrest him and detain him in the Old Capital Prison with the Confederate spies—to many of whom, of course, he was an old friend. Over the next day, as one journalist described it, Sickles "vibrated" between Wikoff's place of imprisonment, the White House, and the house of Mrs. Lincoln's chief gardener, John Watt. Sickles was stitching a deal that was meant to save Mrs. Lincoln. Then he himself was summoned as a witness, disclaimed any knowledge of the source, and was threatened with imprisonment. But he had already arranged that all blame would go elsewhere. He suggested that the Judiciary Committee summon Watt, the White House gardener.

Mr. Watt testified that he had seen the document on the President's desk, had perused it, remembered it—for he claimed to have an extraordinary memory—and recounted it to Wikoff the next day, word for word. Nobody believed his story, and everyone believed he had been levered by Dan into making this preposterous claim so that blame could be deflected from the President's wife.

The hearing had reached an embarrassing stage for Mr. Lincoln, who wrote to the members of the committee and asked them not to bring any further disgrace on him. Wikoff was instantly released. Mary had always been loyal to Watt, even though one of his gardeners sported the blue cockade of the Confederacy while he tended to the White House vegetables. But during his visits to her during the committee hearings, Dan had persuaded her to give him up. With the First Lady's help, Dan gathered evidence of Watt's frauds and used them to intimidate him and offer him a choice of prison or the army. He took the latter, lost his job, and, despite his Southern sympathies, was made to enlist in the Union Army.[35]

One upshot of all this was that Wikoff was no longer as welcome at the White House—this was probably Lincoln's rather than Mary's desire—though Dan Sickles was, if anything, closer to both of them. Lincoln and his wife could not, however, directly vote for his confirmation, and many senators so disliked Mrs. Lincoln that Dan's saving of her could hurt him with the men who would either confirm or deny his rank as a general officer.

Fixing the presidential speech crisis was the sort of work Dan was excited by, but back at Budds Ferry he was full of a restless energy that the regimen of daily parades and drills could not satisfy. Dan went across the river one night in a boat supplied by the naval squadron to land on the opposing shore and observe the enemy. "Although myself rather near-sighted, I soon became sufficiently accustomed to the darkness to distinguish groups of men. . . . They did not seem to be fulfilling the ordinary duty of pickets." Perhaps as a result of this initial probe, Dan was at last asked by Hooker's command to lead a thousand-man reconnaissance in force across the river. Having made the crossing by dark in a flotilla of Union boats, Dan found it possible to set off inland. Near Stafford Courthouse, as day broke, the thousand-man force ran into an outpost of James Longstreet's corps—Dan would often be paired with General Longstreet in the future—and heard the racket of an exchange of angry shots. Two of Dan's scouts rushed back up the road to tell him that he was up against two regiments, but he ordered a continued advance. "A dense column of smoke was seen," he would report, "and it was soon learned that the enemy in retreating through the town had set fire to some buildings which contained their stores." Satisfied with his foray, Dan retreated back to the river. Private Alexander Christ of Company F of the 70th New York was the only man wounded, "and the poor fellow had a hard time in the improvised ambulance over the rough roads to the landing," and—like most wounded NCOs and privates—a hard life ahead. Dan wrote an interesting comment on the effect of this first skirmish upon him. "This was the first time that I or any of my men had been under fire. . . . I was surprised that I'd taken it so coolly. Mind you, I do not say this boastingly, but simply as a man reviewing his sensations under certain conditions." He was well on his way to becoming what a small proportion of soldiers became, to becoming what Hooker already was: a lover of war as the highest state of malehood, as a measure of himself and his young men.[36]

In late winter, Camp Stanton, to which Dan always returned from his adventures into Virginia, his Washington trial, his visits to the White House, had been reduced by downfalls of rain to mud. It requires little imagination to foresee the civilized services Teresa could have rendered such a camp: her irrepressible jolliness at sharing the general's tent, with its board floor; her willingness to emerge at dawn like an Italian-American version of Columbia in a shawl, taking coffee through the Potomac miasmas to the men. Other officers would frequently employ their wives in such roles throughout the war—Libby Meagher was, in the inactive winters, to be found in Virginia, at Brigadier General Meagher's side. Of course, no shred of compounding scandal attended Mrs. Meagher. But it is unlikely that the men of the Excelsior Brigade, in their quagmire encampment on the Potomac, would have been mortified to see Teresa walking the duckboards, her skirts lifted to avoid the mud. If ever the Excelsior needed Teresa, it was in the ennui of January and early February of 1862.

On February 5, 1862, Mary Todd Lincoln had organized an extraordinary night at the White House—the highest night of her career as First Lady. Dan, invited perhaps as reward for his discreet services in regard to the leaked speech, found that he was one of five hundred invited to the all-night dinner. Mary and Abraham Lincoln received guests in the East Room while the Marine Band played in the hall. At midnight the doors of the dining room swung open on a magnificent buffet. Dinner was served until three, and even duty-bound generals like Dan did not leave until daybreak. The only cloud on Mrs. Lincoln's horizon that splendid night was that upstairs her son Willy, eleven years old, was suffering from a high fever. He did not recover from it in coming days; it became more acute, and Willy died on February 20, the second child Mary had lost. Willy was almost certainly a victim of the sewage swamp behind the White House, the evil canal and the polluted stream derisively named the Tiber. At that time, too, the military population of Washington was so great that the sewerage mains had burst and fouled the capital and the Potomac. People of the era were reticent about publishing causes of death, and some speculated that Willy had died of "bilious fever," whatever that might have been. Others thought malaria had taken him, though the symptoms appeared to be very like those of typhoid fever from fecal pollution of the water.

Whatever the cause of Willy's death, Mrs. Lincoln was unable to fit it into an endurable scheme of the world. General Sickles saw Willy, embalmed, laid out in the Green Room, a sprig of laurel on his breast. Dan gave his condolences to Mary Todd Lincoln, who did her best, as good Victorian women were meant to, to hide her grief. Nineteenth-century manuals of mourning advised her against excessive grief. Tears are not for the gaze of others, advised one such book. Mary behaved as well as she could but became ill herself, and her younger remaining son, Tad, took sick with exactly the same sort of fever as his brother. The superintendent of women nurses, an experienced army nurse named Rebecca Pommeroy, came to look after the desperately afflicted Lincoln family. Rebecca was thought of as a good example to Mary; she had lost her husband and three sons. Even so, Mary Lincoln's indiscreet but favorite dressmaker, a former slave named Elizabeth Keckley, claimed that one day Lincoln led his wife to the window, pointed to the Washington Lunatic Asylum, and said, "Mother, do you see that large white building on the hill yonder? Try to control your grief or it will drive you mad and we may have to send you there."

Tad recovered, but Mary, after three months of devastation, began again to talk to such friends as Dan about spiritualism and the chance of getting in contact with Willy and her other dead child, Eddie, through séances.[37]

In the meantime, on March 20, down the road from Washington to Budds Ferry had come a letter from the Adjutant General, dated March 20, 1862, and addressed to Dan.

*Sir:*

*The Senate having on the 17th instant negatived your appointment as Brigadier General of Volunteers, I am instructed by the Secretary of War to inform you that the President does hereby revoke it.*

Dan's sense of the man he was becoming had been so thoroughly invested in his chieftainship of his brigade that, in taking it from him, the

Senate had stolen his validity, and the decision induced in him a panicked energy to make them change their minds. It was a heady experience to watch his five thousand men in review, as he had that day outside the White House. The ordered passage of young males of all sizes and colorings, of varying handsomeness and nobility of spirit, but bonded by their shared oath, took a great time, and gratified and invigorated the soul. To imagine leading them in battle was a martial delight. Dan had been stripped of that possibility by malign men in the Senate. He was angered that when the news of the nonconfirmation came through, Hooker at once appointed Dan's former junior but a professional soldier, Colonel Nelson Taylor of the 72nd New York, to take command of the Excelsior Brigade. It seemed that Hooker considered Taylor a reasonable sort of fellow, but Dan was infuriated. He described Hooker's offending Special Order No. 132 as "illegal, unauthorized and unjust," and said he meant to protest to General McClellan. He got a curt note back from General Hooker that Special Order No. 132 had been issued advisedly.

Naturally, Dan wrote at once to the President, who, after all, owed him a favor. He asked to be allowed "to vindicate at the head of this column of brave and loyal men, the justice and fitness of your generous confidence." But the President could not directly impose his will upon the Senate, and Dan's friend Colonel Charles Graham of New York was himself reduced to resigning in protest over the Senate's decision.

As Sickles, lacking a command but imbued with determination, went back to Washington to fight his cause, General McClellan, who always seemed to covet ground other than that which he presently held, was able to get approval to engage his Army of the Potomac in a massive flanking movement. It would involve transporting his army by steamer down the Virginia coast to the Peninsula—a broad spit of land between the York and James Rivers, and close to Richmond, the seat of rebellion. On the Peninsula, all the east-west roads led into Richmond. If the Union Army suddenly turned up on them, the Rebel capital would be outflanked. To the shallow beaches of the Peninsula, along with the bulk of the Army of the Potomac, went General Thomas Francis Meagher

and his five-thousand-strong Irish Brigade. Meagher, confirmed a brigadier general by the Senate in early February, would be at the core of
events, whereas Dan had to fall back on an interview with Rose Greenhow's former admirer Senator Henry Wilson, chairman of the Military
Affairs Committee. He also sought a meeting with Senator Benjamin
Wade of the Committee on the Conduct of the War, who thought Lincoln too soft for his job, and with other powerful Republicans.

George Sickles admired what his son had accomplished with the
Excelsior and knew how hard Dan might take this unjust rebuff. He
was thus pleased to get a letter from his son that was "anything but de-
sponding." George was loyally gathering a petition condemning the
Senate's decision, and had sent it to, among others, Antonio Bagioli, who
signed it despite Dan's neglect of his daughter. Antonio was certainly indulgent and even doting toward Teresa and Laura, but thought that in
her loneliness his sad daughter was merely expiating her infidelities. On
top of Antonio's support, George was pleased to report, many New York
papers had published editorials condemning the Senate—the "dribbling
apes," as George called them. Horace Greeley of the *Tribune* had signed
a petition to have Dan renominated, and so had William Cullen Bry-
ant, the vituperative editor of the *Evening Post*, who had until now routinely mocked Dan. As for Susan Sickles, said George, she did not
sleep for fear of bloody dreams, and talked about the war endlessly and
nervously.[38]

On April 25, as the Excelsior Brigade was, without Dan, descending
from transports and making its way ashore and into the turpentine
forests of the Peninsula, the President renominated Sickles for a brigadier generalship and sent the documents for confirmation by the Senate.
While Dan waited, his brigade had its first shocking experience of war,
in front of the fortifications of Williamsburg. The rain and wind were
in the soldiers' faces as they defended a road, novices standing up and
blazing away at advancing Confederates, and then advancing and finding themselves cut down in bunches from the side by "a sharp, enfilad-
ing fire of shot and shell . . . from a field fortification opposite."

Their ammunition ran out, and in their sundry states of mind, from hollow to exultant, they filed behind artillery batteries to be resupplied. The losses of the Excelsior that day were 772, which must have shocked Dan. The unimaginable attrition had begun. But Dan was gratified to hear how well the fellows had performed, and the praises they had received from the corps commander, General Heintzelman. On the other hand, Chaplain Twichell would much later speak of wandering through the woods along the Lee's Mill road, and the tumult he felt, "an emotion that words could not describe," at seeing the dead faces of young men with whom he had held conversations in recent days. They lay where they had fallen, their faces smudged by powder and death, and he had suffered that universal human impulse which said that surely the dead were capable of some final movement.

Eight days later, on May 13, the Senate confirmed Dan's nomination by nineteen votes to eighteen. He was finally, by one vote, what he so dearly needed to be—a general. He found a berth at once on a transport steamer for the Peninsula, since it seemed the decisive battles of the war were about to be fought there. Colonel Graham also returned from the protest of resignation to take over his regiment under Dan. In the white-tented encampments outside Williamsburg, Dan enjoyed a resonating welcome from the men of the Excelsior at evening dress parade. As he walked down the line of the New York 71st, the regiment he had originally raised, the tears ran down his cheeks when he noted the vacant places. With a characteristic sense of ceremony and with a sudden emotion, he paused when he came to the regimental colors, took the flag in his hands, and pressed it to his lips.[39]

McClellan, too slowly for Abraham Lincoln, advanced his army up the Peninsula until men could climb trees and see the distant glitter of the dome of the Confederate Capitol in Richmond. The Excelsior occupied a series of not unpleasant camps on the south side of the Peninsula and below the Chickahominy River. Malaria and other fevers were ever present, however. Dan knew that his friend, former Representative Lawrence Branch, now a Confederate general, had tried to turn the Union flank on May 27 with a sudden attack at Hanover Courthouse. Another former colleague, General Roger Pryor, whose wife had so often visited the Stockton Mansion, now commanded a Confederate brigade in Longstreet's division, which was camped in the eastern suburbs of Richmond.

In describing Civil War campaigns of the kind in which Dan was involved and for whose resolution Teresa waited, a writer runs the risk of bamboozling the reader with geographic names and terminology that tell everything except the human feel of events. It is simplest, in the case of this campaign, to say that McClellan's army was lined out north and south of the Chickahominy River, the swampy artery that, in this sector, ran lengthwise down the Peninsula. Hooker's division and the Excelsior were in the far south, to the left of the line. On May 31, the Confederates, with their backs up against the edge of Richmond, tried to break McClellan's army in two. Hooker's division was in reserve the first day, and impatient Dan must have feared that his experience of large-scale battle, for which he had a keen desire and a furious curiosity, would be long delayed. Then, on the second day, most of Hooker's men marched up in the predawn to meet the Confederate Army along the Williamsburg Road, which ran into Richmond. The men of Dan's brigade rushed up breathless and lined themselves out, under the direction of Dan and their colonels, across heavily wooded fields, two regiments forward and the others in reserve. Dan and his young soldiers were exultant and edgy as they waited for sunrise and the outbreak of the contest. Whether they knew it or not, there was nobody behind them or the rest of Joe Hooker's division, and thus they were part of the vulnerable flank of the entire army. Because of the thick foliage between where Dan waited on his horse and the railway station of Fair Oaks, about a mile away, it was hard to see the enemy, but both sides, to their mutual amazement, immediately filled the humid morning air with a prodigious quantity of shot and shell. Stationed nearby, a young Union general Dan knew, Oliver Howard, a former theological student, had his right arm so badly damaged that it had to be amputated. Many humbler men paid more drastic prices still.[40]

As Dan now advanced his men across the fields under awful fire from the hidden enemy, the Confederates at last emerged into the open along the Williamsburg Road, sniffing for the advantage. A previously troublesome Excelsior regiment went screaming at them with bayonets. The enemy were driven back into the woods at eleven-thirty in the morning, and Colonel Hall's men captured prisoners and a horse-drawn omnibus. Previously in use as a Rebel ambulance, the vehicle declared itself to come from the Columbus Hotel, Richmond, Virginia. Sickles was tickled to see it and whimsically sent it on to his corps commander, old General Heintzelman, with a note that said perhaps the general might like to stay at the Columbus once Richmond fell. In his official report, Dan praised all five regiments, though he said two of them were concealed from his view by heavy forest. But it was apparent that they had driven the enemy from their position. "The dashing charge of the Second and Fourth Regiments, the cool and steady advance of the Third, occurred under my immediate observation and could not be surpassed." He had now survived his first large-scale battle, and found himself, after all and very conveniently, suited to such events.[41]

Many generals expected now McClellan would finish off his victory at Fair Oaks by pushing his army up through the Confederate fortifications to capture Richmond. Every soldier wanted it. The Excelsior's historian, Sergeant Henri le Fevre Brown, wrote, "At this time Richmond could have been taken with small loss." Union skirmishers, by climbing trees overlooking the Confederate breastworks, could see that they "had a very small force in them." Dan and others futilely urged General McClellan to authorize the final advance.

At another section of the Union line, Meagher had also had a great success repelling the Rebels. He and Sickles had both become habituated to the furious noise of shells and the audible thud of a ball striking human flesh and invading the body. They had also been presented with the war's new reality—unimagined levels of casualties produced by the variety of modern artillery shells and the latest in rifles and muskets. There was such a stench from rotting bodies in the woods, so many putrid and inhuman sights, that Dan saw men retching uncontrollably. He reported that in the hot and wet weather, the campground "was literally covered with maggots and for several days the only drinking water was ground water." With no safe drinking water, many wounded died of heat exhaustion on their way to the hospital, while many of the healthy were brought down by waterborne diseases. These realities unbalanced sundry other vain men who had previously thought themselves cut out for command. But neither the casualties nor the state of the earth daunted General Sickles. He fancied too that he did not suffer from the fatigue of battle.[42]

Inherent, however, in the question of the unexpected level of wounded was the less exciting question of who would care for them and for their wives and families. One of Dan's civilian committee members in New York, Henry Lieberman, wrote to Dan about the burial of one Lieutenant Haynes of the Excelsior. It took place "in the most plain and obscure manner," said Lieberman. If only he had known, he could have turned out two hundred men as escort, and so brought the comfort of military ceremony to the family. This was a task in which many a general wanted his wife to take an interest—the return of the fallen home for burial, and kindly attention to the bereaved. How wonderful if Mrs. Sickles would consent to take a hand, wrote Lieberman. As well, he urged "that it would be advantageous to both you and Mrs. Sickles if she should visit the sick and wounded of your Brigade, who are located in the city. I suggested it to her, but she prefers hearing from you first."

Clearly Teresa's instincts told her not to act without Dan's permission; she assumed that Dan was operating by a set of rules to which she lacked the key. And there is no record of Dan's response to this genial possibility, the idea of these outgoing and comforting tasks Teresa desired to undertake. For lack of an answer, Teresa wrote to Lieberman, "Upon reflection I think it advisable for me to defer the visit proposed for today, until I hear direct from the General. He will write to me if he desires me to call." Of course, there was no question that Teresa, already applying herself to calves, gravel, and rats with such expiatory energy, would have made an enthusiastic and generous nurse of the sick and wounded. There were, by the end of May 1862, some hundreds of Excelsior wounded to be visited at homes or hospitals in the city, and the numbers were not likely to decline. To read the letters parents and wives wrote to Sickles is to trace this aspect of the hidden ruin of the war, which Teresa might have helped assuage. "My son B. W. Hossey is still home and though the wound is still bad caused by the taking of pieces of bone, the chief issue is that he has had an attack of fever." Another letter to Dan prayed for information on Quartermaster William O'Kell of the 5th Regiment, "from whom his daughter has had no tidings since Williamsburg." The daughter might have been comforted by Teresa, who awaited only Dan's word. So too could have been the parents of one of Sickles's aides-de-camp, Lieutenant Palmer, who, while advancing into the woods late that morning of June 1, ran into a Rebel outpost and was killed by multiple gunshot wounds. His riddled body would be returned to inconsolable parents.[43]

Olive Devoe of the Union Home School had already written to Sickles, complaining that a number of little ones whose fathers were in the Excelsior Brigade were residents of the home and were there because their mothers rarely got a cent from their husbands. "Last evening application was made from Mrs. Tremain to place three little ones here that she feels greatly interested in. Their mother was placed on the 'Island' [the lunatic asylum at Blackwell's Island] for six months." Mrs. Tremain was the wife of Harry Tremain, one of Dan's favorite officers and his aide. How much more apposite might have been an intervention from the general's wife herself. Through the chaplains of his regiment, Dan raised money for Mrs. Devoe's Home School to help the children of Excelsior Brigade soldiers, living and dead, who had fetched up there. Why was Teresa not given the appropriate task of presenting it to Mrs. Devoe, and keeping in touch with her?[44]

The idea must have occurred to Dan, and so again he had his unrevealed but fixed reasons for not accepting it. Though, through the war, Dan had rehabilitated himself and found a way back to the White House, for whatever reason he blocked Teresa's path to redemption through the exercise of war-induced mercies. There were a number of reasons that even a strong-willed wife like Teresa would not have undertaken such missions without her husband's consent. First, the code of marriage at that time established the husband as ultimate authority on what his wife's public behavior should be. Even more than conventional spouses, Teresa would not have wanted to give Dan any grounds for displeasure or encourage him in any way to deny or renounce her or Laura. She would also have feared that without the authority of Dan, her presence among the wounded, the widowed, and the orphaned might have provoked the sort of taunts with which she had been made familiar through the scandals of 1859, and which she still feared.

In the three weeks of inaction following the battle of Fair Oaks, Dan got to know the young Comte de Paris, pretender to the throne of France; his brother the Duc de Chartres; and their uncle the Prince de Joinville, who had, like Lafayette in the Revolutionary War, offered their services to the Union and had been serving on McClellan's staff. But the attack and the end to all civility resumed on June 25, when, at eight-thirty in the morning, Joe Hooker sent Dan's brigade and one other through the woods toward Richmond. Dan's men this time were split on either side of the Williamsburg Road. They were slowed by encounters with pickets, by the problem of getting through a line of Union timber breastworks, and by the mire of White Oak Swamp. To Dan's mortification, the Excelsior fell behind the other brigade, that of Cuvier Grover. The 71st New York had not been engaged at Williamsburg or elsewhere, and now as it went forward in its long blue line, heads lowered and jaws set, it was struck from the side by a fury of fire from a brigade of North Carolinians. Fire from the flank raised, in most men, terror, a feeling of helplessness, of being abandoned by God and fortune. Someone in the regiment—Sickles would never learn who—shouted that they were outflanked and must retreat, and a good part of the 71st panicked and ran for the rear. Dan described it as "disgraceful confusion" and felt humiliated because Joe Hooker was watching. At least the rest of Dan's brigade were firing, advancing shoulder to shoulder, firing again, but an irrational order from McClellan broke off this engagement, named Oak Grove, at ten-thirty.

McClellan would not try for Richmond again. What possessed him now was the desire to save his army and, having moved all his men south of the Chickahominy River, to make it retreat to Harrison's Landing on the James River, a position from which his army could be extracted by federal steamers. The retreat to Harrison's Landing, begun at Oak Grove, would occupy seven days and involve seven battles. Dan's men, like the entire Union Army, retreated each night until the small hours, slept in that uncomfortable mode described in dispatches as "on their arms" until dawn, and rose to fight and retreat again. Dan had the capacity to function on little sleep, but it was a talent sorely tested in those last days of June. In Washington, Lincoln read the dispatches of this withdrawal, based in part on McClellan's huge overestimation of the Confederate strength, with bewilderment and depression. As for Dan and his men, at Gaines's Mill on June 27 they were still defending the Williamsburg Road, but were under orders to retreat back along it. On June 28 they had the job of breaking up their camp and setting a torch to all that could not be carried.[45]

On June 30, near the village of Glendale, Joe Hooker's and Sickles's men were again at the extreme left of the Union line. A parsonage lay off to Dan's left, and to the front of his lines of blue General Branch was improbably commanding the nearest Confederate brigade, on the far side of a little creek called Western Run. Branch had routed a Union brigade in the middle of the line, and more than a thousand of its men stampeded through Hooker's lines, actually shooting some of his men dead in their frenzy. The intimacy of that day's battle, Dan's foliage-limited view of what his men were engaged in, was indicated by the fact that Dan singled out for special mention in his report a private and a corporal who gave excellent service as vulnerable lookouts in trees.[46]

It was now the seventh day, July 1, and Dan's brigade occupied the lee of Malvern Hill, just above Harrison's Landing, and were in reserve until late in the day, when they were put to work near the low crest supporting some Union batteries. Just one of Dan's regiments, the 72nd New York, was sent forward in line against some Confederate troops firing from woods farther down the slope of Malvern Hill, and lost sixty-one men. Once again, as the day before, the Union was so successful in repulsing the Confederate attempt to gain the crest of shallow Malvern

Hill that many Union generals wanted to press the attack, but McClellan was fixed on retreat, and that night at Harrison's Landing steamers landed quantities of new provisions and prepared for the withdrawal of the army. Hooker's division had suffered 2,589 losses in the battles on the Peninsula. Chaplain Twichell regretted the absurd way the army had been managed—"I could not help a feeling of rebellion against the fate that forces the abandonment of ground that costs so much blood and was made so sacred." Twichell was convinced that something or somebody was wrong.

During the campaign on the Peninsula, Hooker got to like Dan better, and invited him frequently to visit his headquarters and share his whiskey at Harrison's Landing. The Irish-American hero Phil Kearny, and the Irishman of Irishmen Thomas Francis Meagher, also dropped by Hooker's tent for the purpose of drinking spirits. Casualties would ultimately take some toll on Meagher's imagination, but Dan was fortunate not to be burdened by that melancholy reality. And he was well liked by the majority of his officers and men. One Private Brannigan wrote to his sister, "General Sickles is the very man to treat his soldiers well, and returns in full their attachment to him."

Dan intended next to go to New York to recruit replacements. Many soldiers had also been struck with illness, and some of those, together with the wounded, had been left behind with volunteer surgeons to be overrun by the Confederates. Twichell later put the number of Dan's effectives in Harrison's Landing as low as two thousand men. There had been mayhem on the Peninsula.[47]

# VII

AFTER A FEW WEEKS IN THE CAMP AT
Harrison's Landing, Sickles returned to New York
on a steamer with General Meagher and one of
Meagher's favorite young officers, Lieutenant Em-
mett, who had been wounded. Dan and Meagher
were in a febrile state, flushed with a devout pride in
their men, the living and the numerous dead. But, arrived back home, Dan was warned even by his father
that the casualty lists from the Peninsula would be a
drag on New York recruiting. And if one of Dan's
purposes in visiting New York was to test the political environment for a possible return to Congress
that fall, he found that politics had become complicated. Mayor Fernando Wood and Dan's old friend
Sam Butterworth were now what the Republican
press called Copperheads, proponents of calling off
the war and letting the South go its way. Since Dan

was thoroughly in favor of that same war, consecrated by the blood of his young men, he could not countenance their position, but it was widely represented in New York and strongly held by some of the Irish. To them, Dan had become a Lincoln man, a crypto-Republican. So he could not expect the broad Democratic support he had once enjoyed.

Dan Sickles had in fact achieved a certain éclat with moderate Republicans. Horace Greeley of the *Tribune* had started a public subscription to present him with an ornamental sword. Greeley had been particularly impressed with a speech Dan gave at the Produce Exchange, where, praising the steady nerve of Abraham Lincoln, Dan confronted the talk of inevitable conscription. "A man may pass through New York, and unless he is told of it, he would not know that this country was at war. . . . In God's name, let the state of New York have it to say hereafter that she furnished her quota to the army without conscription— without resorting to a draft!"[1]

Dan took Chaplain Twichell and some of the brigade wounded to an enlistment rally at the 7th Regiment Armory, above Tompkins Market in Lower Manhattan. The audience was made up of the city's volunteer firemen, and Dan spoke to them for an hour and a half, but did not do much better than Meagher had in the same venue. It would be from the fire companies that much of the resistance to conscription would, in a year's time, derive.

There were sweeter experiences. In the Wintergarden Theatre a performance of *The Hunchback of Notre Dame* was given for the benefit of the Excelsior Brigade, and Dan, a thin, cock-sparrow figure with sword and general's sash, rose in his box to be applauded. Teresa was not at his side. Called on to speak, he told the crowd of the heavy-drinking prewar Southern legislators, sometimes so drunk in the House bars and committee rooms that they passed out on sofas in the anterooms. Others, however, fueled with fire, made it into the chamber and rose to threaten and spread rumors of coming secession at full throat. And the memory of these false former friends of his rose in him that night. He called the war a "Whiskey Rebellion," a rebellion fueled on spirits. "Whiskey everywhere—in the committee rooms, private houses, at a hundred saloons. There never was a state that seceded that did not secede on whiskey. The debate reeked with whiskey. The solemn resolves of statesmanship were taken by men whose brains were feverish from whiskey."[2]

Meanwhile, the Excelsior Brigade arrived at Alexandria near Washington in time to be engaged, almost as soon as it landed, at Bristoe Station, Virginia; and, though not put into the line, the men were under such heavy shellfire that by now barely more than fifteen hundred made up the brave Excelsior. The entire Hooker division was rested and was blessed that it, with Dan and the Excelsior as part of it, was thus not employed in heading off Lee's invasion of the North. For it ended in mid-September with the bloodiest day of all American history, at Antietam Creek, in rural western Maryland. There, for example, Meagher's Irishmen took 550 casualties in a quarter of an hour.

Dan was gratified to find himself caught in the updraft of Hooker's reputation as a fighter. Hooker was elevated to command of the Third Corps, and thus Sickles, his most successful brigade commander, inherited, with Hooker's blessing, the command of the division, its entire three brigades.[3] During much of the time the division was refitting and recuperating in Alexandria, Dan had time to attend Mary Lincoln's salon, what she called "my *beau monde* friends of the Blue Room." Wikoff had by this time been readmitted. Another member was Oliver Halsted, the wild but conversationally accomplished son of a rich New Jersey family. Mary wrote to him on one occasion, "I fancy 'the Blue Room' will look dreary this evening, so if you and the Gov. are disengaged, wander up and see us." The "Gov." referred to was Governor Newell of New Jersey. Another member was Nathaniel Willis, editor of the *Home Journal*, who tried to run counter to the general Washington opinion of Mrs. Lincoln by writing about her as the "Republican Queen in her White Palace." The Blue Room conversation concerned itself with "love, law, literature, war, rulers and thinkers of the time, courts and cabinets, the boudoir and salon, commerce, the church, Dickens and Thackeray."

Sometimes the silver-locked Massachusetts senator, Charles Sumner the abolitionist, would visit, even though he did not often go to receptions in anyone's house. This occasional blessing indicated that he too agreed that Mary Lincoln had surrounded herself with fascinating people. And at other times, though not routinely, women were admitted. "Gov." Newell brought his wife, Joanna, and Assistant Secretary of the Navy Fox, on one occasion, brought Virginia Fox. Not only was it Dan's policy that Mrs. Sickles never come, but her absence was not considered notable and would more likely have haunted Wikoff than Dan. And here again, and for whatever failures of hers and principles of Dan's, Teresa was becoming a woman who, when defined at all, was defined by absences—from the camp, from the capital, from social events at the White House.

Chiefly, it was the fellows and Mary Todd, and the fellows acquired nicknames: "Gov.," "Pet" for Halsted, "Chev" for Wikoff, "Cap" for Sickles, and for Mary herself, "La Reine."[4]

Though capable of manic gaiety, the Queen was barely out of mourning for Willy, and still marked by grief in all she said and did. She was not alone in seeking séances. Many prominent Washingtonians, under the pressure of the huge losses of the war and the considerable infant mortality of their times, had consulted clairvoyants—Mary Jane and Gideon Welles, Senator Ira Harris of New York (whom Dan had once tempted to sit in New York City on the matter of Central Park), and Mrs. James Gordon Bennett. Mary Todd Lincoln's dressmaker, Lizzy Keckley, was another influence on Mrs. Lincoln. Keckley's only son had been killed, and she was confident that through mediums, a Georgetown husband and wife team named the Lauries, she held conversations with her son's disembodied spirit. Earlier in the summer, while Dan Sickles's brigade was fighting on the Peninsula, Mary Lincoln's black carriage was often seen outside the Lauries' house. In fear for his wife's sanity, the President tolerated all this exorbitant behavior. Even so, the Lauries were not the only clairvoyants she had faith in. Lincoln even put up with his wife rushing these people to the White House to tell him about intended Confederate battle plans. For sometimes, when Willy or

Eddie could not be contacted, Mary was able to reach the spirits of deceased Union officers, who sent their advice via the medium to her and Lincoln. The President dared not take the comfort of spiritualism from her.[5]

Mary had, that same summer, consulted a specious medium who claimed to be an English peer, Lord Colchester, newly come across the Atlantic and down to Washington to spread his blessings. Mrs. Lincoln admitted him to the Red Room of the White House for a séance, and also asked him to hold a séance at the Soldiers' Home, where she and the President were staying for part of the summer. Though Willy spoke through Lord Colchester and Mrs. Lincoln was delighted, Dr. Joseph Henry of the Smithsonian claimed Colchester made tapping noises by an apparatus that reacted to the tensing of muscles even when others held his arms and hands. At another séance Colchester ran in the Red Room, an invited journalist had grabbed Colchester's arm and been punched for his trouble. Colchester felt that he had been exposed, though Mrs. Lincoln's belief in the process remained absolute. Not even a letter from Colchester implying that unless she gave him money to go to New York he "might have unpleasant things to say to her" frayed her belief. In the end, Lincoln himself told Colchester that if he was still in town by the following afternoon, he would end up in the Old Capital Prison.

Many surmised that Dan Sickles was driven to take part in séances with Mrs. Lincoln because of his guilt over Key; he wanted to contact the ghost and be given absolution. But this life, with its tests and glories, was adequate to Dan, and he attended with Mrs. Lincoln purely out of a duty of friendship, and possibly at Lincoln's request—to keep an eye on vulnerable Mary.

One of Mary's favorite mediums was diminutive Miss Nettie Colburn, whom the Lauries of Georgetown had introduced at a séance that included Mrs. Lincoln and Caleb B. Smith, the Secretary of the Interior. Nettie herself told of a séance she held in the "Red parlor" of the White House in December 1862. That night, as she entered her trance, sudden ghostly band music filled the room, and the heavy end of the piano in the corner crashed up and down in grotesque time to it. In the midst of this row, Mr. Lincoln appeared and received Nettie kindly. Whereupon she fell again into a trance, and from her mouth, in a male voice, emerged advice on the President's future, a foreshadowing of the Emancipation Proclamation. A gentleman present pointed to a full-length picture of Daniel Webster hanging on the wall. The voice that had emerged from Nettie, the man was sure, was that of Webster.

Dan managed to inject a spirit of skepticism into one of Nettie's sessions in the White House by persuading Mary to allow him to set a test for Nettie Colburn. He concealed himself behind the draperies of the room and asked Nettie, when she arrived, to name who was hiding there. This plot showed that Mrs. Lincoln may, at some level, have begun to doubt. So, while Dan stood hidden there, Mary Todd jovially challenged Nettie to come up with his name. Before Nettie could oblige, Lincoln came into the parlor and apologized for not being able to stay— he had a cabinet meeting, and his cab awaited. At that moment, claimed Nettie, a sudden silence fell upon the group, and she herself was entranced at once. An august male voice emerging from within her slight body counseled Lincoln to amend the condition of the freedmen, the liberated slaves herded together, half clad, on waste ground in the Washington winter. The President thanked the voice and left to go to his cabinet meeting, and Nettie turned her attention to the still-concealed Sickles. As she meditated, one of her familiar voices, Pinky, an Indian maiden, took over Nettie's body and said that the hidden person's name was Crooked Knife. This was considered by most of the company a close enough Indian rendition of the name Sickles. Sickles then revealed himself, and the session continued, various voices emerging from Nettie with news from the Great Beyond. As the guests departed at eleven o'clock, Sickles did the honor of host in Abraham Lincoln's absence, bidding the guests off at Mrs. Lincoln's side.[6]

New men were now coming to prominence, for McClellan, having won at Antietam, was considered remiss by Abraham Lincoln for not having captured Lee's army before it leached away south across the Potomac River. In the wake of what was a fierce disappointment about McClellan's failure, the President decided to review Sickles's division in camp near Fairfax Seminary in northern Virginia. With typical thoroughness, Dan set to work reorganizing his units, recalling most of the men absent on sick leave or in the convalescent camp. He had received a good many fresh recruits, and was glad to declare that his division numbered more than eight thousand infantry.

When the President visited, it occurred to Dan as a military impresario that he could flesh out the ceremony of greeting by borrowing "a few squadrons of cavalry," and then his command would be almost the same as that of General Scott when it had marched on Vera Cruz and captured Mexico City in the war of 1846–47. To greet the arrival of the President on the Virginia shore, Dan led a hundred mounted officers equipped as an escort, together with a regiment of infantry and a battery. "The President came down in his quiet way," said Dan. He was accompanied by only one general and a servant, and was surprised to see the horse that Dan had provided for him, caparisoned in the trappings of a general officer. He was equally intrigued to see himself surrounded by a staff appropriate, as Dan had learned by research, to an emperor at the head of a grand army. The President, as the artillery fired a salute, turned to Dan and exclaimed, "Sickles, I'm not going to take command of the army. What is all this for?" The escort proceeded on the march to Dan's camp a few miles off, and a good many Virginians gathered at the roadside. In an age before newspaper photographs, not one of them knew by sight Lincoln's face, and the President heard an old farmer saying to his neighbor as the column passed, "I guess from the looks of that tall chap and all this fuss, that the Yanks have captured a big prisoner." The President gave his creaky grin and called to the man, "That's so. I'm Jeff Davis!"

It was a study, said Dan, to see the men's faces during the inspection, as the President, an extremely clumsy horseman, rode from right to left of the line. "But," Dan stated in undisguised affection, "if a smile played on their lips, there was love in their eyes, as they rested on that sad, earnest, good face most of them beheld for the first and last time." At the end of the review, Dan invited Lincoln to speak to the men. The President was uneasy about that. "These men are going again to battle, where

I cannot be with them." But as he departed he called Sickles aside and said, "Tell them I think I have never seen a better show."[7]

Now known as the Second Division of Hooker's Third Corps, Dan's eight thousand were sent forward on November 1 into the Virginian hinterland along the Orange & Alexandria Railroad, where they rebuilt bridges, repaired tracks, and guarded the road south. Then they became part of the force that a new general, Ambrose Burnside, moved as far south as the broad Rappahannock, opposite the delightful town of Fredericksburg, nearly halfway between Washington and Richmond. Sickles's division was used in a support role on a crucial day of conflict there, and could again thank the gods of battle for that. For the Confederates had dug in on the heights above the town, called Marye's Heights, and would have one of their greatest successes of the war on December 13, repulsing the Union charge. The brigade of Dan's friend Meagher had a large and tragic part in the fight. "Of the 2,200 men I led into action the day before," Thomas Francis Meagher would write the next day of his Irishmen, "218 now appeared on the ground that morning."[8]

But Dan knew that adequate perils to life and limb awaited him, especially now, when the Union had been so roundly thrashed once more. In a war in which generals commanded troops on a limited front, unaided by such later tools of battle as telephone or wireless, Dan needed to stay close to the action and gain a visual sense of all that was happening in his divisional area. On top of that, he was required by gallantry to expose himself to fire. As one commentator said, generals "carried this aspect of Victorian culture to its counterproductive extreme." Over a hundred Union generals would die in battle.[9]

The Union troops occupied the hills by the Rappahannock, Stafford Heights, for the rest of the winter. Gradually, minds accustomed themselves to the awful losses of Fredericksburg, and there was room for socializing. Officers' wives visited—predictably, Teresa did not. Two of Dan's favorite associates in the camp were a Westphalian nobleman, Prince Felix Salm-Salm, and his fine-featured, vigorous little wife, Princess Salm-Salm, before marriage a circus or vaudeville performer, Agnes Jory of Vermont. Agnes had met the prince in 1862, when he came to

America to fight for the Union, and had been attracted by the old-world bashfulness of the German nobleman. They were married in St. Patrick's Church on Fifth Street, Washington, on August 30, 1862, and, against the tradition of her upbringing, she became a Catholic. A devoted and spirited spouse, she proved her fidelity to her marriage vows by following her prince through innumerable subsequent wars. In this war he commanded the 8th New York Infantry, and his princess from Vermont had been with him in the most advanced position in the Shenandoah Valley earlier in the year, had retreated to Chantilly with him, and had spent Christmas 1862 with him on the Rappahannock. Indeed, all that in a kinder world Teresa could have been for Dan, and all she might have been with a word, was incarnated in what the Princess Salm-Salm was to Prince Felix. She described herself as living with her husband in a hospital tent trimmed with woollen damask, and decorated with a carpet and sofa and a large mirror. By New Year's, she said, "there was scarcely the officer who had not his wife, mother, sister or cousin with him."

Though Dan was one of the officers in camp who lacked a publicly acknowledged woman visitor, an unsigned adoring yet intelligent letter later written by a lover of Dan's from Perth Amboy, New Jersey, indicated he was not celibate in the winter of 1862–63. The letter came from a woman to whom Dan had been attentive and generous in what was either her spinsterhood or widowhood. She addressed him as "My dearest general" and declared, as a result of some "inclosure" he had sent, "You are goodness itself. . . ." This unnamed gentlewoman would by the spring of 1864 have given birth to Dan's child—"our little Julia"—but despite this intimacy, she felt the same anxiety as Teresa about her inability to grasp his inner nature. "I would dearly like for you once in a long while to open the door of the inner sanctuary and give me—your dear one—a glimpse of all the wondrous things. . . . I am beginning to want so much to see you—Philosophy lasts weeks but when it comes to months, time drags." Her care in not signing the letter means that even though it now sits on microfilm in the Library of Congress, she has been able to evade our curiosity as to who she was, and what befell "our little

Julia." But since there is no further reference to the child Julia in the entirety of Dan's papers, it may be that the child died in infancy. For one thing can be said for Dan, on the basis of reading his correspondence: he tried as a matter of honor to make appropriate financial arrangements for friends and lovers, and a love child who survived would have claimed a space in the documents he left.

In any case, whatever his amorous arrangements that winter of 1862–63, his sociability lit up the camp in Stafford Heights. On New Year's Eve, in a huge tent decorated with flags, garlands, flowers, and Chinese lanterns, supper was laid for two hundred people, and Dan sent for Delmonico himself to come down from New York to supervise the banquet. The Princess Salm-Salm declared, "The wines and liquors were in correspondence with the rest, and no less, I suppose, the bill to be paid." The former journalist and French nobleman Colonel Régis de Trobriand agreed that Dan did things "in great style. . . . The collation which he had ordered from Washington was abundant in choice. The champagne and whiskey ran in streams. I wish I could add that they were used in moderation." De Trobriand's comments are a good guide to the way Sickles was estimated as a general. The Frenchman believed his divisional commander was one of the striking figures of the war, "gifted in a high degree with that multiplicity of faculties which had given rise to the saying that a Yankee is ready for anything. . . . Gay, prepossessing, *spirituel,* he rarely fails to make a good impression, even upon those who may be least prepossessed in his favor."[10]

By St. Patrick's Day, the army was still in its camp by the Rappahannock. It was now the duty of General Meagher's Irish Brigade to lay on the celebrations for the entire army, and Dan attended that festive day so associated with the Democratic Party. He found Meagher dressed in the manner of a member of the Irish gentry—in a tall white beaver hat, a blue swallowtail coat with brass buttons, white buckskin breeches, and black top boots. Dan joined Hooker and Meagher and other general officers at a prodigious lunch served under a marquee, and then attended the planned race meeting. In terms of entertainment, Thomas

Francis Meagher, escaped Irish felon, and Sickles, survivor of trial for murder, had a similar spaciousness.

Meagher had his wife, Libby Townsend, at his side as he acted as clerk of the course while three heats were run for the final of the Grand Irish Brigade Steeplechase. Seeing some of his men beneath the ramshackle grandstand, Meagher warned them to get out from beneath it or be crushed by four tons of major generals. The significant thing is that Dan was numbered in those four tons. For on January 26, Burnside had been removed as commander of the Army of the Potomac and, to the outrage of many temperance officers in the army, Hooker was put in his place. Sickles immediately rose in Hooker's wake, to become the commander of the Third Corps, with the rank of major general—the highest rank in the U.S. Army, and a triumph for any officer and his spouse and family. George Sickles was particularly ecstatic, and took proudly to addressing his son by letter as "Dear Major General." Dan had now joined the elevated ranks of seven army corps commanders, of whom only he and German-born Franz Sigel were not graduates of West Point. An equally competent brigade commander, Meagher, remained stuck at the one-star level. He had no profane comet such as Hooker to drag him upward in its tail.[11]

A considerable number of the senior officer corps were conscientious Christians and total abstainers, and to them, for various reasons, Hooker and Sickles were abominations. Nor did they like Hooker's chief of staff, Dan Butterfield, like Dan Sickles a dapper, racy New Yorker, only thirty-two years of age. Charles Francis Adams, Jr., grandson of John Quincy Adams, and a Union cavalry captain, saw Joe Hooker, Dan Sickles, and Dan Butterfield as a trio of depravity, "men of blemished character. During the winter when Hooker was in command, I can say from personal knowledge and experience that the headquarters of the Army of the Potomac was a place to which no self-respecting man would like to go, and no decent woman would go. It was a combination of bar-room and brothel." The nickname Devil Dan was in frequent use among Dan's enemies. No doubt not all the women who came to the headquarters were mothers and wives. But one wonders where Adams's pronouncement put such women as Libby Townsend, the Princess Salm-Salm, one of the most popular of the camp's social set, and sundry other officers' wives.

As unpopular as Hooker may have been with the more proper officers, he was popular with the ranks, immediately cashiering corrupt quartermasters, improving the food, cleaning up the camp and hospitals, and granting furloughs. An amnesty brought many soldiers who had overstayed their leave back to the camp. Among his other achievements, Hooker let General Butterfield reform the army's music. It is claimed that Butterfield was the originator of the bugle call named Taps. Butterfield also devised a system by which each corps had its own fighting patch, worn on the arms of the soldiers. For Dan's Third Corps, the patch was a black diamond.[12]

News came of another intended presidential visit, deep in Virginia by this bloody river. Mrs. Lincoln, along with her son Tad, were to visit the camp with Mr. Lincoln in early April. The Lincolns were to stay at Hooker's headquarters, but the real *maître de plaisirs* (to use the Princess Salm-Salm's term) was General Sickles. When Lincoln and his wife and son arrived at Hooker's headquarters, there was a review of troops, and then the President was led by Major General Sickles to his headquarters tent, where officers' wives were lined up in their best dresses to greet him. Dan was aware of an extreme melancholy in Lincoln, and so was the Princess Salm-Salm, who said that the President in his angular suit of black cloth reminded her of a German schoolteacher. There was in his face, she said, besides kindness and melancholy, "a sly humor, flicking around the corners of his big mouth and his rather small and somewhat tired-looking eyes." During the review of the Second, Third, Fifth, and Sixth Corps, sixty thousand men winding over the hills in splendid equipment, their bayonets bristling like a forest, Princess Salm-Salm had—as an accompanying horsewoman—attracted attention for her graceful and dashing riding. Now, in front of Sickles's headquarters, she told Sickles that Lincoln looked such "a dear good man" that she intended to kiss him. "Would it do any harm?"

"Not a bit of harm," Sickles is reported as saying. "I am only sorry I am not in his place." So she flew up to Lincoln and, with her vaudevillian exuberance, planted a long kiss on his cheek. Lincoln drew back in what one observer called "evident discomposure." Some officers helped the President in his embarrassment by telling him that the princess had made a wager with an officer for a pair of gloves. It happened that Mary Todd Lincoln was not there—she was resting at Hooker's headquarters—but Tad was, and the tale of the beautiful princess reached Mrs. Lincoln.[13]

The next day, according to General Dan Butterfield, everybody at headquarters knew that General Sickles was quite out of favor with Mrs. Lincoln. Lincoln himself had the previous evening been subjected to "an unhappy quarter of an hour." The row could be heard, Butterfield said, outside Lincoln's splendid tent at headquarters, and the President appealed to his wife, "But Mother, hear me."

"Don't 'mother' me," said Mary, in Butterfield's version. "And as for General Sickles, he will hear what I think of him and his lady guests."

Despite Sickles's discomfiture, he was appointed mischievously by Hooker to accompany the Lincolns back to their steamboat at Acquia Creek on the Potomac. On the road, and when the party had boarded the steamer, Mrs. Lincoln would not talk to Dan. He must have been reminded of his times in Coventry during his last session in Congress. As supper was served in the dining room of the steamer, the atmosphere still tense, Lincoln turned to Sickles. "I never knew until last night you were a very pious man," he told Dan. Quite properly Dan told the President that he believed he had been misinformed. "Not at all," said the President. "Mother says you are the greatest psalmist in the army. She says you are more than a psalmist, you are Salm-Salmist." Everybody was grateful to find an excuse for laughter at the President's homely whimsy, and the good humor disarmed Mrs. Lincoln, and her husband and her general were forgiven.

Of all the criticism aimed at Dan, even by Mary Todd, none of it centered upon his neglect of Teresa. She was an unnoted nonpresence. She had achieved a special level of invisibility.[14]

Amid the fun and games of that winter camp, Hooker was planning a serious coup, a great outflanking of Lee's position. While leaving enough troops at Fredericksburg to keep the Confederates locked there, he intended to move the chief part of his army secretly to the northwest, up the Rappahannock in a great right hook, to make a crossing there, and then wheel about and face the enemy. His aim was to end the war, since Lee would need to divide his forces, leaving some in front of Fredericksburg, and so Joe Hooker would triumph by squeezing the split Confederate forces between his main force and the men he left in place at Fredericksburg. Dan, briefed by Dan Butterfield, discussed the movements of his own corps with his three divisional generals, all of them interesting examples of Union generals, and two of them fated to give their lives for Hooker's great plan. The first was Hyram Berry, a former carpenter, bank manager, and Democratic mayor from Maine, thirty-eight years old. David Birney, also under forty, was a lawyer who had been born in Alabama and came from a Southern abolitionist family. Amiel Whipple was a West Pointer, three years older than Dan, whom both Dan and Teresa had known socially in Washington before the war. He was a brilliant surveyor, and had been chief surveyor of the Canadian–U.S. border in the Pacific Northwest.[15]

The skillful, stealthy withdrawal of great numbers of men from in front of Fredericksburg began on April 30. Thousands of campfires were kept burning by small remaining details of Union troops, to create an impression with Lee that nothing had changed on Stafford Heights. One corps remained to undertake "a demonstration" against the town and keep in place Lee's troops there. Dan's Third Corps marched to the west in what Dan saw as good spirits and, with the ease of veterans, crossed the Rappahannock far to the west at a crossing named United States Ford. They massed with the rest of the army in cramped meadows and tangled woods north and south of the little crossroads hamlet of Chancellorsville, on the edge of that great tangle of brush known as the Wilderness. With total success, they had moved largely undetected except by small and confused Confederate patrols, had outflanked the enemy's army, and had placed themselves where Lee did not yet know them to be. The surprise pincer attack against Lee needed only to be triggered. Hooker told his men, "The operations of the last three days have determined that our enemy must either ingloriously fly, or come out from behind his defenses and give us battle on our ground, where certain destruction awaits him." It had certainly been a maneuver worthy of Stonewall Jackson, but this time the Union had pulled it off, as the President had been waiting so long for it to do.

To fuel what generals considered their duty of gallantry, it was essential to every nineteenth-century general that his men should contribute a dossier of praise on his elegant tranquillity in the face of peril. Dan, of course, recognized his duty to behave with casual valor. Many items of such behavior were contributed to Dan's dossier that weekend. A soldier would remember that as the division moved along the sheltered plank road in the afternoon from the north toward Chancellorsville, the infantry did not descend into the sunken road "but instead marched in the fields at its side, allowing use of the main road to the ambulance and wagons." General Sickles, surrounded by his staff, sat chewing his cigar, watching the troops go by, and keeping an eye out to the east. Some enemy batteries in that direction saw his troops and began landing shot among his men. Dan, according to the soldier, without changing his own position, remarked in his peculiar, deliberate tone, "Boys, I think the enemy sees you—you had better take to the road."

Chancellorsville was as confusing as any Civil War battle, but perhaps the best way to understand the event is by seeing the Union line as a shallow, uneven V, facing south from the river. On the afternoon of May 1, Dan's three divisions, over fifteen thousand men, were bivouacked in woods near the top of the V, a little north of Chancellorsville. They were happy men, and they expected the best. A combined assault, from General Sedgwick in front of Fredericksburg and from Hooker's men unfolding like a great hinged machine from the west, like a vast door suddenly unlocked, would certainly have made Lee ingloriously fly. But though Dan did not yet know it, his old friend Hooker, on the edge of these impermeable woods thick with deer, was suddenly stricken by doubt. And that night, an alerted Lee imitated Hooker's movement. He decided to march half his army under the personally eccentric but militarily brilliant General Jackson even farther to the west from the position where Hooker had put himself—basically around the bottom and to the far side of the shallow V. Lee himself would take on Hooker frontally, while Jackson would attack Hooker from behind. Thus, Lee intended to out-pincer the pincer movement Hooker had already achieved—unless, of course, Jackson was detected in the middle of his secret march to outflank the Union Army.

By May 2, the men of Dan's corps had moved down into the right point of the V. General David Birney's division of Dan's corps, for example, was in position among the woods two miles from Chancellorsville on a hilly farm named Hazel Grove, and his scouts and skirmishers in the thickets to the south reported seeing Confederates making their way west by an overgrown road. Dan sent a message to Hooker, asking him to permit an attack. Hooker, in his headquarters in the Chancellor family's house, gave cautious approval.

Though he did not know what the Rebel movement to his south meant, the potentialities of that day, now advancing toward evening, excited Dan. In this terrain choked with vegetation, he sent out a thick screen of pickets made up of the Colonel Berdan's notable Sharpshooters, two entire regiments of marksmen. He also ordered General Amiel Whipple to bring his soldiers down the foliage-choked lanes to join General Birney in whatever was afoot. It was, in fact, Jackson's rear guard against which Dan sent the Sharpshooters and the men of Birney's division. When these troops of Dan's came howling down on the tree-clogged road that Jackson's men were marching along, three hundred Confederate prisoners were instantly captured. Many of them were brought to Dan, where he waited at the Hazel Grove farm. Uncowed, they told him and other officers during interrogation that Jackson was on his way to flank the Yankees on the far, shallower side of the V, and that soon there would be havoc. These men were so assertive in their claim that Dan believed they had been ordered to tell this story and were being deliberately misleading. He and his friend and aide Harry Tremain wrongly came to the conclusion that what he had detected was the enemy fleeing west. He begged Hooker to let him pursue them, and was surprised that the best Joe Hooker did was to tell all his corps commanders, including Dan, to be ready to move in the morning. So Dan's pickets stayed in place, and he ate his rations near the farmhouse, occasionally interrupted by the arrival of reports and dispatch riders.

Even today and on the most modern of mediums, on Civil War sites on the Internet, the merits of Dan's pushing out against Stonewall's men and even of his clinging to the higher ground at Hazel Grove are debated. Most historians squarely blame Hooker's inertia for the failure at Chancellorsville, but many, with some unfairness, see Dan's blowing out the base of the V as creating a dangerous bulge, a "salient," as military historians call it, that allowed the Confederates to attack him from both sides. It also separated his wing of the V from the other wing. A break existed in the line between his and Howard's corps, say his critics, and this led to the ultimate rout of Howard's men.[16]

For it was one-armed and godly General Oliver Howard's heavily German Eleventh Corps to the west of Dan, in the farther arm of the V. Dan's scouts had already reported that as Dan committed his men southward, wanting to chase and destroy Stonewall, a gap had opened between the Third and Howard's men, and Dan had sent David Birney's division to try to fill it. But as the Confederate prisoners had told Dan, Jackson was not in flight, and his Confederates came screaming down on Howard's Eleventh Corps—many of them were brewing their evening coffee at the time—and sent them fleeing blindly eastward through the dense forests toward Sickles. Dan would ever afterward remember the crazed, unreasoning fugitives of the Eleventh Corps running out of the woods to the west, dodging through the lines of Birney's soldiers and swarming over the cleared fields of Hazel Grove where Dan's artillery batteries were parked. "The exulting enemy," wrote Dan, "at their heels mingled yells with their volleys." Dan turned the Maine man Hyram Berry's division around westward to face them. Dan's other men were out of visual contact, and, for a time, a sea of fleeing Eleventh Corps troops separated him entirely from them.

Jackson's attack from the west, in the last week of Jackson's life, was stopped here by Sickles and the fashionable General Alfred Pleasonton, the West Point cavalry general assigned to cooperate with Dan's infantry. Dan's batteries at Hazel Grove shelled the howling lines of Stonewall's men, frightfully rending them apart. The Confederates stopped, fired once more, then returned to the woods and brought their artillery to bear on the fields of Hazel Grove. The fall of shells in Dan's lines was brutal and shocking, and the Union gunners who survived each volley went on working in a stunned, hollow-eyed terror that would revive in their dreams for the rest of their lives. The reliable Pleasonton would always believe that there at Hazel Grove, if Sickles's corps had been reinforced, they could have defeated the whole Rebel army.

The moon came up brightly, and Sickles had authorization for a midnight attack on the Confederate right. Given that screens of woods obscured a clear view of the battlefield even by daylight, many men felt a night attack was as good as a day one. Birney's men rolled forward and recaptured many of the rifle pits abandoned by the Eleventh Corps, together with a number of cannon. Dan seemed to have had a glittering success.

Early the next morning, the Sabbath, May 3, Hooker visited Sickles and looked over the position at Hazel Grove. Dan urged Hooker to let him hold this higher ground, but Hooker told him he would be cut off if anything went wrong between here and the main force around Chancellorsville. Dan believed he was being ordered to retreat from the best position on the entire battlefield. But because of his respect for Hooker, he was not moved by rancor as his men gave up Hazel Grove and retreated. Immediately, the Confederates planted at the farm thirty-one cannon, which at once began deadly work. Dan's men were by now vulnerably lined out in fields around the Chancellorsville crossroads, on a slight rise at Fairview Crest. Here they were reissued ammunition. The night before, Stonewall Jackson had been struck by his own fire, scouting a position near Chancellorsville, and now the Rebels, screaming "Remember Jackson," were about to hurl themselves on the crossroads.

This was the obscene day, ever to be remembered for horror, when artillery fire set the woods ablaze in front of Chancellorsville, the ground becoming fearsomely hot beneath soldiers' feet as the thickets took flame. The wounded of both sides screamed as they were overtaken and burned by walls of fire. The mobile wounded and burned, with blackened faces, were continually passing through the lines, shrieking as they ran toward the ambulances.

Colonel de Trobriand made his contribution to the Sickles dossier of calm courage by telling others how he saw Sickles ride by, smoking his cigar, amid the jarring concussion of Confederate shells. "Everything is going well," said Sickles. Then he confided to de Trobriand that he had handled his troops so well the previous evening that the Frenchman could expect to be promoted and receive a brigadier general's star.[17]

But the Confederates were squeezing Dan's position at Fairview Crest. "The attack came in from the west again as Jackson usually did," wrote Dan succinctly (though Jackson was twelve hours dead), "in heavy columns." They pressed forward in crowds rather than in regular formations. Berry's men stood up and shot them as they roared into the slaughter area in a communal frenzy. Berry himself was fatally shot by a Confederate sharpshooter, and Dan, seized by the massive battle fervor that hung over that place, became crazed when he saw General Joseph Revere, Berry's successor, leading the whole of the 2nd Brigade and portions of two others to the rear, "thus subjecting these proud soldiers, for the first time, to the humiliation of being marched to the rear while their comrades were under fire." Dan rode to intercept Revere, and furiously relieved him of his command. The man would ultimately be court-martialed for misbehavior and sentenced to dismissal. Merciful Lincoln would suspend the sentence to enable Revere to resign.

The experience of giving up high ground and then seeing his men torn apart by guns placed there was a significant one that would explain much of Dan's later behavior. He had an investment in Hooker's succeeding here, since an appropriate glory would be reflected one level down from Hooker to his corps commanders, at least to those heavily engaged in the battle. But it was obvious that Hooker was not succeeding. By this time Confederate shells were landing at the Chancellor house, one of them seeking out Hooker where he stood on the veranda and knocking him senseless for a time. Already his dazed but partially reviving mind was set upon withdrawal. He had been contemptuous of McClellan and every other temporizer, he had been a fire-eater as a divisional and corps commander, but now, to Sickles's private bemusement, timidity claimed Fighting Joe. Even though, back in Fredericksburg, Marye's Heights had fallen to the Union—one end of his planned pincer thus working—Hooker believed his chief duty was what McClellan had believed it his duty to do on the Peninsula: save the army. Dan was disappointed, not least because the formation of the Confederates "was entirely broken up, and from my headquarters they presented to the eye the appearance of a crowd, without definite formation; and if another corps had been available at the moment to have relieved me . . . my judgment was that not only would that attack of the enemy have been triumphantly repulsed, but that we could have advanced on them and carried the day."

Dan's plaint was an echo of a plea the President had uttered: he had said to Hooker that he should commit all his troops, yet two corps, some thirty thousand soldiers, sat by unused that Sunday, since all martial creativity had abandoned Joe Hooker. Driven off Fairview, Dan proposed to retake it with his corps, and his men still felt fury enough to achieve it. But, Hooker having been disabled, the staff told Dan he could not be permitted to go forward again. The losses of the Third Corps in the battle of Sunday were the bulk of that day's casualties.

As Dan withdrew his men into a diminishing salient of Union troops around the Chancellor house, General Amiel Whipple was also shot dead. Dan had now lost two of his three divisional commanders. That night, the revived Hooker invited all his corps commanders to his headquarters tent pitched along the road north of Chancellorsville, the Chancellor house having been abandoned. Hooker had already resolved to withdraw the way he had come, by the fords of the Rappahannock, but he nonetheless consulted his generals. Oliver Howard, George Meade, and John Reynolds argued for an advance. Darius Couch was not sure, but thought an advance could be successfully made. Dan Sickles, still convinced that the position had been lost when he was not supported at Hazel Grove, told the other generals that he argued more from a political than a strategic standpoint. There were sound military reasons for advance, he said, and he did not want to put his opinion against that of men trained in the profession of arms. But the political horizon was dark. Success by the Army of the Potomac was secondary to the avoidance of a disaster. If this army was destroyed, it would be the last one the country could raise, since the great days of recruiting were over. Washington might be captured, and the effect of that loss upon the country and upon Europe was to be dreaded. The rations with which the men had started had already given out. There was no provision for resupplying the troops against a possible advance by Lee and Jackson. On top of all that, in a week, on the next Sunday, in fact, the three years for which men had enlisted would expire for thirty-eight regiments of the army. Better to cross the river again and recuperate, said Dan.

Hooker declared that although the majority of his generals wanted to advance, he intended to withdraw. General Reynolds, lolling on a camp bed in the corner, asked what was the use of calling us together at this time of night when he intended to retreat anyway?[18]

Dan knew that the withdrawal would plunge Abraham Lincoln into a greater melancholy than the Princess Salm-Salm had read on the President's face in April. But a retreat to the safe side of the Rappahannock began, with Sickles's men as part of the rear guard.

Dan's corps, which would now be consolidated into two large divisions, had suffered a loss of 4,039 men killed, wounded, or missing at Chancellorsville. General Amiel Whipple, killed near the Chancellor house, had been a friend of Old Buck's whom Teresa had occasionally met in Washington and thus known since she was a girl. She read of his death in the newspapers, and must have known by the time of Chancellorsville that generals could be killed. Another few inches, and Hooker might have been killed by a shell at the Chancellor house. To what extent Teresa toyed with the idea of a life after Dan, to what extent she was consumed by anxiety over losing Dan, by fear of widowhood, or even by its possibilities, she did not confess in any letter. Later, there would be such manifestations of desperate love from her that one can only conclude that she still fretted over the matter of his safety. Even so, none of the ceremony and glory of being a major general's wife, the spouse of such a glorious creature as a Union corps commander, seemed to attach itself to Teresa. She still walked along the river with her dogs and applied herself to the education of ten-year-old Laura, who loved to paint watercolors so precocious that she could depend on grandparents and other visitors to exclaim and praise them. She derived from her paintings some of the companionship she could not achieve among her peers. Her talent as a painter was handy for a child who needed to be solitary for considerable stretches of time.

The isolated Teresa, and Laura's fond grandmothers, had not been able to prevent her from acquiring the habits of an indulged and pitied single child. These habits were accentuated by her lack of contact with other children and her dawning sense of bearing some questionable history, and of fatherly neglect. She also showed that same prepubescent willfulness which George and Susan had experienced years before in their son. Her father, as her mother and grandfather both told Laura, was a great man, and though it was patently true—it was in all the newspapers, and particularly after Chancellorsville—the idea evoked in Laura ambiguous feelings, as much darkness as pride.

The *Herald*, which had lambasted Dan throughout the 1840s and 1850s, now applauded his conduct at Chancellorsville and advanced his name for command at the highest level, the level for the moment occupied by Hooker. "General Sickles," said his old enemy Bennett, "displayed that quickness of perception, that promptness in action, and that never-failing self-possession which distinguished the great commander. . . . We therefore would call the attention of President Lincoln to General Sickles as the man for this position." The *Herald* also added to Dan's reputation by reporting that a Union officer, taken prisoner and later released, could tell that Jackson's men held a particular spite against General Sickles, and cried, "We'll hang him, Goddamn him, when we catch him."[19] These were the newspaper items, suitably amended for her ears, that George Sickles was pleased to read to Laura, and that fostered in her a bemused sullenness.

Tom Meagher had also fought well in the rear guard at Chancellorsville. His men were now so reduced in number, however, that he demanded they be taken out of the line for rest and to enable recruitment to refill their ranks. When Secretary of War Stanton did not respond to his demand, Meagher offered his resignation, believing that would bring the War Department to its senses. In fact, it made them punish him all the more, by keeping him out of action for most of the remainder of the war. Chancellorsville, which exalted Dan enormously, diminished brave Meagher.[20]

Hooker's dispirited army occupied again the camps at Stafford Heights. Dan's corps was located in an area named Boscobelle, where, as summer came on, sickness took a toll of the men. Dan himself was given medical leave in June after having suffered persistent enteritis in the camp. He took with him to New York, to which he returned lean, fierce, and feverish, two bouquets of pressed flowers that he gave as a present to Laura. Teresa had them framed with a text written by Laura: "Flowers gathered and prepared by my dear Papa—at his camp at Boscobelle—May 25, 1863." Along with a book called *The May Queen*, which Dan had the year before asked Mary Todd Lincoln to sign to "Miss Laura Sickles," these pressed bouquets became dominant artifacts in Laura's adolescence, tokens of who her father was and why he was so much absent.

Feted by the New York Board of Councilmen, Dan kept an eye on movements in Virginia, from which Lee was advancing again into the North. Hooker's army, moving closer to Washington, tracked Lee, expecting an inevitable huge, winner-take-all battle. The *New York Times* was worried about Dan's being too long on leave, because it flatteringly felt that his services could not be dispensed with. "Whether it be in organization and discipline of men," George was proud to read, "or in their cool and skillful handling, from a brigade to an army corps in battle, General Sickles has proven himself a thoroughly competent and complete master of himself and of his position." In the present emergency, the imperiled North could not do better than have him raise and command an army based on the populace of New York, who were "familiar with his successful career as a soldier."[21]

In between official duties downtown, Dan rested at Bloomingdale with Teresa and Laura. For the devoted Teresa, this period was a gala spring, as a shirt-sleeved, thinned-down, convalescent Dan rowed his wife and daughter across the mouth of Striker's Bay on the broad and tranquil Hudson. He found, however, for the first time that Laura did not take him entirely on trust, even though she was frequently taken in by his habitual charm and fascinated by his aides and the sentries on the road above the house.

Teresa was familiar, from reading and speaking to a limited range of friends, with the phenomenon of other heroes, physically wounded or not, coming home from the battles with a baffling reticence and darkness. Wives felt they no longer recognized their husbands. Mysterious angers rose in some veterans, and those who had been peaceable threw unexpected punches. The city was full of fellows who had been on the Peninsula or at Antietam who needed to anesthetize themselves to sleep by sniffing from a can of ether or placing an ether-soaked wad over their faces. But Dan seemed to be the same Dan, and when he was with Teresa, he gave her his full and intense attention, perhaps even sexually. A physical imperfection marred her. She had a cough, a low but persistent fever, and joint pain. He noticed that she took many patent nostrums for the cough.

At the end of his leave, Dan was eager to return to the world he understood, and he caught up with the army at Frederick in Maryland, west of Washington, on the morning of June 28, the very day Hooker was dismissed by Lincoln. Hooker had been for some weeks exaggerating the numbers of the invading enemy as a reason for his excessive caution. Like Meagher, Hooker now offered his resignation, confident that it would not be accepted by the President. It was.

To Dan, Hooker's removal was "a misfortune for the army," but it

tures that would soon have international fame: Rock Creek up to Culp's Hill and on to Cemetery Hill and southward along Cemetery Ridge, ending just before two hills of varying size, Little Roundtop and Big Roundtop. But much of the southern end of this ridge was lower than the rest. Late that night, godly Meade turned up at a farmhouse near the cemetery, worn by an anxiety the confident Dan did not share. Weighing on Meade was the same consideration that had unmanned Hooker: if he committed his troops to fight here, and it turned out to be the wrong choice, the Union itself would be lost.

Dan's men had taken a position on the lower end of Cemetery Ridge, ending their informal line on low ground below Little Roundtop. Along this line they had camped and rested overnight. Whatever nightmares would haunt the survivors of the coming day, for the moment the men displayed the extraordinary composure of veterans. They knew all the old soldiers' saws, including the one about its taking a man's weight in lead to kill him. Of two lines firing frenetically at each other, said the veterans, in ninety-nine cases out of a hundred, the only thing killed was the powder. It was not infrequent that a whole line of the enemy would fire upon a Union line without doing perceptible damage. Artillery, however, altered that proposition.[23]

This Sunday was to be a supreme day for the Union. Although Gettysburg would be fought over three days, July 2 came to be the day the issue was decided, the day of crucial strategies. At eight o'clock in the morning in his bivouac, Dan was snatching sleep after being up the entire night when one of Meade's aides, Meade's own son, arrived to see how Sickles's corps was lining out. Roused, Dan told the aide that he was about to post his men, but he did not know where he should go, given that this end of the ridge was so low—"a hole," in fact, as he told the young man—and a higher ridge existed a little ahead of him by the road. Dan feared it would be a case of Hazel Grove and Chancellorsville all over again. If the Confederates took the higher ridge ahead along the Emmitsburg Road, and in a peach orchard and wheatfield that could be seen from here, they would be able to destroy his men with artillery. Young Captain Meade rode back to his father and returned soon to tell

Dan not to take that higher ground ahead; instead, he was to extend his line along this lower ground in line with General Hancock's Second Corps. Sickles sent a message to Meade that his men would shortly be in position there.

The more Dan looked at it, though, the more he believed his line unsatisfactory. He was in a slough. To abandon the ridge ahead and the road to the enemy would be unpardonable. The force at his disposal was 11,898 men, "insufficient to hold the line along Cemetery Ridge to Roundtop and defend that height, which was obviously the key to our position." He had scouts out, particularly reconnoitering off to his left, in the screen of woods beyond the Emmitsburg Road, where anything might be happening. Cavalry came back to tell him that there were considerable enemy forces hidden over there to his front. Colonel Berdan's Sharpshooters and the 4th Maine went across the peach orchard, over the Emmitsburg Road, and into the woods on the far side. Near a farmhouse on the road, a barefoot boy came up to them and said, "Watch out, there are lots of Rebels in there, in rows."[24]

In view of all this, Dan sent his aides riding to headquarters again and again through the morning, reporting the situation and pleading to be allowed to take the higher ground. He seemed more frustrated than afraid, nor—unlike other generals on the edge of a murderous field— did he write a final letter to his wife or express torment at the idea of his soon-to-be, perhaps, fatherless child. Nostalgia did not delay the concentration of his intellect or will a second. At eleven o'clock, not having received any answers, he rode to Meade's headquarters, situated at a farmhouse near the cemetery.

Meade and Sickles disliked each other and were at temperamental poles. Now, according to Dan, he asked General Meade to come with him and reconnoiter the ground, but Meade dismissively said he was too busy. So Dan requested the chief engineer and the staff artillery officer to visit the ground, and, before he left, asked Meade whether he could dispose his corps according to his own judgment. Meade replied, "Certainly, within the limits of the general instructions I have given to you."

Hunt, the staff artillery officer, and Sickles rode over Dan's part of the field, from the swale and swamp of what Dan considered the hole between Cemetery Ridge and Roundtop and, above all, to the ground ahead, the ridge along the Emmitsburg Road that Dan wanted to occupy. Hunt too liked the advanced ground along the road. It bent nicely at a lane by the peach orchard, and the corps' line of men could be anchored at a clump of rocks named Devil's Den. Hunt pointed out where artillery could be placed to defend the ground by the road, dependent on General Meade's permission.

Dan waited an hour after the staff artillery chief left. No orders came. The troops were "anxious to profit by all the advantages of the ground," and started knocking down any fences between them and the Emmitsburg Road. Over in the direction of the peach orchard there were frequent exchanges of fire between hidden Confederates and Union pickets. Sickles would later plead his case in plain and economic language: "Impossible to wait longer without giving the enemy serious advantages in his attack, I advanced my line toward the highest ground to my front, occupying the Emmitsburg Road at the very point where Longstreet hoped to cross it unopposed."

Dan's men, the survivors of Chancellorsville, were as pleased as Dan to go to the road and the orchard, but this was a most controversial move. It took Sickles out of line with the rest of the Union Army. The decision may have been understandable in terms of Dan's character and his rebelliousness against Meade, but the question as to whether it won or nearly lost the battle is still argued by scholars, and on sites on the Internet. For Dan, by going forward, had left adrift the flank of the rest of the army on Cemetery Ridge. One of his brigade commanders, Régis de Trobriand, would write that Dan's decision "showed more ardor to advance to meet the fight than a nice appreciation of the best means to sustain it." The new situation of the Third Corps "offered some great inconveniences and some great dangers." Dan had perhaps placed his twelve thousand men in some peril, in that they were barely adequate to cover the ground, and in that they would obviously provoke a strenuous attack and an attempt by Lee's lieutenant, James Longstreet, to consume them from the flank.

The rest of the Union Army on Cemetery Ridge was amazed to see Dan go forward to his higher ground along the road and around the peach orchard. Some sober officers thought it a gesture more political than military—to draw attention to himself. After all, he was "a politician, and some other things, exclusive of the Barton Key affair," wrote one officer, "a man after show and notoriety and newspaper fame and the adulation of the mob." But Sickles believed he was being conscientious, and, unlike what would later be said of Longstreet, he did not court the possibility of defeat as a means of teaching his commander a lesson. He had, though, certainly been offended that Meade had been too busy to visit his end of the field, as if the Union left were of small consequence, and so, as a civilian might, he decided that it was mere common sense that he would know the ground better than a man who had not visited it. Above all, he thought of the consequences of his ordered withdrawal from the high ground at Chancellorsville, the more than four thousand casualties. He did not want a repeat of that carnage.[25]

As controversial as Dan's advance was, the concealed march Longstreet had made that day to take on the Union left has been a matter of argument ever since. These two generals, Longstreet and Sickles, jointly held the future of their respective nations in their hands. Longstreet was a professional soldier, an undistinguished graduate of West Point, a major in the Pay Corps at the war's beginning, and two years younger than Dan. He had had a large falling-out with Lee over strategy, and had been pressing on him great strategic plans about continuing northwest to Cincinatti, or else turning southwest and assaulting the Union Army in Tennessee. As for the position here at Gettysburg, Longstreet did not want his commander to take the initiative of attacking the Union Army lined out along Cemetery Ridge. He wanted the Confederate Army to make a massive move completely around the Union's flank—in this case, around Sickles—and take up a strong position somewhere between here and Washington.

But Lee could not be persuaded. Instead, the older general had this morning wanted Longstreet to make a march, concealed by the woods, and attack the Union left flank—that is, Sickles's corps. Longstreet, who possessed a vengeful and mean-hearted streak that some believed would be demonstrated that day to the disadvantage of his own side, was affronted. Over coming years, Dan and James Longstreet would become companions, anchored together in a conspiracy to diminish the reputations of their commanding officers—Sickles with somewhat more justice in Meade's case than Longstreet in Lee's.

Longstreet executed his marching orders sulkily on the morning of July 2, and with as much delay as he could manage. Had he struck Dan's men early, when everything was uncertain, when Meade and Dan were arguing, and staff officers without the power to make the final decision were offering advice to Dan, he could have swept Dan's Black Diamonds away, put cannon on the Roundtops, and driven the entire Union Army off its ridge in bleeding confusion—which was the very thing Lee had envisaged him doing. But Longstreet remained slow. "Thus passed the forenoon of that eventful day," one of his generals would write. As noon passed, one of Lee's staff heard Lee ask, in an uneasy tone, "What *can* detain Longstreet? He ought to be in position now."

Here, said some then and later, was a general who, from pure peevishness, was willing by a chosen delay to play with the lives of his soldiers and bring down death upon them on an immense scale. One of Longstreet's strongest divisions, that of John B. Hood, could now see Dan's line strung out along the Emmitsburg Road and down along the lane past the peach orchard and the wheatfield. It did not stretch to the Big or Little Roundtop, and Hood urged Longstreet to "allow me to turn Roundtops and attack the enemy in flank and rear." Longstreet replied that General Lee's orders were to attack the line along the Emmitsburg Road and that Hood's proposed flanking of Dan could not be permitted. As one modern writer put it, Hood could taste the victory, but Longstreet felt that if he permitted Hood to take it, General Lee would not receive the lesson Longstreet believed he needed to learn. Because Lee had refused the idea of a flanking movement, which would put his army between General Meade's army and Washington,

Longstreet was pretending that this prevented him from outflanking the Union here as well.

While Longstreet tarried, Dan had until after two o'clock to get his men into line. Dan's newly assigned West Point divisional general, Humphreys, had his division along the road, north to south, facing the woods, and here a young woman from the Rogers farmhouse brought out batches of biscuits to feed the men. But by three o'clock, even Dan and his staff, waiting on their horses near the Trostle farmhouse, with the wheatfield to their left, were wondering why it was taking so long for Longstreet's soldiers to begin the day's action.

At that hour, General Meade chose to send for his corps commanders. Dan believed the commanding general had no idea of the imminence of events down along the Emmitsburg Road and along the lane. In fact, Meade had just sent a telegram to Secretary of War Stanton stating that the army was fatigued, and that if he, Meade, found it hazardous to attack, or was satisfied that the enemy was endeavoring to move to his rear and get between him and Washington, "I shall fall back on my supplies at Westminster." Dan would later scathingly write that this telegram showed "that at the supreme moment—3 P.M. July 2— when the enemy was advancing to attack, we had no plan of action, no order of battle. For Meade the battle of July 2 is a surprise, like the battle of July 1."

Unable to reply in writing to the summons from Meade, Dan pointed out to the officer who brought the message that surely he could hear an exchange of fire along the road, the introductory compliments of battle. But Meade insisted, and a second order came for Dan to attend, so he galloped up to headquarters. General Meade, waiting at the door of his farmhouse headquarters, cried, "You need not dismount, General. I hear the sound of cannon on your front. Return to your command. I will join you there at once." Dan was exhilarated to hear those guns—it meant the Union would have to fight here.

By the time he got back to his men, there was quickening fire along the line, and the Confederate cannon beyond the road were beginning to tear terrible holes in Dan's blue lines. General Meade himself arrived on Dan's heels. Dan was waiting not far from the wheatfield, near the creek called Plum Run, when Meade rode up and said succinctly, "General, I am afraid you are too far out."

"Yes," Dan replied. "But I can hold him until reinforcements arrive. I will contract my line, or modify it, if you prefer. My men are easily maneuvered under fire."

General Meade said it was too late, but that he would support him on the left, where Birney's men held the line, and on his right and center, held by Humphreys, with men from neighboring corps. Then Meade galloped away, and Dan heard nothing more of him that day. Meade had left dangling the question of whether Dan had done a good or bad thing. Had Dan also played, in a different and less deliberate sense than Longstreet did, with his men's lives by advancing so far? Or would they have been destroyed had they stayed where Meade wanted them to be? One observer would say that on this would be spilled "a Caspian Sea of ink."

On the banks of the Hudson at Bloomingdale, the same endless, humid afternoon that prevailed at Gettysburg pended over the city and outer parts of Manhattan. It was a promising day for Teresa and Laura to be on Bloomingdale business—visits to animals and to ill neighbors, and preparations for the visits by her parents and others on July Fourth. The child had inherited the salutary interest in domestic animals that was so strong in her mother—a happy circumstance, since Teresa had not recently had the same energy she once did.[26]

The newspapers Teresa had seen that morning were full of late June news, some days out of date, of threatening Confederate movements in Pennsylvania. She had found them hard to read. She was these days possessed of an increasing melancholy and languor. The recently departed Dan was still on her mind and on Laura's. Even though, of all the family, only Susan Sickles seemed to have extreme fears of Dan's death, the possibility of harm coming both to the polity and society of the North and to Dan hung over the day, adding weight to the humid air.

Teresa's feelings—or, more exactly, symptoms—that day were indications that she, like her husband, lay under danger of a great flanking—in her case from one of the pervasive diseases of the era. Tuberculosis, also called consumption or phthisis (a Greek term meaning "wasting away"), was famous, at least in the theater and literature, for attacking the young, the fair, the exuberant, the talented. In fact, it was a predominant disease among Irish immigrants and blacks, arising from the poverty in which they lived, the foulness of the surroundings, the scarcity of warmth and food. Teresa was far from the usual venues of this disease, from the Fourth Ward, where toilets spilled into streets and courtyards, where bacteria from human excrement and urine and from the animal offal of slaughterhouses, all contributing to high mortality. Tuberculosis was, above all, a disease of the lower East Side, the middle East Side known as the Gas House district, and the middle West Side, Hell's Kitchen. Archbishop Hughes, the Catholic archbishop of New York, said, with perhaps too much resignation, that tuberculosis was "the Irish death." Nearly twice as many immigrants as native-born contributed to the city's yearly death toll from the disease of three thousand souls. The working class, having contracted the disease, had no clear mountains, no sun-drenched sanatoria to resort to for a cure. In fact, the use of sanatoria had yet not come into vogue as a means of treating the disease. It was a mercy that laudanum and opiates were freely available across the counter of drugstores to patients who had no other succor. A brown tincture of macerated opium in diluted spirits was imbibed by people of all classes who suffered tubercular symptoms. It was the only effective medicine available, and though it did something for pain and for suppressing the cough, one of its chief influences was to make the patient less fearful and more resigned.

In sylvan Bloomingdale, Teresa would in one sense have been considered by the doctors of the day to be relatively secure from the infection, for the leading experts furiously denied until 1882, when the bacterium was isolated, that tuberculosis was a contagious disease. One important contributor to the disease was, the experts of Teresa's time proclaimed, a hereditary disposition, and though Teresa's parents and grandparents were or had been healthy and long-lived and had never been troubled by tuberculosis, her uncle Lorenzo Da Ponte had died of a form of it. Despite talk of heredity, the unrealized fact was that organisms of the disease were everywhere in the city. If a tubercular person sneezed or coughed, minute droplets containing hundreds of tubercule bacilli would float in the air for hours and even attach themselves to food. For the affluent, it was often the servant who brought the disease out of the squalor of Lower Manhattan into the uptown residences. The early stages of the disease were difficult to detect. One conclusive sign was the fearful cough and the spitting up of blood from ulcerations in the lungs. This expectoration of blood was not uncommonly seen on the streets, and in eating houses and theaters. Once the bacillus found a bridgehead within the body, it entered an alliance with any discontent or ambiguity of soul and, more obviously, with unsuitable domestic arrangements. The chief unsuitable elements in the house at Bloomingdale were its demanding size and draftiness.

Again, however, the baffled experts put less stress on cold drafts in the case of a tubercular gentlewoman, which Teresa was on her way to becoming, than they did on flaws of character in the sufferer. Religiosity and sexual hysteria—"an incontinent search for pleasure"—were other causes they uncomprehendingly invoked. For, apart from religious excess and celibacy, said a leading British specialist, other primary causes were an early addiction to horse riding continuing into young womanhood, inducing habitual masturbation and "paving the way for phthisis." Hence, as Teresa's incipient symptoms developed, the doctors would be predisposed to shake their heads sadly. A horse-riding, sexually notorious soul whose husband had abandoned her to whatever solitary solace she could achieve.

It had been only recently, in 1854, that Hermann Brehmer, a German sufferer from the disease, had cured himself by spending time in high, dry air in the Himalayas, and had been moved to build the first sanatorium and to recommend altitude, clean air, and good food. But

Teresa, in whom the symptoms were not yet fully visible, was in any case already surrounded by relatively wholesome air and ate wholesome food.[27]

In Washington that same day, as Teresa by the Hudson felt the onset of the unusual languor that was an early symptom of her disease, and as Dan waited with a warrior exaltation for bloody chaos to begin by the Emmitsburg Road, Mary Todd Lincoln was thrown from her carriage in Washington. It was not known whether the bolts of her carriage seat had been intentionally loosened by a saboteur with Mr. Lincoln in mind or whether it was an accident, but it would lead to serious illness. Lincoln himself was saved from injury because he spent that day in the telegraph office of the War Department, waiting for news from Gettysburg. There, on the field itself, at midafternoon, the pattern of the afternoon's havoc was established. General Hood's rebels struck Sickles's men, or, specifically, David Birney's men, with a sudden ferocity. De Trobriand, commanding one of Sickles's brigades, thought the enemy came rushing up like demons from hell, but many of Birney's men were Pennsylvanians, fighting resolutely for home ground.[28]

Still, the fury of fire from the Confederate lines, the determination of their advance toward the wheatfield (later to be known as *the* Wheatfield), and their pressure on Sickles's men at the hinge of their line among the trees of the peach orchard (hereafter, Peach Orchard) were such that Dan had continually to transfer men from Humphreys's end of the line to reinforce Birney. Dan's friend Charles Graham, formerly of the Brooklyn Navy Yard, was a brigade commander under Birney in the Wheatfield, a triangular parcel of land about four hundred yards on each of its three sides. He rolled back a number of attacks. But a third of all Birney's men had within an hour been struck and variously shattered by shells or minié balls. Graham, the Tammany engineer, already wounded once, was pitched to the ground in the Peach Orchard when his horse was shot. Stunned and blood-soaked, he could barely see or move as men from Mississippi swarmed over his position and captured him.

Three brigadier generals ordered to help Dan's men were shot dead in short order that afternoon. As some of the newcomers wavered, de Trobriand in the Wheatfield was depicted almost in caricature as yelling, "Third Michigan, change front to right! . . . Change quick, or you will be gobbled up. Don't you see you are flanked? Ze whole Rebel army is in your rear!" Ultimately the position would be tenuously held, and de Trobriand's brigade, like other men of Sickles's corps, were ordered to march to the rear for resupplying. They moved across fields in which their reinforcements from the Fifth Corps lay down on the stubbly and stony ground in lines to enable the surviving Black Diamonds to pass among them.

Many of Dan's units managed an orderly withdrawal back across the creek named Plum Run Creek. Others, he saw, were stampeded. But it cannot be denied that by nightfall the federal line would lie more or less where Meade had that morning envisaged it should lie, with the difference that the Roundtops were firmly held by the Union.[29]

Before Dan's troops withdrew (or were driven back, according to which view was accepted), Dan was still astride his horse in the Trostle farmyard, an unlit cigar in his mouth, maintaining without apparent effort a deliberate but tautly aware frame of mind. He later depicted what happened next in the plainest language, leached of all trauma. "I am wounded. I turn over my command to Birney and am carried to the rear, knowing that victory is ours." Indeed it was, for the Confederates had not managed to turn the Union flank, and it was the Third Corps and its reinforcements that had denied Longstreet's men the victory. What had happened to Dan, however, was that a twelve-pound cannonball that had failed to explode came visibly lolloping, far too fast to be avoided by Dan and his mounted staff, across the farmyard from the direction of the Confederate artillery on Seminary Ridge and shattered and tore to pulp Dan's right leg in its blue fabric. Curiously, by one of those anomalies veterans were used to, it left his horse unmarked. Dan was conscious of the damage, yet was not overwhelmed with pain and did not lose consciousness. Already in a heightened, feverish state from the battle he was fighting, perhaps he found it all the easier to marshal the chemicals appropriate to trauma. A captain of the 70th New York, standing nearby, nonetheless feared that the men still fighting on the Third Corps line might be affected if too many of them heard the rumor that their general had been—as it seemed—mortally wounded. The captain formed a detail of a sergeant and six soldiers, who covered Dan with a blanket and carried him to the shade of the Trostle farmhouse. This was, above all, in the hour of his wound, a moment of which the right sort of general could make a myth of his easy gallantry, and Dan managed it, his cigar still stuck between his lips by grimace or by stubbornness. When he arrived by the wall of the house, he appeared merely moderately upset and told one of the men to buckle a saddle strap tightly over the upper thigh as a tourniquet. Major Harry Tremain then turned up with a message and was filled with horror to see what had befallen Sickles. Dan ordered Tremain, "Tell General Birney he must take command."[30]

A stretcher arrived, Dan had an NCO light his cigar, and that was how he was carried away, cap over his eyes, cigar in mouth, hands folded on chest. A little to the rear, bleeding heavily despite the strap around his upper thigh, but still not showing acute pain, he was placed in an ambulance with a medical aide, who began pouring brandy down his throat to counteract the shock. Tremain also got into the ambulance, since he thought Dan would expire on its bloody boards, and he did not want him to die without a face he knew. "Solemn words," said Tremain, "not to be written in my story, were softly spoken to me amid the din of cannon." Dan was pleased to see Father O'Hagen, chaplain of the 74th New York, ride up to offer spiritual comforts. There seemed to be a consensus that the general would die, but Dan did not appear oppressed by it.

Certainly he was now about to experience the mercy of a field hospital, of exactly the kind of place outside which Walt Whitman, hospital orderly, sighted a heap of amputated feet, legs, arms, and hands—the mark of a site of horrors. The Third Corps field hospital consisted of a string of tents near the Taneytown Road, a little way behind the Roundtops. Light was fading, and the doctors inspected Dan by the illumination of candles stuck on bayonets. Tremain caught the odor of chloroform, which the more advanced Union surgeons were merciful enough to use. After chloroform was administered to Dan, Dr. Thomas Sim, the corps' medical director, using a new method of rounded amputation, cut off the leg at a third of the way up the thigh. He had just read that the Army Medical Museum in Washington was advertising for samples, and so, instead of throwing the limb into a heap, he had it wrapped in a wet blanket and placed in a small coffin for shipment to Washington. Dan's shattered leg lived on as a museum exhibit and remains on display at the Walter Reed Hospital in Washington.

Overnight, as the anesthetic wore off, the pain of Dan's amputation became intolerable. He now felt at one with the thousands of agonized men of Gettysburg, Chancellorsville, and other nightmares, and he was filled with vague but deep anxieties. After he was given two opium pills for the pain, Sim believed it essential to get him away from the infections of the field hospital. In the morning he was placed on a stretcher and began the journey to the nearest Union-controlled railroad depot at Littlestown, twelve miles away. He had been moved to the hospital, following his wound, fairly deftly and without pain, but this time he could be transported only at a creeping pace. As well as Dr. Sim, who had left his deputy in charge of the Third Corps hospital, Tremain and two other aides, handsome Alexander Moore and plump Tom Fry, accompanied Dan, and ten shifts of four men each were used to transport him, with enormous care, over the difficult ground. Whenever cavalry came rattling past, Dr. Sim would cry out to them and to the stretcher bearers themselves to go steadily. "A stumble might kill the patient." There were frequent rests, of an extent not afforded the wounded of other ranks, in secluded and shady places. They traveled only four miles that first day, as, at Gettysburg, the final Confederate assault on the center began, ending in the defeat of Lee's army. At the Wheatfield, Mathew Brady would take a famous photograph of the already bloating young dead of Dan's corps.

The next morning Dan at first felt well and insisted on shaving himself, and that day the railroad and its strings of rail coaches full of wounded was reached. Dan and his accompanying surgeon and aides traveled to Washington on what Tremain called "an ordinary passenger car." The jolting of the train pained Dan, and he was fed morphine. Two days after the battle, the party reached Washington. Dan could sense, that Sunday morning, even through his opium haze, the exhilaration of the capital, the excitement apparent on the faces of people at the train station. There were frantic cheers from those waiting for or arriving on trains as he was carried forth. Had he known, he would have been ecstatic to learn that the *New York Times* was already laying print for the next day that said, "New York State and City owe a debt of peculiar gratitude to General Sickles. He it is that, in the most signal manner, has proved what militia are capable of when led by a brave man." There was hope, "amounting almost to confidence, that his life and services will be spared to the country." The *Times* could not express more than "hope" because of the problems surgeons often had with amputations. Since such injuries were covered with lint scraped from materials not always sterile, the chance of gangrene and of an agonizing and fevered death was always present for the recent amputee.[31]

Rooms in a lodging house on Eighth Street had been organized for Dan. He continued to lie on the stretcher on top of a mattress placed on the floor, and a medical orderly kept the stump wet—what Surgeon Sim called "irrigating the wound." There was discussion about lifting him off the floor and into a bed, but since Sim felt he might not be up to it, he was tended quietly where he was. He seemed to be alert and happy in a feverish way.

Late that Sunday afternoon, an aide came into the room with the news that the President and his son Tad were downstairs. If many professional soldiers were blaming Dan for taking his corps forward, the President, an advocate of "forward," did not fret much about the matter. Lincoln, aware that Dan, right or wrong, had given spirited aid to the survival of the United States, was willing to leave his sick wife at the White House to spend time with Dan. He had been following Meade's dispatches and, concerned, as so often before, by the man's excessive caution, was planning to urge him to pursue Lee. "You have given the enemy a stunning blow at Gettysburg. Follow it up, and give him another before he can reach the Potomac."

No visitor could have been more welcome to Dan in his semideliri-ous state, alternating between euphoria and fretfulness, than the Presi-dent. Lincoln walked in, bent over, shook hands with Sickles, asked him about his wound, and then sat in a chair at the side of the mattress while Tad stood by, no doubt amazed at the pallid transformation of this man he had seen around the White House. Sickles had a cigar lit up for the occasion, and was eager to answer the President's questions about the battle. That very afternoon, with his hold on life tenuous, Dan began his campaign to discredit the dilatory Meade before Meade discredited the rash Sickles. Meade himself would not lose much time arguing his point. In his official dispatch he would state, "General Sickles, misinterpreting his orders, instead of placing the Third Corps on the prolongation of the Second, had moved it nearly three-quarters of a mile in advance, an er-ror which nearly proved fatal in the battle." But Meade, Dan implied or said outright to the President that afternoon, had had no plan of battle for Gettysburg. Sickles explained now to the nation's father how he had seen it as a matter of necessity to advance to the high ground. According to one of his aides, he spoke of the general impact of the battle itself, and its probable political consequences, "with a lucidity and ability remark-able in his condition. . . . Occasionally he would wince with pain and call sharply to his orderly to wet his stump with water. But he never dropped his cigar nor lost the thread of his narrative. . . . He certainly got his side of the story of Gettysburg well into the President's mind." Lincoln gravely thanked Dan, asked if there was anything he needed, was thanked in return, and departed.[32]

Before the day was out, Henry Wikoff called in. Not only was the chevalier still a favorite of Mary Todd Lincoln's, but, although he was too old now for military service, his entrée to the various embassies of Washington inevitably made him a useful source of intelligence to the Union. In Dan's sickroom, he almost certainly asked if Dan at last wanted Teresa at his side. For whatever reason, Dan still didn't. Wikoff sent off telegrams to the *Herald* and to Teresa so that she would not have the shock of reading the first definitive news of Dan's wound in the next day's paper. Other visitors to Dan were War Secretary Edwin Stanton and James Topham Brady, of Dan's old legal team, and General Thomas Francis Meagher, who came down from New York bringing confections and wine. Dan asked Brady's help with a fund to buy delicacies, medicines, and comforts for the nearly three thousand wounded of the Third Corps. Brady returned to New York and made a speech in the Stock Exchange, raising a considerable sum, which was sent to General Birney, who had inherited Dan's corps.

Dan had become more subject to depression and anxiety. He blamed them not on his wound or on what he had witnessed, but on his having been anesthetized. One of his recurrent concerns was how he and his men would survive the controversy over the forward position he had taken at Gettysburg. He was also haunted by the feverish idea that the remains of his corps had been involved in a new military disaster following Gettysburg. He must have expressed this concern to Stanton and others, who told the President about it, so that, on July 10, Lincoln took the trouble to write a note of reassurance to him. "I understand you are troubled with some reports that the Third Corps has sustained a disaster or a repulse. I can only say that I have watched closely, and believe I've seen all the dispatches of the military telegraph office up to a half hour ago . . . and I have heard of no such disaster or repulse. I add that I do not believe there had been any such. Yours truly, A. Lincoln."

Indeed, Lincoln wished that the Third Corps and all the other corps *had* been involved in some military expedition. For on July 14, Meade let Lee recross the Potomac unmolested and go home. When the President visited Sickles the next day, Tremain heard Lincoln groan and tell Sickles that this failure to get Lee was the greatest disaster of the war.

As Dan's health improved, Teresa may have harbored a hope that this new incapacity would make her husband dependent on her. That he had not sent for her certainly cast doubt on the idea, but, with only one leg, he would have to lead a less restless and peripatetic life and a more domestic one. So she might yet become what she passionately desired to be: a helpmeet. Dan did not seem averse to going back to New York and Bloomingdale. He was practicing on crutches in his room for a train journey there. On July 22, he turned up by slow carriage at the White

House and went in. He was moving without the approval of his doctor, and an erratic motion, like that of a coach, could cause agony in his only partly healed wound. But he managed to look dashing on crutches and would all his life prefer them to any prosthetic device. Cynics said that he preferred to proceed in this painful manner, with his trouser leg pinned up, to ensure that no one who met him could forget that he had placed his body in intimate peril for the Union.[33]

Having said goodbye to the President, Dan went home by train. The journey caused him difficulties, but he and his aides safely reached Jersey City, where a revenue cutter waited to take him in triumph to New York. As he tottered toward the gangplank, bystanders cheered. His New York friends Brady and Meagher, Hart and Wikoff, were aboard the cutter, as were many others. The cabin had been laid out as a dining room, and a splendid meal was served while the cutter made directly for Ninety-first Street on the Hudson. On the way, speeches were made, with Brady acting as toastmaster.

This was a dangerous time for the city, since in the days following Gettysburg there had been a crisis over conscription. It had begun on Monday, July 13, when German and Irish rioters had organized a protest against the draft. The situation had degenerated, so that at the climax of a week of riot and resistance, masses of New Yorkers fought a force of the Union Army, with high but unspecified casualties among the civilians. The Board of Councilmen thought that legless Sickles might serve as a chastening example to the rebellious city, and they were quick to proffer thanks to him and to order a gold medal struck in his honor.[34]

# VIII

BUT ANY RESIDUAL HOPE THAT TWENTY-
six-year-old Teresa may have harbored of Dan's becoming a private man was soon dispelled. At home,
he was as restless and irritable as other soldier husbands. He clumped about the house with an absorbed
air, and in his postwound edginess, he experienced
swings of mood. He had already confessed to one
of his officers, in a letter written from Bloomingdale, that he wanted to be back with the corps the
very first day his strength would permit. His stump
was extremely painful, particularly when a storm
approached, and while it was in progress. Because it
had not yet shrunk to its natural size, he could not yet
be measured for an artificial leg. "Nor has it acquired
sufficient hardness to enable me to ride in a carriage
faster than a walk over any but a park road." He still
insisted on catching carriages down to the city, either

to be feted or to spend time in George Sickles's office on Nassau Street. Short of his brothers in the field, he felt most at ease with his father.[1]

After less than two weeks, he sat down in his study at Bloomingdale and wrote an energetic letter to Edwin Stanton. "It will not be long before I am ready for work again—can you give me a command? . . . Meanwhile, please do not permit General Meade to break up my corps—which I hear he contemplates." He became obsessed about his friend Charles Graham, captured while wounded in the Peach Orchard, and pleaded with Stanton to expedite the prisoner exchange, since some evil stories had arisen from Confederate prisoner-of-war camps around Richmond.

Obviously, it would be forever impossible for Dan to become a private man dependent on his wife. He did not especially seek her company, and his pain and her persistent cough and occasional prostrations separated them further. On August 11, he departed Bloomingdale and its humid summer and made for Lake George in the Adirondacks, accompanied not by Teresa but by two young captains, brilliantly accoutered. When Dan turned up, helped in and out of the carriage by his officers, at the Fort William Henry Hotel, the affluent guests fibrillated with excitement. By now, he understood that his old capacity to charm people and to appeal to women sexually had not vanished with his leg. Nor did he fall back upon his disability as a means of avoiding a hyperactive country vacation. He played tenpins and billiards, negotiating his way up and down the green and the billiard table on his crutches, by now familiar implements. He went hunting and fishing almost every day, and shot two deer. He sent the head of a buck to Lorenzo Delmonico, with whom the Excelsior Brigade had built up such a debt in the conflict's early days.

In the ballroom of the Fort William Henry Hotel a dance was held in Dan's honor, and at its close he was required to speak. For the first time, he staked out a position on what the Union's attitude to the South should be—not vengeance, but magnanimity, justice, and conciliation. "The army will prove that they who are fearless in conflict are generous in victory." His pleasant, off-the-cuff, modest, but well-reasoned speech, delivered to the glittering faces of the guests, showed that he understood what the great postwar question would be, and it was reported by the *New York Times*.[2]

Dan and his officers moved on to Saratoga Springs, the most fashionable resort in the United States, and on returning to New York in September, he was pleased to welcome General Charles Graham, who had been exchanged, as Dan had recommended. He learned that his personal stock had become even more heightened in the city, and, though he did not know it, an indication of this was that George Templeton Strong was at last moved to mention him well in his journal: "I suppose Sickles, with his one leg, is among our best volunteer officers. His recuperative powers are certainly wonderful. Four years ago he was a ruined man in every sense, a pariah whom to know was discreditable."[3]

On October 18, Dan, determined to take up his career as a soldier and with his stump three and a half months healed, traveled south to Fairfax Station in Virginia to seek back his command from General Meade and to see the men of the Third Corps. There were rumors about Meade's having said that if Dan had not lost his leg at Gettysburg, he would have been court-martialed. The meeting between Meade and Dan was thus polite but cool. Dan admitted that he was not up to a full-scale campaign but wondered whether he could have his corps back, if only for the next battle. But even Dan's friends thought his valor outmatched his physical capacity. He could not ride; he could not march. Meade mentioned the Confederacy's General Richard Ewell, who had recuperated for nine months from the loss of an arm before taking up his command again.[4]

Dan was not satisfied. He was deeply affected, however, to find that the men had pooled their resources to buy him a barouche. It was pulled by two matched pairs of horses, and in it he proceeded along the lines of his men, accompanied by General Birney. One soldier said it was only his weakened condition that prevented the men from lifting him out of the vehicle and carrying him shoulder-high through the camp.

He returned to Washington in the same carriage, even more determined to have Meade dismissed for his timidity. Visiting the White

House two days later, Secretary of the Navy Gideon Welles found Dan in Abraham Lincoln's upstairs office, discussing the question of who had chosen the battle site at Gettysburg. Dan argued that the credit should go to General Oliver Howard, who had occupied the ridge of the Gettysburg cemetery on July 1. Then he himself had sent a message to Meade, supporting Howard and recommending the place, though predicting that the lower ground to the south would be the problem. Although Welles admitted that allowance always needed to be made for Sickles when he had an interest, "his representations confirmed my impressions of Meade, who means well, and, in his true position, that of a secondary commander, is more of a man than Sickles represents him."[5]

After Dan's rebuff by Meade, back in New York, the distancing between Teresa and himself creaked toward finality. Dan took up residence downtown in the Brevoort House, excusing his action by his need to be handy to the factory where he could be fitted for a prosthetic limb. Teresa and Laura bravely repeated the feasible story but knew the truth in their hearts. At the Brevoort, Dan declined an official dinner, but the band of the 7th New York Regiment assembled, and, on the last evening of October, "an eager multitude, of which the gentler sex formed no inconsiderable part," waited outside the hotel for the serenading of the hero. Knowing Dan's passion for opera, Signor Graffula, conductor of the band, played selections from *Tannhäuser*, *William Tell*, *Marta*, *The Enchantress*, and a series of other popular operas, and as Dan appeared on the balcony, "Hail to the Chief" was played. Dan had ascended to a level where, without irreverence, the presidential theme could be performed to honor him. Asked to speak, Dan expressed his contempt for the Copperheads, who would countenance a divided nation. "Rather than see the Republic so degraded, let the last citizen perish; lay waste the continent; recall the red man from his long exile; and give back to the proud lords of the forest and plain the heritage we took from their fathers."

Dan retired indoors in the midst of the applause, and without any irony the band struck up "The Star-Spangled Banner," product of Key's father.[6] It did not seem that Dan was ever haunted at the playing of this anthem, yet if ever the ghost of Key was sent packing from the scene, it was that night. Nor was any citizen profane or curmudgeonly enough to cry, "Remember Key?" or "General, where is your wife?"

When not at the Brevoort House, Dan spent time in Washington, staying at Edwin Stanton's house on K Street or at the White House. Mary Todd Lincoln had not been cured of séances since Dan had last seen her. Sometimes, when Willy and Eddie returned to speak to her, they brought with them her dead half brother, Aleck, everyone's favorite, a Confederate killed in a skirmish near Baton Rouge in Louisiana. She had by now lost three of her Confederate half brothers. Sam Todd died at Shiloh. David Todd, who had for a time run a Confederate prisoner-of-war camp at Richmond, was rumored to have tortured Yankee prisoners and had perished at Vicksburg. And then Aleck. Nor did the embarrassment of her family connections end there. General Benjamin Helm, who had recently been killed at Chattanooga, had been married to Mary's half sister Emilie. Mary Todd Lincoln could not formally mourn any of these rebels; much of the Republican press thought her too sympathetic to the Confederacy to begin with. But after General Helm's funeral, Emilie Todd Helm needed to get a pass to cross the Union lines and return to the family home in Lexington. Lincoln had himself sent her a pass, protecting her person and property except for slaves, but it could not be acted upon until Emilie gave the requisite oath of allegiance to the government of the United States. A small fire-eating woman in the tradition of the Todds, she refused to take the oath, and the President broke procedure and ordered that she be brought to Washington by official escort anyhow. In this he was influenced by Mary, both by the force of her personality and by her need for consolation. And so in December 1863, to the astonishment of Dan and other Lincoln friends, the wife of a Confederate general entered the White House as a guest.

The two women had not seen each other since the war began; since, in fact, the late General Helm had turned down the President's offer of a high rank in the Union Army. Emilie found her half sister in an anxious condition. Mary Todd obviously feared the descent of more and more sorrows. "Kiss me, Emilie," said Mary, "and tell me that you love me. I seem to be the scapegoat for both North and South." Mary and Emilie tried to avoid mention of the war, but Emilie untactfully had an argument with young Tad about who was really President. Emilie's attention was also drawn to General Sickles, who came clumping in and out of the household in a way that made her remark, "He seems on very intimate terms here."

And Dan noticed Mary's Emilie, who wore the black garments of widowhood. One day, Emilie was summoned to the Blue Room because, as one of the White House servants told her, there was a visitor inquiring after an old friend in the South. By now, she confessed, she was sick of people looking sideways at her, but this sounded innocent, and she went down to the Blue Room, where she found Senator Ira Harris of New York and the one-legged general sitting with Mary. Senator Harris wanted to ask after former U.S. Vice President Breckinridge, who was now a Confederate general—indeed, the divisional general under whose command her husband had died. Widow Helm told the senator that since she had not herself met General Breckinridge, she could give him no news of the general's health.

Harris went on pressing her, and—according to combative Emilie Helm—a contest developed. "Well, we have whipped the rebels at Chattanooga, and I hear, madam, the scoundrels ran like scared rabbits." It was hardly a sensitive reference, given that Chattanooga had widowed Emilie, but genial old Northern Democrats like Harris had been rendered less forgiving by the brutal level of casualties and by anxiety for relatives serving in the army. Emilie responded, "It was the example, Senator Harris, that you set them at Bull Run and Manassas." Mary tried to change the subject, but Harris turned to her and asked, "Why isn't Robert in the army?" Mary Lincoln went "as white as death." She had already confessed to Emilie that this was the coming threat she most feared—the loss of Robert to the war. He was a twenty-year-old undergraduate at Harvard who until now had been able with some credibility to claim that an astigmatic eye prevented him from volunteering his services.

A tremulous Mary replied to Harris, "Robert is making his preparations now to join the army, Senator Harris; he is not a shirker as you seem to imply, for he has been anxious to go for a long time. If fault there be, it is mine. I have insisted that he should stay in college a little longer, as I think an educated man can serve his country with more intelligent purpose than an ignoramus."

She could tell that neither Senator Harris, who sometimes went to the theater with the Lincolns, nor her friend Sickles agreed with this proposition. Dan's corps had had college boys in its ranks, many serving as enlisted men, who had suspended scholarship for the duration of the war. Sickles was too close a friend to disagree with her openly, however, particularly in front of others. But not so Harris. "I have only one son and he is fighting for his country," he told Mrs. Lincoln, before turning to Mrs. Helm. "And, madam, if I had twenty sons they should all be fighting the rebels."

"And if I had twenty, Senator Harris, they should all be opposing yours," said Mrs. Helm. She rushed from the room, and Mary Lincoln pursued her and embraced her.

Sickles had too recent a memory of his own pain and of all the fine young men who had been defaced, disemboweled, or torn apart along the Emmitsburg Road, in the Wheatfield and the Peach Orchard. He was agitated as he went upstairs to tell the unwell Abe Lincoln, who was lying down, about the incident downstairs. Abe laughed and shook his head. "The child has a tongue like the rest of the Todds," he said. Dan flashed with an irritability that had become more common since his injury. "You should not have that Rebel in your house." The President absorbed this and said, "Excuse me, General Sickles, my wife and I are in the habit of choosing our own guests. We do not need from our friends either advice or assistance in the matter."[7]

This brush did not seem to sour relations between the Lincolns and Dan Sickles. He frequently escorted Mr. and Mrs. Lincoln to the theater that winter, and later in the season, writing from the Brevoort House in New York, he was confident of being listened to by Mr. Lincoln when he proposed himself for the job of military commissioner, a not-yet-existent post he had devised, aimed at reconstructing the relationship between North and South. The President, in an attempt to accommodate Dan, at the end of January sent him a cable: "Could you, without its being inconvenient or disagreeable to yourself, immediately take a trip to Arkansas for me?" Dan wanted to accept, but he had been summoned to give testimony before the Joint Committee on the Conduct of the War, which was, like Dan himself, anxious to prove that General Meade had been a lackluster commander at Gettysburg.[8]

Almost five years to the day after he had shot Philip Barton Key, Dan rolled up to the Capitol in a carriage, his trouser leg pinned up. Whatever accommodation he was coming to with his wood-and-leather prosthetic leg, it was not politic to wear it today, when the visible absence of a limb might underpin the earnestness of his answers to the Joint Committee's questions.

Rising up the Capitol steps on his crutches, attended by Colonel Harry Tremain, Dan attracted the reverent admiration of the legislators, legislative aides, and citizens of the nation who happened to be coming to and going from the Capitol that morning. He entered the lobby and advanced toward the appointed room, where a quorum of the committee, made up of seven members drawn from both chambers, were sitting that morning. It would have been an aberration if both zealous Senators Zachariah Chandler and Benjamin Wade had not been present for the evidence of this potentially crucial ally against a general, Meade, whom they disliked on both political and performance grounds. After a short wait in an anteroom, Dan was invited into the fire-breathing committee's presence.

The committee began its questioning with an attempt to restore the status of Joe Hooker. What was the condition of the army after the disaster at Fredericksburg, when, down in that wintry camp on the Rappahannock, Hooker was given the command? Dan was pleased to answer that when General Hooker took command, "the condition of the army presented several features indicating demoralization. Desertions were very numerous; the general tone of conversation in the camps was that of dissatisfaction and complaint." He told the committee how effective Hooker had been in restoring morale. But the committee, feeding Dan precisely the questions he wanted, asked why, if Hooker was such an accomplished leader of the army, the Chancellorsville campaign had ended badly. Dan obligingly argued that the fault was not Hooker's. The loss of Chancellorsville was due to "the giving way of the Eleventh Corps on Saturday." The men of Howard's Eleventh Corps had come streaming back through the woods as "a mass of fugitives." Dan asserted that by the time Sunday dawned, General Hooker was already doomed to defense and withdrawal. But wasn't it true that Hooker had a taste for strong liquor? the committee asked. "I have never known him on duty to be in the least degree affected by intoxicating liquors."

The committee members thanked General Sickles. He had helped them to lay some groundwork for the restoration of Joe Hooker and the dismissal of Meade, whom they considered a secret proslaver and a delayer. But they required more from Dan. So he came back the following day, the eve of the anniversary of Key's death, and opened his second stanza of evidence by mentioning the circular Meade had sent out to his generals on July 1. "Already," said Dan, "it is no longer his intention to assume the offensive." Meade intended to back off and disengage. Despite conflicting orders and Meade's contradictory messages and impulses, Dan "had written a communication to General Meade, begging by all means to concentrate his army there and fight a battle, stating that in my opinion it was a good place to fight." Dan detailed his movement orders from and meetings with Meade that day. He declared that the order to retreat was already drafted, and that Meade was cemented in place at Gettysburg only by the enemy attack that occurred on that second day and made retreat impossible.

It was when the committee moved to the period after Gettysburg that Dan really enjoyed himself. His answers were not those of a man who had been taken off the field in shock and pain and shipped back to Washington, but were delivered with a certainty that seemed to imply that he had somehow still been there on July 3 and 4 to judge what should happen next. Yet he believed his wound, and the wounds of his corps, entitled him to an opinion.

"Question: In your opinion, as a military man, what do you think of the propriety of again encountering the enemy at the [Potomac] river before he recrossed?

"Answer: He should have been followed up closely, and vigorously attacked before he had an opportunity to recross the river. . . . If we could whip them at Gettysburg, as we did, we could much more easily whip a running and demoralized army seeking a retreat which was closed by a swollen river."

Then how did General Sickles account for the fact that a meeting of corps commanders had decided by a two-thirds vote not to make such an assault? General Sickles could not say how that happened; he reminded them that he was off the field, wounded.

To the committee's thanks, Sickles departed in a gray Washington dusk not unlike the one in which he had stamped home from the Capitol with temporary lunacy in his face. Now he went to his dinner in expectation of Meade's fall. This one-legged man on crutches was more eminently revered than he had ever been derided, and he might rise to any height, military or civil, under the aegis of Mr. Lincoln, who liked combative generals. He had shown both in the White House and on the Capitol steps that he could move with one leg more lithely than the hesitant, delaying Meade.[9]

Dan's assault on the dilatory Meade was splendidly reinforced by the evidence of General Abner Doubleday, whose fame in America would be associated with the founding of the national game, baseball, but who at this time harbored serious military ambitions. He came before the committee as a misused officer. On the first day of Gettysburg, he had, as senior surviving officer, taken over command of the First Corps, but had been replaced when Meade appointed instead a less senior officer. "I think there have been proslavery cliques controlling that army," said General Doubleday, "composed of men who, in my opinion, would have been willing to have a compromise in favor of slavery." He also argued that early in the battle Meade had singled him out as one of "a couple of scapegoats. . . . In case the next day's battle turned out unfavorably, he wished to mark his disapprobation of the first day's fight."

By March 4, the joint committee felt it had sufficient evidence regarding Gettysburg to call for Meade's dismissal. Senators Wade and Chandler recorded that they believed it their duty to visit both the President and the Secretary of War and lay before them "the substance of the testimony taken before them and . . . demand the removal of General Meade and the appointment of someone more competent." They declared they were not advocates of any particular general, even though they nominated Hooker as someone suitable. But if the President considered any general more competent for the command, "then let him be appointed. . . . Unless the state of things be changed it would become their duty to make the testimony public." They were thus not above threatening President Lincoln with the press.

When Mr. Lincoln delayed on the matter, the idea came naturally to Dan, or to someone close to him, of using the press; of producing a long article on Gettysburg from Dan's point of view. Its publication may have been deliberately delayed to coincide with General Meade's appearances before the committee. Dan also helpfully pointed out to Senator Chandler that his friend General Dan Butterfield had turned up at Willard's. Butterfield had been recuperating from a wound suffered at Gettysburg, and he had lost his position of chief of staff to Meade. He was now to command a mere division under General William Tecumseh Sherman, and such lowly work made him fretful and hostile to Meade. Butterfield did not have permission to be in Washington, but these niceties did not matter much to politicians like Dan and Butterfield. Dan suggested to the committee that Butterfield "be subpoenaed regularly," which would validate his being in town.

General Meade, still in command, was summoned to begin his testimony on March 5. He knew he would be given a hard time. As good as accused by Senator Wade of intending, on the morning of the July 2, to order the retreat of the army from Gettysburg, Meade denied any recollection of having issued such an order. He had, he said, made great efforts to mass his army on Gettysburg on the night of July 1, so it was improbable that he would order it to retreat unless the enemy did something to require him to. He also argued that the defenses the enemy had put in place strengthened his opinion that any renewed attack on Lee after the battle "would have resulted disastrously to our arms." He believed that Lee had ten to fifteen thousand men more than he himself had.

On March 12, an extensive article on the battle of Gettysburg, signed Historicus, appeared in the *New York Herald*. This long item, whoever wrote it, described the enterprising General Sickles making his wise decision to leave Emmitsburg and advance to help Howard, who had greeted him with the flattering statement "Here you are, General— always reliable, always first." Historicus declared that he had seen a circular of General Meade's, issued on the morning of July 1 to his corps commanders, stating that his advance had accomplished all the objects he had contemplated—namely, the salvation of Harrisburg and Philadelphia. Now he would desist altogether from the offensive. Gettysburg had become a great and holy incident in the American imagination by the winter of 1863–64, when the article appeared, so it was a grave matter to imply that Meade had not wanted his army to be there. Almost at the moment when Sickles's left flank was struggling with the right flank of the enemy, said Historicus, Meade was planning to retire, and this was the only plan he had. Historicus, as partial justification for Dan's move forward, quoted Meade's throwaway line to Dan: "Oh, generals are all out to look for the attack to be made where they are." At the time, the entire right wing of the enemy was concentrated on the devoted Third Corps, wrote Historicus, and Meade could not have cared less for the thunder that was about to descend upon them. Only later did Meade begin "to pour in reinforcements whose presence in the beginning of the action would have saved thousands of lives."

Historicus went on to describe what had happened on July 3 and 4 in the manner of an eyewitness, so perhaps the writer was an officer friend of Dan's who had been present on the battlefield on those two days. He concluded scathingly, "Had General Meade been more copious in his report and less reserved as to his own important acts, the necessity for this communication would not have existed."

Reading this long piece, Meade had no doubt that it and "other articles of the same kind in the New York papers were written or dictated by General Sickles; nevertheless, you will not be able to fix on him the authorship, and nothing would suit him better than to get into a personal or newspaper controversy." Meade asked Stanton and Lincoln to set up a court of inquiry, but Mr. Lincoln replied, "It is natural you should feel some sensibility on this subject, but I am not impressed . . . with the belief that your honor demands, or the public interest demands, such an inquiry."[10]

Dan's agitation against Meade was to have massive and not quite expected results for the nation. Mr. Lincoln did not yield to the importuning of the Committee on the Conduct of the War or of Dan, that is, not in the terms in which they hoped he would. He was weary of that committee, and, as much as he might listen to Sickles man to man, he did not choose to hear his views as filtered through Wade and Chandler. Meade continued in command of the Army of the Potomac, so, for all the permanent damage he did Meade, Dan might as well have spent the winter with Teresa. On the other hand, he and the committee did cause Lincoln to come up with another plan. Lincoln would supersede Meade by bringing in a supreme, newly created three-star general, a man not given to timidity or to flights of imagination, a fellow who had operated with great success in the West, General Ulysses S. Grant. Grant would have ultimate responsibility over Meade's Army of the Potomac.

Dan showed every sign of being satisfied with this result; his contempt for Meade was genuine. Dan met Grant at a White House levee in the East Room, where Grant, a socially awkward and strangely reticent man, was forced to stand on a sofa so that the crowd could get a view of him. When Secretary of War Stanton introduced Sickles, Dan told Grant, "Besieged by friends, even you must surrender, General."

Grant showed Sickles his sore hand and said, with an atypical neatness of phrasing, "Yes, I have been surrendering for two hours until I have no arms left." Later, Dan would plead with Grant to save the Third Corps, but without effect. It was the sort of decision Grant left to Meade.

In the end, the depleted divisions of Dan's corps were consolidated into the Second Corps under Major General Hancock, and the Black Diamonds of the Third Corps vanished.[11]

But in April, in an attempt to keep feverish Dan usefully employed, Mr. Lincoln sent him on a swing through the Union-held South to report both on the condition of the army there and on the prospects for reconstruction. He was told particularly to see whether Andrew Johnson, the Union-installed governor of Tennessee, could be checked in his severity against the local people, since Lincoln, unlike many other Republicans, wanted the South to be treated in a conciliatory manner.

In the winter just ending, Teresa had been subject to an increasing number of fevers and colds, and to the loss of appetite whose medical description was anorexia, brought on by appetite-suppressant drugs and by the disease itself. When she had Dr. Payne or Dr. Bradhurst in, the doctor prescribed strong doses of medicinal purgatives, and bleeding or cupping, the application of heated glass cups, "to draw out deep-seated infections," to carefully chosen sites, cut with a lancet, on the chest or back. As the cup cooled, blood and tissue fluid oozed up and, doctors believed, among other matter voided were the vicious tubercular cells. Like all other sufferers, Teresa continued to take futile infusions of unpalatable cod liver oil, and, of course, the tinctures of morphine either prepared by apothecaries or presented as patent medicines. Mrs. Bagioli was her nurse, and so were Laura and a female servant. Her spittle was streaked with blood.

If the doctors suggested going to the country, she did not do so. Compared to cholera or typhus, tuberculosis was considered a gentle and slow condition. But it brought with it a feverish invigoration of the imagination, as the famous Brontë sisters had shown. Even at this stage of the disease, poor Teresa's vivid dreams would have evoked a hunger for tenderness and touch, which seemed to be unsatisfied.

Over time, Mrs. Bagioli and visitors such as the loyal Chevalier Wikoff noticed her features becoming sharper, bonier, though not enough yet to cancel her reputation for allure. Just the same, her eyes were beginning to sink in her face and to resemble flowers bruised by winter's first frost. Her breasts, famous and fantasized-upon, were slowly sinking, as if the rib cage were collapsing. She was in the hands of what Dickens called "a disease in which death and life are so strangely blended that death takes the hue of life and life the gaunt and grisly form of death; a disease which medicine never cured, wealth never warded off or poverty could cause exemption from."[12]

In Memphis, Dan, not yet fully acquainted with the latest reports of his wife's illness, was greeted with full honors by the occupying Union Army. Whatever others may have once said of his own accommodating morality, Dan found that Memphis was a morass, with many federal officers taking money from Southern profiteers to release certain goods for sale at phenomenal prices into the dwindling Confederacy. He had nonetheless been turned into an absolutist by what he had seen of the rebellion, and was morally appalled that officers would profit by this commerce. He warned the President, "This intercourse enriches a mercenary horde, who follow in the rear of our force, corrupting by the worst temptations those in authority." Dan visited Sherman's rampaging army in their lines at Resaca, Georgia. He inspected the city of Helena in Arkansas, New Orleans, then Crescent City, the navy yard at Pensacola, and, finally, Charleston. He warned Lincoln and Stanton about the problem of an abiding hatred of the North among the parts of the South that had been captured.[13]

By the time he returned, the Republicans had just about decided that in 1864 they would again nominate Lincoln, with Dan's recent host Andrew Johnson of Tennessee, a Union Democrat, as his running mate. The Democrats selected General McClellan, but no matter Dan's political history, he believed there was only one man to bring the war to a successful conclusion, which was the only issue that meant anything. In the peculiar but not unique position of a Democrat who would vote for a Republican, he became a leading figure of the extensive group named Democrats for Lincoln, which included his friend General Meagher. On November 1, 1864, at the Cooper Institute in New York, they held a massive rally at which Dan was the chief speaker. "As regards to the Chicago Democrat convention which is appointing McClellan as their candidate," said Dan, those who would rather stay at home, who would rather not pay taxes, were all "accommodated under that platform. . . . Every sneak in the republic who wants a hiding place, can get under that platform. [Cheers and laughter] No man, not even its candidate, has the courage to stand upon it. [Cheers and laughter]"[14]

And so Lincoln was reelected, and as the war thundered on to its climax, Dan still felt underused and could not turn to the normal recourse, in the company of wife and daughter, that men with any taste for a humble life and intimate joys would willingly have sought. Though sometimes at Bloomingdale, he lived mainly downtown at the Brevoort House, and no doubt told Teresa that was better for her, given her restlessness and cough. He possibly believed it, too, but Laura would judge him harshly. Not so George Sickles. He had the usual attitude to Teresa's condition—that, with God's will, the slow-burning and not very specific disease would, by good rest and medicine, and the basic strength of her constitution, be vanquished.

Dan, in his restlessness, wrote on December 9 to the newly reelected President: "I beg respectfully to remind you that I am still unassigned. . . . I hope to be spared the humiliation of being dropped from the rolls amongst the list of useless officers." The President was motivated by Dan's part at Gettysburg to find another task for him, and asked him to undertake a taxing mission. Lincoln needed an emissary to go on government business to Panama and Colombia. Greater Colombia, or New Granada, as the Federation of Colombia, Costa Rica, and Panama styled itself, formed one loose federal state ruled from the highland capital of Bogotá, Colombia. He was to leave by January with the purpose of persuading the Panamanian authorities to allow Union troops to cross the Isthmus of Panama, something they had recently prohibited. He was then to travel to Bogotá and raise, with the federal authorities there, the possibility of Colombia's offering a home to freed black slaves, who were now pooling in Washington and in Northern cities. He was, in one way, well equipped in that he had as a congressman got on well with the Colombian ambassador in Washington, the urbane Manuel Murillo, who was now president of Colombia.

In another way, it was an extraordinary task to ask of a one-legged man, given the extent to which donkeys, canoes, and sampan-like craft were used for travel in Central and South America. Some thought it a make-work mission devised to pacify or even neutralize Dan, more than to meet any national need. The malicious believed rumors of a sexual relationship between Mrs. Lincoln and Dan. In their version, Abe was getting a rival out of town. Whatever the case, Dan was hungry for the mission and suffered no doubts about his capacity, whether diplomatic or physical. He may have thought that if he made this journey into the Andes, no one could ever say he was not fit to campaign. George Sickles, of similar rugged soul, was proud of his son's having been offered such a potentially important task.

Chevalier Wikoff went to the *Herald* office in New York to talk up Dan's mission and to correct an impression that Mr. Lincoln wanted Dan to lay the groundwork for a pan-American alliance against the European powers. The *Herald* did not mention a significant sidebar to Dan's mission. The commissioners of Central Park, which were these days heavily covered with hospital tents full of wounded, had authorized him, in view of his continuing interest in the park's zoo, to acquire from professional trappers in Colombia whatever items of South American fauna he could.

Wikoff was in place to accompany Teresa and Laura to the midwinter dock for Dan's departure. The young wife was winter-pale and had an ethereal air. She was fortified with laudanum to help her negotiate the freezing wharf and the gangplank. Since she had lost a little of her rounded desirability, Bogotá was precisely the dry mountain locale she might have benefited from, but even if Dan had contemplated inviting her on the journey, there lay between her and the Andean height at which Bogotá was located a belt of potentially fatal tropics. She may nonetheless have daydreamed of going, remembering that when Meagher had gone on a mission to Costa Rica and Panama on the eve of the war, to try to negotiate a railway across the Panamanian province of

Chiriqui, and lucky Libby Meagher had seen the splendid forests and spectacular birds of Central America, and had resided for a time in the presidential palace in San José, Costa Rica.

Though the men at the wharf knew Teresa was run-down, in an age when a woman's premature decline could have many causes, they did not yet know with certainty that she had consumption. Nor did Wikoff mention any such condition in his friendly letters to the traveling general. He did notice that at the ship, "Thérèse," as he always called her, was unusually affected by Dan's departure. "The tears came streaming down her face the whole time she remained on the pier." Like Mrs. Lincoln, she was full of "sad presentiments" and, as Wikoff noticed, was not in the habit of showing her feeling as fully as did the First Lady, and thus she "must be deeply stirred for it to escape in tears. Laura, too, was crying, the first time I ever knew her to do so." Wikoff had heard that there was an argument about the house at Bloomingdale, involving the Bagiolis and Teresa. Perhaps the parents had partially underwritten the original purchase, and now, having fallen on tougher times, and needing to take in lodgers at their recently acquired house on Thirty-second Street, may have wanted to realize their money from Bloomingdale. It was typical that Wikoff should be attuned to the argument taking place between Teresa and Mrs. Bagioli, whom he described to Dan as "vulgar and coarse . . . complicated and unfeeling." Hence, Dan's importuning of the President for a job, something that would put him back on full pay, may have arisen from economic causes as well as ambition. "It will be a dreadful blow if you are obliged to lose it [Bloomingdale]," said the genial Wikoff to Dan. He assured Dan that he would go up there on the Sunday after Dan's departure on the mission "and do all I can to alleviate your absence. . . . Write fully and often to Terese."

However temporarily strained her relationship with her mother, Teresa had a reliable backup in George and Susan Sickles. They continued to be doting grandparents, and George would always be loyal to Laura's interests even when she clashed with Dan. But he was a dutiful father, and saw to it that as Dan made his way south, at every stage there would be a paternal letter waiting. Still addressing Dan as "My dear

General," the letters included admiring news, such as the rumor in the *Times* that Dan would be nominated for the mayoralty of New York. George also included such details as "Laura visits her grandma as a general thing on Saturday." Occasionally the little girl stayed overnight, and her general health—George was pleased to report—was good.[15]

Dan and his aides concluded their consultations with the local authorities in Colón, Panama, by March. As Secretary Seward had instructed him to do, he made clear to the Panamanians that the United States would intervene to keep the route open, but the Panamanians told him horror stories of the behavior of drunken gringos along the railway route across the isthmus. He concluded that these stories were not opportunistic complaints, for the Panamanians were sympathetic to the United States. The Panamanian and other New Granada ministers and bureaucrats with whom he met had a sense that the prosperity of the United States was a direct result of the liberal institutions of that nation, and they wanted their region to flourish by the same means. Dan was authorized to offer, in principle, damage compensation for the behavior of Americans on the isthmus, and the Panamanians considered that just. Some time after Dan's visit, the amount due was settled at $14 million.

Having crossed to South America by steamer, Dan wrote to George describing, for his entertainment, the important Colombian port of Cartagena, with its old Spanish forts. From there, he and his aides caught the steamer up the coast and into the broad mouth of the Magdalena, the river path to the capital. The river's lower reaches were steamy, swampy, and dangerous to health, an appropriate environment for malaria and yellow fever. The general went untouched by these perils. As well as possessing a strong constitution, he had none of the hypochondria of Barton Key and many others of his contemporaries. More than four hundred miles along the river, against a strong tide, lay not the capital Bogotá but the final approaches to it. Dan, of course, cigar at lip, and adroit and athletic on his crutches, took enthusiastically to life on the steamer, and was fascinated at every river stop it made to take on produce and tobacco.

New Granada was, in the 1860s, an immensely more hopeful place than some of its constituent parts became in the late twentieth century. It had liberated its slaves as early as 1851, and its constitution acknowledged a full range of civil liberties. A revolution led by the renowned progressive Tomás de Mosquera confiscated much church property and radically separated church and state. In terms of the racial politics of the day, Colombia made a good harbor for former slaves, particularly because such a high proportion of its people were mestizos (Indian-white), mulattos (white-black), and zambo (black-Indian).

The Magdalena's rapids near the town of Honda required passengers to transfer either by mule or by jaunting carts, and Dan managed the mules by strapping on his prosthetic leg. He and his party left the ascending river and traveled by mule and cart a spectacular seventy miles to Bogotá, climbing passes in the cordilleras, from which they could see mountains stretch away an eternity to the west, and descending at last into the valley where the capital was located. Dan got an impression of a mass of tiled roofs, and saw above the city the potent local mountains of Monserrate and Guadalupe.

The president, Manuel Murillo, as well as having been the Colombian ambassador in Washington, had visited it as late as the winter of 1863–64, negotiating recognition of the new Colombian government and looking for guarantees against the possibility that clients of Colombian companies might sue the country for nondelivery because of the federal blockade of the South. Murillo authorized a considerable number of ceremonial events to honor the famous visiting general. In meetings at the presidential residence near the cathedral, Murillo explained to Dan that New Granada's various regional components had such power that they could, as in the case of Panama, make decisions bearing on foreign relations, such as banning the transit of Americans and American troops. It was an issue, said Murillo, on which Bogotá could not give absolute guarantees or dictate Panama's policies. But important advice and reports could be prepared in collaboration with Dan to minimize future problems. Dan found, too, that in principle Murillo was open to the concept of American freed-slave immigration to Colombia. But the matter would need to be discussed in his cabinet and subjected to the advice of the Colombian bureaucracy. In the end, no final arrangement was ever reached, and little came of the concept. Yet representing its virtues and arguing its value occupied Dan and his staff for three months.

Dan relished life in that high Hispanic capital. He spent his time in conferences and social visits and in excursions into the surrounding country with trappers. But sometimes he had too much leisure, since the mail came only once a month or even less often, given that the river was full of bars of mud and the steamer schedules problematic. On May 2, he wrote to Stanton that he would be back in Cartagena to leave by steamer for the United States on June 1, unless there were more instructions from the Secretary of State waiting for him in Panama. "I shall have the honor to report to you for duty before the 1st of July. I trust you may then have occasion to employ me usefully in the field. You and I burnt the first powder in this war, on our side, and so I wish to be with you, 'in at the death' of the rebellion." Dan, knowing nothing of the final days of the war or of the national tragedy that had overtaken the people, told Stanton that he would report to him on two legs, because in that mountain capital, he boasted, he had made progress in the use of his prosthetic limb. He had ridden through the mountain passes in every direction out of Bogotá, on Peruvian and Granadian horses and "all sort of mules." He doubted that even General Meade could now doubt his ability to ride far enough to the front to post a battery or make a reconnaissance. He was heartened by the latest war news he had received, but it was the news of February's actions, the fall of Charleston and Columbia, in South Carolina, and of Wilmington. He did not know two crucial items of news—that Grant had succeeded in strangling Lee's army into surrender at Appomattox, and that President Lincoln, to whom he had been close enough to importune and upbraid him, had been killed by a pro-Southern actor named Booth during a night at the theater. While watching a comedy titled *Our American Cousin*, Lincoln was shot in the back of the head, and Mary, at his side, had screamed, "Oh, my God, and have I given my husband to die?" Had Dan been in Washington, he might well have been in that fatal presidential box at Ford's Theatre, as was his friend Senator Harris, to see the nation's noblest heart discharge its blood. As Dan savored Bogotá and conversed with Murillo and his cabinet about emancipation, the isthmus, and the fauna of the cordilleras, his friend Mary Lincoln was a demented, howling widow, so frantic that cabinet ministers, generals, and doctors were shocked by her uncontrolled grief, both as her husband lay dying and afterward.[16]

The American consul in Santa Marta, down on the coast, sent notification upriver to the capital of the end of the war, but not of Mr. Lincoln's death. Receiving the news of peace, Dan may have experienced mixed feelings, but he took a carriage at once to President Murillo's palace, and Murillo, who had great admiration for Lincoln and his cause, made arrangements to announce and celebrate the victory and the coming peace by means of a banquet for the diplomatic corps.

Carrying letters for Secretary of State William Seward, Dan left for Honda late in May at the head of wagons laden with captured animals, and there he was handed another American dispatch, one that told him not only that President Lincoln had been murdered, but that there had been a series of attacks on Union leaders. An attempt had been made on the life of Secretary Seward and on that of his friend Stanton, the dispatch said. The report about Stanton was not true, but Secretary of State Seward had been severely wounded, while lying ill at home in Washington, by a fellow conspirator of John Wilkes Booth. The conspirator invaded Seward's sickroom at the same time that Booth shot Lincoln. Whether Dan learned the details then or later, it must have been, even for such a strong-minded man, a redolent detail to discover that Seward's wounds had been inflicted in the same building in which Key had died. For during his cabinet career, Secretary Seward stayed in the old Clubhouse on Lafayette Square.

On the steamer home, Dan was accompanied by his crates full of riverine and Andean animals for the Central Park menagerie—tree sloths, anteaters, monkeys, tapirs, agoutis, and a jaguar. As he approached New York, Dan grew more uneasy about his potential reception by the new President, Andrew Johnson, who had come to the White House after barely six weeks in the post of Vice President and as a result of his chief's assassination. Dan had got to know Johnson in Tennessee the previous year, knew that he was proud of his humble origins as a former tailor, self-educated—a history for which others mocked him. Being one of those Democrats severely alienated by the ferocity of the rebellion, Johnson had at one stage said that the South should be managed after the war with fire and rope. Those Radical Republicans who wanted to see the South humiliated in every sense were hopeful that he would introduce more rigorous policies toward the conquered areas than they had seen prefigured in the case of Lincoln.[17]

That summer, following the established pattern of earlier ones, Dan visited Teresa and Laura. He was conscious that by now Teresa's problems had worsened, and his friends later indicated that he was resolved to arrange for her the best care. She was possessed of the listlessness and flushed face typical of her disease, and she went about the house, still trying to attend to domestic matters, with a glazed eye and a rasping breath that the humidity exacerbated. She was also possessed by what the tubercular Brontë sisters' physician called a "tinge of religious melancholy." She had become a more devout Catholic, and her bedroom was strewn with rosaries, missals, scapulars, holy cards, and medals, all alien to Dan's tradition, and her bed was sprinkled by Mrs. Bagioli with holy water. Friendly doctors still jovially misinformed Dan and Laura about the prospects of Teresa's recovery. After all, the medical journals, including the *Lancet*, carried news of a number of new treatments under consideration in England, including mixtures of quinine and beef tea, and the pumping of various mixtures into patients' mouths, the most common ingredients for such forcible pumping including hydrogen, coal gas, iodine, creosote, and carbolic acid. Teresa was, after all, naturally robust, and if the right treatment could be hit upon, the disease would withdraw quite quickly.[18]

Bloomingdale seemed secure from a forced sale, and would be rendered more secure if Dan was given yet another post. And at the end of the summer, Secretary of War Stanton nominated him for one—the military governorship of South Carolina. This state, which had been the mother of the rebellion, would be a turbulent province to administer, but

Dan was exhilarated by the prospect. He had fought off the tag of immobility and uselessness that the loss of his leg had encouraged people to plant on his forehead. No doubt his Andean journey had helped prove that he was not ready to be made inactive. By early September, he was on his way to Charleston, to the harbor where the entire calamity had been introduced by the firing on Sumter. There were valid reasons for not taking Teresa this time, even had he decided to. The task in Charleston and in Colombia, turned to ashes by Sherman's order, would give Dan even less time for a sick wife than he had previously been able to provide. As well, though Charleston was warmer than New York, it had been tried by other consumption sufferers, who found that its moist winters and heavy-aired summers were not notably helpful. And then the region had been reduced by war to a primitive economy in which most goods, including medicines, were scarce.

Arriving by steamer with his staff, Dan found Charleston a demoralized city, with a bitter sense of its own debasement. Parts of the town were in rubble from Union bombardments by land and sea, but despite the damage that had been done to it, General Sickles could tell it had not yet been cured of its hubris. Nonetheless, the harbor was empty—there was nothing to export, and the traditional aristocracy, who possessed town houses or lived in mansions around the verge of the city, had been reduced to wearing the homespun clothing previously worn by poor farmers and slaves. The only wealthy people on the landscape were the war profiteers and those Yankee investors looking for cheap property, markets that could only improve. Derisively, they were called carpetbaggers. Resenting them, willing to beat them to death, the remnants of the Southern army loitered in the streets in tattered gray or butternut. As well, the former slaves who milled around town often seemed disoriented and displaced by freedom—a point the advocates of slavery did not fail regularly to make to visiting Northerners.

Dan knew the powers he took to South Carolina were prodigious, with the only brake upon them the cabinet in Washington and hostile commentary in South Carolina itself and in the national press. The South Carolinians understood his position, and many resented him accordingly. He took up residence in a handsome surviving house on Charlotte Street and established his headquarters at the Citadel, the grand Southern military academy, one of the glories of antebellum Charleston, that had largely remained intact, being far from the range of the U.S. naval blockade. Dan was early visited by planters who came with stories of their former power and complaints about the behavior of the Negroes. One planter Dan would remember presented himself with the boast he had spent forty years in the South Carolina legislature, had entertained President Van Buren in his mansion, and had owned hundreds of slaves. He produced, as a sign of his former wealth and intellectual liveliness, a repeater watch, a watch that struck the hour. The man, whom Dan described as "haughty," even though Dan had enjoyed a considerable and friendly acquaintance with such people before the war, complained that his slaves hung on to their former quarters but refused to work. They were insolent; they carried shotguns; occasionally they burned their own huts. When Sherman's army was approaching, this much-reduced Southern dignitary told Dan, he had set fire to his ancestral mansion so that it would not be defiled. He said, "I could maintain discipline among my Negroes without coming to you, but you have taken away my authority as a master, and you have substituted nothing in its place."

"Then," Dan depicted himself as saying, "I would advise you to give your Negroes a good example to imitate. For instance, if you don't want them to burn their huts, don't burn your own house. . . . If you don't want them to carry double-barreled shotguns, don't carry a double-barreled shotgun yourself when you drive out." The planter remarked, "If other Yankee generals didn't know more than you do, I don't understand how the South got licked." The story—and perhaps it is a parable—is indicative of the style Dan tried to bring to his administration of South, and later of North, Carolina.[19]

Dan was also visited in his office, and wherever he traveled, by the minority of anti-secession, pro-Union men who had remained loyal to the United States and had been severely persecuted throughout the war. Such men existed in every Southern state, though there were more in

North Carolina and Tennessee than in South Carolina. In some cases it was the widows, harrowed by years of suffering, who came to him. Some of these loyal Union folk took to demonstrating that there was a new order in place by breaking the old shibboleths of race. As one Southern writer complained, they "ate and drank, walked and rode, went to public places and ostensibly affiliated with Negroes." This incited a range of savage retaliations by former Rebels, and a corresponding law-and-order challenge for Dan and his men.

A journalist who visited the Carolinas recorded a sense that Dan, too, must have recognized—that the rural Southerners lived in a far more primitive condition than their counterparts in Maine or Vermont. "Thus, Charleston has much intelligence, and considerable genuine culture; but go twenty miles away, and you are in the land of the barbarians. . . . In South Carolina there is very little pretense of loyalty. I believe I found less than fifty men who admitted any love for the Union." A state convention of pro-Union or, at the very least, realistic Southerners had already elected a civil governor with whom Dan would need to collaborate. Fortunately, he was a competent man of the realistic kind, a former Speaker of the House and a neighbor of Dan's from Lafayette Square, James L. Orr, who, before the cataclysm and prior to Dan and Teresa's occupation, had rented the Stockton Mansion. Orr had been a Confederate, had served the entire war with increasing doubt in the Southern Senate in Richmond, and had now—treasonably, according to the fire-eaters; sensibly, according to the less rabid—taken the oath to the United States again and brought his considerable gifts to rebuilding his state. By and large he got on well sharing power with Dan, and he remembered the day of Dan's acquittal, when he had been one of his congratulators.

To keep order from the Citadel in this prime rebel province, as of January 1, 1866, Dan had a force of 352 officers and 7,056 men. They were scattered throughout this triangle of a state, in one restive little town after another, as far as the foothills of the Appalachians. His mandate was that this force should be deployed to protect the freed black men and women, and loyal whites, from the anger of disaffected rural populations and veterans. He wanted to show that in this regard a new era had dawned, and a general order he issued, appropriately, on January 1, 1866, declared the state's Black Code null and void, and decreed that "all laws shall be applicable to all inhabitants." Negroes were to have the same judicial recourse as whites, and all occupations were to be opened to them. They were also to possess a novel freedom for ex-slaves: freedom of movement, exemption from any special taxes, and immunity from arrest on the basis of the poor and vagrancy laws.[20]

His general order created, as he expected, howls of outrage in the South Carolina hinterland, let alone in Charleston and Columbia. Dan had earlier warned Stanton and President Lincoln that there was an intractability of feeling in the South. And as his first summer in Charleston began, he told Stanton again that the Southern people yielded to the United States only a reluctant and sullen allegiance. "In my Department, I have not seen the American flag raised by a Carolinian. If it floated over a dwelling, or a hotel, or a shop, the population would avoid the place as they would shun a pesthouse filled with lepers."

Since he and his soldiers could not prevent every outrage, Dan began to intervene, personally or through officers, in district court hearings to protect former slaves and those who were sympathetic to them. When a district court headed by Judge A. P. Aldridge sentenced a white man to flogging for his association with blacks, Dan sent a company of troops to intervene, clear the court, and prevent the punishment. This caused Judge Aldridge to complain to Washington about assaults on the independence of the judiciary. Then two Northern visitors, suspected carpetbaggers, were beaten up in a Columbia shanty barroom, and a magistrate released on bail the young men who had done it. Dan removed the Columbia magistrate from office and sent the culprits before a military court, which sentenced them to six months in Fort Macon. He knew his actions would once more unleash a torrent of complaints from Southerners to the Attorney General in Washington. He and other military governors were in an impossible situation. The *Realpolitik* of

America then was that Radical Republicans wanted the South crushed, while Southerners, who had inherited intact their judicial system, did not like to see it interfered with at all.

Dan had traveled so far since his pro-Southern days as to see the South Carolinians who attacked the new social order as incarnations of an intolerance that, "illustrated in countless affrays, was long permitted in Southern communities, to hunt down with cruel violence persons venturing to maintain opinions not in harmony with local sentiment." To him the incarnations of this "cruel violence" were a pre-KKK group named the Regulators, who rode over the countryside to combat the "Negro menace." During 1866 and into the new year, as Dan's military force was reduced in strength, so did the Regulators roam more widely and demonstrate throughout the farmlands of South Carolina.

The daily stream of petitioners who came to Dan's office at the Citadel did not diminish, and he treated them courteously and became socially friendly with some. By June 1866, his power had been increased; he was placed in command of the newly created Second Military Department, which included both North and South Carolina. He could hardly get to New York at all, for although North Carolina was easier to administer than its sister, the spring and summer resonated with the deeds of the hooded Regulators. In North Carolina the governor he collaborated with was a principled Quaker named Jonathan Worth, who had throughout opposed the rebellion and whose desire was to see North Carolina return to such a degree of loyalty and prosperity as once again to be a sovereign state in the nation. North Carolinians were more willing to declare themselves pro-Union, and to tell visitors that they "had always prophesied the downfall of the so-called Confederacy and had always desired the success of the Union arms."

The news from New York was that Teresa continued poorly. To outsiders, though, sometimes the disease seemed to bring its own consolation. One French author declared that in contrast to "diseases of crude and baser kind which clog and soil the mind, phthisis is an illness of the lofty and noble parts: it calls forth a state of elevation, tenderness and love." Edgar Allan Poe had written of "the terrible beauty of consumption," from which his wife, Virginia, suffered. It made her, he recorded, "delicately, morbidly angelic." The forms of sensuality were being eroded from Teresa. She had become more angular; that sumptuous, full-fleshed look so admired by Victorian men was gone, but she smiled like an angel, not least in Laura's direction. As Teresa rested from the efforts of mounting the stairs and attempts at managing the house in the way she had so easily done in the past, her thirteen-year-old daughter watched and made her judgments about her father. If one wanted to be harsh, one could say that Dan had, since their reconciliation, avoided every notable chance to acknowledge Teresa as his wife. And Laura wanted to be harsh. As for Teresa, had she wanted to go to Charleston that winter, she was too proud to be importunate and demand to be brought there, however temporarily. She knew she could not fulfill the functions of the general's consort as she could have a few years back. But in her clear hours, even for a sunny soul like hers, the rustication in Bloomingdale, the purdah of the suburbs, must have seemed connected to her interminable decay; body and spirit were in perverse conspiracy against her.

Typically, Dan had found other associations. He had been visited in the Sherman-shattered, burned, and ruined Columbia, for example, by a young, forthright Southerner named Allie Grant, a gentlewoman down on her luck, as were most of her Southern sisters. She later wrote to him asking for employment with a Dan-like directness of her own, and requesting that he "write to her as soon as possible, for I long to hear something absorbing and compulsory to fill my head and hands, and occupy my thoughts." Allie was one of the recipients of the ration certificates Dan distributed from his office, for in some ways, in that hungry landscape, his job resembled that of a modern nongovernmental organization or aid body.[21]

In the summer of 1866, President Johnson offered Dan the post of Minister to the Netherlands. Dan suspected it was a mechanism to get him out of the Carolinas because of complaints that he was both too soft on Southerners and too tyrannical over them. He immediately approached General Grant and asked whether the offer of the posting arose from any dissatisfaction with his performance. In conflict with the President over policy in the South, Grant replied that he himself would regret to see Sickles replaced. In the letter refusing the diplomatic posting, Dan pleaded that the $3,500 per year which his wife and family would need to remain in New York would leave him only $4,000 to run an official establishment at a foreign court, and that he would therefore run short.

As another fall came on, Allie Grant of Columbia was still an intermittent friend to Dan. "I really thought you'd entirely forgotten the '*beggar.*' I am very happy to learn that I was laboring under a mistake," she wrote to Dan. He had set up a post for her, which she intended to accept with great pleasure. "I was inclined to call and see you again while you were up here, but some of the Delegates [to the state convention] were talking already about my first visit. . . . People are generally too pragmatical in Columbia." She had spotted him talking with a former Confederate general outside the hotel, a fellow she had quarreled with over politics, so she had not stopped to converse. "Columbia is awfully dull," wrote Allie. "And I do wish I was down in Charleston. P.S. I think you had better come to Columbia for a while, and I will let you see me, not in *disguise* though." The general, even without a leg, was still a charmer of women, as long as they had a sportive attitude.

But not all Dan's generosity to Southern women was opportunistic. He was supporting the aging widow of an eminent Southern anti-secessionist judge, Jane Pettigru, who suffered from an abiding disease—perhaps tuberculosis—and who told Dan, "What I would do without the two Rations a day I could not tell." Perhaps on the basis of his experience with Teresa, Dan had also been kind enough to prescribe opiates for her health problems. "The laudanum you kindly advised me to be supplied with," said Mrs. Pettigru, "I would die without."[22]

That fall and winter it was still the turbulent and surly condition of South Carolina that occupied most of his time, though the raids of the Regulators became less common. He was involved in many further arguments, arresting some of the leading citizens of Edgefield, South Carolina, and taking them out of that jurisdiction to Columbia on charges of complicity in the murder of Union soldiers. He was reduced to threatening the white citizens of Edgefield, Lawrence, and Newberry that their freed slaves would be provided with rations, housing, and protection at the expense of those districts unless they behaved more reasonably.

He felt, too, a deep and visceral offense at continuing demonstrations of disloyalty by people in Charleston, and refused to turn a blind eye to the abuse of the symbols of the Union. He arrested the editor of the *South Carolinian* for commending a war remembrance at which the Confederate flag was displayed. When, in the following spring, the Charleston fire companies marched, he required them to carry the Union flag, and a fireman who mutilated it was held for a month without trial and publicly reprimanded.

In November 1866, the month when President Johnson optimistically declared that the rebellion no longer existed, Dan's force had been reduced to 2,700 men, for the official end of rebellion meant that he could turn over to the civil authorities all law cases and jails, except on the sea islands off the coast. Not least among Dan's problems was that Union troops sometimes provoked black freedmen to behave provocatively in front of Southerners, generally with a reaction that fell not upon the Union soldiers, but upon the freedmen. Yet he placed great reliance on his troops as keepers of order and believed that in the case of North and South Carolina, they were the reason for "the fortunate exemption of this Department from the riots and collisions which have occurred elsewhere." Indeed, by the early winter of 1866–67, civil strife began to diminish, law and order being enforced, not always perfectly but with less public resistance, by law officers people knew to be locals instead of the despised bluecoats. Much of the duty of his men now consisted of exhuming the shallowly buried bodies of Sherman's men and reinterring them properly.[23]

In New York, Laura had become, in the eyes of her ailing, bemused mother, a model of Dan's energy and stubbornness, and her inchoate and bewildered taste for life and activity, acquired both from Dan and from the Da Pontes and Bagiolis, expressed itself in her abiding enthusiasm for painting. This was a testing time for a child who was solitary and both assertive and shy. Teresa intended, if possible, to send her to the nuns at Manhattanville, so that like her—or, at least, like her had she not fallen for the trap of her own luscious and open nature—Laura might grow up with a network of genial friends to absorb and direct her liveliness, and to give her a sense of living a normal, unjudged life.

Even now, Teresa, when feeling well and in remission from languor, tried to go out, wearing heavy boots, inquiring into the health of one of her dogs, or tramping the lanes to visit a sick neighbor. But mainly she was subject to those days of unspecific exhaustion that had become more common during the summer of 1866 and as the autumn began. She had slipped into a near-permanent invalid state by the onset of winter.

But she was still hungry for urbane visitors. Comforted by her Catholic devotions, eased by medicines, and feeling remote from the sins and blood and shame of 1859, she held few grudges, and one of the men who visited her that winter was James Topham Brady, a fellow of such delicacy of feeling that he remained concerned about the harsh treatment to which he had subjected her name during the trial. Brady himself had had uncertain health—indeed, he had only two more winters to live—and typically wished to be at peace with all souls. He gave Teresa and Laura a copy of his *A Christmas Dream*, a takeoff on *A Christmas Carol* published in 1860. Brady's book was suffused with concern for poor and unfortunate women and with a sense of loss. The tale began with a girl pauper on a busy street who was churlishly refused a coin at Christmas by a man mounting a carriage. Soon after, the same carriage ran her down and careened onward, and the narrator records the injustice of this scene of privileged arrogance, poverty, and misfortune. From there, the scene moves to a New York restaurant, and the storyteller has a dream in which a man, or a spirit carrying a sack, accosts him, telling him that tonight he has seen the "sufferings earned by the heartlessness of bloated avarice," and taking him back to Christmases past.

Thus it was other and, in many ways, more innocent men than Dan who charmed and diverted Teresa that pale winter. Manny Hart, Henry Wikoff, and the bachelor Brady all made the hard, cold journey by coach up icy Broadway from Lower Manhattan, but since none of them warned Dan urgently of her condition, they may have judged it something chronic, or believed, by the glitter of Teresa's splendid eyes, that she would recover from it in spring. That was very likely her attitude, too, or her conscious hope. It was hard for anyone to believe that lovely Teresa was seriously vulnerable. "I imagined her as little likely to die as myself," wrote Emily Brontë, who knew everything about tuberculosis, of the consumptive Frances Earnshaw in *Wuthering Heights*. "She was rather thin but young-complexioned and her eyes sparkled like diamonds." Just so did Teresa's, especially in lively company.[24]

But Teresa became totally bedridden at the height of that winter, in January 1867. Over a week, she declined unexpectedly and at a fierce rate. Maria Bagioli nursed her anxiously, and the ineffectual doctors of Bloomingdale came and went. Though newspapers and friends in that time were always delicate about naming an exact cause of death, in case the squalor of symptoms detracted from the nobility of the deceased, she was said to have caught a pulmonary infection that made her condition suddenly more acute. Bloodstained discharges came from her mouth. The features were "cyanosed," to use the doctors' term, blue and pinched, and the flesh seemed to fall away from the bones of her face, as if gravity were winning the battle against her. She endured strong chest pains, and her heart palpitated wildly. Poignantly, it was often during these more extreme phases of the disease that reputable doctors would open a vein in the patient's arm and bleed her, in theory to reduce the symptomatic pressure in the system, but managing to reduce the patient's capacity to struggle against the disease. A priest came, bidden by Mrs. Bagioli, and gave Teresa the last rites, the sacred oil on eyes, nose, mouth, hands, feet. This scandalous woman Teresa, whose name still burned in the American imagination, her vivid eroticism only partly erased by the calamities of the Civil War, all at once lost consciousness of the world for which she was well fitted, and became, in one vast, tormented, but unknowing breath, a cold-weather corpse, an eroded landscape.

She was laid out in her coffin in Bloomingdale's Applewood Room, awaiting the arrival of her husband, who had been summoned by telegram and was already on a train with an alacrity for which she had always hoped in life. The news had stunned him; he had not expected her death so soon, or that she would die of this condition.

The newspapers of New York thought that it would require more bravery and fortitude of Dan to endure this loss heroically than he had needed to oppose the charge of thousands in the roar of battle. Dan was, in his particular way, grief-stricken, and wept unaffectedly. He was not a fellow to wallow in regret, but Teresa's death was so unfair, not least to Teresa herself. She had just turned thirty-one years, the press recorded, and had been in failing health for some time, and a recent cold "took root in her constitution" and led to the melancholy fact of her death.

The funeral took place at St. Joseph's Church on Sixth Avenue, near her parents' house, on the morning of February 9, 1867. She lay in a handsome rosewood coffin, covered with greenhouse flowers. Her pall-bearers included the recently elevated Brigadier General Harry Tremain, Major General Alfred Pleasonton, Brigadier General Charles K. Graham, James Topham Brady, and her Bloomingdale friend Tom Field, who had once brought back from Dan's prison cell in Washington letters Dan had written her. Requiem mass was said by the Reverend Father Farrell, who paid due regard to the devout Teresa, the afflicted husband, the daughter Laura, the aged Sickleses, and Mr. and Mrs. Bagioli. A choir sang plainchant, enriched by selections from Rossi and Caracono, and the anthem "Pray for Me" was rendered under the musical direction of grief-stricken Mr. Bagioli with a touching sweetness and to profound effect. Obviously Father Farrell had known Teresa well, both socially and possibly through the confessional. Here was a woman with the face of a saint, he said, who had lived in patient expiation. He spoke with some tenderness of her, but the surviving husband, the faithful soldier of the Republic, attracted particular comment even from Father Farrell. "Now he was called upon to render unto Him who gave her, the chiefest treasure which had blessed his life. It became him as a man to bow in Christian submission to the decree of Divine Wisdom, and to look for support under this severe trial to the Hand which had sustained him hitherto." The newspapers made much of the way in which, accompanied by his daughter, Sickles arose on his crutches and followed down the aisle "all that was mortal of her whom he had loved so well. . . . His feelings now broke forth and he wept, and the large congregation rushed tumultuously from the building after him, testifying in various ways the hold he had upon their hearts, and the extent to which they shared his affliction." Her coffin was taken to the Catholic cemetery on Second Avenue, now long since built over.[25]

# FINALE

BY THE TIME OF TERESA'S DEATH, DAN
had so redeemed himself that her going did not elicit
any press retrospectives on the murder of Key. After
so many murders in blue and gray, Key was let rest.
Dan now took Laura to Charleston with him, and
Southerners would long after remember the handsome girl who sometimes sat at Dan's table during official dinners and began to attend the Sisters of
Mercy. (The nuns had immediately involved Dan in
an attempt to get a congressional appropriation for
the rebuilding of the Charleston orphan asylum destroyed in the war.)[1]

Dan was still occupied by office, as both North
and South Carolina held constitutional conventions
selected by all male citizens, excluding those unwill-
ing to swear adherence to the Thirteenth Amendment to the Constitution, granting emancipation and

equal rights to former slaves. The legislatures of both states, when elected, would be required, in drafting their new constitutions, to accept the Thirteenth Amendment. By the time this happened, Dan had got into trouble with the federal Attorney General by interfering with South Carolina's Judge Bryan, who held him in contempt when he refused to appear in answer to a writ of habeas corpus issued in favor of four men convicted by the military commission for the murder of some soldiers. He had been complained of before for lesser intrusions into the judicial system, and this was the onset of a public quarrel with the Southern judiciary that, in the end, he would not win. One friend described him at this stage as "a wise, sagacious commander, placed in a most delicate and responsible position among a touchy, testy, fiery people," and praised him for possessing "the wisdom of Solomon, the patience of Job, the astuteness of Talleyrand and the audacity of the Devil." But even those qualities could not pacify all parties.

General Grant approved of him and came down to Charleston in the summer of 1867 to see his protégé. For the occasion, Sickles invited to dinner a number of eminent Charlestonians—James Orr; Trenholm, the former Confederate Secretary of Treasury; McGrath, the last Rebel governor of South Carolina; and a man named Truscott, a former Confederate diplomat. A former South Carolina governor and former U.S. congressman named William Aiken wrote that he did not possess a coat in which to attend the dinner. He, once the owner of a thousand slaves, had only a suit of homespun. Thus he sent his regrets. But Sickles assured Aiken that Grant would be happy to meet him in his everyday suit, and indeed Grant himself, knowing how much damage the war had done to Southern fashion, accommodatingly came to dinner wearing no epaulettes and with his coat unbuttoned.[2]

Differences between Grant and Johnson over the treatment of the South ripened. Johnson had begun his presidency as an advocate of severe measures in the South, but his regard for small farmers made him a contradictory patchwork of moderation and severity. He came to consider Dan both too severe and too arbitrary. There were similar complaints about a range of military governors, including Generals Philip Sheridan and John Pope. Three months after Teresa's death, when Johnson returned to his birthplace at Raleigh, North Carolina, and was met by the military governor Sickles, Johnson mentioned that he had been requested by a delegation of farmers to intercede with the general to allow them to use firearms to shoot crows in their cornfields. Sickles implied that the President had been taken in: "Your Excellency, no formal permission is necessary. Shooting crows in cornfields is not being prohibited."

But Johnson was certainly angry with Sickles for having issued, in the spring of 1867, General Order Number Ten. This edict imposed a twelve-month moratorium on imprisonment and foreclosure for debt. It was not so much the wise measure itself, which saved many of the smaller farmers. It was that Dan had issued the order without consulting Washington. Governor James Orr would praise this order for keeping "the small means of farmers and planters . . . from the process of the courts. They were thereby enabled to subsist their families, and grow the present crop." Dan had also wisely taken a measure that his late friend Meagher, recently drowned in the Missouri while serving as acting governor of Montana, had earlier urged upon the British government at the time of the Irish Famine. That was, he restricted the manufacture of liquor to keep more grain available as food. It was, again, not the content of these decrees, though that was considered serious enough in some quarters, but rather the absolutist style in which they were issued which raised alarm in sections of Johnson's Cabinet. General Pope and General Sheridan were criticized for similar decisions in their departments. The unease created by these edicts of military governors was compounded by criticism of their having superseded the courts. Johnson demanded Dan's, Sheridan's, and Pope's resignations, and on August 12 dismissed Dan before Dan offered to go.[3]

At the time, opinion in New York was against what had happened. "General Sickles's resignation as a District Commander is premature in every respect," announced the *New York Times*. "Nothing has yet occurred that warrants it." Johnson himself was more disapproved of than Sickles, and Dan was yet again celebrated, the remarkable widower returned to New York. But, political beast that he was, he also went down to Washington to work with some of the Radical Republicans, former enemies, for the impeachment of Johnson in March 1868. The movement to impeach the President would fail by one vote.[4]

A passionate supporter of his Republican friend and old commander Grant, Sickles, when Grant came to the presidency, was offered the post of minister to Mexico but refused it, with his accustomed directness, as an inadequate reward. So he was now appointed minister to Spain—for Cuba had revived as an issue, and Grant hoped Dan would at last bring it to the United States. This was an important and senior post, but the *New York World* was able to destroy a civic reception planned for Sickles at the Everett House by publishing an account of "his career as rowdy, mail robber, spy, murderer, confidence man, 'general,' satrap, politician, etc." President Grant was not, however, dissuaded from appointing Dan to the post.

In the U.S. legation near the Prado in Madrid, Dan was presented not to Queen Isabella II, to whom he had been presented as a legation secretary in 1854 but who had been driven into exile by the uprising, but to the new president, General Juan Prim. Dan was able to convince Prim of the wisdom of the sale of Cuba, but wondered whether the general's cabinet would support it. They did not do so.

Dan had another source of income in these years. He had been put on a retainer to inquire into the running of the Erie Railroad by the notorious railroad baron Jay Gould and his partner James Fisk. Dan wrote to his old friend General Alfred Pleasonton, who had defended Hazel Grove with him at the battle of Chancellorsville and was now commissioner of Internal Revenue, urging him to look into the bookkeeping and tax matters of the Erie Railroad. While in Spain trying to buy unbuyable Cuba, he lobbied other old friends from a distance to bring down the notorious Gould. General Prim was in the meantime assassinated, and Prince Amadeo of Savoy, son of the King of Italy, became the new Spanish monarch. But nothing was settled about Cuba.

At one of his weekly ambassadorial parties, Dan met Caroline de Creagh, the dark-haired adopted daughter of an Irish-Spanish family. He began to court her, but on a trip to Paris, when he met the deposed Queen Isabella II, who possessed a sexual appetite to rival his own, he had no inhibition about beginning an affair, and shuttled back and forth between Madrid and Paris on the express. They were a splendid pair. Isabella did not seem to have been rendered any more neurotic by having succeeded as a toddler to a throne under continual attack than Dan had been by his part in the Civil War. It was a splendid validation for an amputee lover to know that he was adequate to a queen, even a deposed one. But in this, as in his relationship with the late Fanny White, he showed that his sense of diplomatic propriety was not acute. He was mocked internationally as *le roi américain de l'Espagne* or, as American papers reported it, the Yankee King of Spain. Seventeen-year-old Laura, who lived with her father in the U.S. legation as she had lived with him in South Carolina and New York, must have heard the rumors.[5]

Despite all, in the autumn of 1871, it was announced that the U.S. ambassador to Spain would marry Señorita de Creagh. For unspecified reasons, there was a hasty marriage at the legation, performed by the Patriarch of the Indies, the highest dignitary of Catholicism in Madrid. The bride was described as "one of Spain's fairest daughters," who had been matched "with one of America's bravest sons." Laura Sickles was present for the wedding; indeed, she seemed to like Señorita de Creagh. Susan Sickles had also arrived, and became from that point on a habitual member of Dan's household.

If his enemies can be believed, Dan showed himself once more an inappropriate fellow for matrimony. A letter written to Secretary of State Hamilton Fish by an outraged anonymous American who had just visited Spain charged that Dan, although supposedly happily remarried, was not a fit person to represent the United States because of his unrepentant depravity. "Can the Department of State be aware, or rather ignorant, of the infamous character of Gen. Dan E. Sickles? While in Madrid his conduct with women has been simply disgraceful. For months before his marriage with Caroline de Creagh, who is heartily sick of her bargain, poor girl, he lived in open and notorious adultery with Madame or Señora Domeriquy, a Cuban conspirator, even at the U.S. Legation, to the shame of our countrymen abroad. An American by the name of Belknap supplied this creditable Minister with child virgins for the purpose of prostitution. His conduct with lewd women of the town was, and even is, shocking. Are we to have another Philip Barton Key affair in Spain?" If so, Caroline de Creagh was not playing along by seeking a lover of her own, since the only adulterer in her garden seemed to be Dan.[6]

He was still working on behalf of railroad shareholders to bring down the scandalous Jay Gould. He returned home on leave to show his bride his city and to attend to the Erie Railroad matter. Jay Gould, a slight and soft-spoken man of thirty-six years, had hived off some $60 million from the line, robbed stockholders, consumed smaller railroads, and destroyed competitors. He got his legal immunity from the protection of Tammany Hall, the machine that had once protected Dan, and from its current boss, William Marcy Tweed. Dan had built an alliance of directors who had fallen out with Gould, and had collected interested parties who supplied him with affidavits concerning Gould's financial crimes. In March 1872, Dan's allies among the directors tricked Gould into calling a board meeting, and on his crutches, and accompanied by allies, interested parties, and police, Dan entered the headquarters of the Erie Railroad, which were located in the white marble Grand Opera House at Twenty-third Street. With him were a phalanx of famous stockholders, including Generals McClellan and Dix, and Tom Meagher's brother-in-law, Samuel Mitchell Barlow.

The anti-Gould directors who had conspired with Dan sat down at once in the boardroom and, in Gould's absence, voted all positions vacant. A new set of reform-minded directors was hurriedly elected. Hearing cheers from the boardroom and fearing some such coup, Gould locked himself in his office, but Dan had the ornate door broken in with a crowbar so that the man could be told of his fall and asked to leave. This was an astonishing operation, and Dan was rewarded with stock and other prizes, and thus achieved the financial substance he had sought all his life. Some said the British government, an investor in the railroad, had gratefully given Dan the title to the house he occupied on Fifth Avenue. But as much as the *Times* and the *Tribune* praised him for delivering the Erie stockholders from the blight of Gould, the *World* was still attacking Dan, describing him as a pimp—a reference to the old accusation that he had lived or campaigned off the earnings of Fanny White. John Graham published a letter in the *World*, threatening legal action, which brought from George Templeton Strong the memorable line "One might as well try to spoil a rotten egg as to damage Dan's character." Caroline de Creagh, unfamiliar with the details of Dan's past, was particularly abashed to find him attacked so slightingly and with such vituperation.[7]

In Spain in 1873, another republican uprising caused King Amadeo to flee to Portugal, and again the great chimera of Cuba rose up. Dan felt that the pressure from Washington on King Amadeo had not been adequate to produce the long-desired result. He told the Secretary of State that if, at this promising moment, the President did not intend to initiate a policy of rigorous influence directed at Spain on the matter of Cuba, "I wish you would instruct me to present my letter of recall in January or February. I confess I'm tired of my useless work here and of these vacillating people."

Dan regained his enthusiasm when he paid a promising call on President Figueres, the new liberal head of state, to carry the pleasant news of America's recognition of the government. But events betrayed him. For just then the master and fifty-two American passengers and crewmen of the *Virginius*, involved in sneaking arms and revolutionaries into Cuba, were lined up against a wall in Havana and shot. The American press was appalled by the image of Spanish soldiers jamming their guns into the dead men's mouths and shooting their skulls out. The *Herald* of New York hallooed Sickles on his way when he decided on his own authority to close the American embassy in protest. Unhappily for Dan, his action was read by the Secretary of State as an attempt to make policy and to involve the United States in a war for Cuba. The government of Spain dealt directly with Washington on the matter, bypassing

Dan, and was quick to negotiate compensation for the *Virginius*. Dan felt betrayed that Secretary of State Fish had not apprised him of or involved him in the negotiations for a final settlement of the *Virginius* crisis. Fish, in return, believed that Dan had not informed him of some of the more conciliatory gestures the Spaniards had made.[8]

Thus undermined, Dan became *persona non grata* to the Spaniards. His career in Madrid ended in 1874, and he left for Paris with his wife, his mother, and his increasingly resentful, knowing, but beautiful daughter. Dan sought to raise money in London and in Paris for a canal across the isthmus of Panama, but he was also close to Queen Isabella, now a Junoesque woman of forty-four years. Before and after she was deposed, she lived apart from her husband, a Bourbon prince. When Dan visited her in Paris, it was at the mansion she had bought and occupied, the Hôtel Basilewski on Avenue Kléber, now the Palais de Castille.

In 1875, while the Sickles family was still living in Paris, Caroline de Creagh bore the general a daughter named Eda, and the following year a son, whom Dan named George Stanton, in honor of both his father and Secretary of War Stanton. The presence of these children delivered Laura from what she thought of as a solitary struggle with her father, the negligent and philandering husband of her dead mother. She embraced Caroline's son and daughter, had endless patience with them, and was much adored in return by her younger half brother and half sister. She argued, however, both with her stepmother and her father. Dan is rumored to have intervened in a romance between Laura and a young Spanish officer, possibly a love affair undertaken in part as vengeance against her father. The dispute grew to such a pitch, the struggle so primal, that Laura returned to New York on an allowance to live with her grandmother. It seems more than likely, given the depth of her father's alienation from her, that she may have at the time threatened to inform Dan's wife of certain Sickles truths.

There were other separations. Susan Sickles, who lived with her son in Paris, did not seek to go back to George, and Dan began uneasily to suspect that his father had not remained faithful to his mother.

She was in her early seventies when she became ill and died in a Paris sanatorium.[9]

Through the frenzied shifts of Spanish politics, in 1875 the son of Isabella II, to whom she had abdicated her throne, returned to Madrid to be crowned Alfonso XII. But Dan had no more influence in the affairs of Spain and the United States. He stayed on in Paris for four more years. He helped the French politician Louis Adolphe Thiers prevent a visit by Grant at a time that would have given legitimacy to the conservative Marshal MacMahon in a French presidential election. For his service in persuading Grant to divert through Belgium and Germany and not come near France until after the election, Dan received the office of Commander of the Legion of Honor. Caroline de Creagh was by now seeing perhaps as little of her husband as Teresa used to. Dan, stouter and balder than the lean whippet who had been wounded at Gettysburg, spent some time back in America for an 1878 reunion of the Third Army Corps Union in Newburgh, New York.

He particularly wanted to go to America for the period leading to the election campaign of 1880. He had a temperamental hunger to be involved, and was seeking another government post, having become bored with the role of Yankee in European exile. Caroline refused to go with him. Her mother was ill in Madrid, but on top of that, "I learned that my husband had been untrue to me." In the early winter of 1879, by mutual consent, Dan said his farewells to Caroline, *au revoir* to little Eda and George Stanton, and left them in Europe. He had failed yet again as a family man, but since he considered that a lesser fault, it did not burden or delay him.

By then Laura was living in Brooklyn with Mrs. Bagioli, Antonio having died. Laura had married badly and been already "abandoned" by her husband. She was buying drink with the allowance her father sent her, and she painted small pictures and sold them in a Brooklyn market. With a severity he did not show to men, Dan turned his back on hapless Laura.

The native son returning was in his sixtieth year, but unconquered by years, regret, or nostalgia. He settled at the corner of Fifth Avenue and Ninth Street, in a spacious house, and decorated the walls with animal hides from his travels and hunting expeditions, and with the military and political gleanings of a life rich in incident. No record appeared on those walls of what had been lost, unless it was the well-known photograph of his fibula and tibia, a favorite exhibit on display in the Army Medical Museum in Washington, which in the nineteenth century was one of the must-see attractions of the capital. That loss, like all the others, had failed to rob him of efficacy.[10]

At the Republican convention in Chicago, where Dan's friend Grant intended to attempt a return to the presidency, an unexpected candidate emerged, James A. Garfield. This was bad news for Dan. He did not know Garfield—the first President since Pierce with whom he was not on close terms. He could expect nothing from the man, not least because he had stuck by Grant to the end. Grant himself was content to begin life as a Wall Street broker, and he could console himself with his private life. The idea that Dan, even in his sixties, should gather together his family and become a paterfamilias was one which simply did not register with him.[11]

George Sickles, the wellspring of his son's illimitable vigor, was eighty-one years old. He lived in New Rochelle, where he owned sizable property, and commuted to Nassau Street every day. After meals, he flapped his arms like a rooster and crowed to prove what rude good health he enjoyed. To further demonstrate the issue, he remarried. His bride was a turbulent Irish woman who had perhaps been his mistress for some years. Forty-eight-year-old Mary Sheraton Sawyer brought into the marriage three daughters. Dan did not approve of this union, and never got on well with her. A cousin, William Sickles, felt bound to write to Dan: "I see by this morning's papers that at the wedding which took place yesterday [was one] William Sickles, and I am happy that it was not me that was present but Uncle Oliver's son who has always toadied to Mrs. Sawyer. I would not have you think for the world that I would ever be present at a ceremony which placed that party in the position formerly held by your dear Mother."

Meanwhile, under presidential administrations that knew him not,

Dan remained busy with committees, and he attended the opera a great deal with the Vanderbilts, who always reserved a chair for him in their box. One night when Dan was in a private box at the Standard Theatre, he saw below him in the stalls Robert Key, the son of Phillip Barton Key. People noticed when the young man looked up with his father's eyes at his father's killer. "They recognized each other undoubtedly," wrote one commentator, "but neither gave any sign of recognition."[12]

It was not reproaches attaching to the Key affair that distressed Dan. It was more the emergence of histories of the Civil War, even those written by friends, that cast doubt on his actions on that famous July 2. De Trobriand, writing his account, *Four Years with the Army of the Potomac,* declared that after the advance to the Peach Orchard and the Emmitsburg Road, "the new disposition of the Third Corps offered some great inconveniences and some great dangers." Harry Tremain would be more diplomatic in his book, *Two Days of War: A Gettysburg Narrative and Other Excursions,* which was hard on Meade. Tremain quoted General Longstreet, who was locked now with Sickles in a comradeship across the lines of enmity to ensure that they did not bear the blame for July 2. Longstreet had written of Dan, "I believe it is now conceded that the advanced position at the peach orchard, taken by your Corps and under your orders, saved that battlefield to the Union cause."

Dan at least had the advantage over Meade, in that Meade was more than ten years dead. But Dan knew this argument over his line along the higher ground near the Emmitsburg Road was one that would never go away. On one side, a former officer of the Third Corps, General John Watts De Peyster, came to his aid by giving Dan credit for seeing "that the battle must be fought where it was received" and for hanging on to Longstreet's wing with such "bulldog pertinacity" and inflicting such losses as to diminish the "maneuvering aggressive power" of the enemy. But an aide of Meade's, Colonel Benedict, published documents defending Meade in such vigorous terms that Dan felt the need to respond energetically himself. In the course of the eternal argument about the Emmitsburg Road, the Peach Orchard, the Wheatfield, he was appointed chairman of the New York State Monuments Commission, in charge of the design and erection of monuments to New York regiments on the battlefield of Gettysburg. The earnestness with which he had brought the dinginess and squalor of the battlefield to the attention of the public added credibility to his claims of having earlier been creatively involved in Central Park. A grateful state gave him the job of trying to amend the condition of the Gettysburg battlefield, especially those parts of it on which New Yorkers had fought.[13]

After a year of turbulent marriage to Mrs. Sawyer, the apparently immortal George Sickles died. Dan, full of the customary sorrow and ambiguity of a son who loved and sometimes quarreled with his father, arranged a fine funeral and bought dinner for 150 mourners at the Huguenot Hotel. His relations with his father was perhaps not only the most enduring of his life, but those marked by the greatest frankness. To his credit, George Sickles had retained a grandfatherly love for Laura, and had sometimes written to Dan on Laura's behalf, as he did in 1883: "I do not know in what manner the lady has turned your feelings against her, but I do know that whatever the cause may have been in the past, it has continued quite as long as a father can afford to remember anger against his child." Laura, said George, was suffering for the necessities of life, her health was poor, she had no money to live on except from the few paintings she had taken to doing, from which the income was quite small. Thin from alcoholism and bad diet, she had come to visit the elderly George Sickles, accompanied by a woman servant who had attended to Teresa in her final illness, and her grandfather had given Laura $50 and the nurse $5. If Dan would not help Laura out of fatherly feeling, said George in his letter to his son, perhaps he should also be aware that this history could attract a paragraph of print: "General Sickles's daughter starving—her father at Number 131 Fifth Avenue living on $100,000." Dan's reply to such appeals from his father was adamant. "Let me remind you that I wrote you sometime before, in reply to a similar communication, upon the same subject, that my decision was then made, was irrevocable." The sternness again, and of a tragically iron quality too. "Once more—for all—I repeat, that I have done my whole duty toward the person in whose behalf you write. As far as I'm concerned she is dead and buried. Happily, you have nothing to forgive. You can therefore be generous. As for the reference to paragraphs in corners of newspapers, pray reserve such menaces for others." His love for his father and George's for him had always survived such exchanges, but now George's beloved, admiring, and contrary voice was gone.

Laura also suffered through George's death. She had always felt a desperate affection for and gratitude to her grandfather, who regularly sent money. "It is very kind, my darling Grandpa, for you to think of me now that you are ill—and I appreciate it deeply and *sincerely*." Laura hoped to see George Sickles when he came home from the sanatorium "ready, as you say, to 'enter upon a new life and a long one.' " She was not well, she told her grandfather often, but in one letter wrote that she was hard at work for Easter and had painted many pretty little pictures for the market. "I shall be pleased on Easter Sunday to offer you one of my little paintings as a token of joy at your recovery." Laura signed off with "A thousand kisses and bushels of love."[14]

It is not known to what extent Laura was helped in George's will, but unless he was too heavily influenced by his wife, who had three daughters of her own, Laura would have been provided for in some way. As for Dan, the mystery remains as to what young Laura's crime could have been. Surely it was more than her affair with the Spanish officer. For while, in his letter to George, he was fulminating against Laura, he had jewelry on order at Theodore Starr's emporium on Fifth Avenue. Starr wrote to ask for his indulgence for a few days further regarding some earrings Dan had on order. "In riveting the onyx for the ear screw, it was broken and a new piece has had to be cut." The earrings were not a gift for Caroline de Creagh.

When Laura died of alcoholism and, perhaps, tuberculosis in 1891 in her rented room in Brooklyn, her father did not attend her funeral. Whatever wrong he believed she had done him was not absolved by death.[15]

But that same year, while dedicating a memorial to the 42nd New

York Regiment at Gettysburg, he made a memorable oration for other dead, the young masses killed in the first three days of July, twenty-eight years past. He declared that the haphazard, state-by-state management of this holiest of battlefields should be now given to the undivided control of the federal government, and he resolved that he would stand for Congress with this issue as one of his chief platforms. To coincide with the unveiling of the monument, he was awarded the Medal of Honor for his part in the battle, for having displayed "most conspicuous gallantry on the field, vigorously contesting the advance of the enemy and continuing to encourage his troops after being himself severely wounded."

The conditions that had made him a Union Democrat in the Civil War and a Democrat for Lincoln and Grant—the next worst thing to a Republican, in some Democrats' eyes—no longer existed in 1892, when he stood again for Congress as a Democrat. It was a chance for him to attack the pernicious proposition that it was the Republicans who had won the war. "Gettysburg was the decisive battle of the war, as admitted on all sides, and who fought it? On the right wing was General Slocombe commanding an army corps, a Democrat; on the left was General Reynolds, till he was killed, a Democrat . . . in the Devil's Den was a man named Sickles, a Democrat."[16]

In 1893, then, in his seventy-fifth year, Dan went off to Washington as a legislator under the Republican presidency of Benjamin Harrison. The last time he had been here, Congress had rung with the rancor of secessionists, the outrage of abolitionists. In the 1850s he had been considered a dangerous man; now he was an old, avuncular soldier with special issues and no broad agenda. If his sexual appetites were still exorbitant for a man his age, the world was not as likely to detect or be outraged by them. Representative Champ Clark would describe the relationship between his little boy, who played around the House a great deal, wearing kilts, and a number of members of Congress, but particularly Sickles. "Frequently he would go over to the old soldier's seat, climb upon his lap, toy with his spectacles, crutches and watch-chain. He generally came back with his pockets bulging with candy, apples, oranges, and other gimcracks."

Dan left Congress in 1894, having been defeated in his reelection bid. The House had been something of a disappointment to him compared with the old days, when he had served on the Foreign Affairs Committee and had had the ear of the President.[17]

He still practiced the law, chaired the New York Monuments Commission, went to the theater, and spent his summer on energetic holidays at Lake Placid or in the Adirondacks. From there, in his mid-seventies, he told a friend, Horatio C. King, "If I had a girl or two with me I wouldn't return at all." But he could not stay away from politics and, in 1896, turned away from another Democrat candidate, William Jennings Bryan, and campaigned for a handsome young Republican politician from Ohio by the name of William McKinley. He joined one-armed General Oliver Howard and a number of other aging heroes of the war in McKinley's rail car across the United States. At this advanced age, too, he traveled to Cuba, and brought back a fifteen-foot boa constrictor for the Central Park Zoo.

As disenchanted as Caroline de Creagh remained with her marriage, she ensured that her children dutifully and affectionately wrote to Dan. Eda and George Stanton Sickles (Stanton to friends) were cultivated Euro-American children who could correspond easily in French, Spanish, and English, and their letters told him of leg injuries, colds, and the travails and enthusiasms of childhood. In 1897, Eda, whom he had not seen for seventeen years, arrived in New York with her new husband, a British diplomat. She was very beautiful, twenty-two years of age, and any trace of Laura that showed in her face did not depress the general at all. He took her down to Old Point Comfort, Virginia, where the Third Corps was having its reunion, and showed her off to all his old comrades, then took her to Washington, introduced her to dignitaries, and attended a reception at the British embassy with her. He would not, however, see Caroline or son Stanton until eleven years later, in 1908, a fact that bespoke no urgency on his part.[18]

In that time, at the end of one century, with the beginning of an apparently limitless one imminent, Dan's sense of association was strongest not with his children but with men like former Confederate general

James Longstreet. In Atlanta one year early in the 1890s, the two old men were guests at the Irish Society's St. Patrick's Day banquet. Afterward, unable to get a cab, they walked together to Sickles's hotel, Dan still on his preferred crutches. At the hotel, a somewhat tipsy Sickles said, "Longstreet, the streets of Atlanta are very dark and it is very late, and you are somewhat deaf and rather infirm; now I must escort you to your headquarters."

Longstreet said, "All right, come on and we'll have another handshake over the bloody chasm." So they returned to Longstreet's hotel, hobbling along together and perhaps enjoying a libation at the end of the journey. Then Longstreet said, "Sickles, the streets of Atlanta are very dark and you are lame, and a stranger here, and do not know the way back to your hotel. I must escort you home." And so they struggled out into the night again.

"Old fellow, I hope you are sorry for shooting off my leg at Gettysburg. I suppose I will have to forgive you, for it's Sunday."

"Forgive me? You ought to thank me for leaving you one leg to stand on, after the way you behaved to me."

Many were deeply touched at the Gettysburg reunion of 1893 when these two old generals helped each other up one of the hills named Roundtop, arriving, despite their age, with an alacrity Longstreet had not shown on the day itself. "Sickles," said Longstreet, "you can well afford to help me up here now. If you had not kept me away so long . . . on the 2nd July 1863, the war would have lasted longer than it did. . . ."[19]

The two were iconically matched again in March 1901, at the second inauguration of President McKinley, then at the West Point Centennial, and in 1902, on May 30, reviewing the veterans of the Spanish-American War from the same platform as President Theodore Roosevelt. It was their last meeting, for Longstreet would die of old age in 1904.

Sickles remained an ally of the Confederate general's young second wife, Helen Longstreet, acquiring for her a postmastership in Georgia and providing several Longstreet-redeeming quotations for her book on the relationship between Lee and Longstreet. Indeed, said Dan improbably, given General Meade's uncertainty, if Longstreet had delayed another hour before making his attack, he might have found the Union Army pulled out to Pipe Creek, the position chosen by General Meade on June 30. Even in defending Longstreet, Dan raised the old proposition he had been uttering for forty-one years—that Meade meant to retreat and did not intend to fight at Gettysburg, and that it was his subordinates, including Dan, who made the battle occur![20]

In the early twentieth century, Dan was looked after at his home in New York by two black servants, Moseley and Sarah, and by a middle-aged widow, Eleanor Wilmerding, who was said to have loved the general "with a jealous, undying, and devoted affection." Though there seems to have been a sexual component in the relationship, there was, as in all Dan's relations with women, a lack of reciprocated devotion from Dan. The aging general's meals were cooked by a former soldier named Captain Denton, and it was Denton who explained Dan's lack of total emotional dependence upon Mrs. Wilmerding. He would tell a researcher nearly four decades later that he had seen in the general's chamber dresser a whole drawer filled with lady's black stockings and another with lady's gloves. They had been left behind over time by lovers and were testimony to Dan's erotic capacity in his advancing years. But his gastronomic tastes were shrinking, for in those last years, said Denton, he liked plain, wholesome meals, not the Delmonico and Maison Dorée style of food he had relished for most of his life. Now it was oyster stew, lamb stew, fried oysters, rice pudding—the straightforward, the sustaining.[21]

But he was not done yet with entertaining notable Americans. Through the Reverend Joseph Twichell, formerly of the Excelsior Brigade, and pastor of the fashionable Asylum Hill Congregational Church in Hartford, Mr. Samuel Clemens, Mark Twain, began to hear Twichell's colorful tales of Dan Sickles. When Twain later moved to New York, just across Ninth Street from where the general lived, and got to know him personally, he brought his incisive whimsy to his description of Sickles's house. "You couldn't walk across that floor anywhere without stumbling over the hard heads of lions and things . . . it was as if a menagerie had undressed in the place. . . . It was a kind of museum, and yet it was not the sort of museum which seemed dignified enough to be the museum of a great soldier—and so famous a soldier. It was the sort of museum which should delight and entertain little boys and girls. I suppose that that museum reveals a part of the general's character and make. He is sweetly and winningly childlike."

Mark Twain admired Dan's well-constructed sentences. His talk was full of interest and bristling with points, Twain found, but the delivery had a certain monotonous quality that became oppressive after a time. The great writer and humorist was reminded of what a friend had said about Wagner's music: "I have been told that Wagner's music is better than it sounds." That seemed to fit the general's manner of speech exactly. "His talk is much better than it is. . . . His talk does not sound entertaining, but it is distinctly entertaining."

Sickles's other gift, thought Twain, was to talk about nothing but himself and yet at the same time sound modest, inoffensive, and "unexasperating." "He seemed to me . . . just the kind of man who would risk his salvation in order to do some 'last words' in an attractive way." If he made ungenerous remarks about any officers from the war, he did so with dignity and courtesy, but Twain percipiently thought that "the general valued his lost leg a way above the one that is left. I am perfectly sure that if he had to part with either of them, he would part with the one that he has got."[22]

The son who would eventually come to the United States to meet him, Stanton Sickles, worked in the American embassy in Spain, possessed immense fondness for all members of the Sickles clan, and had a spaciousness of soul like that of his grandfather. When he arrived in America with his mother in 1908, he wrote excitedly in French in his journal, in uppercase letters: "FIRST INTERVIEW OF MY DEAR PARENTS AFTER 27 YEARS, AT HALF PAST TWELVE AT OUR HOTEL."

The second Mrs. Sickles agreed to be reunited with her husband if he would dismiss Mrs. Wilmerding, who so far forgot her position as to constantly refer to the general as "Dear." Dan, more intractable than ever at eighty-eight years, would not dismiss her. So Caroline de Creagh Sickles continued to live at the Albert Hotel on Eleventh Street, and Dan remained in his nearby house, enjoying the housekeeping mercies of Mrs. Wilmerding. It was rumored that he had made out a new will, which left everything to that lady. Not that this was necessarily a splendid prospect for her. Dan had lost on the stock market a considerable amount of what he had made from the Gould coup and inherited from his father. He held in trust the inheritance of both Eda and George Stanton Sickles, but was waiting for the right time to sell the chief property of 109 acres in New Rochelle. Yet he was reckless with money, distributing it to veterans who appeared outside his house for handouts on Sunday mornings. When a friend of his, Representative William Sulzer of New York, presented a bill in Congress proposing that Dan be retired with the rank of lieutenant general, a move that would raise his pension to $7,500, it was not simply because this was a worthy honor, but because it would provide Dan with essential income. The attempt to elevate Dan to three-star rank failed in the House in February 1910.[23]

Dan had lost some of his money to importunate women. Some years earlier he had advanced more than $9,900 to Eleanor Wilmerding. His last great folly of expenditure on women involved a plausible artist named Princess Lenott Parlaghy. She set up a studio in the Plaza Hotel, where Dan often dined, and she asked whether he would sit for her. Dan behaved toward the princess with a breathtaking extravagance. She said she had always wanted a lion cub, so he turned up with a litter of six, acquired somehow from his zoo connections. And after the general had his portrait painted by Princess Parlaghy, he passed on the names of two hundred friends who might like to undergo the same process.

His greatest indulgence was, however, to stand as guarantor for the princess's debts. In the spring of 1910, the managing director of the Plaza advised Dan that the amount Princess Parlaghy owed the hotel "stood at a little over $5,500, and as her business manager informs me it may be three to eight days before she receives her remittance. I thought I would let you know the amount of her indebtedness covered by your guaranty."

The Knickerbocker Trust Company told Dan six months later that the princess had deposited with it a sum of $750 for him—a repayment against this or some other advance by Dan. It was not enough to count. A year after covering the princess's debt, he was pleading with one August Hecksher of Fifth Avenue for an extension on two notes Hecksher held for $7,700 plus interest. In 1912 the Bowery Savings Bank initiated foreclosure proceedings against the general, and the Bank of the Metropolis attached his property for his failure to pay $5,050.[24]

Caroline Sickles, still living in the hotel close to Dan but not as his wife, came to his aid. She paid a judgment for $8,200, and took a second mortgage on the general's house to save him from eviction. She pawned her jewels to pay the debt of $5,050. But Dan demonstrated no gratitude; instead he cast bitter doubt on Caroline's motives. "I pawn my jewels to save his treasures," an affronted Caroline was quoted in the *Times* as saying. "The general has his pension to live on, and I can do nothing further for him." As for the rest, she said, she would welcome him if he wished to make his home with her. "But I will not put up all my money to save his house to have it occupied by him and his housekeeper to the exclusion of me."[25]

A worse and final financial crisis hung over Dan. State Controller William Somer discovered, late in 1912, that there was a discrepancy in the books of the New York State Monuments Commission: $445,641 had been budgeted to the commission, of which Sickles was the chief, but the general's expense vouchers amounted to only $417,165. Missing was more than $28,000. Loyal Stanton Sickles offered $5,000 as a gesture against the missing funds, but that did not stop the state attorney general from taking action against the entire commission, including its ninety-three-year-old chairman. The court order for the civil arrest of Dan was issued on the last Saturday of January 1913. General Sickles nonetheless had a quiet Sunday at home, and took care to have the curtains raised so that he could sit at the window by a little table containing a large vase of flowers. An American flag was draped on either side of him, and to show that he was still a man to be reckoned with, he smoked a cigar. A police patrol wagon from Mercer Street stood outside the house most of the afternoon, and a lieutenant of police had a conference with Dan, but no arrest was made.

The city sheriff, Harburger, told the press that he would not bully the old man, that the general would be treated as an honored guest rather than as a prisoner. The sheriff nonetheless declared that, with great regret, he would arrest Dan the following morning and place him in the Ludlow Street Jail. "Do you really expect to put him in a cell?" asked a journalist. "My goodness, no," said the sheriff. The general would have all the comforts of a good home.

Controller Somer, who had discovered the discrepancy, started a subscription to help Dan pay the debt, and donated the first $100 himself. A telegram came to Dan from Gainesville, Georgia, from Helen B. Longstreet: "Am wiring the Attorney General of New York that I will raise money among the ragged, destitute, maimed veterans who followed Lee, to pay the amount demanded if the New York officials will allow us sufficient time. . . . The Republic, whose battles you fought, will not permit your degradation." Sheriff Harburger spent another day trying to be busy to escape the necessity of arresting Dan Sickles, and in the state Senate there was a motion calling on the attorney general to suspend action against the old general. Dan's friend Sulzer, now governor of New York, expressed his concern for what awaited Dan, but said that he could do nothing to prevent an arrest.

"Fifty years ago," declared Senator Murtaugh in Albany, "the name of General Sickles was one to conjure with. Fifty years hence our children, and our children's children, will stand with uncovered heads before monuments erected to the memory of General Sickles, for which this State will spend far more money than now is required to extricate the hero of Gettysburg from his trouble."[26]

But even among Dan's allies there was dissent. Mrs. Longstreet was outraged by a statement of Stanton Sickles that his father had procured the position of postmaster of Gainesville for her, that in "passing the plate in the South" she was merely repaying a favor, and that the money collected would benefit only Mrs. Wilmerding. She did not know Stanton, said Mrs. Longstreet. She did not know Wilmerding. All she knew was that General Sickles was her husband's best friend among all the Union generals after the war was over "and we became one nation again."

Attorney General Thomas Carmody in Albany stood against the tide of sympathy for Dan. "General Sickles had appropriated a large amount for his own use. This he has not attempted to justify or to defend." The sheriff now attended to arresting Dan in the most benign manner. He went to the house, into a back room, where General Sickles was seated in a huge chair, wearing a black suit, an eye shade, and a strip of plaster on his left cheek. Grasping him by the hand, the sheriff placed him under arrest. But then he arranged that Dan be granted bail without having to leave his residence, which would become his *de facto* prison for a short time. A $30,000 bond was arranged through a surety company official, who produced the papers and had them signed by all parties. Sheriff Harburger apologetically told Dan that a sum of $5.29 was due as a bond fee. "Ah, yes," the general said. "Eleanor! Please get me $5.29."

"Yes, dear," Mrs. Wilmerding replied, and fetched the money.[27]

Dan had fought off the state and his wife. But he believed that Caroline and Stanton intended to get control of his house, and that was a battle he would not be able to win from beyond the grave. In July 1913, he went to Gettysburg, accompanied by his valet, Moseley, and by Mrs. Wilmerding, to attend the celebration of the fiftieth anniversary of the battle. He listened to a speech by a new President, Woodrow Wilson. At a related ceremony, he sat in honor on the porch of the Rogers house, behind the Emmitsburg Road, where a girl had once baked biscuits for some of General Humphrey's men as they waited for Longstreet's attack. He watched white-headed men, veterans of the Confederate Army, hobble across the space between Seminary Ridge and Cemetery Ridge, reproducing Pickett's charge. As they reached Cemetery Ridge, they were not shot down but were embraced by aged survivors of the Union line. Dan's friend Horatio King was there, and so was the Reverend Joseph Twichell. Helen Longstreet, not yet aged, was writing up the event for a Southern newspaper. She was aware of Horatio King's verses to Dan:

> I see him on that famous field,
> The bravest of the brave,
> Where Longstreet's legions strove to drive
> The Third Corps to its grave.
> The fight was bloody, fierce and long,
> And Sickles' name shall stay
> Forever in the hall of fame
> As he who saved the day.[28]

Mrs. Wilmerding perished the next winter of a sudden pneumonic infection. Dan made a new will, naming his three grandchildren—that is, Stanton's and Eda's children—as heirs and leaving bequests to his servant Moseley and to Horatio King, who had written the verse representing Dan's version of Gettysburg.

He suffered a cerebral hemorrhage in April 1914, and Caroline and Stanton at last moved into the house. He died less than two weeks later, on May 3, a little after nine o'clock at night.

Because of a vanity that had led him to misrepresent his age, the *Times* confidently but wrongly gave his years as ninety-one. The journalists at the *Times* fondly remembered the previous March, when a rumor had got around that Dan was at the point of death, and a *Times* reporter had called his home on the telephone. Dan had answered. "Yes, this is General Sickles. Am I ill? Nonsense. I was never better in my life. There's nothing to that story." This time, however, the story was soundly based.

So now at last he joined Teresa and Key, Abe and Mary Todd Lincoln (who had died of a stroke in 1882), Meagher, James Topham Brady, Wikoff, Queen Isabella II, Laura, and other vivid spirits. But Teresa did not intrude upon his obsequies as he had upon hers. If he got the larger share of mention at her funeral, at his she was barely a whisper. Five days after his death, his body was transported to Washington. He was buried at the Arlington National Cemetery with gun carriage and riderless horse, escort and volleys of rifle fire, and it was his triumphant and militant career that dominated the event.[29]

For the sake of his courage, the Republic honored his vivid character and forgave him the failures of his heart.

# LAST WORD

TYPICALLY, DAN MADE AN UNQUIET GHOST, his life, particularly his actions on July 2, 1863, casting up a legion of disputative voices to ensure that his name still has resonance. A recent dispute can serve as a case in point. In 1993 a report in the *Times* of 1914 was seized on by two New Yorkers named Davis and Shad, the latter Sickles's great-great-nephew and only known survivor, to demonstrate that his widow, Caroline de Creagh, had wanted Dan buried near the New York Monument on the Gettysburg battlefield. The battle between the Gettysburg Military Park and Mr. Davis on the issue of moving Dan to Gettysburg continued for some years, with the Gettysburg Military Park conceding that Dan's remains could go into the Soldiers' National Cemetery Annex, or his ashes could be strewn in the original cemetery, which had been closed to burials since 1903. Davis was contemptuous of the bureaucrat who gave him this answer, saying, "He wouldn't have a job if it wasn't for Dan Sickles." The dispute is unsettled and will probably never come to conclusion, and Dan is still in Arlington, beneath his discreet military stone, which mentions merely his name, rank, Medal of Honor, and date of death. But to arise yet again easefully from that place, Dan needs only the invocation of his name at a history seminar, at a Civil War buffs' meeting, or on an Internet Civil War chat site, and from the heat of people's breaths he rises again to full and controversial life.[1]

The gentler and pleasant spirit of Teresa is not as easily invoked, and insofar as these pages have been able, within the limits of evidence, to commemorate this beautiful, pleasant, and intelligent girl, the author is happy.

# NOTES

## CHAPTER I

1. Philip Shriver Klein, *President James Buchanan,* p. 117; John W. Forney, *Anecdotes of Public Men,* pp. 317, 318; W. A. Swanberg, *Sickles the Incredible,* p. 92; Marilyn Wood Hill, *Their Sisters' Keepers: Prostitution in New York City, 1830–1870,* p. 281; *New York World,* June 30, 1869.

2. *Harper's Weekly,* April 9, 1859; Joseph Louis Russo, *Lorenzo Da Ponte, Poet and Adventurer,* passim.

3. G. W. D. Andrews to Sickles, August 13, 1853, Daniel E. Sickles Papers, Manuscripts Division, New-York Historical Society (hereafter NYHS).

4. Ronald H. Bayor and Timothy J. Meagher, *The New York Irish,* pp. 122–123; Hill, pp. 77, 82, 110, 134; James Dabney McCabe, *Lights and Shadows of New York Life,* p. 583.

5. Robert Ernst, *Immigrant Life in New York City, 1825–1863,* pp. 14, 20, 21; *Harper's Weekly,* April 9, 1859.

6. *Harper's Weekly,* April 9, 1859.

7. Russo, pp. 12, 30; Felix G. Fontaine, *De Witt's Special Report: Trial of Daniel E.*

*Sickles for Shooting Philip Key, Esq., U.S. District Attorney of Washington D.C.,* pp. 54–55.

8. Russo, pp. 151ff.; Thomas Keneally, *The Great Shame,* p. 289; *Harper's Weekly,* April 9, 1859.

9. Swanberg, p. 81; Ernst, p. 170; James M. McPherson, *The Battle-cry of Freedom,* p. 60; Gustavus Myers, *The History of Tammany Hall,* p. 171; *Harper's Weekly,* April 9, 1859.

10. *Harper's Weekly,* April 9, 1859; *New York World,* June 30, 1869.

11. Ernst, pp. 163–165; Bayor and Meagher, pp. 88, 102; Keneally, p. 249.

12. Ernst, pp. 164–166; Thomas Lowe Nichols, *Forty Years of American Life,* pp. 160–162.

13. McPherson, pp. 60–62; Myers, p. 171.

14. Myers, p. 187; *New York Herald* (hereafter *NYH*), August 24, 1852; Bayor and Meagher, pp. 122–123; Ernest A. McKay, *The Civil War and New York City,* pp. 1, 3; *Harper's Weekly,* April 9, 1859.

15. *New York World,* June 30, 1869; David Graham to Sickles, October 25, 1851, Daniel Edgar Sickles Papers, Manuscripts and Archives Division, New York Public Library, Astor, Lenox, and Tilden Foundations (hereafter NYPL).

16. Hill, pp. 102–103; *New York World,* June 30, 1869.

17. *New York World,* June 30, 1869; George Templeton Strong, *Diary of George Templeton Strong: Selections,* Vol. 2, p. 438; Swanberg, pp. 83–84.

18. Swanberg, p. 84; Nat Brandt, *The Congressman Who Got Away with Murder,* p. 22; Stephen Fiske, *Off-Hand Portraits of Prominent New Yorkers,* p. 284; Irving Katz, *August Belmont: A Political Biography,* p. 42; Fiske, pp. 27–29.

19. Swanberg, p. 84; Forney, pp. 68–69, 317–318; McCabe, pp. 475, 476.

20. J. L. Carpentier to Sickles, March 19, 1852, NYPL; Richard Schell to Sickles, July 23, 1853, NYPL.

21. Hill, pp. 102, 103, 395; Strong, Vol. 2, pp. 440–441; George Sickles to Sickles, April 14, 1862, NYPL; *New York Times* (hereafter *NYT*), March 15, 1859.

22. *Harper's Weekly,* April 9, 1859; Jane McCerren to Miss T. Bagioli, December 15, 1852, NYPL; Teresa Sickles to Florence, May 3, 1856, NYPL.

23. *Harper's Weekly,* April 9, 1859; Strong, Vol. 2, pp. 440–441.

24. *New York World,* June 30, 1869; *NYH,* March 1, 1859; *New York Sun,* March 15, 1853; H. C. Banks to Sickles, March 16, 1853, NYPL.

25. McPherson, pp. 118–119; L. A. Gobright, *Recollection of Men and Things at Washington During the Third of a Century,* pp. 134–135; President Pierce from Sickles, March 13, 1853, NYPL.

26. *Harper's Weekly,* April 9, 1859; *NYH,* March 1 and March 2, 1853; Swanberg, p. 85; Brandt, p. 19; *New York Post* (hereafter *NYP*), March 1 and March 17, 1859.

27. Fiske, pp. 285, 286; *NYT,* March 15, 1859; Teresa Sickles to Sickles, August 1853, NYPL; Edgcumb Pinchon, *Dan Sickles, Hero of Gettysburg and "Yankee King of Spain,"* pp. 134–135; Forney, p. 318.

28. Undated Sickles essay, "The Founder of Central Park, in New York," D. E. Sickles Papers, Library of Congress (hereafter LC).

29. Notes on a cross travel system, Manhattan, Daniel E. Sickles Papers, NYHS.

30. Sickles to Robert Dillon, March 14, 1853, NYPL.

31. Sickles to George Sickles from Gadsby's Hotel, February 1853, NYPL; undated letter, Gandicini to Sickles, NYPL; George Sickles to Sickles, April 11, 1853, NYPL.

32. Gobright, pp. 135–136.

## CHAPTER II

1. Klein, pp. 117, 118, 130–132.

2. Forney, pp. 317–318; Fiske, p. 29.

3. Edmund Porter to Sickles, July 23, 1853, NYPL; Teresa Sickles to Sickles, August 1853, NYPL.

4. Sickles's notes, December 3, 1852, to August 4, 1853, NYPL; signed note in favor of Antonio Bagioli, August 18, 1853, NYHS; Ernst, pp. 79, 80; Mary Ellwill to Sickles, April 14, 1853, NYPL.

5. *Dictionary of American Biography,* Vol. 10, pp. 197–198.

6. Swanberg, pp. 90–91; Brandt, p. 29.

7. Hill, pp. 160–162.

8. Swanberg, p. 91; *New York World,* June 30, 1869; Pinchon, p. 34.

9. Forney, pp. 318–319.

10. Keneally, pp. 251, 262–263.

11. McPherson, p. 110; Katz, p. 42; Don Carlos Seitz, *The James Gordon Bennetts, Father and Son,* p. 130; Swanberg, pp. 93–95.

12. Swanberg, p. 94; Benjamin Perley Poore, *Reminiscences of Sixty Years in the National Metropolis,* Vol. 1, p. 444.

13. McPherson, pp. 105–110; Swanberg, pp. 98, 99.

14. *NYH,* November 4, 1854.

15. *NYH,* July 25, August 7, and November 8, 1854.

16. *Harper's Weekly,* April 9, 1859.

17. *Harper's Weekly,* April 9, 1859.

18. Strong, Vol. 2, p. 441; Pinchon, p. 53.

19. McPherson, pp. 107, 108; Fiske, pp. 26–31; Katz, p. 42; Swanberg, p. 99.

20. Swanberg, pp. 99, 100; Fiske, p. 286; *New York World,* June 30, 1869; *Harper's Weekly,* April 9, 1859.

21. Hill, pp. 101, 282, 387, 397.

22. Swanberg, p. 99; undated Sickles essay, "The Founder of Central Park, in New York," LC.

23. D. Wemyss Jobson, *The Allan Trials,* pp. 31, 56, 57.

24. Swanberg, pp. 102–103; *Harper's Weekly,* April 9, 1859; *Appleton's Cyclopaedia of American Biography,* Vol. 3, p. 102.

25. Teresa Sickles to Florence, May 3, 1856, NYPL; Swanberg, pp. 102–103; *New York World,* June 30, 1869.

26. Undated Sickles essay, "The Founder of Central Park, in New York," LC.

27. D. E. Sickles, *Remarks of Hon. Daniel E. Sickles in the Senate of the State of New York on the Bill "to Prevent Illegal Voting in the City of New York," Commonly Known as the Registry Bill.*

28. Swanberg, p. 104; Ernst, p. 20; Hopper Striker Mott, *The New York of Yesterday: A Descriptive Narrative of Old Bloomingdale,* pp. 17, 18; *Frank Leslie's Illustrated Paper,* March 26, 1859.

29. Ellen E. Plante, *The Victorian Home,* passim; Teresa Sickles to Sickles, April 20, 1861, NYHS; Teresa Sickles to Florence, July 9, 1861, NYPL.

30. Teresa Sickles to Florence, late 1856, NYPL.

31. Klein, p. 220; Swanberg, p. 103.

32. McPherson, pp. 106–109.

33. McPherson, pp. 156–162; Swanberg, p. 105.

34. Jean A. Baker, *Mary Todd Lincoln: A Biography,* p. 137; Teresa Sickles to Florence, late 1856, NYPL.

## CHAPTER III

1. Swanberg, p. 2; Baker, pp. 137, 138; McPherson, p. 123.

2. Charles Dickens, *American Notes,* pp. 149, 152, 153.

3. Mary S. C. Logan, *Thirty Years in Washington; Or, Life and Scenes in Our National Capital,* p. 63; Sara Agnes Pryor, *Reminiscences of Peace and War,* p. 3.

4. Brandt, pp. 37–38; Pinchon, p. 69.

5. Swanberg, pp. 5, 6.

6. Swanberg, pp. 4, 5.

7. Virginia Clay-Clopton, *A Belle of the Fifties: Memoirs of Mrs. Clay of Alabama,* pp. 95–97; Swanberg, pp. 3–4; Gobright, pp. 160–162.

8. *NYH,* March 1, 1859; *NYT,* March 2, 1859; *New York Tribune,* March 2 and March 3, 1859.

9. *Harper's Weekly,* March 12, 1859.

10. McPherson, pp. 170, 171, 174–176.

11. Fontaine, Haskin and Hoover evidence, pp. 38, 39; Swanberg, pp. 10–13; *Dictionary of American Biography,* Vol. 4, p. 471.

12. Clay-Clopton, pp. 43–45, 56, 115; Pryor, p. 53; Poore, p. 111; Ishbel Ross, *Rebel Rose: Life of Rose O'Neal Greenhow, Confederate Spy,* p. 72.

13. *NYT,* May 9 and May 12, 1857; *NYP,* May 13, 1857.

14. Daniel Edgar Sickles, *The Court of Common Pleas in the Matter of Charles Devlin Street Commissioner, Argument of Daniel Sickles,* p. 42.

15. Brandt, pp. 61–67; *NYP,* March 1, 1859; *NYH,* March 1, 1859; *Harper's Weekly,* March 12, 1859; *Frank Leslie's Illustrated Newspaper,* March 26, 1859; Fontaine, Hoover evidence, p. 40; Keneally, p. 285.

16. Brandt, pp. 61–67.

17. Isaac Frederick Marcosson, *"Marse Henry": A Biography of Henry Watterson,* p. 63; Clay-Clopton, p. 47; Swanberg, pp. 19, 21; Fontaine, pp. 36, 37; *Harper's Weekly,* March 12, 1859.

18. Poore, p. 25; *NYH,* March 1, 1859; *NYP,* March 1, 1859; Brandt, p. 63; Clay-Clopton, p. 86.

19. McPherson, pp. 164–167.

20. McPherson, pp. 165–167.

21. Brandt, pp. 44–46; Pryor, p. 51.

22. Clay-Clopton, pp. 88–89.

23. Fontaine, Thompson's evidence, pp. 70–71; Clay-Clopton, pp. 96–97; *NYH,* March 1, 1859; *Harper's Weekly,* March 12, 1859; *Frank Leslie's Illustrated Paper,* March 19, 1859.

24. Clay-Clopton, p. 47; *Frank Leslie's Illustrated Newspaper,* March 26, 1859; Fontaine, pp. 36, 37.

25. *Frank Leslie's Illustrated Paper,* March 19, 1859; Teresa Sickles to Florence, July 9, 1861, NYPL.

26. Fontaine, p. 48; undated letter (in folder of letters from first half of 1850s), anonymous woman to Sickles, NYPL.

27. Fontaine, Haskin evidence, p. 70.

28. Fontaine, Haskin evidence, pp. 36, 37; *Frank Leslie's Illustrated Newspaper,* March 26, 1859.

29. Clay-Clopton, pp. 98, 128–134; McPherson, p. 168; John von Sonntag de Havilland, *A Metrical Description of a Fancy Ball Given at Washington, 9th April, 1858,* pp. 5–6, 10, 13, 15, 17, 20, 39.

30. Ernst, pp. 66–68; Bayor and Meagher, pp. 93, 95, 96; Hill, pp. 82, 83; Fontaine, Thompson evidence, pp. 70–71.

31. Swanberg, p. 33; Fontaine, Dougherty's evidence, pp. 38, 39; *NYH,* June 13, 1858; Daniel E. Sickles, *Speech of the Hon. Daniel Sickles of New York on the Neutrality Laws, Delivered in the House of Representatives, January 6, 1858;* McKay, p. 3.

32. *NYH,* September 1, 1859; Fontaine, Dougherty evidence, pp. 38, 39; *Harper's Weekly,* March 12, 1859; *New York Tribune,* March 3, 1859; *NYP,* March 5, 1859.

33. *NYT,* November 20, 1858.

34. Lawrence O'Brien Branch, "Letters, 1856–1860," *North Carolina Historical Quarterly,* Vol. 10, No. 1 (January 1933), pp. 49, 64.

35. Teresa Sickles to Florence, undated but internal evidence indicates February 1859, NYPL.

36. Fontaine, Mrs. Brown evidence, pp. 53, 66, 67, Miss Seeley evidence, p. 70, Wooldridge evidence, pp. 48, 49.

37. *NYT,* February 28, 1859; *NYH,* February 28, 1859; Fontaine, Cooney evidence, p. 72.

38. Fontaine, arguments of counsel, pp. 35, 75, 76; *NYT,* February 28, 1859.

39. McPherson, pp. 193–195.

40. *NYT,* February 28, 1859; *New York Tribune,* March 21, 1859.

## CHAPTER IV

1. Brandt, p. 62; Fontaine, defense opening, p. 34, Titball evidence, p. 20, Wooldridge evidence, pp. 48, 49, 72, 73.

2. Brandt, p. 100; Swanberg, pp. 45–46.

3. Fontaine, Smith Pyne evidence, p. 40.

4. Clay-Clopton, pp. 97–98.

5. *New York Tribune,* March 2, 1859; *NYT,* February 28, 1859.

6. Fontaine, Emerson evidence, p. 72.

7. Clay-Clopton, p. 98; *New York Tribune,* March 3, 1859; *NYT,* February 28, 1859.

8. *Harper's Weekly,* March 12, 1859; R.P.G. letter, Sickles papers, NYHS.

9. Fontaine, Ridgeley evidence, p. 46.

10. Fontaine, McElhone evidence, p. 75; *Washington Evening Star,* February 26, 1859; Fontaine, Wooldridge evidence, pp. 48, 72, 73.

11. Fontaine, Wooldridge evidence, pp. 74, 75.

12. Fontaine, Wooldridge evidence, pp. 74, 75, Cooney evidence, p. 72.

13. Fontaine, Cooney evidence, p. 72, Wooldridge evidence, pp. 74, 75, Dougherty evidence, p. 39.

14. Fontaine, Wooldridge evidence, pp. 74, 75, Lewis and Smith evidence, pp. 84, 85, Mohun evidence, p. 42.

15. Fontaine, Duffy evidence, p. 42, Ridgeley evidence, p. 46.

16. Fontaine, Ridgeley evidence, p. 46, Duffy evidence, p. 42, tabled confession of Teresa, pp. 42, 43.

17. Fontaine, Duffy and Ridgeley evidence, pp. 42, 46; *Harper's Weekly,* March 12, 1859; *Appleton's Cyclopaedia of American Biography,* Vol. 1, p. 310; *NYT,* March 3, 1859; *NYH,* March 2, 1859.

18. Clay-Clopton, p. 43; Fontaine, defense opening, pp. 18, 20, 21, Cuyler evidence, pp. 51, 52; Brandt, p. 114; Fontaine, Pendleton evidence, p. 79; *NYP,* March 5, 1859.

19. Fontaine, Berret evidence, p. 52; *NYT,* March 3, 1856; Fontaine, Ridgeley, Duffy, Wooldridge, and Cooney evidence, pp. 42, 46, 48, 72, 73; Poore, p. 26; *NYH,* March 6, 1859.

20. *NYT,* March 2, 1859; Fontaine, evidence of eyewitnesses, pp. 16–23, 48, 83, Wooldridge evidence, pp. 49, 74–75; *NYP,* February 28, 1859; *NYH,* February 28, 1859.

21. Swanberg, p. 55.

22. *NYH,* February 28 and March 2, 1859; Clay-Clopton, p. 97; Fontaine, McClusky evidence, p. 77, Brodhead evidence, p. 87.

23. Fontaine, McBlair evidence, pp. 83, 84, Walker evidence, pp. 40, 41, Berret evidence, p. 52; *New York Tribune,* March 2, 1859; *NYH,* March 2, 1859.

24. *NYH,* March 2, 1859; *Harper's Weekly,* March 12, 1859.

25. Fontaine, Berret evidence, p. 83, Goddard evidence, p. 40, Walker evidence, pp. 40, 41; *Harper's Weekly,* March 12 and March 19, 1859; Poore, pp. 26, 531; McPherson, pp. 151, 152; Gobright, pp. 160–162.

26. *NYT,* February 28, 1859; Baker, p. 71.

27. Fontaine, Woodward evidence, pp. 22, 23; *Washington Evening Star,* February 28, 1859.

# CHAPTER V

1. *NYT,* February 28, 1859; *NYH,* March 2, 1859.
2. Fontaine, counsel's argument, p. 23, Greenleaf evidence, p. 82; *NYT,* February 28, 1859; *Frank Leslie's Illustrated Newspaper,* March 26, 1859.
3. Brandt, p. 133; *NYH,* March 1, 1859; *Harper's Weekly,* March 12, 1859.
4. *NYH,* March 1, 1859.
5. *NYH,* March 1, 1859; *NYP,* February 28 and March 1, 1859; Strong, Vol. 2, p. 438.
6. Brandt, p. 145; *NYP,* March 5 and March 2, 1859; Strong, Vol. 2, pp. 440–441; *New York Tribune,* March 3, 1859; *NYP,* March 2, 1859; *NYH,* March 2, 1859; *NYT,* March 15, 1859; Brandt, pp. 145, 146; Strong, Vol. 2, pp. 440–441; *NYT,* March 15, 1859.
7. *Harper's Weekly,* March 12, 1859; *Frank Leslie's Illustrated Newspaper,* March 26, 1859; *NYT,* March 15, 1859; *New York Tribune,* March 2, 1859.
8. Strong, Vol. 2, pp. 440, 441; *New York Tribune,* March 2, 1859; *NYT,* March 15, 1859.
9. *Frank Leslie's Illustrated Newspaper,* March 12, 1859; *NYH,* March 2, 1859; *New York Tribune,* March 2, 1859.
10. *Harper's Weekly,* March 12, 1859; *NYP,* March 12, 1859.
11. *Frank Leslie's Illustrated Newspaper,* March 26, 1859.
12. *Frank Leslie's Illustrated Newspaper,* March 12, 1859.
13. Gobright, pp. 192–193; Brandt, p. 151.
14. *Frank Leslie's Illustrated Newspaper,* April 9, 1859; *Harper's Weekly,* April 16, 1859; Bar Association of the City of New York, *In Memoriam, James T. Brady: Report of Proceedings at a Meeting of the New York Bar,* pp. 13, 21–22; *Dictionary of American Biography,* Vol. 1, pp. 583–584.
15. Henry Ward Beecher and James Topham Brady, *Addresses on Mental Culture for Women,* speeches delivered October 26, 1858, pp. 20, 24, 37, 38; *Harper's Weekly,* April 16, 1859; *Frank Leslie's Illustrated Newspaper,* April 9, 1859.
16. Fontaine, Mann testimony, pp. 67–68, Pendleton testimony, p. 79; *Harper's Weekly,* March 26 and April 16, 1859; Poore, p. 29.
17. *Frank Leslie's Illustrated Newspaper,* March 26, 1859; *Harper's Weekly,* March 19, 1859; *Harper's Weekly,* March 12, 1859.
18. Pinchon, pp. 134–136.

19. *Harper's Weekly,* March 26, 1859; *NYH,* April 5, 1859.

20. *Frank Leslie's Illustrated Newspaper,* April 9, 1859; *Harper's Weekly,* April 9, 1859; *NYH,* April 5 and April 8, 1859; *NYT,* April 5, 1859.

21. *NYH,* March 15 and April 5, 1859.

22. Fontaine, p. 6; *Frank Leslie's Illustrated Newspaper,* April 9, 1859; *Harper's Weekly,* April 9, 1859; *NYH,* April 6, 1859.

23. *NYH,* April 5, 1859; Brandt, p. 166; Fontaine, p. 6.

24. Fontaine, pp. 7, 8.

25. Fontaine, p. 8; *NYH,* April 5, 1859.

26. Fontaine, pp. 9, 10; *NYH,* April 27, 1859.

27. Fontaine, pp. 11–15.

28. Fontaine, address of counsel, pp. 15–16; Pinchon, p. 134.

29. Fontaine, Reed, and other eyewitness evidence, pp. 16–21.

30. Fontaine, Woodward evidence, p. 21.

31. Fontaine, Coolidge evidence, p. 22.

32. Fontaine, Coolidge evidence and argument of counsel, pp. 22–24.

33. *NYH,* April 11, 1859.

34. Fontaine, address of counsel, pp. 25–30; *NYP,* April 11, 1859.

35. *New York World,* June 30, 1869; *NYH,* March 15, 1859.

36. Fontaine, address of counsel and letters offered as evidence, pp. 32–37.

37. Fontaine, Haskin evidence, p. 38.

38. Fontaine, Walker evidence, p. 41; *NYP,* April 19, 1859.

39. *NYH,* April 14, 1859; Fontaine, argument of counsel, pp. 42–43.

40. Fontaine, argument of counsel, pp. 44–46; *Frank Leslie's Illustrated Newspaper,* April 23, 1859; *Harper's Weekly,* April 23, 1859.

41. Fontaine, Duffy evidence, pp. 46–49, arguments of counsel, pp. 49–51.

42. Fontaine, Wilson and Ratley evidence, pp. 52, 53.

43. Fontaine, Brown evidence and arguments of counsel, pp. 55–66; *NYH,* April 14, 1859.

44. *Harper's Weekly,* April 23, 1859; Fontaine, Brown evidence, pp. 66, 67.

45. Fontaine, McDonald evidence, p. 78.

46. Fontaine, Doyle, Winder, and other eyewitness evidence, pp. 81, 84, 85.

47. Fontaine, Lewis and other evidence, pp. 85, 86.

48. Fontaine, arguments of counsel, pp. 86, 87.

49. *Washington Star,* April 25, 1859; Fontaine, counsels' summation, pp. 89–90.

50. Fontaine, counsels' summation, pp. 90–100.

51. Fontaine, counsels' summation and judge's directions, pp. 103–105.

52. Fontaine, verdict, p. 106; *NYH,* April 27, 1859; *New York Tribune,* April 27, 1859; *NYT,* April 27, 1859.

53. *New York Tribune,* April 28, 1859; *NYH,* April 27, 1859; *NYT,* April 28, 1859; *Harper's Weekly,* May 14, 1859.

CHAPTER VI

1. Swanberg, p. 67.

2. *NYH,* July 12, 1859; *NYT,* July 13, 1859.

3. Strong, Vol. 2, pp. 456–457; *NYH,* July 19, 1859; *Harper's Weekly,* July 17, 1859.

4. *NYH,* July 20, 1859.

5. Brandt, p. 197; Colonel George Hickory to Sickles, August 7, 1859, NYPL; Stephen Gooding to Sickles, July 21, 1859, NYPL.

6. Brandt, pp. 198–199.

7. *Harper's Weekly,* December 24, 1859.

8. Mary Boykin Miller Chesnut, *A Diary from Dixie,* pp. 246–247.

9. McPherson, pp. 209, 210, 216, 217, 220, 221; Daniel E. Sickles, *Remarks of the Hon. Daniel E. Sickles of New York on the Relations of the North and the South, and the Duty of the North in the Present Crisis,* pp. 8, 11, 13, 15, 16.

10. McPherson, pp. 227–233.

11. McPherson, p. 233; Daniel Edgar Sickles, *Speech of the Hon. Daniel E. Sickles of New York on the State of the Union,* pp. 9–16.

12. McPherson, pp. 234, 235.

13. Daniel E. Sickles, *The Republic Is Imperishable, Speech of the Honorable Dan E. Sickles of New York on the State of the Union, January 16, 1861,* pp. 2, 10, 12, 13, 16.

14. Sickles, *The Republic Is Imperishable,* p. 12; McPherson, p. 266; undated typescript, "Address to 'Gentlemen of the Institute,' " LC.

15. Sickles, *A Speech Delivered to the House of Representatives, February 5, 1861, by Mr. Sickles of New York on Mr. Colfax's Postal Service Suspension Act,* p. 8.

16. Swanberg, p. 111, 112; McPherson, pp. 274, 275; Hill, pp. 103, 281–282.

17. McKay, p. 77; Teresa to Sickles, April 21, 1861, NYHS.

18. McPherson, p. 260; Keneally, pp. 327, 328, 346.

19. Swanberg, pp. 115, 116; Régis de Trobriand, *Four Years with the Army of the Potomac,* p. 427.

20. Swanberg, pp. 115–117; Henri le Fevre Brown, *History of the Third Regiment,*

*Excelsior Brigade, 72nd New York Volunteer Infantry, 1861–1865,* pp. 9, 10; List of Excelsior Brigade Prisoners Paroled and Given Transport Home, 1862, NYPL; Keneally, p. 329.

21. Swanberg, pp. 117, 118; Baker, pp. 228, 239; J. G. Holland, *Life of Abraham Lincoln,* pp. 90, 123; McPherson, pp. 321–323.

22. Swanberg, pp. 119, 120.

23. "The Old Excelsior Brigade," undated typescript, LC; *Harper's Weekly,* April 9, 1859.

24. Teresa Sickles to Florence, July 9, 1861, NYPL; Baker, pp. 218, 231–234; William O. Stoddard, *Inside the White House in War Times: Memoirs and Reports of Lincoln's Secretary,* pp. xiv, xv; Henry Wikoff, *My Courtship and Its Consequences,* pp. 29, 73, 194–198, 311–315; Henry Wikoff, *The Adventures of a Roving Diplomatist,* passim.

25. Swanberg, pp. 122–124; John Woodward to Sickles, May 1, 1862, NYPL; Henry Steele Commager, *The Blue and the Gray,* Vol. 1, pp. 116–117.

26. *New York World,* June 30, 1869.

27. Swanberg, pp. 126; *New York Tribune,* July 22, 1861; Sickles's list of signals, NYPL.

28. Logan, pp. 63–64; Noah Brooks, *Washington in Lincoln's Time,* pp. 13, 16.

29. Baker, pp. 119, 191; Stoddard, p. 33; Swanberg, p. 29.

30. Swanberg, p. 128; Walter Herbert, *Fighting Joe Hooker,* p. 54; Laura Sickles to Sickles, October 27, 1861, NYPL; Susan Sickles to Dan, November 5, 1861, NYPL.

31. Herbert, p. 54; Brown, p. 30.

32. Swanberg, p. 134.

33. Sickles to Wikoff, January 30, 1862, LC; Herbert, pp. 62, 63.

34. Ross, pp. 71, 76, 77, 118, 121; Poore, p. 111.

35. Poore, pp. 142, 143; Baker p. 191; Ruth Painter Randall, *Mary Lincoln: Biography of a Marriage,* p. 255.

36. "Report of a Reconnoiter, Headquarters Excelsior Brigade," February 28, 1862, NYPL; copy of Hooker's letter, April 1, 1862, NYHS; "Looking for Beauregard," undated typescript, LC.

37. Keneally, pp. 377, 378; Baker, pp. 206–212.

38. Herbert, pp. 66–68; Hooker to Sickles, April 6, 1862, LC; Swanberg, p. 140; Stephen W. Sears, *To the Gates of Richmond,* pp. 18–20; George Sickles to Sickles, April 14, 1862, NYPL.

39. Brown, pp. 29, 41; Swanberg, pp. 146, 147.

40. Sears, pp. 117, 135–138; Herbert, p. 97.

41. Brown, p. 40; United States, War Department, *The War of the Rebellion: A Compilation of the Official Records of the Union and Confederate Armies,* Series 1, Vol. 11, Pt. 3, p. 190; Herbert, pp. 101–103.

42. Sears, pp. 149, 150; Brown, pp. 51, 52; Keneally, pp. 352–354; United States, *War of the Rebellion,* Series 1, Vol. 11, Pt. 1, p. 830.

43. Henry Liebeman to Sickles, May 21, 1862, NYPL; Teresa Sickles to Liebeman, May 19, 1862, LC; Swanberg, pp. 151, 157; father of Lieutenant Hossey to Sickles, June 4, 1862, NYPL; J. Gaylor to Sickles, May 19, 1861, NYPL; Swanberg, p. 151; Herbert, pp. 101, 102.

44. Olive Devoe to Sickles, April 22, 1862, NYPL.

45. Herbert, pp. 101–103, 110; Swanberg, p. 151; Sears, pp. 187–189.

46. Herbert, pp. 110, 111; Brown, pp. 52, 54.

47. Herbert, pp. 111, 175; Sears, p. 345; Swanberg, pp. 153, 154, 156.

## CHAPTER VII

1. Herbert, pp. 114, 115; McKay, p. 176; *New York Tribune,* August 7, 1862.

2. Swanberg, pp. 159, 160; Keneally, pp. 365, 366; McKay, pp. 198, 199; Iver Bernstein, *The New York Draft Riots,* pp. 18–22; *New York Tribune,* August 16, 1862.

3. Keneally, p. 374; Herbert, pp. 114, 115, 152.

4. Baker, pp. 231, 232.

5. Ruth Randall, p. 219.

6. Nettie Colburn Maynard, *Was Abraham Lincoln a Spiritualist? Curious Revelations from the Life of a Trance Medium,* pp. 71–74, 128–132; Ruth Randall, pp. 293, 294; Baker, pp. 219–221.

7. McPherson, p. 562; Brown, pp. 78–80.

8. Brown, p. 80; McPherson, pp. 571–574; Keneally, pp. 374–375.

9. Gabor S. Borritt, ed., *Lincoln's Generals,* p. 70.

10. Princess Felix Salm-Salm, *Ten Years of My Life,* pp. 26–27, 29, 40, 41; unsigned letter, a woman to Sickles, October 3, 1864, LC; de Trobriand, pp. 398, 426, 427.

11. Keneally, p. 380; Herbert, p. 175; letters of George Sickles to Sickles, late January 1863 onward, NYPL; Swanberg, p. 170.

12. Swanberg, pp. 169, 173, 174; United States, *Report of the Joint Committee on the Conduct of the War,* Vol. 1, Sickles evidence, pp. 3–15.

13. Salm-Salm, pp. 43, 44; Brooks, pp. 54–70; Julia Lorrilard Saffort Butterfield, *A Biographical Memorial of General Daniel Butterfield,* p. 160.

14. Butterfield, pp. 161–162.

15. Theodore Ayrault Dodge, *The Campaign of Chancellorsville,* pp. 32, 33; Herbert, pp. 175, 176.

16. United States, *War of the Rebellion,* Series 1, Vol. 25, Pt. 1, p. 387; Herbert, pp. 194–195; Dodge, pp. 134–136; Swanberg, p. 180; Gary R. Rice, "Devil Dan Sickles' Deadly Salients," www.thehistorynet.com; Sickles chat site on www.suite101.com.

17. Dodge, pp. 137, 143, 145; Swanberg, p. 189.

18. United States, *War of the Rebellion,* Series 1, Vol. 25, Pt. 1, p. 392; Dodge, p. 227; Herbert, pp. 212–216, 218; de Trobriand, p. 427.

19. Dodge, p. 17; George Stanton Sickles to Sickles, June 5, 1901, LC; Colonel Whipple to Sickles, August 3, 1853, NYPL; George Sickles to Sickles, November 22, 1883, LC; *NYH,* May 9 and May 26, 1863.

20. Keneally, pp. 394–395.

21. George Stanton Sickles to Sickles, June 5, 1901, LC; Laura Sickles to George Sickles, March 14, 1883, LC; George Sickles to Sickles, November 22, 1883, LC; Jack D. Walsh, *Medical Histories of Union Generals,* pp. 302, 303; *NYT,* May 31 and June 17, 1863.

22. Herbert, p. 336; United States, *War of the Rebellion,* Series 1, Vol. 27, Pt. 3, pp. 399, 420; Henry Edwin Tremain, *Two Days of War: A Gettysburg Narrative and Other Excursions,* p. 14; Daniel Edgar Sickles, "Further Recollections of Gettysburg," *North American Review,* No. 151 (March 1891), pp. 250–262; Borritt, p. 72.

23. Brown, p. 104; Sickles, "Further Recollections," pp. 262, 263; Gary W. Gallagher, ed., *The Second Day at Gettysburg,* pp. 314–317; Commager, Vol. 1, pp. 314–316.

24. Sickles, "Further Recollections," p. 263; United States, *Report of the Joint Committee on the Conduct of the War,* Butterfield evidence, Vol. 1, p. 427; Swanberg, p. 209.

25. Sickles, "Further Recollections," p. 264; Herbert, p. 211; de Trobriand, p. 494; Swanberg, p. 210.

26. Gallagher, pp. 69–70; Swanberg, p. 211; Sickles, "Further Recollections," p. 265; Tremain, pp. 37, 41, 53.

27. Thomas Dormandy, *The White Death: A History of Tuberculosis,* pp. 2, 8–9, 42, 43, 45, 48, 49, 150, 151; Bayor and Meagher, p. 157.

28. Borritt, pp. 70, 71; de Trobriand, p. 494; Glenn Tucker, *High Tide at Gettysburg,* p. 272; Tremain, pp. 60–61; Sickles, "Further Recollections," pp. 266, 267.

29. Sickles, "Further Recollections," pp. 267, 268; Tremain, pp. 88–89; Brown, p. 105.

30. Walsh, pp. 302–303; Tremain, pp. 88, 89, 94.

31. Swanberg, pp. 221, 222, 223; David S. Reynolds, *Walt Whitman's America,* p. 411; *NYT,* July 6, 1863.

32. United States, *War of the Rebellion,* Series 1, Vol. 27, Pt. 1, pp. 82, 16.

33. Tremain, pp. 100, 101, 105; Swanberg, p. 223; Roy P. Basler, *The Collected Works of Abraham Lincoln,* Vol. 6, p. 53; *NYH,* July 19, 1863.

34. *NYH,* July 24 and July 29, 1859.

## CHAPTER VIII

1. *NYT,* August 1, 1863; Swanberg, p. 227.

2. Swanberg, p. 226; *NYT,* August 12 and September 9, 1863.

3. *NYT,* September 9, 1863; Strong, Vol. 3, p. 351; *New York Tribune,* October 19, 1863.

4. De Trobriand, p. 530; Swanberg, pp. 233, 235; United States, *Report of the Joint Committee on the Conduct of the War,* Vol. 1, p. 304.

5. Swanberg, p. 234, 236; O. W. Davis to Sickles, August 21, 1863, NYPL; de Trobriand, p. 546.

6. *NYT,* November 1, 1863.

7. Baker, pp. 223, 224; Ruth Randall, pp. 334–335; Katherine Helm, *The True Story of Mary, Wife of Lincoln,* pp. 22, 226–228, 231, 334, 335.

8. Swanberg, pp. 244, 245; Ruth Randall, p. 338; Basler, Vol. 7, p. 160.

9. United States, *Report of the Joint Committee on the Conduct of the War,* Vol. 1, pp. 3–5, 296, 300, 302; Richard Allen Sauers, *A Caspian Sea of Ink: The Meade-Sickles Controversy,* pp. 41–43.

10. United States, *Report of the Joint Committee on the Conduct of the War,* Vol. 1, pp. xix, 311, 312, 337, 349; Swanberg, p. 253; *NYH,* March 12, 1864; United States, *War of the Rebellion,* Series 1, Vol. 27, Pt. 1, pp. 137, 139; Sauers, pp. 41–46.

11. Swanberg, p. 259; Adam Badeau, *Grant in Peace: From Appomattox to Mount McGregor,* p. 382; Clarence E. N. Macartney, *Grant and His Generals,* p. 99.

12. Swanberg, pp. 261, 262; Dormandy, pp. 44, 46, 92, 102.

13. Sickles to President Lincoln, May 16, 1864, LC.

14. Swanberg, p. 262; *NYH,* November 2, 1864.

15. Swanberg, pp. 268, 269; Keneally, pp. 318, 319, 321; Stephen J. Randall, *Colombia and the United States: Hegemony and Interdependence,* p. 48; George Sickles to Sickles, April 24, 1865, NYPL; William Hobart Royce to Edgcumb Pinchon,

December 6, 1941, William Hobart Royce Papers, NYPL; Badeau, p. 238; Wikoff to Sickles, January 22, 1865, NYPL; George Sickles to Sickles, April 24, 1865, NYPL.

16. Stephen Randall, pp. 38, 49, 50; David W. Bushnell, *The Making of Modern Colombia,* pp. 106, 107, 120; Harvey F. Kline, *Colombia: Portrait of Unity and Diversity,* p. 13; F. Lorraine Petre, *The Republic of Colombia,* pp. 83–85, 123; William Lindsay Scruggs, *The Colombian and Venezuelan Republics,* p. 49.

17. Swanberg, pp. 271, 273; Baker, p. 243; Badeau, p. 238; Robert Selph Henry, *The Story of Reconstruction,* pp. 248, 259; Edward L. Gambill, *Conservative Ordeal: Northern Democrats and Reconstruction, 1865–1869,* p. 98.

18. Dormandy, pp. 47, 48, 49, 102, 103, 106; *NYH,* February 10, 1867.

19. Swanberg, p. 275; Anon., "Three Months Among the Reconstructionists," *Atlantic Monthly,* February 1866, pp. 237–245; "A Planter's Grievance," Sickles Papers, LC; Sickles to Assistant Adjutant General, June 18, 1867, LC.

20. Francis Butler Simkins and Robert Hilliard Woody, *South Carolina During Reconstruction,* pp. 57–59, 65–68; "Three Months Among the Reconstructionists," pp. 237–245.

21. Swanberg, p. 284; Simkins and Woody, pp. 57–59, 69; "Three Months Among the Reconstructionists," pp. 237–245; Allie Grant to Sickles, September 22, 1865, NYPL.

22. Swanberg, pp. 281, 282; Badeau, p. 385; Simkins and Woody, p. 64; Dormandy, pp. 83, 84, 93, 94; Allie Grant to Sickles, October 2, 1866, NYPL; Jane Pettigru to Sickles, March 21, 1867, NYPL.

23. Simkins and Woody, pp. 56–60, 65, 66.

24. *NYH,* February 10, 1867; James T. Brady, *A Christmas Dream,* p. 32; Dormandy, pp. 92, 93.

25. *NYH,* February 10, 1867.


FINALE


1. Dr. Bermingham, Vicar-General of Charleston, to Sickles, March 5, 1869, NYHS; Sr. Xavier to Sickles, March 11, 1869, NYHS.

2. Simkins and Woody, pp. 68, 69; Badeau, pp. 383, 384; Seaver to Sickles, April 28, 1867, NYHS.

3. Swanberg, pp. 287, 288; Simkins and Woody, p. 68; James Orr to Sickles, September 7, 1867, NYHS; Seaver to Sickles, April 28, 1867, NYHS; Grant to

Sickles, August 13, 1867, LC; Sickles to Adjutant General of the Army, copied by Sickles to President Johnson, June 19, 1867, LC.

4. *NYT,* June 21, September 4, September 8, and September 24, 1867; Sickles to Adjutant General, September 11, 1867, LC; Swanberg, pp. 294–297; Badeau, pp. 383–386; Macartney, p. 99.

5. Swanberg, pp. 302–308, 314–318, 320, 321; *New York World,* June 25 and June 30, 1869; Badeau, p. 387; *NYP,* July 2, 1869; Sickles to State Department, August 9, 1869, LC; Sickles to Wikoff, January 3, 1871, NYPL; Sickles to Pleasanton, January 21, 1871, NYPL.

6. Susan Sickles to Sickles, February 1872, LC; *NYH,* December 19, 1871; Swanberg, p. 344.

7. Swanberg, pp. 335–338; *NYT,* March 12, 1872; *NYH,* March 12, 1872; Strong, Vol. 4, p. 422.

8. Swanberg, pp. 348, 349; *NYT,* December 23, 1873.

9. Swanberg, pp. 351–355; William Hobart Royce to Edgcumb Pinchon, December 6, 1941 and July 26, 1942, William Hobart Royce Papers, New York Public Library; George Stanton Sickles to Sickles, June 5, 1901, LC.

10. Swanberg, pp. 355–357; Badeau, p. 387; William P. Shreve, *The Story of the Third Army Corps Union,* pp. 38, 49; *New York World,* May 4, 1914; George Stanton Sickles to Sickles, June 5, 1901, LC.

11. Swanberg, pp. 359–360.

12. William Sickles to Sickles, December 22, 1881, LC; William Hobart Royce to Edgcumb Pinchon, December 18, 1941, William Hobart Royce Papers, New York Public Library; Fiske, p. 287.

13. De Trobriand, p. 494; Swanberg, p. 363, 364; Tremain, p. 68; Major General John Watts De Peyster, "The Third Corps and Sickles at Gettysburg," *Volunteer,* Vol. 1, No. 11, p. 308, No. 13, p. 358; Sauers, pp. 59, 60, 82.

14. George Sickles to Sickles, November 22, 1883, LC; Sickles to George Sickles, November 25, 1883, LC; Laura Sickles to George Sickles, March 14, 1883, LC; William Hobart Royce to Edgcumb Pinchon, December 6, 1941, William Hobart Royce Papers, New York Public Library;

15. Theodore B. Starr to Sickles, June 19, 1882, LC; William Hobart Royce to Edgcumb Pinchon, December 6, 1941, William Hobart Royce Papers, New York Public Library;

16. *NYT,* November 7, 1892; www.arlingtoncemetery.com.

17. Undated press clipping, c. 1900, quoting Champ Clark, NYHS; *NYH,* November 7, 1894.

18. Sickles to King, undated letter, LC; Swanberg, pp. 368–370; Shreve, p. 71; George Stanton Sickles to Sickles, June 17, 1881, and March 20, 1882, LC.

19. Helen Dortch Longstreet, *Lee and Longstreet at High Tide: Gettysburg in the Light of the Official Records,* pp. 19–20.

20. Longstreet, pp. 20, 21, 22; James Longstreet to Sickles, September 19, 1902, LC; *NYT,* January 29, 1913.

21. William Hobart Royce to Edgcumb Pinchon, October 22, 1941, William Hobart Royce Papers, New York Public Library; *NYT,* January 28, 1913.

22. Justin Kaplin, *Mr. Clemens and Mark Twain,* p. 83; William Hobart Royce to Edgcumb Pinchon, December 6, 1941, William Hobart Royce Papers, New York Public Library; Swanberg, pp. 378, 379.

23. George Stanton Sickles to Sickles, undated note, LC; *NYT,* May 4, 1914; William Hobart Royce to Edgcumb Pinchon, October 22, 1941, William Hobart Royce Papers, New York Public Library; Private Calendar No. 174, House of Representatives, 61st Congress, 2nd Session.

24. Receipt, Eleanor Wilmerding to Sickles, August 12, 1907, LC; Fred Sterry/Plaza Hotel to Sickles, June 28, 1910, LC; Knickerbocker Trust Company to Sickles, January 12, 1911, LC; Lenott Parlaghy to Sickles, February 11, 1911, LC; Sickles to August Hecksher, June 29, 1912, LC; Annie Conover to Sickles, undated, NYPL; William Hobart Royce to Edgcumb Pinchon, December 18, 1941, William Hobart Royce Papers, New York Public Library.

25. *NYT,* January 26, 1913.

26. *NYT,* January 29, 1913.

27. Thomas Carmody to Daniel F. Hays, April 25, 1913, Sickles Papers, LC; *NYT,* January 27, January 28, January 29, and January 30, 1913; J. D. McHenry to Sickles, February 14, 1913, LC.

28. *NYH,* July 1, 1913; Swanberg, pp. 388–390.

29. *NYT,* May 4 and May 5, 1914; www.arlingtoncemetery.com.

## LAST WORD

1. *NYT,* May 5, 1914; www.arlingtoncemetery.com.

# BIBLIOGRAPHY

## Major Collections

Daniel Edgar Sickles Papers, Manuscripts Division, Library of Congress
(abbreviated LC)
Daniel Edgar Sickles Papers, Manuscripts and Archives Division, New York Public
Library, Astor, Lenox, and Tilden Foundations (abbreviated NYPL)
Daniel E. Sickles Papers, New-York Historical Society (abbreviated NYHS)

## Newspapers and Journals

*Congressional Globe*
*Frank Leslie's Illustrated Newspaper*
*Harper's Weekly*
*New York Herald (NYH)*
*New York Post (NYP)*
*New York Times (NYT)*
*New York Tribune*
*New York World*
*Washington Star*

Adams, George W. *Doctors in Blue.* New York, 1952.

Anderson, Frank Maloy. *Mystery of a Public Man.* Minneapolis, 1948.

*Appleton's Cyclopaedia of American Biography.* New York, 1873.

Badeau, Adam. *Grant in Peace: From Appomattox to Mount McGregor.* Hartford, Conn., 1887.

Baker, Jean A. *Mary Todd Lincoln: A Biography.* New York, 1987.

Bar Association of the City of New York. *In Memoriam, James T. Brady: Report of Proceedings at a Meeting of the New York Bar.* New York, 1869.

Basler, Roy P., ed. *The Collected Works of Abraham Lincoln.* Vols. 5–7. Springfield, Ill., 1953–55.

Bayor, Ronald H., and Meagher, Timothy J. *The New York Irish.* Baltimore, 1996.

Beecher, Henry Ward, and Brady, James Topham. *Addresses on Mental Culture for Women.* Speeches delivered October 26, 1858. New York, 1859.

Bennett, James Gordon. *The People of the State of New York on the Complaint of Daniel E. Sickles, versus James Gordon Bennett.* New York, 1857.

Bernstein, Iver. *The New York Draft Riots.* New York, 1990.

Borritt, Gabor S., ed. *Lincoln's Generals.* New York, 1994.

Bowers, Claude Gernade. *The Tragic Era: The Revolution After Lincoln.* Cambridge, 1929.

Brady, James Topham. *A Christmas Dream.* New York, 1860.

Brandt, Nat. *The Congressman Who Got Away with Murder.* Syracuse, N.Y., 1991.

Brooks, Noah. *Washington in Lincoln's Time.* Ed. Herbert Mitgang. New York, 1958.

Brown, Henri le Fevre. *History of the Third Regiment, Excelsior Brigade, 72nd New York Volunteer Infantry, 1861–1865.* Jamestown, N.Y., 1902.

Bushnell, David W. *The Making of Modern Colombia.* Berkeley, Calif., 1990.

Butterfield, Julia Lorrilard Saffort. *A Biographical Memorial of General Daniel Butterfield.* New York, 1904.

Chesnut, Mary Boykin Miller. *A Diary from Dixie.* London, 1905.

Clay-Clopton, Virginia. *A Belle of the Fifties: Memoirs of Mrs. Clay of Alabama.* Ed. Ada Sterling. New York, 1905.

Clemmer, Mary. *Ten Years in Washington.* Hartford, Conn., 1874.

Commager, Henry Steele. *The Blue and the Gray.* 2 vols. Indianapolis, 1973.

Daly, Maria Lydig. *Diary of a Union Lady, 1861–1865.* Ed. Harold Earl Hammond. New York, 1962.

Dickens, Charles. *American Notes.* New York, 1996.

*Dictionary of American Biography.* 10 vols. New York, 1937.

Dormandy, Thomas. *The White Death: A History of Tuberculosis.* New York, 2000.

Dodge, Theodore Ayrault. *The Campaign of Chancellorsville.* Boston, 1881.

Ernst, Robert. *Immigrant Life in New York City, 1825–1863.* Syracuse, N.Y., 1994.

Fiske, Stephen. *Off-Hand Portraits of Prominent New Yorkers.* New York, 1884.

Fontaine, Felix G. *De Witt's Special Report: Trial of Daniel E. Sickles for Shooting Philip Key, Esq., U.S. District Attorney of Washington D.C.* New York, 1859.

Forney, John W. *Anecdotes of Public Men.* New York, 1873.

Gallagher, Gary W., ed. *The Second Day at Gettysburg.* Kent, Ohio, 1993.

Gambill, Edward L. *Conservative Ordeal: Northern Democrats and Reconstruction, 1865–1869.* St. Cloud, Minn., 1981.

Gobright, L. A. *Recollection of Men and Things at Washington During the Third of a Century.* Washington, D.C., 1869.

Hansel, W. U. *A Pennsylvania Presbyterian President: An Inquiry into the Religious Sentiments and Character of James Buchanan.* Philadelphia, 1907.

Havilland, John von Sonntag de. *A Metrical Description of a Fancy Ball Given at Washington, 9th April, 1858.* Washington, D.C., 1858.

Helm, Katherine. *The True Story of Mary, Wife of Lincoln.* New York, 1928.

Henry, Robert Selph. *The Story of Reconstruction.* New York, 1938.

Herbert, Walter. *Fighting Joe Hooker.* New York, 1944.

Hill, Marilyn Wood. *Their Sisters' Keepers: Prostitution in New York City, 1830–1870.* Los Angeles, 1993.

Holland, J. G. *Life of Abraham Lincoln.* Springfield, Ill., 1886.

Jobson, D. Wemyss. *The Allan Trials.* New York, 1857.

Kaplin, Justin. *Mr. Clemens and Mark Twain.* New York, 1996.

Katz, Irving. *August Belmont: A Political Biography.* New York, 1968.

Keneally, Thomas. *The Great Shame and the Triumph of the Irish in the English-Speaking World.* New York, London, Sydney, 1999.

King, Horatio. *Turning on the Light: A Dispassionate Survey of President Buchanan's Administration from 1860 to Its Close.* Philadelphia, 1895.

Klein, Philip Shriver. *President James Buchanan.* University Park, Pa., 1962.

Kline, Harvey F. *Colombia: Portrait of Unity and Diversity.* Boulder, Colo., 1983.

Knoop, Jeanne W. *I Follow the Course Come What May.* New York, 1998.

Lincoln, Abraham. *Complete Works*. Ed. John G. Nicolay and John Hay. 2 vols. New York, 1894.

Logan, Mary S. C. *Thirty Years in Washington; Or, Life and Scenes in Our National Capital*. Hartford, Conn., 1901.

Longstreet, Helen Dortch. *Lee and Longstreet at High Tide: Gettysburg in the Light of the Official Records*. Gainesville, Ga., 1904.

Macartney, Clarence E. N. *Grant and His Generals*. New York, 1953.

McCabe, James Dabney. *Lights and Shadows of New York Life; Or, The Sights and Sensations of the Great City*. New York, 1872.

McKay, Ernest A. *The Civil War and New York City*. Syracuse, N.Y., 1990.

McPherson, James M. *The Battle-cry of Freedom*. New York, 1988.

Marcosson, Isaac Frederick. *"Marse Henry": A Biography of Henry Watterson*. New York, 1951.

Maynard, Nettie Colburn. *Was Abraham Lincoln a Spiritualist? Curious Revelations from the Life of a Trance Medium*. Philadelphia, 1891.

Milton, George Fort. *The Age of Hate: Andrew Johnson and the Radicals*. Hamden, Conn., 1965.

Mott, Hopper Striker. *The New York of Yesterday: A Descriptive Narrative of Old Bloomingdale*. New York, 1908.

Myers, Gustavus. *The History of Tammany Hall*. New York, 1901.

Nichols, Thomas Lowe. *Forty Years of American Life*. New York, 1969.

Nicolay, John G., and Hay, John. *Complete Works of Abraham Lincoln*. 12 vols. New York, 1905.

Petre, F. Lorraine. *The Republic of Colombia*. London, 1906.

Pfanz, Harry W. *The Battle of Gettysburg*. Conshohocken, Pa., 1994.

Pinchon, Edgcumb. *Dan Sickles, Hero of Gettysburg and "Yankee King of Spain."* New York, 1945.

Plante, Ellen E. *The Victorian Home*. Philadelphia, 1995.

Poore, Benjamin Perley. *Reminiscences of Sixty Years in the National Metropolis*. 2 vols. Philadelphia, 1886.

Pryor, Sara Agnes. *Reminiscences of Peace and War*. New York, 1904.

Randall, Ruth Painter. *Mary Lincoln: Biography of a Marriage*. Boston, 1953.

Randall, Stephen J. *Colombia and the United States: Hegemony and Interdependence*. Athens, Ga., 1992.

Reynolds, David S. *Walt Whitman's America*. New York, 1995.

Ross, Ishbel. *Rebel Rose: Life of Rose O'Neal Greenhow, Confederate Spy*. New York, 1954.

Russo, Joseph Louis. *Lorenzo Da Ponte, Poet and Adventurer.* New York, 1922.

Salm-Salm, Princess Felix. *Ten Years of My Life.* New York, 1877.

Sauers, Richard Allen. *A Caspian Sea of Ink: The Meade-Sickles Controversy.* Baltimore, 1989.

Scruggs, William Lindsay. *The Colombian and Venezuelan Republics.* Boston, 1900.

Sears, Stephen W. *To the Gates of Richmond.* New York, 1992.

Seitz, Don Carlos. *The James Gordon Bennetts, Father and Son.* Indianapolis, 1928.

Shreve, William P. *The Story of the Third Army Corps Union.* Boston, 1910.

Sickles, Daniel E. *Speech of the Hon. Daniel Sickles of New York on the Neutrality Laws, Delivered in the House of Representatives, January 6, 1858.* Pamphlet. Washington, 1858.

Sickles, Daniel Edgar. *Remarks of Hon. Daniel E. Sickles in the Senate of the State of New York on the Bill "to Prevent Illegal Voting in the City of New York," Commonly Known as the Registry Bill.* Albany, 1856.

Sickles, Daniel Edgar. *The Court of Common Pleas in the Matter of Charles Devlin Street Commissioner, Argument of Daniel Sickles.* New York, 1857.

Sickles, Daniel Edgar. *Remarks of the Hon. Daniel E. Sickles of New York on the Relations of the North and South, and the Duty of the North in the Present Crisis, Delivered in the House of Representatives, December 13, 1859.* Washington, D.C., 1860.

Sickles, Daniel Edgar. *Speech of the Hon. Daniel E. Sickles of New York on the State of the Union, Delivered in the House of Representatives, December 10, 1860.* Washington, D.C., 1860.

Sickles, Daniel Edgar. *A Speech Delivered to the House of Representatives, February 5, 1861, by Mr. Sickles of New York on Mr. Colfax's Postal Service Suspension Act.* Washington, D.C., 1861.

Sickles, Daniel Edgar. *The Revolution of 1860, a Speech Delivered by Mr. Sickles of New York in the House of Representatives, January 16, 1861.* Washington, D.C., 1861.

Sickles, Daniel Edgar. *The Republic Is Imperishable, Speech of the Honorable Dan E. Sickles of New York on the State of the Union, January 16, 1861.* Washington, D.C., 1861.

Simkins, Francis Butler, and Woody, Robert Hilliard. *South Carolina During Reconstruction.* Chapel Hill, N.C., 1932.

Stoddard, William O. *Inside the White House in War Times: Memoirs and Reports of Lincoln's Secretary.* Ed. Michael Burlingame. Lincoln, Neb., 2000.

Strong, George Templeton. *Diary of George Templeton Strong: Selections.* Ed. Allan Nevins and Milton Halsey Thomas. 4 vols. New York, 1952.

Swanberg, W. A. *Sickles the Incredible.* New York, 1984.

Tremain, Henry Edwin. *Two Days of War: A Gettysburg Narrative and Other Excursions.* New York, 1905.

Trobriand, Régis de. *Four Years with the Army of the Potomac.* Boston, 1889.

Tucker, Glenn. *High Tide at Gettysburg.* New York, 1958.

United States, War Department. *The War of the Rebellion: A Compilation of the Official Records of the Union and Confederate Armies.* 128 vols. Washington, D.C., 1880–1901.

United States. *Report of the Joint Committee on the Conduct of the War.* 3 vols. Washington, D.C., 1865.

Walsh, Jack D. *Medical Histories of Union Generals.* Kent, Ohio, 1996.

Wikoff, Henry. *The Adventures of a Roving Diplomatist.* New York, 1857.

Wikoff, Henry. *My Courtship and Its Consequences.* New York and Boston, 1855.

## ARTICLES

Anon. "Three Months Among the Reconstructionists." *Atlantic Monthly,* February 1866, pp. 237–245.

Balderstone, Thomas. "The Sad Shattered Life of Teresa Sickles." *American History Illustrated,* Vol. 17, No. 5 (September 1982), pp. 40–45.

Branch, Lawrence O'Brien. "Letters, 1856–1860." *North Carolina Historical Quarterly,* Vol. 10, No. 1 (January 1933).

De Peyster, Major General John Watts. "The Third Corps and Sickles at Gettysburg." *Volunteer,* Vol. 1, Nos. 11–13.

Longacre, Ed. "Damnable Dan Sickles." *Civil War Times Illustrated,* Vol. 23, No. 3 (May 1984).

Rice, Gary R. "Devil Dan Sickles' Deadly Salients." www.thehistorynet.com.

Sickles, Daniel Edgar. "Further Recollections of Gettysburg." *North American Review,* No. 151 (March 1891), pp. 250–286.

# INDEX

West Point, 227, 261, 264, 268, 275, 280, 346

Whig Party, 54, 59

Whipple, Amiel, 264, 266, 270, 271

White, Charles J., 145

White, Fanny
  as brothel owner and prostitute, 2, 3, 16, 18, 39, 215
  death of, 215
  in London, 2–3, 17, 35–36, 38, 39, 42–43
  Sickles's relationship with, 2–3, 16–17, 23, 26, 32, 33, 40, 44, 47, 55, 83, 215, 335, 337

White House, 75, 76, 77, 81, 104, 127, 128, 156, 224–25, 238, 292–93, 298, 299, 307
  Blue Room of, 224, 230, 253, 300
  séances held by Mary Todd Lincoln at, 254–56, 299

Whitman, Walt, 288

Wikoff, Henry "Chevalier," 50, 102, 106, 143, 163, 172, 177, 187, 196, 200, 204, 230, 293, 311, 353
  arrest of, 235–36
  background of, 34–35, 225
  Mary Todd Lincoln's friendship with, 224–25, 228, 230, 235–36, 253, 291
  Teresa Sickles's relationship with, 33,

34, 35, 65, 83, 216, 224–25, 254, 308, 312, 326

Wiley, William, 15, 20, 97, 157, 196, 197, 198, 200, 204, 226
  as militia recruiter, 218–19, 220, 222–23
  Sickles denounced by, 227

Wilkes, Charles, 76

Williamsburg, Va., 241–42, 247, 248

Willis, Nathaniel, 253

Wilmerding, Eleanor, 347, 348–49, 351–52, 353

Wilson, Frederick, 185

Wilson, Henry, 233, 234, 241

Wilson, Jesse, 188

Wilson, Woodrow, 352

Wintergarden Theatre, 252

women, 326
  Civil War roles of, 238, 258–59, 261–62
  limited employment opportunities of, 5–6
  at Sickles's trial, 172–73

women's rights movement, 153

Wood, Fernando, 15, 96, 97, 251

Woodward, Thomas, 136–37, 169–70

Wooldridge, George, 70–71, 86, 87, 88, 110–14, 120, 121, 123, 125, 127, 132–33, 157, 166, 171–72, 180, 189

Worth, Jonathan, 322